MYTHS
and
FACTS

A GUIDE TO THE
Arab-Israeli Conflict

By **Mitchell G. Bard**

American-**I**sraeli **C**ooperative **E**nterprise (AICE)

2810 Blaine Dr.
Chevy Chase, MD 20815

http://www.JewishVirtualLibrary.org

ISBN 0-9712945-6-9

Printed in the United States of America

American Israeli Cooperative Enterprise (AICE)
2810 Blaine Dr.
Chevy Chase, MD 20815
Tel. 301-565-3918
Fax. 301-587-9056
Email. aiceresearch@gmail.com
http://www.JewishVirtualLibrary.org

Other studies available from AICE (all are now available on our web site):

- **Israel Studies:** An Anthology
- **Partners for Change:** How U.S.-Israel Cooperation Can Benefit America
- **Learning Together:** Israeli Innovations In Education That Could Benefit Americans
- **Breakthrough Dividend:** Israeli Innovations In Biotechnology That Could Benefit Americans
- **Experience Counts:** Innovative Programs For The Elderly In Israel That Can Benefit Americans
- **Building Bridges:** Lessons For America From Novel Israeli Approaches To Promote Coexistence
- **Good Medicine:** Israeli Innovations In Health Care That Could Benefit Americans
- **Rewriting History in Textbooks**
- **On One Foot:** A Middle East guide for the perplexed or How to respond on your way to class, when your best friend joins an anti-Israel protest
- **TENURED OR TENUOUS:** Defining the Role of Faculty in Supporting Israel on Campus

Production, new cover art and maps by North Market Street Graphics
Original Book Logo Design, Cover concept, Typography, Map Illustration: *Danakama / Nick Moscovitz / NYC*

Table of Contents

MAPS

Preface

"The great enemy of truth is very often not the lie—deliberate, contrived and dishonest—but the myth—persistent, persuasive and repeated."

—President John F. Kennedy[1]

I am often asked to name the most prevalent myth about the Middle East. The answer is the suggestion, in one form or another, that Israelis do not want peace.

No one craves peace more desperately than Israelis, who have lived through seven wars and an ongoing campaign of terror for more than six decades. This is why, as this book discusses, Israel has repeatedly sought compromises, often at great risk, that would bring an end to the conflict.

Each time a new peace initiative is launched, our hopes are raised that we will not need to publish another edition of *Myths and Facts*, which was first printed more than 40 years ago. We remain hopeful that Israel's neighbors will accept a Jewish state in their midst and take advantage of the great opportunities for working together for mutual benefit. Unfortunately, the "Arab Spring" has created new uncertainty and potential danger for Israel. The upheaval in Egypt has put the Israel-Egypt peace treaty in jeopardy, the takeover of Lebanon by Hezbollah has increased the threat from the north while turmoil in Syria has erased any short-term expectation of peace on that front. Meanwhile, the threat of a nuclear Iran looms over the entire region.

In the meantime, old myths, including ancient blood libels, continue to be recycled, and new calumnies invented. These must not be allowed to go unanswered if we are to progress toward coexistence.

Myths and Facts pulls no punches when it comes to addressing Israel's responsibility for events and policies that tarnish its image. Friends of Israel do not try to whitewash the truth, but they do try to put events in proper context. That is also our goal. When friends criticize Israel, it is because they want the country to be better. Israel's detractors do not have that goal; they are more interested in delegitimizing the country, placing a wedge between Israel and its allies, and working toward its destruction. The campaign to delegitimize Israel has intensified in recent years and prompted us to include a chapter devoted to the myths promulgated by the advocates of boycotts, divestment and sanctions directed at Israel.

[1]President John F. Kennedy, Commencement Address at Yale University, (June 11, 1962).

This new edition covers the basics of the history of the conflict and offers documented facts to respond to the most common myths. It is not meant to be comprehensive, and we have intentionally made this volume shorter while making additional information available in the **Jewish Virtual Library (www.JewishVirtualLibrary.org)**. Material that previously appeared in appendices, such as quotations reflecting Arab/Muslim attitudes toward Israel, and the text of treaties, UN Resolution 242 and the Hamas Covenant can be found online. Information about Jews in Arab countries was also deleted but can be found in the JVL.

We continually update the online edition of *Myths* and archive older facts as well as material we could not fit in the book. We anticipate offering translations online as well. For now, previous editions are available in Spanish, German, Portuguese, Russian, French, Swedish and Hebrew. In addition, we have a listserv for weekly myths/facts and other periodic updates. To sign up, visit the Library.

I would like to acknowledge the contributions of the distinguished group of past editors: Sheila Segal, Wolf Blitzer, Alan Tigay, Moshe Decter, M.J. Rosenberg, Jeff Rubin, Eric Rozenman, Lenny Davis and Joel Himelfarb. I would also like to thank Rafi Danziger, Rebecca Weiner, Isaac Wolf, David Shyovitz, Alden Oreck, Elihai Braun, Sarah Szymkowicz, Avi Hein, Joanna Sloame, Stephanie Persin, Ariel Scheib, David Krusch, Jonathan Lord, Allison Krant, Yariv Nornberg, Jennifer Feinberg, Elie Berman, Sybil Ottenstein, Stephanie Kogan, and Zachary Scheinerman for their invaluable assistance in the AICE editions.

AICE is especially grateful to the sponsors of this edition: The Herbert Bearman Foundation, Inc., of Baltimore, Maryland and Evelyn and Dr. Shmuel Katz from Bal-Harbour Florida, who contributed in loving memory of the AUSCH and KATZ family members O.B.M. H.Y.D. who perished during the Holocaust in Europe. May their greatness be an inspiration to all people of good will.

"Facts are stubborn things," observed John Adams, "and whatever may be our wishes, our inclinations, or the dictates of our passion, they cannot alter the state of facts and evidence."* The following pages lay out the stubborn facts about the Arab-Israeli conflict. They are the best weapons we have to insure that truth triumphs over fiction.

Mitchell G. Bard
October 2011

---

*John Adams, "Argument in Defense of the Soldiers in Boston Massacre Trial," (December 1770).

1. Israel's Roots

MYTH

"The Jews have no claim to the land they call Israel."

FACT

A common misperception is that all the Jews were forced into the Diaspora by the Romans after the destruction of the Second Temple in Jerusalem in the year 70 C.E. and then, 1,800 years later, the Jews suddenly returned to Palestine demanding their country back. In reality, the Jewish people have maintained ties to their historic homeland for more than 3,700 years.

The Jewish people base their claim to the Land of Israel on at least four premises: 1) the Jewish people settled and developed the land; 2) the international community granted political sovereignty in Palestine to the Jewish people; 3) the territory was captured in defensive wars and 4) God promised the land to the patriarch Abraham.

Even after the destruction of the Second Temple in Jerusalem, and the beginning of the exile, Jewish life in the Land of Israel continued and often flourished. Large communities were reestablished in Jerusalem and Tiberias by the ninth century. In the 11th century, Jewish communities grew in Rafah, Gaza, Ashkelon, Jaffa and Caesarea. The Crusaders massacred many Jews during the 12th century, but the community rebounded in the next two centuries as large numbers of rabbis and Jewish pilgrims immigrated to Jerusalem and the Galilee. Prominent rabbis established communities in Safed, Jerusalem and elsewhere during the next 300 years.

By the early 19th century—years before the birth of the modern Zionist movement—more than 10,000 Jews lived throughout what is today Israel.[1] The 78 years of nation-building, beginning in 1870, culminated in the reestablishment of the Jewish State.

Israel's international "birth certificate" was validated by the promise of the Bible; uninterrupted Jewish settlement from the time of Joshua onward; the Balfour Declaration of 1917; the League of Nations Mandate, which incorporated the Balfour Declaration; the United Nations partition resolution of 1947; Israel's admission to the UN in 1949; the recognition of Israel by most other states; and, most of all, the society created by Israel's people in decades of thriving, dynamic national existence.

"Nobody does Israel any service by proclaiming its 'right to exist.'

Israel's right to exist, like that of the United States, Saudi Arabia and 152 other states, is axiomatic and unreserved. Israel's legitimacy is not suspended in midair awaiting acknowledgement. . . .

There is certainly no other state, big or small, young or old, that would consider mere recognition of its 'right to exist' a favor, or a negotiable concession."

—**Abba Eban**[2]

MYTH

"Palestine was always an Arab country."

FACT

The term "Palestine" is believed to be derived from the Philistines, an Aegean people who, in the 12th Century B.C.E., settled along the Mediterranean coastal plain of what are now Israel and the Gaza Strip. In the second century C.E., after crushing the last Jewish revolt, the Romans first applied the name *Palaestina* to Judea (the southern portion of what is now called the West Bank) in an attempt to minimize Jewish identification with the land of Israel. The Arabic word *Filastin* is derived from this Latin name.[3]

The Hebrews entered the Land of Israel about 1300 B.C.E., living under a tribal confederation until being united under the first monarch, King Saul. The second king, David, established Jerusalem as the capital around 1000 B.C.E. David's son, Solomon, built the Temple soon thereafter and consolidated the military, administrative and religious functions of the kingdom. The nation was divided under Solomon's son, with the northern kingdom (Israel) lasting until 722 B.C.E., when the Assyrians destroyed it, and the southern kingdom (Judah) surviving until the Babylonian conquest in 586 B.C.E. The Jewish people enjoyed brief periods of sovereignty afterward until most Jews were finally driven from their homeland in 135 C.E.

Jewish independence in the Land of Israel lasted for more than 400 years. This is much longer than Americans have enjoyed independence in what has become known as the United States.[4] In fact, if not for foreign conquerors, Israel would be more than 3,000 years old today.

Palestine was never an exclusively Arab country, although Arabic gradually became the language of most of the population after the Muslim invasions of the seventh century. No independent Arab or Palestinian state ever existed in Palestine. When the distinguished Arab-American historian, Princeton University Prof. Philip Hitti, testified against partition before the Anglo-American Committee in 1946, he said: "There is no such thing as 'Palestine' in history, absolutely not."[5]

Prior to partition, Palestinian Arabs did not view themselves as having a separate identity. When the First Congress of Muslim-Christian Associations met in Jerusalem in February 1919 to choose Palestinian representatives for the Paris Peace Conference, the following resolution was adopted:

> We consider Palestine as part of Arab Syria, as it has never been separated from it at any time. We are connected with it by national, religious, linguistic, natural, economic and geographical bonds.[6]

In 1937, a local Arab leader, Auni Bey Abdul-Hadi, told the Peel Commission, which ultimately suggested the partition of Palestine: "There is no such country as Palestine! 'Palestine' is a term the Zionists invented! There is no Palestine in the Bible. Our country was for centuries part of Syria."[7] The representative of the Arab Higher Committee to the United Nations echoed this view in a statement to the General Assembly in May 1947, which said Palestine was part of the Province of Syria and the Arabs of Palestine did not comprise a separate political entity. A few years later, Ahmed Shuqeiri, later the chairman of the PLO, told the Security Council: "It is common knowledge that Palestine is nothing but southern Syria."[8]

Palestinian Arab nationalism is largely a post-World War I phenomenon that did not become a significant political movement until after the 1967 Six-Day War.

MYTH

"The Palestinians are descendants of the Canaanites and were in Palestine long before the Jews."

FACT

Palestinian claims to be related to the Canaanites are a recent phenomenon and contrary to historical evidence. The Canaanites disappeared from the face of the earth three millennia ago, and no one knows if any of their descendants survived or, if they did, who they would be.

Sherif Hussein, the guardian of the Islamic Holy Places in Arabia, said the Palestinians' ancestors had only been in the area for 1,000 years.[9] Even the Palestinians themselves have acknowledged their association with the region came long after the Jews. In testimony before the Anglo-American Committee in 1946, for example, they claimed a connection to Palestine of more than 1,000 years, dating back no further than the conquest of Muhammad's followers in the 7th century.[10] Over the last 2,000 years, there have been massive invasions (e.g., the Crusades) that killed off most of the local people, migrations, the plague, and other manmade or natural disasters. The entire local population was replaced many times over. During the British mandate alone, more than 100,000 Arabs emigrated from neighboring countries and are today considered Palestinians.

By contrast, no serious historian questions the more than 3,000-year-old Jewish connection to the Land of Israel, or the modern Jewish people's relation to the ancient Hebrews.

MYTH

"The Balfour Declaration did not give Jews the right to a homeland in Palestine."

FACT

In 1917, Britain issued the Balfour Declaration:

> His Majesty's Government views with favor the establishment in Palestine of a national home for the Jewish people, and will use their best endeavors to facilitate the achievement of this object, it being clearly understood that nothing shall be done which may prejudice the civil and religious rights of existing non-Jewish communities in Palestine or the rights and political status enjoyed by Jews in any other country.

The Mandate for Palestine included the Balfour Declaration. It specifically referred to "the historical connections of the Jewish people with Palestine" and to the moral validity of "reconstituting their National Home in that country." The term "reconstituting" shows recognition of the fact that Palestine had been the Jews' home. Furthermore, the British were instructed to "use their best endeavors to facilitate" Jewish immigration, to encourage settlement on the land and to "secure" the Jewish National Home. The word "Arab" does not appear in the Mandatory award.[11]

The Mandate was formalized by the 52 governments at the League of Nations on July 24, 1922.

MYTH

"Arabs in Palestine suffered because of Jewish settlement."

FACT

For many centuries, Palestine was a sparsely populated, poorly cultivated and widely-neglected expanse of eroded hills, sandy deserts and malarial marshes. As late as 1880, the American consul in Jerusalem reported the area was continuing its historic decline. "The population and wealth of Palestine has not increased during the last forty years," he said.[12]

The Report of the Palestine Royal Commission quotes an account of the Maritime Plain in 1913:

> The road leading from Gaza to the north was only a summer track suitable for transport by camels and carts ... no orange groves, orchards or vineyards were to be seen until one reached [the Jewish village of] Yabna [Yavne]. ... Houses were all of mud. No windows were anywhere to be seen. ... The ploughs used were of wood. ... The yields were very poor. ... The sanitary conditions in the village were horrible. Schools did not exist. ... The western part, towards the sea, was almost a desert. ... The villages in this area were few and thinly populated. Many ruins of villages were scattered over the area, as owing to the prevalence of malaria, many villages were deserted by their inhabitants.[13]

Surprisingly, many people who were not sympathetic to the Zionist cause believed the Jews would improve the condition of Palestinian Arabs. For example, Dawood Barakat, editor of the Egyptian paper *Al-Ahram,* wrote: "It is absolutely necessary that an entente be made between the Zionists and Arabs, because the war of words can only do evil. The Zionists are necessary for the country: The money which they will bring, their knowledge and intelligence, and the industriousness which characterizes them will contribute without doubt to the regeneration of the country."[14]

Even a leading Arab nationalist believed the return of the Jews to their homeland would help resuscitate the country. According to Sherif Hussein, the guardian of the Islamic Holy Places in Arabia:

> The resources of the country are still virgin soil and will be developed by the Jewish immigrants. One of the most amazing things until recent times was that the Palestinian used to leave his country, wandering over the high seas in every direction. His native soil could not retain a hold on him, though his ancestors had lived on it for 1000 years. At the same time we have seen the Jews from foreign countries streaming to Palestine from Russia, Germany, Austria, Spain, America. The cause of causes could not escape those who had a gift of deeper insight. They knew that the country was for its original sons (*abna'ihilasliyin*), for all their differences, a sacred and beloved homeland. The return of these exiles (*jaliya*) to their homeland will prove materially and spiritually [to be] an ex-

perimental school for their brethren who are with them in the fields, factories, trades and in all things connected with toil and labor.[15]

As Hussein foresaw, the regeneration of Palestine, and the growth of its population, came only after Jews returned in massive numbers.

Mark Twain, who visited Palestine in 1867, described it as: "... a desolate country whose soil is rich enough, but is given over wholly to weeds—a silent mournful expanse.... A desolation is here that not even imagination can grace with the pomp of life and action.... We never saw a human being on the whole route.... There was hardly a tree or a shrub anywhere. Even the olive and the cactus, those fast friends of the worthless soil, had almost deserted the country."[16]

MYTH

"Zionism is racism."

FACT

In 1975, the UN General Assembly adopted a resolution slandering Zionism by equating it with racism. Zionism is the national liberation movement of the Jewish people, which holds that Jews, like any other nation, are entitled to a homeland.

History has demonstrated the need to ensure Jewish security through a national homeland. Zionism recognizes that Jewishness is defined by shared origin, religion, culture and history. The realization of the Zionist dream is exemplified by nearly six million Jews, from more than 100 countries, who are Israeli citizens.

Israel's Law of Return grants automatic citizenship to Jews, but non-Jews are also eligible to become citizens under naturalization procedures similar to those in other countries. Israel's policy is not unique; many other countries, including Germany, Greece, Ireland and Finland have special categories of people who are entitled to citizenship.

More than one million Muslim and Christian Arabs, Druze, Baha'is, Circassians and other ethnic groups also are represented in Israel's population. The presence in Israel of thousands of Jews from Ethiopia, Yemen and India is the best refutation of the calumny against Zionism. In a series of historic airlifts, labeled Operations Moses (1984), Joshua (1985) and Solomon (1991), Israel rescued more than 20,000 members of the ancient Ethiopian Jewish community.

Zionism does not discriminate against anyone. Israel's open and democratic character, and its scrupulous protection of the religious and political rights of Christians and Muslims, rebut the charge of exclusivity. Moreover, anyone—Jew or non-Jew, Israeli, American, or Chinese, black, white, or purple—can be a Zionist.

Writing after "Operation Moses" was revealed, William Safire noted:

"...For the first time in history, thousands of black people are being brought to a country not in chains but in dignity, not as slaves but as citizens."[17]

By contrast, the Arab states define citizenship strictly by native parentage. It is almost impossible to become a naturalized citizen in Arab states such as Algeria, Saudi Arabia and Kuwait. Several Arab nations have laws that facilitate the naturalization of foreign Arabs, with the specific exception of Palestinians. Jordan, on the other hand, instituted its own "law of return" in 1954, according citizenship to all former residents of Palestine, except for Jews.[18]

The 1975 UN resolution was part of the Soviet-Arab Cold War anti-Israel campaign. Almost all the former non-Arab supporters of the resolution have apologized and changed their positions. When the General Assembly voted to repeal the resolution in 1991, only some Arab and Muslim states, as well as Cuba, North Korea and Vietnam were opposed.

MYTH

"The Zionists could have chosen another country besides Palestine."

FACT

In the late 19th century, the rise of anti-Semitism led to a resurgence of pogroms in Russia and Eastern Europe, shattering promises of equality and tolerance. This stimulated Jewish immigration to Palestine from Europe.

Simultaneously, a wave of Jews immigrated to Palestine from Yemen, Morocco, Iraq and Turkey. These Jews were unaware of Theodor Herzl's political Zionism or of European pogroms. They were motivated by the centuries-old dream of the "Return to Zion" and a fear of intolerance. Upon hearing that the gates of Palestine were open, they braved the hardships of travel and went to the Land of Israel.

The Zionist ideal of a return to Israel has profound religious roots. Many Jewish prayers speak of Jerusalem, Zion and the Land of Israel. The injunction not to forget Jerusalem, the site of the Temple, is a major tenet of Judaism. The Hebrew language, the Torah, laws in the Talmud, the Jewish calendar and Jewish holidays and festivals all originated in Israel and revolve around its seasons and conditions. Jews pray toward

Jerusalem and recite the words "next year in Jerusalem" every Passover. Jewish religion, culture and history make clear that it is only in the land of Israel that the Jewish commonwealth can be built.

In 1897, Jewish leaders formally organized the Zionist political movement, calling for the restoration of the Jewish national home in Palestine, where Jews could find sanctuary and self-determination, and work for the renascence of their civilization and culture.

MYTH

"Herzl himself proposed Uganda as the Jewish state as an alternative to Palestine."

FACT

Theodor Herzl sought support from the great powers for the creation of a Jewish homeland. He turned to Great Britain, and met with Joseph Chamberlain, the British colonial secretary and others. The British agreed, in principle, to permit Jewish settlement in East Africa.

At the Sixth Zionist Congress at Basle on August 26, 1903, Herzl proposed the British Uganda Program as a *temporary emergency refuge* for Jews in Russia in immediate danger. While Herzl made it clear that this program would not affect the ultimate aim of Zionism, a Jewish entity in the Land of Israel, the proposal aroused a storm of protest at the Congress and nearly led to a split in the Zionist movement. The Uganda Program, which never had much support, was formally rejected by the Zionist movement at the Seventh Zionist Congress in 1905.

MYTH

"The Arabs saw the Balfour Declaration as a betrayal of their rights."

FACT

Emir Faisal, son of Sherif Hussein, the leader of the Arab revolt against the Turks, signed an agreement with Chaim Weizmann and other Zionist leaders during the 1919 Paris Peace Conference. It acknowledged the "racial kinship and ancient bonds existing between the Arabs and the Jewish people" and concluded that "the surest means of working out the consummation of their national aspirations is through the closest possible collaboration in the development of the Arab states and Palestine." Furthermore, the agreement looked to the fulfillment of the Balfour Declaration and called for all necessary measures " ... to encourage and stimulate immigration of Jews into Palestine on a large scale, and as quickly as possible to settle Jewish immigrants upon the land through closer settlement and intensive cultivation of the soil."[19]

Faisal had conditioned his acceptance of the Balfour Declaration on the fulfillment of British wartime promises of independence to the Arabs. These were not kept.

Critics dismiss the Weizmann-Faisal agreement because it was never enacted; however, the fact that the leader of the Arab nationalist movement and the Zionist movement could reach an understanding is significant because it demonstrated that Jewish and Arab aspirations were not necessarily mutually exclusive.

> *"Our settlers do not come here as do the colonists from the Occident to have natives do their work for them; they themselves set their shoulders to the plow and they spend their strength and their blood to make the land fruitful. But it is not only for ourselves that we desire its fertility. The Jewish farmers have begun to teach their brothers, the Arab farmers, to cultivate the land more intensively; we desire to teach them further: together with them we want to cultivate the land—to 'serve' it, as the Hebrew has it. The more fertile this soil becomes, the more space there will be for us and for them. We have no desire to dispossess them: we want to live with them."*
>
> **—Martin Buber**[20]

MYTH

"The Zionists were colonialist tools of Western imperialism."

FACT

"Colonialism means living by exploiting others," Yehoshofat Harkabi has written. "But what could be further from colonialism than the idealism of city-dwelling Jews who strive to become farmers and laborers and to live by their own work?"[21]

Moreover, as British historian Paul Johnson noted, Zionists were hardly tools of imperialists given the powers' general opposition to their cause. "Everywhere in the West, the foreign offices, defense ministries and big business were against the Zionists."[22]

Emir Faisal also saw the Zionist movement as a companion to the Arab nationalist movement, fighting against imperialism, as he explained in a letter to Harvard law professor and future Supreme Court Justice Felix Frankfurter on March 3, 1919, one day after Chaim Weizmann presented the Zionist case to the Paris conference. Faisal wrote:

> The Arabs, especially the educated among us, look with deepest sympathy on the Zionist movement.... We will wish the Jews a hearty welcome home.... We are working together for

a reformed and revised Near East and our two movements complete one another. *The Jewish movement is nationalist and not imperialist.* And there is room in Syria for us both. Indeed, I think that neither can be a real success without the other (emphasis added).[23]

In the 1940s, the Jewish underground movements waged an *anti-colonial* war against the British. The Arabs, meanwhile, were concerned primarily with fighting the Jews rather than expelling the British imperialists.

MYTH

"The British promised the Arabs independence in Palestine."

FACT

The central figure in the Arab nationalist movement at the time of World War I was Hussein ibn 'Ali, the Sherif of Mecca in 1908. As Sherif, Hussein was responsible for the custody of Islam's shrines in the Hejaz and was one of the Muslims' spiritual leaders.

In July 1915, Hussein sent a letter to Sir Henry MacMahon, the High Commissioner for Egypt, informing him of the terms for Arab participation in the war against the Turks. The letters between Hussein and MacMahon that followed outlined the areas that Britain was prepared to cede to the Arabs in exchange for their help.

The Hussein-MacMahon correspondence conspicuously fails to mention Palestine. The British argued the omission had been intentional, thereby justifying their refusal to grant the Arabs independence in Palestine after the war.[24] MacMahon explained:

> I feel it my duty to state, and I do so definitely and emphatically, that it was not intended by me in giving this pledge to King Hussein to include Palestine in the area in which Arab independence was promised. I also had every reason to believe at the time that the fact that Palestine was not included in my pledge was well understood by King Hussein.[25]

Notes

1. Dan Bahat, ed. *Twenty Centuries of Jewish Life in the Holy Land,* (Jerusalem: The Israel Economist, 1976), pp. 61–63.
2. *New York Times,* (November 18, 1981).
3. Yehoshua Porath, *The Emergence of the Palestinian-Arab National Movement, 1918-1929,* (London: Frank Cass, 1974), p. 4.
4. Max Dimont, *Jews, God and History,* (NY: Signet, 1962), pp. 49–53.
5. Moshe Kohn, "The Arabs' 'Lie' of the Land," *Jerusalem Post,* (October 18, 1991).
6. Randall Price, *Fast Facts on the Middle East Conflict,* (Harvest House Publishers: 2003), p. 25.

7. Moshe Kohn, "The Arabs' 'Lie' of the Land," *Jerusalem Post*, (October 18, 1991).

8. Avner Yaniv, *PLO*, (Jerusalem: Israel Universities Study Group of Middle Eastern Affairs, August 1974), p. 5.

9. *Al-Qibla*, (March 23, 1918), quoted in Samuel Katz, *Battleground-Fact and Fantasy in Palestine*, (NY: Bantam Books, 1977), p. 126.

10. British Government, *Report of the Anglo-American Committee of Enquiry, 1946, Part VI*, (April 20, 1946).

11. Howard Sachar, *A History of Israel: From the Rise of Zionism to Our Time*, (NY: Alfred A. Knopf, 1979), p. 129.

12. Ben Halpern, *The Idea of a Jewish State*, (MA: Harvard University Press, 1969), p. 108.

13. Palestine Royal Commission Report, p. 233.

14. Neville Mandel, *The Arabs and Zionism Before World War I*, (University of California Press: 1976), p. 8.

15. *Al-Qibla*, (March 23, 1918), quoted in Samuel Katz, *Battleground-Fact and Fantasy in Palestine*, (NY: Bantam Books, 1977), p. 126.

16. Mark Twain, *The Innocents Abroad*, (London, 1881).

17. *New York Times*, (January 7, 1985).

18. Jordanian Nationality Law, Article 3(2) of Law No. 6 of 1954, Official Gazette, No. 1171, January 1, 1954.

19. Chaim Weizmann, Trial and Error, (NY: Schocken Books, 1966), pp. 246–247; Howard Sachar, *A History of Israel: From the Rise of Zionism to Our Time*, (NY: Alfred A. Knopf, 1979), p. 121.

20. From an open letter from Martin Buber to Mahatma Gandhi in 1939, accessed at GandhiServe.com.

21. Yehoshafat Harkabi, *Palestinians And Israel*, (Jerusalem: Keter, 1974), p. 6.

22. Paul Johnson, *Modern Times: The World from the Twenties to the Nineties*, (NY: Harper & Row, 1983), p. 485.

23. Naomi Comay, *Arabs Speak Frankly on the Arab-Israeli Conflict*, (Printing Miracle Ltd., 2005), p. 8.

24. George Kirk, *A Short History of the Middle East*, (NY: Frederick Praeger Publishers, 1964), p. 314.

25. "Report of a Committee Setup to Consider Certain Correspondence Between Sir Henry McMahon and the Sharif of Mecca in 1915/1916," U.K. Parliament, March 16, 1939.

2. The Mandatory Period

MYTH

"The British helped the Jews displace the native Arab population of Palestine."

FACT

Herbert Samuel, a British Jew who served as the first High Commissioner of Palestine, placed restrictions on Jewish immigration "in the 'interests of the present population' and the 'absorptive capacity' of the country."[1] The influx of Jewish settlers was said to be forcing the Arab fellahin (native peasants) from their land. This was at a time when less than a million people lived in an area that now supports more than nine million.

The British actually limited the absorptive capacity of Palestine when, in 1921, Colonial Secretary Winston Churchill severed nearly four-fifths of Palestine—some 35,000 square miles—to create a brand new Arab entity, Transjordan. As a consolation prize for the Hejaz and Arabia (which are both now Saudi Arabia) going to the Saud family, Churchill rewarded Sherif Hussein's son Abdullah for his contribution to the war against Turkey by installing him as Transjordan's emir.

The British went further and placed restrictions on Jewish land purchases in what remained of Palestine, contradicting the provision of the Mandate (Article 6) stating that "the Administration of Palestine . . . shall encourage, in cooperation with the Jewish Agency . . . close settlement by Jews on the land, including State lands and waste lands not acquired for public purposes." By 1949, the British had allotted 87,500 acres of the 187,500 acres of cultivable land to Arabs and only 4,250 acres to Jews.[2]

Ultimately, the British admitted the argument about the absorptive capacity of the country was specious. The Peel Commission said: "The heavy immigration in the years 1933–36 would seem to show that the Jews have been able to enlarge the absorptive capacity of the country for Jews."[3]

MYTH

"The British allowed Jews to flood Palestine while Arab immigration was tightly controlled."

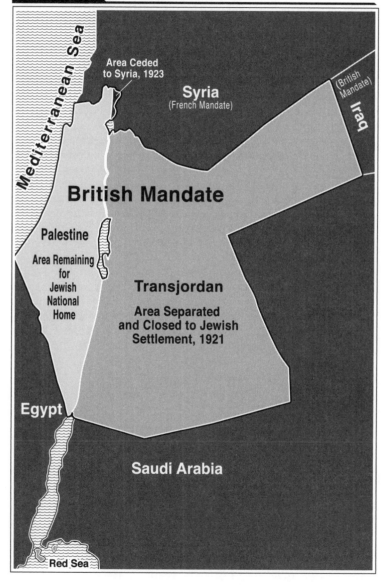

Map 1 Great Britain's Division of the Mandated Area 1921-1923

FACT

The British response to Jewish immigration set a precedent of appeasing the Arabs, which was followed for the duration of the Mandate. The British placed restrictions on Jewish immigration while allowing Arabs to enter the country freely. Apparently, London did not feel that a flood of Arab immigrants would affect the country's absorptive capacity.

During World War I, the Jewish population in Palestine declined because of the war, famine, disease and expulsion by the Turks. In 1915, approximately 83,000 Jews lived in Palestine among 590,000 Muslim and Christian Arabs. According to the 1922 census, the Jewish population was 84,000, while the Arabs numbered 643,000.[4] Thus, the Arab population grew exponentially while that of the Jews stagnated.

In the mid-1920s, Jewish immigration to Palestine increased primarily because of anti-Jewish economic legislation in Poland and Washington's imposition of restrictive quotas.[5]

The record number of immigrants in 1935 (see table) was a response to the growing persecution of Jews in Nazi Germany. The British administration considered this number too large, however, so the Jewish Agency was informed that less than one-third of the quota it asked for would be approved in 1936.[6]

The British gave in further to Arab demands by announcing in the 1939 White Paper that an independent Arab state would be created within 10 years, and that Jewish immigration was to be limited to 75,000 for the next five years, after which it was to cease altogether. It also forbade land sales to Jews in 95 percent of the territory of Palestine. The Arabs, nevertheless, rejected the proposal.

Jewish Immigrants to Palestine[7]

1919	1,806	1931	4,075
1920	8,223	1932	12,533
1921	8,294	1933	37,337
1922	8,685	1934	45,267
1923	8,175	1935	66,472
1924	13,892	1936	29,595
1925	34,386	1937	10,629
1926	13,855	1938	14,675
1927	3,034	1939	31,195
1928	2,178	1940	10,643
1929	5,249	1941	4,592
1930	4,944		

By contrast, throughout the Mandatory period, Arab immigration was unrestricted. In 1930, the Hope Simpson Commission, sent from London to investigate the 1929 Arab riots, said the British practice of ignoring the uncontrolled illegal Arab immigration from Egypt, Transjordan and Syria had the effect of displacing the prospective *Jewish* immigrants.[8]

The British Governor of the Sinai from 1922–36 observed: "This illegal immigration was not only going on from the Sinai, but also from Transjordan and Syria, and it is very difficult to make a case out for the misery of the Arabs if at the same time their compatriots from adjoining states could not be kept from going in to share that misery."[9]

The Peel Commission reported in 1937 that the "shortfall of land is . . . due less to the amount of land acquired by Jews than to the increase in the Arab population."[10]

MYTH

"The British changed their policy after World War II to allow the survivors of the Holocaust to settle in Palestine."

FACT

The gates of Palestine remained closed for the duration of the war, stranding hundreds of thousands of Jews in Europe, many of whom became victims of Hitler's "Final Solution." After the war, the British refused to allow the survivors of the Nazi nightmare to find sanctuary in Palestine. On June 6, 1946, President Truman urged the British government to relieve the suffering of the Jews confined to displaced persons camps in Europe by immediately accepting 100,000 Jewish immigrants. Britain's Foreign Minister, Ernest Bevin, replied sarcastically that the United States wanted displaced Jews to immigrate to Palestine "because they did not want too many of them in New York."[11]

Some Jews were able to reach Palestine, many smuggled in by way of dilapidated ships organized by members of the Jewish resistance organizations. Between August 1945 and the establishment of the State of Israel in May 1948, 65 "illegal" immigrant ships, carrying 69,878 people, arrived from European shores. In August 1946, however, the British began to intern those they caught in camps in Cyprus. Approximately 50,000 people were detained in the camps, 28,000 of whom were still imprisoned when Israel declared independence.[12]

MYTH

"As the Jewish population in Palestine grew, the plight of the Palestinian Arabs worsened."

FACT

The Jewish population increased by 470,000 between World War I and World War II, while the non-Jewish population rose by 588,000.[13] In fact, the permanent Arab population increased 120 percent between 1922 and 1947.[14]

This rapid growth of the Arab population was a result of several factors. One was immigration from neighboring states—constituting 37 percent of the total immigration to pre-state Israel—by Arabs who wanted to take advantage of the higher standard of living the Jews had made possible.[15] The Arab population also grew because of the improved living conditions created by the Jews as they drained malarial swamps and brought improved sanitation and health care to the region. Thus, for example, the Muslim infant mortality rate fell from 201 per thousand in 1925 to 94 per thousand in 1945 and life expectancy rose from 37 years in 1926 to 49 in 1943.[16]

The Arab population increased the most in cities where large Jewish populations had created new economic opportunities. From 1922–1947, the non-Jewish population increased 290 percent in Haifa, 131 percent in Jerusalem and 158 percent in Jaffa. The growth in Arab towns was more modest: 42 percent in Nablus, 78 percent in Jenin and 37 percent in Bethlehem.[17]

MYTH

"Jews stole Arab land."

FACT

Despite the growth in their population, the Arabs continued to assert they were being displaced. From the beginning of World War I, however, part of Palestine's land was owned by absentee landlords who lived in Cairo, Damascus and Beirut. About 80 percent of the Palestinian Arabs were debt-ridden peasants, semi-nomads and Bedouins.[18]

Jews actually went out of their way to avoid purchasing land in areas where Arabs might be displaced. They sought land that was largely uncultivated, swampy, cheap and, most important, without tenants. In 1920, Labor Zionist leader David Ben-Gurion expressed his concern about the Arab *fellahin,* whom he viewed as "the most important asset of the native population." Ben-Gurion said "under no circumstances must we touch land belonging to *fellahs* or worked by them." He advocated helping liberate them from their oppressors. "Only if a *fellah* leaves his place of settlement," Ben-Gurion added, "should we offer to buy his land, at an appropriate price."[19]

It was only after the Jews had bought all of the available uncultivated land that they began to purchase cultivated land. Many Arabs were willing to sell because of the migration to coastal towns and because they needed money to invest in the citrus industry.[20]

When John Hope Simpson arrived in Palestine in May 1930, he observed: "They [Jews] paid high prices for the land, and in addition they paid to certain of the occupants of those lands a considerable amount of money which they were not legally bound to pay."[21]

In 1931, Lewis French conducted a survey of landlessness for the British government and offered new plots to any Arabs who had been "dispossessed." British officials received more than 3,000 applications, of which 80 percent were ruled invalid by the Government's legal adviser because the applicants were not landless Arabs. This left only about 600 landless Arabs, 100 of whom accepted the Government land offer.[22]

In April 1936, a new outbreak of Arab attacks on Jews was instigated by a Syrian guerrilla named Fawzi al-Qawukji, the commander of the Arab Liberation Army. By November, when the British finally sent a new commission headed by Lord Peel to investigate, 89 Jews had been killed and more than 300 wounded.[23]

The Peel Commission's report found that Arab complaints about Jewish land acquisition were baseless. It pointed out that "much of the land now carrying orange groves was sand dunes or swamp and uncultivated when it was purchased.... there was at the time of the earlier sales little evidence that the owners possessed either the resources or training needed to develop the land."[24] Moreover, the Commission found the shortage was "due less to the amount of land acquired by Jews than to the increase in the Arab population." The report concluded that the presence of Jews in Palestine, along with the work of the British Administration, had resulted in higher wages, an improved standard of living and ample employment opportunities.[25]

"It is made quite clear to all, both by the map drawn up by the Simpson Commission and by another compiled by the Peel Commission, that the Arabs are as prodigal in selling their land as they are in useless wailing and weeping" (emphasis in the original).

—Transjordan's King Abdullah[26]

Even at the height of the Arab revolt in 1938, the British High Commissioner to Palestine believed the Arab landowners were complaining about sales to Jews to drive up prices for lands they wished to sell. Many Arab landowners had been so terrorized by Arab rebels they decided to leave Palestine and sell their property to the Jews.[27]

The Jews were paying exorbitant prices to wealthy landowners for small tracts of arid land."In 1944, Jews paid between $1,000 and $1,100 per acre in Palestine, mostly for arid or semiarid land; in the same year, rich black soil in Iowa was selling for about $110 per acre."[28]

By 1947, Jewish holdings in Palestine amounted to about 463,000 acres. Approximately 45,000 of these acres were acquired from the Mandatory Government; 30,000 were bought from various churches and 387,500 were purchased from Arabs. Analyses of land purchases from 1880 to 1948 show that 73 percent of Jewish plots were purchased from large landowners, not poor *fellahin*.[29] Those who sold land included the mayors of Gaza, Jerusalem and Jaffa. As'ad el-Shuqeiri, a Muslim religious scholar and father of PLO chairman Ahmed Shuqeiri, took Jewish money for his land. Even King Abdullah leased land to the Jews. In fact, many leaders of the Arab nationalist movement, including members of the Muslim Supreme Council, sold land to Jews.[30]

MYTH

"The British helped the Palestinians to live peacefully with the Jews."

FACT

In 1921, Haj Amin el-Husseini first began to organize *fedayeen* ("one who sacrifices himself") to terrorize Jews. Haj Amin hoped to duplicate the success of Kemal Atatürk in Turkey by driving the Jews out of Palestine just as Kemal had driven the invading Greeks from his country.[31] Arab radicals were able to gain influence because the British Administration was unwilling to take effective action against them until they began a revolt against British rule.

Colonel Richard Meinertzhagen, former head of British military intelligence in Cairo, and later Chief Political Officer for Palestine and Syria, wrote in his diary that British officials "incline towards the exclusion of Zionism in Palestine." In fact, the British encouraged the Palestinians to attack the Jews. According to Meinertzhagen, Col. Waters-Taylor (financial adviser to the Military Administration in Palestine 1919-23) met with Haj Amin a few days before Easter, in 1920, and told him "he had a great opportunity at Easter to show the world ... that Zionism was unpopular not only with the Palestine Administration but in Whitehall and if disturbances of sufficient violence occurred in Jerusalem at Easter, both General Bols [Chief Administrator in Palestine, 1919-20] and General Allenby [Commander of Egyptian Force, 1917-19, then High Commissioner of Egypt] would advocate the abandonment of the Jewish Home. Waters-Taylor explained that freedom could only be attained through violence."[32]

Haj Amin took the Colonel's advice and instigated a riot. The British withdrew their troops and the Jewish police from Jerusalem, allowing the Arab mob to attack Jews and loot their shops. Because of Haj Amin's overt role in instigating the pogrom, the British decided to arrest him. Haj Amin escaped, however, and was sentenced to 10 years imprisonment in absentia.

A year later, some British Arabists convinced High Commissioner Herbert Samuel to pardon Haj Amin and to appoint him Mufti. By contrast, Vladimir Jabotinsky and several of his followers, who had formed a Jewish defense organization during the unrest, were sentenced to 15 years' imprisonment.[33]

Samuel met with Haj Amin on April 11, 1921, and was assured "that the influences of his family and himself would be devoted to tranquility." Three weeks later, riots in Jaffa and elsewhere left 43 Jews dead.[34]

Haj Amin consolidated his power and took control of all Muslim religious funds in Palestine. He used his authority to gain control over the mosques, the schools and the courts. No Arab could reach an influential position without being loyal to the Mufti. His power was so absolute "no Muslim in Palestine could be born or die without being beholden to Haj Amin."[35] The Mufti's henchmen also ensured he would have no opposition by systematically killing Palestinians from rival clans who were discussing cooperation with the Jews.

As the spokesman for Palestinian Arabs, Haj Amin did not ask that Britain grant them independence. On the contrary, in a letter to Churchill in 1921, he demanded that Palestine be reunited with Syria and Transjordan.[36]

The Arabs found rioting to be an effective political tool because of the lax British response toward violence against Jews. In handling each riot, the British prevented Jews from protecting themselves, but made little or no effort to prevent the Arabs from attacking them. After each outbreak, a British commission of inquiry would try to establish the cause of the violence. The conclusion was always the same: the Arabs were afraid of being displaced by Jews. To stop the rioting, the commissions would recommend that restrictions be placed on Jewish immigration. Thus, the Arabs came to recognize that they could always stop the influx of Jews by staging a riot.

This cycle began after a series of riots in May 1921. After failing to protect the Jewish community from Arab mobs, the British appointed the Haycraft Commission to investigate the cause of the violence. Although the panel concluded the Arabs had been the aggressors, it rationalized the cause of the attack: "The fundamental cause of the riots was a feeling among the Arabs of discontent with, and hostility to, the Jews, due to political and economic causes, and connected with Jewish immigration, and with their conception of Zionist policy...."[37] One consequence of the violence was the institution of a temporary ban on Jewish immigration.

The Arab fear of being "displaced" or "dominated" was used as an excuse for their merciless attacks on peaceful Jewish settlers. Note, too, that these riots were not inspired by nationalistic fervor—nationalists would have rebelled against their British overlords—they were motivated by racial strife and misunderstanding.

In 1929, Arab provocateurs succeeded in convincing the masses that the Jews had designs on the Temple Mount (a tactic still used today). A Jewish religious observance at the Western Wall, which forms a part of the Temple Mount, served as a pretext for rioting by Arabs against Jews that spilled out of Jerusalem into other villages and towns, including Safed and Hebron.

Again, the British Administration made no effort to prevent the violence and, after it began, the British did nothing to protect the Jewish population. After six days of mayhem, the British finally brought troops in to quell the disturbance. By this time, virtually the entire Jewish population of Hebron had fled or been killed. In all, 133 Jews were killed and 399 wounded in the pogroms.[38]

After the riots were over, the British ordered an investigation, which resulted in the Passfield White Paper. It said the "immigration, land purchase and settlement policies of the Zionist Organization were already, or were likely to become, prejudicial to Arab interests. It understood the Mandatory's obligation to the non-Jewish community to mean that Palestine's resources must be primarily reserved for the growing Arab economy. . . ."[39] This, of course, meant it was necessary to place restrictions not only on Jewish immigration but on land purchases.

MYTH

"The Mufti was not anti-Semitic."

FACT

In 1941, Haj Amin al-Husseini, the Mufti of Jerusalem, fled to Germany and met with Adolf Hitler, Heinrich Himmler, Joachim Von Ribbentrop and other Nazi leaders. He wanted to persuade them to extend the Nazis' anti-Jewish program to the Arab world.

The Mufti sent Hitler 15 drafts of declarations he wanted Germany and Italy to make concerning the Middle East. One called on the two countries to declare the illegality of the Jewish home in Palestine. He also asked the Axis powers to "accord to Palestine and to other Arab countries the right to solve the problem of the Jewish elements in Palestine and other Arab countries in accordance with the interest of the Arabs, and by the same method that the question is now being settled in the Axis countries."[40]

In November 1941, the Mufti met with Hitler, who told him the Jews were his foremost enemy. The Nazi dictator rebuffed the Mufti's requests for a declaration in support of the Arabs, however, telling him the time was not right. The Mufti offered Hitler his "thanks for the sympathy which he had always shown for the Arab and especially Palestinian cause, and to which he had given clear expression in his public speeches.... The Arabs were Germany's natural friends because they had the same enemies as had Germany, namely.... the Jews...." Hitler told the Mufti he opposed the creation of a Jewish state and that Germany's objective was the destruction of the Jewish element residing in the Arab sphere.[41]

In 1945, Yugoslavia sought to indict the Mufti as a war criminal for his role in recruiting 20,000 Muslim volunteers for the SS, who participated in the killing of Jews in Croatia and Hungary. He escaped from French detention in 1946, however, and continued his fight against the Jews from Cairo and later Beirut.

MYTH

"The bombing of the King David Hotel was part of a deliberate terror campaign against civilians."

FACT

British troops invaded the Jewish Agency on June 29, 1946, and confiscated large quantities of documents. At about the same time, more than 2,500 Jews from all over Palestine were placed under arrest. A week later, news of a massacre of 40 Jews in a pogrom in Poland reminded the Jews of Palestine how Britain's restrictive immigration policy had condemned thousands to death.

As a response to what it viewed as British provocations, the Irgun decided to target the King David Hotel. Besides guests, the hotel housed the British military command and the British Criminal Investigation Division and was the place where information about Jewish Agency operations, including intelligence activities in Arab countries, was taken.

Irgun leader Menachem Begin stressed his desire to avoid civilian casualties. In fact, the plan was to warn the British so they would evacuate the building before it was blown up. Three telephone calls were placed, one to the hotel, another to the French Consulate, and a third to the *Palestine Post,* warning that explosives in the King David Hotel would soon be detonated.

On July 22, 1946, the calls were made. The call into the hotel was apparently received and ignored. Begin quotes one British official who supposedly refused to evacuate the building, saying: "We don't take orders from the Jews."[42] As a result, when the bombs exploded, the casualty toll was high: a total of 91 killed and 45 injured. Among the casualties were 15 Jews. Few people in the hotel proper were injured by the blast.[43]

In contrast to Arab attacks against Jews, which were widely hailed by

Arab leaders as heroic actions, the Jewish National Council denounced the bombing of the King David.[44]

For decades the British denied they had been warned. In 1979, however, a member of the British Parliament introduced evidence that the Irgun had indeed issued the warning. He offered the testimony of a British officer who heard other officers in the King David Hotel bar joking about a Zionist threat to the headquarters. The officer who overheard the conversation immediately left the hotel and survived.[45]

Notes

1. Aharon Cohen, *Israel and the Arab World*, (NY: Funk and Wagnalls, 1970), p. 172; Howard Sachar, *A History of Israel: From the Rise of Zionism to Our Time*, (NY: Alfred A. Knopf, 1979), p. 146.
2. Moshe Auman, "Land Ownership in Palestine 1880-1948," in Michael Curtis, et al., *The Palestinians*, (NJ: Transaction Books, 1975), p. 25.
3. *Palestine Royal Commission Report* (the Peel Report), (London: 1937), p. 300. Henceforth Palestine Royal Commission Report.
4. Arieh Avneri, *The Claim of Dispossession*, (Tel Aviv: Hidekel Press, 1984), p. 28; Yehoshua Porath, *The Emergence of the Palestinian-Arab National Movement, 1918-1929*, (London: Frank Cass, 1974), pp. 17-18.
5. Porath (1974), p. 18.
6. Cohen, p. 53.
7. Yehoshua Porath, *Palestinian Arab National Movement: From Riots to Rebellion: 1929-1939*, vol. 2, (London: Frank Cass and Co., Ltd., 1977), pp. 17-18, 39.
8. John Hope Simpson, *Palestine: Report on Immigration, Land Settlement and Development*, (London, 1930), p. 126.
9. C. S. Jarvis, "Palestine," *United Empire* (London), Vol 28 (1937), p. 633.
10. *Palestine Royal Commission Report*, p. 242.
11. George Lenczowski, *American Presidents and the Middle East*, (NC: Duke University Press, 1990), p. 23.
12. Cohen p. 174.
13. Dov Friedlander and Calvin Goldscheider, *The Population of Israel*, (NY: Columbia Press, 1979), p. 30.
14. Avneri, p. 254.
15. Curtis, p. 38.
16. Avneri, pp. 264; Cohen p. 60.
17. Avneri, pp. 254-55.
18. Moshe Aumann, *Land Ownership in Palestine 1880-1948*, (Jerusalem: Academic Committee on the Middle East, 1976), pp. 8-9.
19. Shabtai Teveth, *Ben-Gurion and the Palestinian Arabs: From Peace to War*, (London: Oxford University Press, 1985), p. 32.
20. Porath, pp. 80, 84; See also Hillel Cohen, *Army of Shadows: Palestinian Collaboration with Zionism, 1917-1948*, (Berkeley, University of California Press, 2008).
21. Hope Simpson Report, p. 51.
22. Avneri, pp. 149-158; Cohen, p. 37; based on the Report on Agricultural Development and Land Settlement in Palestine by Lewis French, (December 1931, Supplementary; Report, April 1932) and material submitted to the Palestine Royal Commission.
23. Netanel Lorch, *One Long War*, (Jerusalem: Keter, 1976), p. 27; Sachar, p. 201.
24. *Palestine Royal Commission Report* (1937), p. 242.
25. *Palestine Royal Commission* (1937), pp. 241-242.

26. King Abdallah, *My Memoirs Completed,* (London, Longman Group, Ltd., 1978), pp. 88-89.
27. Porath (77), pp. 86-87.
28. Aumann, p. 13.
29. Abraham Granott, *The Land System in Palestine,* (London, Eyre and Spottiswoode, 1952), p. 278.
30. Avneri, pp. 179-180, 224-225, 232-234; Porath (77), pp. 72-73; See also Hillel Cohen, *Army of Shadows: Palestinian Collaboration with Zionism, 1917-1948,* (Berkeley, University of California Press, 2008).
31. Jon Kimche, *There Could Have Been Peace: The Untold Story of Why We Failed With Palestine and Again With Israel,* (England: Dial Press, 1973), p. 189.
32. Richard Meinertzhagen, *Middle East Diary 1917-1956,* (London: The Cresset Press, 1959), pp. 49, 82, 97.
33. Samuel Katz, *Battleground-Fact and Fantasy in Palestine,* (NY: Bantam Books, 1977), pp. 63-65; Howard Sachar, *A History of Israel: From the Rise of Zionism to Our Time,* (NY: Alfred A. Knopf, 1979), p. 97.
34. Paul Johnson, *Modern Times: The World from the Twenties to the Nineties,* (NY: Harper & Row, 1983), p. 438.
35. Larry Collins and Dominique Lapierre, *O Jerusalem!,* (NY: Simon and Schuster, 1972), p. 52.
36. Kimche, p. 211.
37. Ben Halpern, *The Idea of a Jewish State,* (MA: Harvard University Press, 1969), p. 323.
38. Sachar, p. 174.
39. Halpern, p. 201.
40. "Grand Mufti Plotted To Do Away With All Jews In Mideast," *Response,* (Fall 1991), pp. 2-3.
41. Record of the Conversation Between the Fuhrer and the Grand Mufti of Jerusalem on November 28, 1941, in the Presence of Reich Foreign Minister and Minister Grobba in Berlin, *Documents on German Foreign Policy, 1918-1945,* Series D, Vol. XIII, London, 1964, p. 881ff in Walter Lacquer and Barry Rubin, *The Israel-Arab Reader,* (NY: Penguin Books, 2001), pp. 51-55.
42. Menachem Begin, *The Revolt,* (NY: Nash Publishing, 1977), p. 224.
43. J. Bowyer Bell, *Terror Out Of Zion,* (NY: St. Martin's Press), p. 172.
44. Anne Sinai and I. Robert Sinai, *Israel and the Arabs: Prelude to the Jewish State,* (NY: Facts on File, 1972), p. 83.
45. Benjamin Netanyahu, ed., "International Terrorism: Challenge And Response," Proceedings of the Jerusalem Conference on International Terrorism, July 25, 1979, (Jerusalem: The Jonathan Institute, 1980), p. 45.

3. Partition

"The United Nations unjustly partitioned Palestine."

FACT

As World War II ended, the magnitude of the Holocaust became known. This accelerated demands for a resolution to the question of Palestine so the survivors of Hitler's Final Solution might find sanctuary in a homeland of their own.

The British tried to work out an agreement acceptable to both Arabs and Jews, but their insistence on the former's approval guaranteed failure because the Arabs would not make any concessions. The British subsequently turned the issue over to the UN in February 1947.

The UN established a Special Commission on Palestine (UNSCOP) to devise a solution. Delegates from 11 nations* went to the area and found what had long been apparent: The conflicting national aspirations of Jews and Arabs could not be reconciled.

When they returned, the delegates of seven nations—Canada, Czechoslovakia, Guatemala, The Netherlands, Peru, Sweden and Uruguay—recommended the establishment of two separate states, Jewish and Arab, to be joined by economic union, with Jerusalem an internationalized enclave. Three nations—India, Iran and Yugoslavia—recommended a unitary state with Arab and Jewish provinces. Australia abstained.

The Jews of Palestine were not satisfied with the small territory allotted to them by the Commission, nor were they happy that Jerusalem was severed from the Jewish State; nevertheless, they welcomed the compromise. The Arabs rejected UNSCOP's recommendations.

The *ad hoc* committee of the UN General Assembly rejected the Arab demand for a unitary Arab state. The majority recommendation for partition was viewed as a more just solution and subsequently adopted by a vote of 33–13 with 10 abstentions on November 29, 1947.[1]

---

*Australia, Canada, Czechoslovakia, Guatemala, India, Iran, the Netherlands, Peru, Sweden, Uruguay and Yugoslavia.

Map 2 The Partition Plan - 1947
UN General Assembly Resolution 181

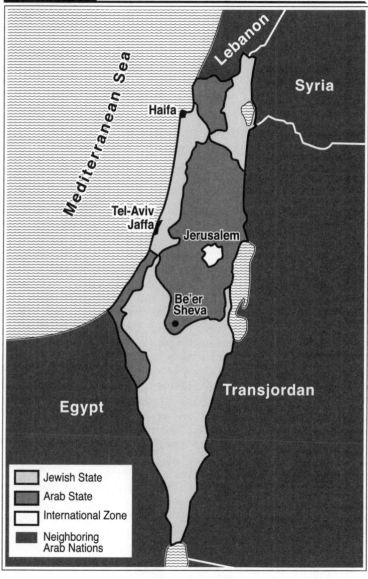

Lebanon

Syria

Mediterranean Sea

Haifa

Tel-Aviv
Jaffa

Jerusalem

Be'er
Sheva

Egypt

Transjordan

Jewish State

Arab State

International Zone

Neighboring
Arab Nations

> *"It is hard to see how the Arab world, still less the Arabs of Palestine, will suffer from what is mere recognition of accomplished fact—the presence in Palestine of a compact, well organized, and virtually autonomous Jewish community."*
>
> **London Times editorial**[2]

MYTH

"The partition plan gave the Jews most of the land, including all the fertile areas."

FACT

The partition plan took on a checkerboard appearance largely because Jewish towns and villages were spread throughout Palestine. This did not complicate the plan as much as the fact that the high living standards in Jewish cities and towns had attracted large Arab populations, which ensured that any partition would result in a Jewish state that included a substantial Arab population. Recognizing the need to allow for additional Jewish settlement, the majority proposal allotted the Jews land in the northern part of the country, the Galilee, and the large, arid Negev desert in the south. The remainder was to form the Arab state.

These boundaries were based solely on demographics. The borders of the Jewish State were arranged with no consideration of security; hence, the new state's frontiers were virtually indefensible. Overall, the Jewish State was to be comprised of roughly 5,500 square miles (about 55 percent of Palestine), and the population was to be 538,000 Jews and 397,000 Arabs. Approximately 92,000 Arabs lived in Tiberias, Safed, Haifa and Bet Shean, and another 40,000 were Bedouins, most of whom were living in the desert. The remainder of the Arab population was spread throughout the Jewish state. The Arab State was to be 4,500 square miles with a population of 804,000 Arabs and 10,000 Jews.[3]

Critics claim the UN gave the Jews fertile land while the Arabs were allotted hilly, arid land. To the contrary, approximately 60 percent of the Jewish state was to be the desert in the Negev while the Arabs occupied most of the agricultural land.[4]

Further complicating the situation was the UN majority's insistence that Jerusalem remain apart from both states and be administered as an international zone. This arrangement left more than 100,000 Jews in Jerusalem isolated from their country and circumscribed by the Arab state.

According to British statistics, more than 70 percent of the land in what would become Israel belonged to the mandatory government. Those lands reverted to Israeli control after the departure of the British. Another 9 percent of the land was owned by Jews and about 3 percent by Arabs who became citizens of Israel. That means only about 18 percent belonged to Arabs who left the country before and after the Arab invasion of Israel.[5]

MYTH

"Israel usurped all of Palestine in 1948."

FACT

Nearly 80 percent of what was the historic land of Palestine and the Jewish National Home, as defined by the League of Nations, was severed by the British in 1921 and allocated to what became Transjordan. Jewish settlement there was barred. The UN partitioned the remaining 20-odd percent of Palestine into two states. With Jordan's annexation of the West Bank in 1950, and Egypt's control of Gaza, Arabs controlled more than 80 percent of the territory of the Mandate, while the Jewish State held a bare 17.5 percent.[6]

MYTH

"The Palestinian Arabs were never offered a state and therefore have been denied the right to self-determination."

FACT

The Peel Commission in 1937 concluded the only logical solution to resolving the contradictory aspirations of the Jews and Arabs was to partition Palestine into separate Jewish and Arab states. The Arabs rejected the plan because it forced them to accept the creation of a Jewish state, and required some Palestinians to live under "Jewish domination." The Zionists opposed the Peel Plan's boundaries because they would have been confined to 1,900 out of the 10,310 square miles remaining in Palestine. Nevertheless, the Zionists decided to negotiate with the British, while the Arabs refused to consider any compromises.

In 1939, the British White Paper called for the establishment of an Arab state in Palestine within 10 years, and for limiting Jewish immigration to no more than 75,000 over the following five years. Afterward, no one would be allowed in without the consent of the Arab population. Though the Arabs had been granted a concession on Jewish immigration, and been offered independence—the goal of Arab nationalists— they repudiated the White Paper.

With partition, the Palestinians were given a state and the opportunity for self-determination. This too was rejected.

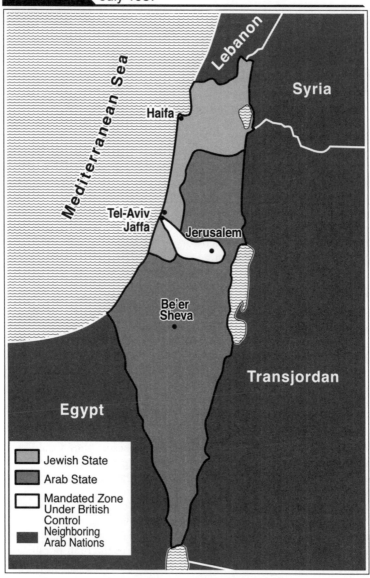

Map 3 — Peel Commission Partition Plan July 1937

Legend:
- Jewish State
- Arab State
- Mandated Zone Under British Control
- Neighboring Arab Nations

MYTH

"The majority of the population in Palestine was Arab; therefore, a unitary Arab state should have been created."

FACT

At the time of the 1947 partition resolution, the Arabs did have a majority in western Palestine, as a whole—1.2 million Arabs versus 600,000 Jews.[7] But the Jews were a majority *in the area allotted to them* by the resolution, and in Jerusalem.

The Jews never had a chance of reaching a majority in the country given the restrictive immigration policy of the British. By contrast, Palestine's Arab population, which had been declining prior to the Mandate in 1922, grew exponentially because Arabs from all the surrounding countries were free to come—and thousands did—to take advantage of the rapid economic development and improved health conditions stimulated by Zionist settlement.

The decision to partition Palestine was not determined solely by demographics; it was based on the conclusion that the territorial claims of Jews and Arabs were irreconcilable, and that the most logical compromise was the creation of two states. Ironically, that same year, 1947, the Arab members of the United Nations supported the partition of the Indian sub-continent and the creation of the new, predominantly Muslim state of Pakistan.

MYTH

"The Arabs were prepared to compromise to avoid bloodshed."

FACT

As the partition vote approached, it became clear little hope existed for a political solution to a problem that transcended politics: the Arabs' unwillingness to accept a Jewish state in Palestine and the refusal of the Zionists to settle for anything less. The implacability of the Arabs was evident when Jewish Agency representatives David Horowitz and Abba Eban made a last-ditch effort to reach a compromise in a meeting with Arab League Secretary Azzam Pasha on September 16, 1947. Pasha told them bluntly:

> The Arab world is not in a compromising mood. It's likely, Mr. Horowitz, that your plan is rational and logical, but the fate of nations is not decided by rational logic. Nations never concede; they fight. You won't get anything by peaceful means or compromise. You can, perhaps, get something, but only by the force of your arms. We shall try to defeat you. I am not

sure we'll succeed, but we'll try. We were able to drive out the Crusaders, but on the other hand we lost Spain and Persia. It may be that we shall lose Palestine. But it's too late to talk of peaceful solutions.[8]

Notes

1. Voting in *favor* of partition: Australia, Belgium, Bolivia, Brazil, Byelorussian SSR, Canada, Costa Rica, Czechoslovakia, Denmark, Dominican Republic, Ecuador, France, Guatemala, Haiti, Iceland, Liberia, Luxembourg, Netherlands, New Zealand, Nicaragua, Norway, Panama, Paraguay, Peru, Philippines, Poland, Sweden, Ukrainian SSR, Union of South Africa, USSR, USA, Uruguay, Venezuela.

   Voting against partition: Afghanistan, Cuba, Egypt, Greece, India, Iran, Iraq, Lebanon, Pakistan, Saudi Arabia, Syria, Turkey, Yemen.

   Abstained: Argentina, Chile, China, Columbia, El Salvador, Ethiopia, Honduras, Mexico, UK, Yugoslavia. *Yearbook of the United Nations, 1947-48,* (NY: United Nations, 1949), pp. 246-47.
2. *London Times,* (December 1, 1947).
3. Howard Sachar, *A History of Israel: From the Rise of Zionism to Our Time,* (NY: Alfred A. Knopf, 1998), p. 292.
4. Aharon Cohen, *Israel and the Arab World,* (Boston: Beacon Press, 1976), p. 238.
5. Moshe Aumann, "Land Ownership in Palestine, 1880-1948," (Academic Committee on the Middle East: Israel, 1974), p. 18.
6. Historic Palestine comprised what is today Jordan (approximately 35,640 square miles), Israel (8,019 square miles), Gaza (139 square miles) and the West Bank (2,263 square miles).
7. Arieh Avneri, *The Claim of Dispossession,* (NJ: Transaction Books, 1984), p. 252.
8. David Horowitz, *State in the Making,* (NY: Alfred A. Knopf, 1953), p. 233.

4. The War of 1948

MYTH

"The Jews started the first war with the Arabs."

FACT

The Arabs made clear they would go to war to prevent the establishment of a Jewish state. The chairman of the Arab Higher Committee said the Arabs would "fight for every inch of their country."[1] Two days later, the holy men of Al-Azhar University in Cairo called on the Muslim world to proclaim a *jihad* (holy war) against the Jews.[2] Jamal Husseini, the Arab Higher Committee's spokesman, had told the UN prior to the partition vote the Arabs would drench "the soil of our beloved country with the last drop of our blood...."[3]

Husseini's prediction began to come true almost immediately after the UN adopted the partition resolution on November 29, 1947. The Arabs declared a protest strike and instigated riots that claimed the lives of 62 Jews and 32 Arabs. Violence continued to escalate through the end of the year.[4]

The first large-scale assaults began on January 9, 1948, when approximately 1,000 Arabs attacked Jewish communities in northern Palestine. By February, the British said so many Arabs had infiltrated they lacked the forces to run them back.[5]

In the first phase of the war, lasting from November 29, 1947, until April 1, 1948, the Palestinian Arabs took the offensive, with help from volunteers from neighboring countries. The Jews suffered severe casualties and passage along most of their major roadways was disrupted.

On April 26, 1948, Transjordan's King Abdullah said:

> All our efforts to find a peaceful solution to the Palestine problem have failed. The only way left for us is war. I will have the pleasure and honor to save Palestine.[6]

On May 4, 1948, the Arab Legion attacked Kfar Etzion. The defenders drove them back, but the Legion returned a week later. After two days, the ill-equipped and outnumbered settlers were overwhelmed. Many defenders were massacred after they had surrendered.[7] This was prior to the invasion by the regular Arab armies that followed Israel's declaration of independence.

The UN blamed the Arabs for the violence. The UN Palestine Commission, which was never permitted by the Arabs or British to go to

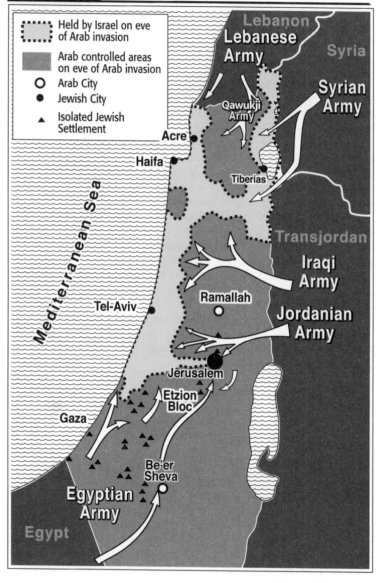

Map 4

The Arab Invasion
May 15, 1948

Held by Israel on eve
of Arab invasion

Arab controlled areas
on eve of Arab invasion

O Arab City

● Jewish City

▲ Isolated Jewish
Settlement

Lebanon

Lebanese
Army

Syria

Syrian
Army

Qawukji
Army

Acre

Haifa

Tiberias

Mediterranean Sea

Transjordan

Iraqi
Army

Ramallah

Jordanian
Army

Tel-Aviv

Jerusalem

Etzion
Bloc

Gaza

Be'er
Sheva

Egyptian
Army

Egypt

Palestine to implement the resolution, reported to the Security Council on February 16, 1948, that "powerful Arab interests, both inside and outside Palestine, are defying the resolution of the General Assembly and are engaged in a deliberate effort to alter by force the settlement envisaged therein."[8]

The Arabs were blunt in taking responsibility for the war. Jamal Husseini told the Security Council on April 16, 1948:

> The representative of the Jewish Agency told us yesterday that they were not the attackers, that the Arabs had begun the fighting. We did not deny this. We told the whole world that we were going to fight.[9]

The British commander of Jordan's Arab Legion, John Bagot Glubb admitted:

> Early in January, the first detachments of the Arab Liberation Army began to infiltrate into Palestine from Syria. Some came through Jordan and even through Amman ... They were in reality to strike the first blow in the ruin of the Arabs of Palestine.[10]

Despite the disadvantages in numbers, organization and weapons, the Jews began to take the initiative in the weeks from April 1 until the declaration of independence on May 14. The Haganah captured several major towns including Tiberias and Haifa, and temporarily opened the road to Jerusalem.

The partition resolution was never suspended or rescinded. Thus, Israel, the Jewish State in Palestine, was born on May 14, as the British finally left the country. Five Arab armies (Egypt, Syria, Transjordan, Lebanon and Iraq) immediately invaded Israel. Their intentions were declared by Abd Al-Rahman Azzam Pasha, Secretary-General of the Arab League: "It will be a war of annihilation. It will be a momentous massacre in history that will be talked about like the massacres of the Mongols or the Crusades."[11]

MYTH

"The United States was the only nation that criticized the Arab attack on Israel."

FACT

The United States, the Soviet Union and most other states recognized Israel soon after it declared independence on May 14, 1948, and immediately condemned the Arabs for their aggression. The United States urged a resolution charging the Arabs with breach of the peace.

Soviet delegate Andrei Gromyko told the Security Council, May 29, 1948:

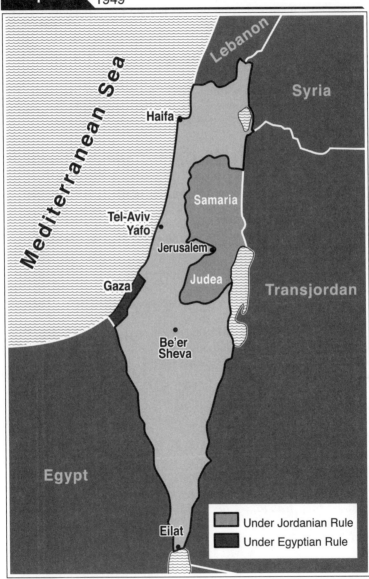

Map 5 Armistice Lines 1949

Lebanon

Syria

Mediterranean Sea

Haifa

Samaria

Tel-Aviv Yafo

Jerusalem

Judea

Transjordan

Gaza

Be'er Sheva

Egypt

Eilat

Under Jordanian Rule
Under Egyptian Rule

This is not the first time that the Arab states, which organized the invasion of Palestine, have ignored a decision of the Security Council or of the General Assembly. The USSR delegation deems it essential that the council should state its opinion more clearly and more firmly with regard to this attitude of the Arab states toward decisions of the Security Council.[12]

On July 15, the Security Council threatened to cite the Arab governments for aggression under the UN Charter. By this time, the Israel Defense Forces (IDF) had succeeded in stopping the Arab offensive and the initial phase of the fighting ended.

MYTH

*"The West's support of Israel allowed the
Jews to conquer Palestine."*

FACT

The Jews won their war of independence with minimal help from the West. In fact, they won despite actions that undermined their military strength.

Although the United States vigorously supported the partition resolution, the State Department did not want to provide the Jews with the means to defend themselves. "Otherwise," Undersecretary of State Robert Lovett argued, "the Arabs might use arms of U.S. origin against Jews, or Jews might use them against Arabs."[13] Consequently, on December 5, 1947, the U.S. imposed an arms embargo on the region.

Many opponents of the Jewish state in the State Department saw the embargo as a means of obstructing partition. President Truman, however, supported it because he hoped it could avert bloodshed. This was naive given Britain's rejection of Lovett's request to suspend weapons shipments to the Arabs and subsequent agreements to provide additional arms to Iraq and Transjordan.[14]

The Arabs had no difficulty obtaining all the arms they needed. In fact, Jordan's Arab Legion was armed and trained by the British, and led by a British officer. At the end of 1948, and beginning of 1949, British RAF planes flew with Egyptian squadrons over the Israel-Egypt border. On January 7, 1949, Israeli planes shot down four of the British aircraft.[15]

The Jews, on the other hand, were forced to smuggle weapons, principally from Czechoslovakia. When Israel declared its independence in May 1948, the army did not have a single cannon or tank. Its air force consisted of nine obsolete planes. Although the Haganah had 60,000 trained fighters, only 18,900 were fully mobilized, armed and prepared for war.[16] On the eve of the war, chief of operations Yigael Yadin told David Ben-Gurion: "The best we can tell you is that we have a 50–50 chance."[17]

The Arab war to destroy Israel failed. Indeed, because of their aggression, the Arabs wound up with less territory than they would have had if they had accepted partition.

The cost to Israel, however, was enormous. "Many of its most productive fields lay gutted and mined. Its citrus groves, for decades the basis of the Yishuv's Jewish community economy, were largely destroyed."[18] Military expenditures totaled approximately $500 million. Worse yet, 6,373 Israelis were killed, nearly one percent of the Jewish population of 650,000.

Had the West enforced the partition resolution or given the Jews the capacity to defend themselves, many lives might have been saved.

The Arab countries signed armistice agreements with Israel in 1949, starting with Egypt (Feb. 24), followed by Lebanon (March 23), Jordan (April 3) and Syria (July 20). Iraq was the only country that did not sign an agreement with Israel, choosing instead to withdraw its troops and hand over its sector to Jordan's Arab Legion. None of the Arab states would negotiate a peace agreement.

MYTH

"The Arab economic boycott was imposed in response to the creation of Israel."

FACT

The Arab boycott was formally declared by the newly formed Arab League Council on December 2, 1945: "Jewish products and manufactured goods shall be considered undesirable to the Arab countries." All Arab "institutions, organizations, merchants, commission agents and individuals" were called upon "to refuse to deal in, distribute, or consume Zionist products or manufactured goods."[19] As is evident in this declaration, the terms "Jewish" and "Zionist" were used synonymously. Thus, even before the establishment of Israel, the Arab states had declared an economic boycott against the Jews of Palestine.

The boycott, as it evolved after 1948, is divided into three components. The primary boycott prohibits direct trade between Israel and the Arab nations. The secondary boycott is directed at companies that do business with Israel. The tertiary boycott involves the blacklisting of firms that trade with other companies that do business with Israel.[20]

The objective of the boycott has been to isolate Israel from its neighbors and the international community, and deny it trade that might be used to augment its military and economic strength. While undoubtedly isolating Israel and separating the Jewish State from its most natural markets, the boycott failed to undermine Israel's economy to the degree intended.

In 1977, Congress prohibited U.S. companies from cooperating with the Arab boycott. When President Carter signed the law, he said the "issue goes to the very heart of free trade among nations" and that it was designed to "end the divisive effects on American life of foreign boycotts aimed at Jewish members of our society."[21]

The boycott has gradually crumbled and few countries outside the Middle East comply with it. The primary boycott—prohibiting direct relations between Arab countries and Israel—cracked when nations such as Qatar, Oman and Morocco negotiated deals with Israel. Saudi Arabia, pledged to end its economic boycott as a condition for membership in the World Trade Organization but, after winning acceptance, continued its prior policy.[22] Meanwhile, the boycott remains technically in force.[23]

Notes

1. *New York Times,* (December 1, 1947).
2. *Facts on File Yearbook,* (NY: Facts on File, Inc., 1948), p. 48.
3. J.C. Hurewitz, *The Struggle For Palestine,* (NY: Shocken Books, 1976), p. 308.
4. *Palestine Post,* (January 2, 7, 27; April 1; May 1, 1948).
5. *Facts on File 1947,* p. 231.
6. Howard Sachar, *A History of Israel: From the Rise of Zionism to Our Time,* (NY: Alfred A. Knopf, 1979), p. 322.
7. Netanel Lorch, *One Long War,* (Jerusalem: Keter Books, 1976), p. 47; Ralph Patai, ed., *Encyclopedia of Zionism and Israel,* (NY: McGraw Hill, 1971), pp. 307-308.
8. Security Council Official Records, Special Supplement, (1948), p. 20.
9. Security Council Official Records, S/Agenda/58, (April 16, 1948), p. 19.
10. John Bagot Glubb, *A Soldier with the Arabs,* (London: Staughton and Hodder, 1957), p. 79.
11. "Interview with Abd al-Rahman Azzam Pasha," *Akhbar al-Yom (Egypt),* (October 11, 1947); translated by R. Green.
12. Security Council Official Records, SA/Agenda/77, (May 29, 1948), p. 2.
13. *Foreign Relations of the United States 1947,* (DC: GPO, 1948), p. 1249. Henceforth FRUS.
14. Mitchell Bard, *The Water's Edge And Beyond,* (NJ: Transaction Books, 1991), pp. 171175; *FRUS,* pp. 537-39; Robert Silverberg, *If I Forget Thee O Jerusalem: American Jews and the State of Israel,* (NY: William Morrow and Co., Inc., 1970), pp. 366, 370; Shlomo Slonim, "The 1948 American Embargo on Arms to Palestine," *Political Science Quarterly,* (Fall 1979), p. 500.
15. Sachar, p. 345.
16. Larry Collins and Dominique Lapierre, *O Jerusalem!,* (NY: Simon and Schuster, 1972), p. 352.
17. Golda Meir, *My Life,* (NY: Dell, 1975), pp. 213, 222, 224.
18. Sachar, p. 452.
19. Terence Prittie and Walter Nelson, *The Economic War Against The Jews,* (London: Corgi Books, 1977); Dan Chill, *The Arab Boycott of Israel,* (NY: Praeger, 1976), p. 10.
20. Prittie and Nelson, pp. 47-48; Sol Stern, "On and Off the Arabs' List," *The New Republic,* (March 27, 1976), p. 9; Kennan Teslik, *Congress, the Executive Branch and Special Interests,* (CT: Greenwood Press, 1982), p. 11.
21. Bard, pp. 91-115.
22. "Congress to Saudis: End Israel Boycott," *Jerusalem Post,* (April 6, 2006).
23. "Saudis Flout Vow to End Israel Boycott," *Jerusalem Post,* (May 29, 2006).

5. The 1956 War

MYTH

"Arab governments were prepared to accept Israel after the 1948 war."

FACT

In the fall of 1948, the UN Security Council called on Israel and the Arab states to negotiate armistice agreements. Thanks to UN mediator Ralph Bunche's insistence on direct bilateral talks between Israel and each Arab state, armistice agreements between Israel and Egypt, Jordan, and Syria were concluded by the summer of 1949. Iraq, which had also fought against Israel, refused to follow suit.

Meanwhile, on December 11, 1948, the General Assembly adopted a resolution calling on the parties to negotiate peace and creating a Palestine Conciliation Commission (PCC), which consisted of the United States, France and Turkey. All Arab delegations voted against it.

After 1949, the Arabs insisted that Israel accept the borders in the 1947 partition resolution and repatriate the Palestinian refugees before they would negotiate an end to the war they had initiated. This was a novel approach that they would use after subsequent defeats: the doctrine of the limited-liability war. Under this theory, aggressors may reject a compromise settlement and gamble on war to win everything in the comfortable knowledge that, even if they fail, they may insist on reinstating the status quo ante.

MYTH

"The threat from Israel, and the withdrawal of the United States' offer to build the Aswan Dam, drove Egypt to seek arms from the Soviet Union in 1955. This started the Middle East arms race."

FACT

In 1955, Nasser turned to the Soviet Union in anger because the United States had armed Iraq, Egypt's hated rival, and promoted the Baghdad Pact. Nasser opposed that agreement, as he did any defense alliance with the West.

Egypt began to receive Soviet Bloc arms in 1955. The United States, hoping to maintain a degree of influence in Egypt and to induce Nasser to reduce his arms acquisitions, offered to build the Aswan Dam. But

Nasser increased his arms orders and spurned a U.S. peace initiative. Egypt had embarked on a policy of "neutralism," which meant that Nasser intended to get aid from both East and West if he could, while maintaining his freedom to attack the West and assist Soviet efforts to gain influence in the Arab and Afro-Asian worlds. As a result of these actions, and Nasser's increasing hostility to the West, the United States withdrew the Aswan offer. Egypt then nationalized the Suez Canal.

Immediately after Nasser made his 1955 arms deal, Israel appealed to the United States—not for a gift of arms, but for the right to purchase them. The U.S. recognized the need to maintain an arms balance, but it referred Israel to France and other European suppliers. It was not until 1962 that the United States agreed to sell Israel its first significant American system, the HAWK anti-aircraft missile.

MYTH

"Israel's military strike in 1956 was unprovoked."

FACT

Egypt had maintained its state of belligerency with Israel after the armistice agreement was signed. The first manifestation of this was the closing of the Suez Canal to Israeli shipping. On August 9, 1949, the UN Mixed Armistice Commission upheld Israel's complaint that Egypt was illegally blocking the canal. UN negotiator Ralph Bunche declared: "There should be free movement for legitimate shipping and no vestiges of the wartime blockade should be allowed to remain, as they are inconsistent with both the letter and the spirit of the armistice agreements."[1]

On September 1, 1951, the Security Council ordered Egypt to open the Canal to Israeli shipping. Egypt refused to comply.

The Egyptian Foreign Minister, Muhammad Salah al-Din, said early in 1954 that:

"The Arab people will not be embarrassed to declare: We shall not be satisfied except by the final obliteration of Israel from the map of the Middle East."[2]

In 1955, Egyptian President Gamal Abdel Nasser began to import arms from the Soviet Bloc to build his arsenal for a future confrontation with Israel. In the short-term, however, he employed a new tactic to prosecute Egypt's war with Israel. He announced it on August 31, 1955:

Egypt has decided to dispatch her heroes, the disciples of Pharaoh and the sons of Islam and they will cleanse the land of Palestine.... There will be no peace on Israel's border because we demand vengeance, and vengeance is Israel's death.[3]

These "heroes" were Arab terrorists, or *fedayeen,* trained and equipped by Egyptian Intelligence to engage in hostile action on the border, and to

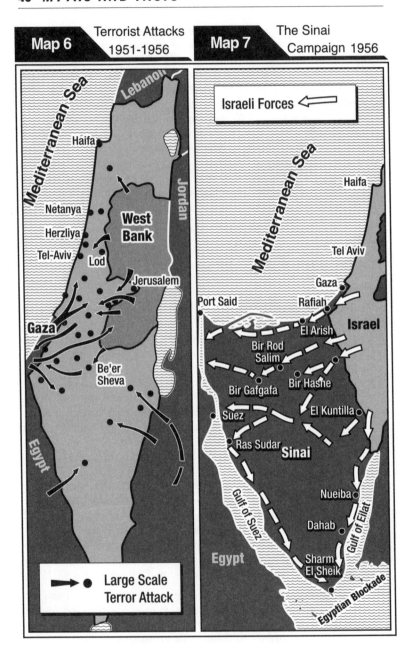

Map 6 — Terrorist Attacks 1951-1956

Mediterranean Sea

Lebanon

Haifa

Netanya

Herzliya

Tel-Aviv

Lod

West Bank

Jordan

Jerusalem

Gaza

Be'er Sheva

Egypt

➤ ● Large Scale Terror Attack

Map 7 — The Sinai Campaign 1956

Israeli Forces ⇐

Mediterranean Sea

Haifa

Tel Aviv

Gaza

Rafiah

Port Said

El Arish

Israel

Bir Rod Salim

Bir Gafgafa

Bir Hashe

Suez

El Kuntilla

Ras Sudar

Sinai

Nueiba

Dahab

Egypt

Gulf of Suez

Gulf of Eilat

Sharm El Sheik

Egyptian Blockade

infiltrate Israel to commit acts of sabotage and murder. The *fedayeen* operated mainly from bases in Jordan, so that Jordan would bear the brunt of Israel's retaliation, which inevitably followed. The terrorist attacks violated the armistice agreement provision that prohibited the initiation of hostilities by paramilitary forces; nevertheless, it was Israel that was condemned by the UN Security Council for its counterattacks.

The escalation continued with the Egyptian blockade of Israel's shipping lane in the Straits of Tiran, and Nasser's nationalization of the Suez Canal in July 1956. On October 14, Nasser made clear his intent:

> I am not solely fighting against Israel itself. My task is to deliver the Arab world from destruction through Israel's intrigue, which has its roots abroad. Our hatred is very strong. There is no sense in talking about peace with Israel. There is not even the smallest place for negotiations.[4]

Less than two weeks later, on October 25, Egypt signed a tripartite agreement with Syria and Jordan placing Nasser in command of all three armies.

The blockade of the Suez Canal and Gulf of Aqaba to Israeli shipping, combined with the increased *fedayeen* attacks and the bellicosity of Arab statements, prompted Israel, with the backing of Britain and France, to attack Egypt on October 29, 1956. The Israeli attack on Egypt was successful, with Israeli forces capturing the Gaza Strip, much of the Sinai and Sharm al-Sheikh. A total of 231 Israeli soldiers died in the fighting.

Israeli Ambassador to the UN Abba Eban explained the provocations to the Security Council on October 30:

> During the six years during which this belligerency has operated in violation of the Armistice Agreement there have occurred 1,843 cases of armed robbery and theft, 1,339 cases of armed clashes with Egyptian armed forces, 435 cases of incursion from Egyptian controlled territory, 172 cases of sabotage perpetrated by Egyptian military units and fedayeen in Israel. As a result of these actions of Egyptian hostility within Israel, 364 Israelis were wounded and 101 killed. In 1956 alone, as a result of this aspect of Egyptian aggression, 28 Israelis were killed and 127 wounded.[5]

MYTH

"The United States' blind support for Israel was apparent during the Suez War."

FACT

President Eisenhower was upset by the fact that Israel, France and Great Britain had secretly planned the campaign to evict Egypt from the Suez

Canal. Israel's failure to inform the United States of its intentions, combined with ignoring American entreaties not to go to war, sparked tensions between the countries. The United States subsequently joined the Soviet Union (ironically, just after the Soviets invaded Hungary) in a campaign to force Israel to withdraw. This included a threat to discontinue all U.S. assistance, UN sanctions and expulsion from the UN (see exchanges between Ben-Gurion and Eisenhower[6]).

U.S. pressure resulted in an Israeli withdrawal from the areas it conquered without obtaining any concessions from the Egyptians. This sowed the seeds of the 1967 war.

One reason Israel did give in to Eisenhower was the assurance he gave to Prime Minister David Ben-Gurion. Before evacuating Sharm al-Sheikh, the strategic point guarding the Straits of Tiran, Israel elicited a promise that the United States would maintain the freedom of navigation in the waterway.[7] In addition, Washington sponsored a UN resolution creating the United Nations Emergency Force (UNEF) to supervise the territories vacated by the Israeli forces.

The war temporarily ended the activities of the *fedayeen;* however, they were renewed a few years later by a loosely knit group of terrorist organizations that became known as the Palestine Liberation Organization (PLO).

Notes

1. "Israel's Complaint to the U.N. Security Council on the Suez Canal Blockade; S-2241," Israel Ministry of Foreign Affairs, (July 11, 1951).
2. *Al-Misri,* (April 12, 1954), cited in, "Mideast-History's Lesson," *Florida Times Union,* (May 7, 2002).
3. *Middle Eastern Affairs,* (December 1956), p. 461.
4. *Middle Eastern Affairs,* (December 1956), p. 460.
5. *Security Council Official Records,* S/3706, (October 30, 1956), p. 14.
6. Jewish Virtual Library, www.jewishvirtuallibrary.org/jsource/History/bgiketoc.html.
7. Janice Gross Stein and Raymond Tanter, *Rational Decision Making: Israel's Security Choices,* (OH: Ohio State University, 1976), p. 163.

6. The Six-Day War and the War of Attrition, 1967–1970

MYTH

"Arab governments recognized Israel after the Suez War."

FACT

Israel consistently expressed a desire to negotiate with its neighbors. In an address to the UN General Assembly on October 10, 1960, Foreign Minister Golda Meir challenged Arab leaders to meet with Prime Minister David Ben-Gurion to negotiate a peace settlement. Egyptian President Nasser answered on October 15, saying that Israel was trying to deceive the world, and reiterating that his country would never recognize the Jewish State.[1]

The Arabs were equally adamant in their refusal to negotiate a separate settlement for the refugees. Nasser made clear that solving the refugee issue was not his concern. "The danger of Israel," he said, "lies in the very existence of Israel as it is in the present and in what she represents."[2]

Meanwhile, Syria used the Golan Heights, which tower 3,000 feet above the Galilee, to shell Israeli farms and villages. Syria's attacks grew more frequent in 1965 and 1966, while Nasser's rhetoric became increasingly bellicose: "We shall not enter Palestine with its soil covered in sand," he said on March 8, 1965. "We shall enter it with its soil saturated in blood."[3]

Again, a few months later, Nasser expressed the Arabs' aspiration: ". . . the full restoration of the rights of the Palestinian people. In other words, we aim at the destruction of the State of Israel. The immediate aim: perfection of Arab military might. The national aim: the eradication of Israel."[4]

MYTH

"Israel's military strike in 1967 was unprovoked."

FACT

A combination of bellicose Arab rhetoric, threatening behavior and, ultimately, an act of war left Israel no choice but preemptive action. To do this successfully, Israel needed the element of surprise. Had it waited for

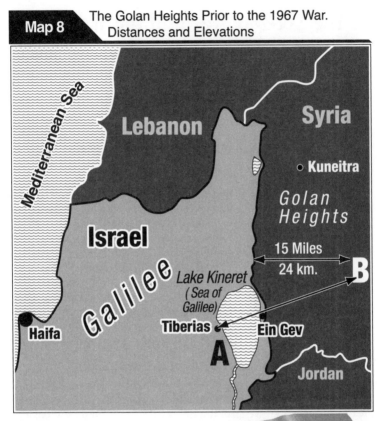

Map 8   The Golan Heights Prior to the 1967 War. Distances and Elevations

Mediterranean Sea

Lebanon

Syria

○ **Kuneitra**

Golan Heights

Israel

15 Miles
24 km.

B

Galilee

*Lake Kineret
(Sea of
Galilee)*

Tiberias

Ein Gev

A

● **Haifa**

Jordan

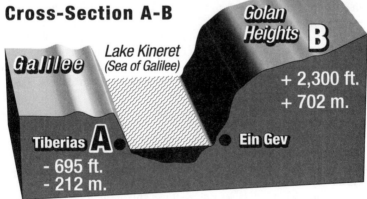

Cross-Section A-B

Golan Heights **B**

*Lake Kineret
(Sea of Galilee)*

Galilee

+ 2,300 ft.
+ 702 m.

Tiberias A

Ein Gev

- 695 ft.
- 212 m.

an Arab invasion, Israel would have been at a potentially catastrophic disadvantage.

In addition to Nasser's verbal threats, Israel was under actual attack from Arab terrorists. In 1965, 35 raids were conducted against Israel. In 1966, the number increased to 41. In just the first four months of 1967, 37 attacks were launched.[5]

Meanwhile, Syria's attacks on Israeli kibbutzim from the Golan Heights provoked a retaliatory strike on April 7, 1967, during which Israeli planes shot down six Syrian MiGs. Shortly thereafter, the Soviet Union—which had been providing military and economic aid to both Syria and Egypt—gave Damascus information alleging a massive Israeli military buildup in preparation for an attack. Despite Israeli denials, Syria decided to invoke its defense treaty with Egypt.

On May 15, Israel's Independence Day, Egyptian troops began moving into the Sinai and massing near the Israeli border. By May 18, Syrian troops were prepared for battle along the Golan Heights.

Nasser ordered the UN Emergency Force, stationed in the Sinai since 1956, to withdraw on May 16. Without bringing the matter to the attention of the General Assembly, as his predecessor had promised, Secretary-General U Thant complied with the demand. After the withdrawal of the UNEF, the Voice of the Arabs proclaimed (May 18, 1967):

> As of today, there no longer exists an international emergency force to protect Israel. We shall exercise patience no more. We shall not complain any more to the UN about Israel. The sole method we shall apply against Israel is total war, which will result in the extermination of Zionist existence.[6]

An enthusiastic echo was heard on May 20 from Syrian Defense Minister Hafez Assad:

> Our forces are now entirely ready not only to repulse the aggression, but to initiate the act of liberation itself, and to explode the Zionist presence in the Arab homeland. The Syrian army, with its finger on the trigger, is united. . . . I, as a military man, believe that the time has come to enter into a battle of annihilation.[7]

On May 22, Egypt closed the Straits of Tiran to all Israeli shipping and all ships bound for Eilat. This blockade cut off Israel's only supply route with Asia and stopped the flow of oil from its main supplier, Iran. The following day, President Johnson declared the blockade illegal and tried, unsuccessfully, to organize an international flotilla to test it.

Nasser was fully aware of the pressure he was exerting to force Israel's hand. The day after the blockade was set up, he said defiantly: "The Jews threaten to make war. I reply: Welcome! We are ready for war."[8]

Nasser challenged Israel to fight almost daily. "Our basic objective will be the destruction of Israel. The Arab people want to fight," he said on May 27.[9] The following day, he added: "We will not accept any ... coexistence with Israel ... Today the issue is not the establishment of peace between the Arab states and Israel. ... The war with Israel is in effect since 1948."[10]

King Hussein of Jordan signed a defense pact with Egypt on May 30. Nasser then announced:

> The armies of Egypt, Jordan, Syria and Lebanon are poised on the borders of Israel ... to face the challenge, while standing behind us are the armies of Iraq, Algeria, Kuwait, Sudan and the whole Arab nation. This act will astound the world. Today they will know that the Arabs are arranged for battle, the critical hour has arrived. We have reached the stage of serious action and not declarations.[11]

President Abdur Rahman Aref of Iraq joined in the war of words: "The existence of Israel is an error which must be rectified. This is our opportunity to wipe out the ignominy which has been with us since 1948. Our goal is clear—to wipe Israel off the map."[12] On June 4, Iraq joined the military alliance with Egypt, Jordan and Syria.

The Arab rhetoric was matched by the mobilization of Arab forces. Approximately 250,000 troops (nearly half in Sinai), more than 2,000 tanks and 700 aircraft ringed Israel.[13]

By this time, Israeli forces had been on alert for three weeks. The country could not remain fully mobilized indefinitely, nor could it allow its sea lane through the Gulf of Aqaba to be interdicted. Israel's best option was to strike first. On June 5, 1967, the order was given to attack Egypt.

MYTH

"Nasser had the right to close the Straits of Tiran to Israeli shipping."

FACT

In 1956, the United States gave Israel assurances that it recognized the Jewish State's right of access to the Straits of Tiran. In 1957, at the UN, 17 maritime powers declared that Israel had a right to transit the Strait. Moreover, the blockade violated the Convention on the Territorial Sea and Contiguous Zone, which was adopted by the UN Conference on the Law of the Sea on April 27, 1958.[14]

The closure of the Strait of Tiran was the *casus belli* in 1967. Israel's attack was a reaction to this Egyptian first strike.

Map 9 Israel Before June 1967

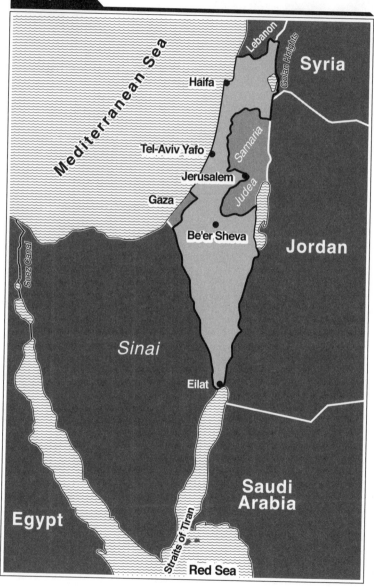

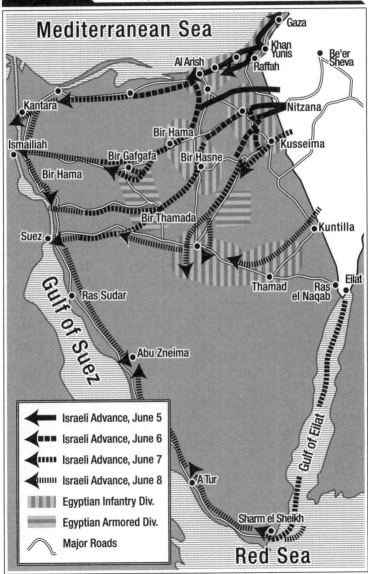

Map 10 The Egyptian Front
June 5-8, 1967

President Johnson acknowledged as much after the war (June 19, 1967):

> If a single act of folly was more responsible for this explosion than any other it was the arbitrary and dangerous announced decision that the Strait of Tiran would be closed. The right of innocent maritime passage must be preserved for all nations.[15]

MYTH

"The United States helped Israel defeat the Arabs in six days."

FACT

The United States tried to prevent the war through negotiations, but it could not persuade Nasser or the other Arab states to cease their belligerent statements and actions. Still, right before the war, President Johnson warned: "Israel will not be alone unless it decides to go alone."[16] Then, when the war began, the State Department announced: "Our position is neutral in thought, word and deed."[17]

Moreover, while the Arabs were falsely accusing the United States of airlifting supplies to Israel, Johnson imposed an arms embargo on the region (France, Israel's other main arms supplier, also embargoed arms to Israel).

By contrast, the Soviets were supplying massive amounts of arms to the Arabs. Simultaneously, the armies of Kuwait, Algeria, Saudi Arabia and Iraq were contributing troops and arms to the Egyptian, Syrian and Jordanian fronts.[18]

MYTH

"Israel attacked Jordan to capture Jerusalem."

FACT

Prime Minister Levi Eshkol sent a message to King Hussein saying Israel would not attack Jordan unless he initiated hostilities. When Jordanian radar picked up a cluster of planes flying from Egypt to Israel, and the Egyptians convinced Hussein the planes were theirs, he then ordered the shelling of West Jerusalem. It turned out the planes were Israel's, and were returning from destroying the Egyptian air force on the ground. Meanwhile, Syrian and Iraqi troops attacked Israel's northern frontier.

Had Jordan not attacked, the status of Jerusalem would not have changed during the course of the war. Once the city came under fire, however, Israel needed to defend it, and, in doing so, took the opportunity to unify the city, ending Jordan's 19-year occupation of the eastern part.

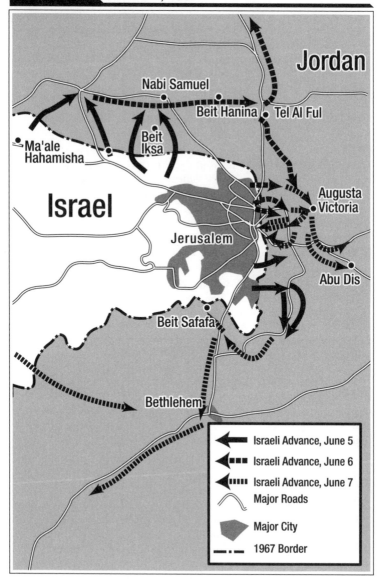

Map 11 The Battle for Jerusalem
June 5-7, 1967

Jordan

Nabi Samuel

Beit Hanina • Tel Al Ful

Ma'ale
Hahamisha

Beit
Iksa

Israel

Augusta
Victoria

Jerusalem

Abu Dis

Beit Safafa

Bethlehem

	Israeli Advance, June 5
	Israeli Advance, June 6
	Israeli Advance, June 7
	Major Roads
	Major City
	1967 Border

MYTH

"Israel did not have to fire the first shot in June 1967."

FACT

By using the element of surprise, Israeli forces managed to break through the enemy lines after just six days of fighting and were in a position to march on Cairo, Damascus and Amman. A cease-fire was invoked on June 10.

The victory came at a very high cost. In storming the Golan Heights, Israel suffered 115 dead—roughly the number of Americans killed during Operation Desert Storm. Altogether, Israel lost twice as many men—777 dead and 2,586 wounded—in proportion to her total population as the U.S. lost in eight years of fighting in Vietnam.[19] Also, despite the incredible success of the air campaign, the Israeli Air Force lost 46 of its 200 fighters.[20] Had Israel waited for the Arabs to strike first, as it did in 1973, and not taken preemptive action, the cost would certainly have been much higher and victory could not have been assured.

MYTH

"Israel expelled peaceful Arab villagers from the West Bank and prevented them from returning after the war."

FACT

After Jordan launched its attack on June 5, approximately 325,000 Palestinians living in the West Bank fled.[21] These were Jordanian citizens who moved from one part of what they considered their country to another, primarily to avoid being caught in the cross fire of a war.

A Palestinian refugee who was an administrator in a UNRWA camp in Jericho said Arab politicians had spread rumors in the camp. "They said all the young people would be killed. People heard on the radio that this is not the end, only the beginning, so they think maybe it will be a long war and they want to be in Jordan."[22]

Some Palestinians who left preferred to live in an Arab state rather than under Israeli military rule. Members of various PLO factions fled to avoid capture by the Israelis. Nils-Göran Gussing, the person appointed by the UN Secretary-General to investigate the situation, found that many Arabs also feared they would no longer be able to receive money from family members working abroad.[23]

Israeli forces ordered a handful of Palestinians to move for "strategic and security reasons." In some cases, they were allowed to return in a few days, in others, Israel offered to help them resettle elsewhere.[24]

Israel now ruled more than three-quarters of a million Palestinians—most of whom were hostile to the government. Nevertheless, more

Map 12 Cease-Fire Lines After the Six-Day War
1967

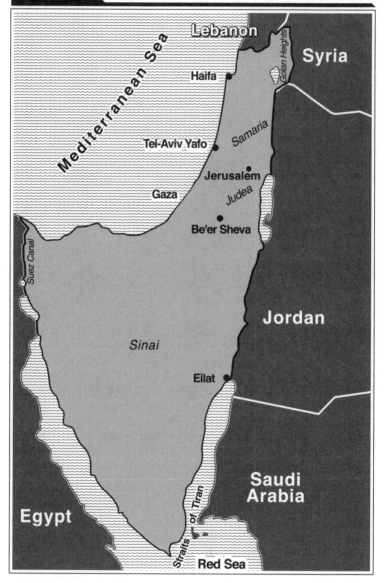

than 9,000 Palestinian families were reunited in 1967. Ultimately, more than 60,000 Palestinians were allowed to return.[25]

After the Six-Day War ended, President Johnson announced his view of what was required next to end the conflict:

"Certainly, troops must be withdrawn; but there must also be recognized rights of national life, progress in solving the refugee problem, freedom of innocent maritime passage, limitation of the arms race and respect for political independence and territorial integrity."[26]

MYTH

"During the 1967 War, Israel deliberately attacked the USS Liberty."

FACT

The Israeli attack on the *USS Liberty* was a grievous error, largely attributable to the fact that it occurred in the midst of the confusion of a full-scale war in 1967. Ten official United States investigations and three official Israeli inquiries have all conclusively established the attack was a tragic mistake.

On June 8, 1967, the fourth day of the Six-Day War, the Israeli high command received reports that Israeli troops in El Arish were being fired upon from the sea, presumably by an Egyptian vessel, as they had a day before. The United States had announced that it had no naval forces within hundreds of miles of the battle front on the floor of the United Nations a few days earlier; however, the *USS Liberty,* an American intelligence ship under the dual control of the Defense Intelligence Agency/Central Intelligence Agency and the Sixth Fleet, was assigned to monitor the fighting. As a result of a series of United States communication failures, whereby messages directing the ship not to approach within 100 miles were not received by the *Liberty,* the ship sailed to within 14 miles off the Sinai coast. The Israelis mistakenly thought this was the ship shelling its soldiers and war planes and torpedo boats attacked, killing 34 members of the *Liberty's* crew and wounding 171. Ships from the Sixth Fleet were directed to launch four attack aircraft with fighter cover to defend the *Liberty,* but the planes were recalled after a message was received at the White House that the Israelis had admitted they had attacked the ship.

Tapes of the radio transmissions made prior, during and after the attack do not contain any statement suggesting the pilots saw a U.S. flag before the attack on the ship. During the raid, a pilot specifically says, "there is no flag on her!" The recordings also indicate that once the pilots became concerned about the identity of the ship, by virtue of reading its hull number, they terminated the attack and they were given an order to leave the area.[27]

A CIA report on the incident issued June 13, 1967, found that an overzealous pilot could mistake the *Liberty* for an Egyptian ship. In 1981, the National Security Agency concluded: "While these [signal intelligence of Israeli communications] reports revealed some confusion on the part of the pilots concerning the nationality of the ship, they tended to rule out any thesis that the Israeli Navy and Air Force deliberately attacked a ship they knew to be American."[28]

Initially, the Israelis were terrified that they had attacked a *Soviet* ship and might have provoked the Soviets to join the fighting.[29] Once the Israelis were sure what had happened, they reported the incident to the U.S. Embassy in Tel Aviv and offered to provide a helicopter for the Americans to fly out to the ship and to supply any help they required to evacuate the injured and salvage the ship. The offer was accepted and a U.S. naval attaché was flown to the *Liberty*.

In October 2003, the first Israeli pilot to reach the ship broke his 36-year silence on the attack. Brig.-Gen. Yiftah Spector said he had been told an Egyptian ship was off the Gaza coast. "This ship positively did not have any symbol or flag that I could see. What I was concerned with was that it was not one of ours. I looked for the symbol of our navy, which was a large white cross on its deck. This was not there, so it wasn't one of ours." The *Jerusalem Post* obtained a recording of Spector's radio transmission in which he said, "I can't identify it, but in any case it's a military ship."[30]

Secretary of Defense Robert McNamara told Congress on July 26, 1967: "It was the conclusion of the investigatory body, headed by an admiral of the Navy in whom we have great confidence, that the attack was not intentional." Twenty years later, he repeated his belief that the attack was a mistake, telling a caller on the "Larry King Show" that he had seen nothing in the 20 years since to change his mind that there had been no "coverup."[31]

In January 2004, the State Department held a conference on the *Liberty* incident and also released new documents, including CIA memos dated June 13 and June 21, 1967, which say that Israel did not know it was striking an American vessel. The historian for the National Security Agency, David Hatch, said the available evidence "strongly suggested" Israel did not know it was attacking a U.S. ship. Two former U.S. officials, Ernest Castle, the United States Naval Attaché at the U.S. Embassy in Tel Aviv in June 1967, who received the first report of the attack from Israel, and John Hadden, then CIA Chief of Station in Tel Aviv, also agreed with the assessment that the attack on the *Liberty* was a mistake.[32]

Israel apologized for the tragedy and paid nearly $13 million in humanitarian reparations to the United States and to the families of the victims in amounts established by the U.S. State Department. The matter was officially closed between the two governments by an exchange of diplomatic notes on December 17, 1987.

Many of the survivors of the *Liberty* remain bitter, and are convinced the attack was deliberate. None of Israel's accusers, however, can explain why Israel would deliberately attack an American ship at a time when the United States was Israel's only friend and supporter in the world. Confusion in a long line of communications, which occurred in a tense atmosphere on both the American and Israeli sides is a more probable explanation.

> *"The Arabs say they want their territory back, but they don't want to talk to us, and they don't want to negotiate with us, and they don't want to recognize us. They want peace by immaculate conception."*
>
> **—Abba Eban**[33]

MYTH

"After the 1967 war, Israel refused to negotiate a settlement with the Arabs."

FACT

By the end of the war, Israel had captured enough territory to more than triple the size of the area it controlled, from 8,000 to 26,000 square miles. The victory enabled Israel to unify Jerusalem as well as capture the Sinai, the Golan Heights, the Gaza Strip and the West Bank. Israel hoped the Arab states would enter peace negotiations. Israel signaled to the Arab states its willingness to relinquish virtually all the territories it acquired in exchange for peace. As Moshe Dayan put it, Jerusalem was waiting only for a telephone call from Arab leaders to start negotiations.[34]

But these hopes were dashed in August 1967 when Arab leaders meeting in Khartoum adopted a formula of three noes: "no peace with Israel, no negotiations with Israel, no recognition of Israel. . . ."[35]

As former Israeli President Chaim Herzog wrote: "Israel's belief that the war had come to an end and that peace would now reign along the borders was soon dispelled. Three weeks after the conclusion of hostilities, the first major incident occurred on the Suez Canal."[36]

MYTH

*"The Palestinians were willing to negotiate
a settlement after the Six-Day War."*

FACT

The Arab League created the Palestine Liberation Organization (PLO) in Cairo in 1964 as a weapon against Israel. Until the Six-Day War, the PLO engaged in terrorist attacks that contributed to the momentum toward conflict. Neither the PLO nor any other Palestinian groups campaigned for Jordan or Egypt to create an independent Palestinian state in the West Bank and Gaza. The focus of Palestinian activism was on the destruction of Israel.

After the Arab states were defeated in 1967, the Palestinians did not alter their basic objective. With one million Arabs coming under Israeli rule, some Palestinians believed the prospect for waging a popular war of liberation had grown. Toward that end, Yasser Arafat instigated a campaign of terror from the West Bank. During September-December 1967, 61 attacks were launched, most against civilian targets such as factories, movie theaters and private homes.[37]

Israeli security forces gradually became more effective in thwarting terrorist plans inside Israel and the territories. Consequently, the PLO began to pursue a different strategy—attacking Jews and Israeli targets abroad. In early 1968, the first aircraft was hijacked by Palestinian terrorists.

MYTH

"Israel was responsible for the War of Attrition."

FACT

Egypt's President Gamal Nasser thought that because most of Israel's army consisted of reserves, it could not withstand a lengthy war of attrition. He believed Israel would be unable to endure the economic burden, and the constant casualties would undermine Israeli morale. To pursue this strategy of slowly weakening Israel, Nasser ordered attacks on Israel that were calibrated so that they would not provoke an all-out Israeli war in response.

As early as July 1, 1967, Egypt began shelling Israeli positions near the Suez Canal. On October 21, 1967, Egypt sank the Israeli destroyer *Eilat*, killing 47. A few months later, Egyptian artillery began to shell Israeli positions along the Suez Canal and Israeli military patrols were ambushed. This bloody War of Attrition, as it became known, lasted three years. The Israeli death toll between June 15, 1967, and August 8, 1970, when a cease-fire was declared, was 1,424 soldiers and more than 100 civilians. Another 2,000 soldiers and 700 civilians were wounded.[38]

MYTH

"Egypt terminated the War of Attrition and offered peace to Israel, only to have Jerusalem spurn these initiatives."

FACT

In the summer of 1970, the United States persuaded Israel and Egypt to accept a cease-fire. This cease-fire was designed to lead to negotiations under UN auspices.

On August 7, however, the Soviets and Egyptians deployed sophisticated ground-to-air missiles in the restricted 32-mile-deep zone along the west bank of the Suez Canal. This was a violation of the cease-fire agreement, which barred the introduction or construction of any military installations in this area. The "most massive anti-aircraft system ever created" provided air coverage for Egypt's surprise attack against Israel in 1973.[39]

Despite the Egyptian violations, the UN-sponsored talks resumed— additional evidence that Israel was anxious to make progress toward peace. The talks were swiftly short-circuited, however, by UN Special Envoy Gunnar Jarring, when he accepted the Egyptian interpretation of Resolution 242 and called for Israel's total withdrawal to the pre-June 5, 1967, demarcation lines.

On that basis, Egypt expressed its willingness "to enter into a peace agreement with Israel" in a February 20, 1971, letter to Jarring. But this seeming moderation masked an unchanging Egyptian irredentism and unwillingness to accept a real peace, as shown by the letter's sweeping reservations and preconditions. The crucial sentences about a "peace agreement with Israel" were neither published nor broadcast in Egypt. Moreover, Egypt refused to enter direct talks. Israel attempted to at least transform the struggling Jarring mission into indirect talks by addressing all letters not to Jarring, but to the Egyptian government. Egypt refused to accept them.

Just after the letter to Jarring, Anwar Sadat, Egypt's new president, addressed the Palestine National Council (PNC) meeting in Cairo. He promised support to the PLO "until victory" and declared that Egypt would not accept Resolution 242.[40]

Five days after Sadat suggested he was ready to make peace with Israel, Mohammed Heikal, a Sadat confidant and editor of the semi-official *Al-Ahram,* wrote:

> Arab policy at this stage has but two objectives. The first, the elimination of the traces of the 1967 aggression through an Israeli withdrawal from all the territories it occupied that year. The second objective is the elimination of the traces of the 1948 aggression, by the means of the elimination of the State of Israel itself. This is, however, as yet an abstract, undefined

objective, and some of us have erred in commencing the latter step before the former.[41]

Sadat was only willing to sign a peace agreement if Israel capitulated to all his demands. This was unacceptable to Israel and suggested that Sadat was not genuinely interested in peace.

Notes

1. *Encyclopedia Americana Annual 1961,* (NY: Americana Corporation, 1961), p. 387.
2. Speech by Nasser to the United Arab Republic National Assembly, March 26, 1964, quoted in Yehoshafat Harkabi, *ArabAttitudes To Israel,* (Jerusalem: Keter Publishing House, 1972), p. 27.
3. Howard Sachar, *A History of Israel: From the Rise of Zionism to Our Time,* (NY: Alfred A. Knopf, 1979), p. 616.
4. Samuel Katz, *Battleground-Fact and Fantasy in Palestine,* (NY: Bantam Books, 1985), pp. 10-11, 185.
5. Netanel Lorch, *One Long War,* (Jerusalem: Keter, 1976), p. 110.
6. Isi Leibler, *The Case For Israel,* (Australia: The Globe Press, 1972), pp. 60-61.
7. Ibid.
8. Abba Eban, *Abba Eban,* (NY: Random House, 1977), p. 331.
9. Leibler, p. 60.
10. Leibler, p. 18.
11. Leibler, p. 60.
12. Leibler, p. 61.
13. Chaim Herzog, *The Arab-Israeli Wars,* (NY: Random House, 1982), p. 149.
14. *United Nations Conference on tshe Law of the Sea,* (Geneva: UN Publications 1958), pp. 132-134.
15. Yehuda Lukacs, *Documents on the Israeli-Palestinian Conflict 1967-1983,* (NY: Cambridge University Press, 1984), pp. 17-18; Eban, p. 358.
16. Eban, p. 358.
17. Lyndon B. Johnson, *The Vantage Point: Perspectives of the Presidency 1963-1969,* (NY: Holt, Rinehart and Winston, 1971), p. 299.
18. Sachar, p. 629.
19. Katz, p. 3.
20. *Jerusalem Post,* (April 23, 1999).
21. *Encyclopedia Americana Annual 1968,* p. 366.
22. George Gruen, "The Refugees of Arab-Israeli Conflict," (NY: American Jewish Committee, March 1969), p. 5.
23. Gruen, p. 5.
24. Gruen, p. 4.
25. *Encyclopedia Americana Annual 1968,* p. 366.
26. Lyndon B. Johnson, *Public Papers of the President,* (DC: GPO 1968), p. 683.
27. Hirsh Goodman, "Messrs. Errors and No Facts," *Jerusalem Report,* (November 21, 1991); Arieh O' Sullivan, "Exclusive: Liberty attack tapes revealed," *Jerusalem Post,* (June 3, 2004).
28. "Attack on a SIGINT Collector, the U.S.S. Liberty," "Special Series Crisis Collection," National Security Agency, p. 64.
29. Dan Kurzman, *Soldier of Peace: The Life of Yitzhak Rabin,* (NY: HarperCollins, 1998), pp. 224-227; Rabin, p. 108-109; *Washington Post,* (November 6, 1991); L. Wainstain, "Some Aspects of the U.S. Involvement in the Middle East Crisis, May-June 1967," Institute for Defense Analysis, (February 1968).

30. *Jerusalem Post* (October 10, 2003). See also Nathan Guttman, "Memos show Liberty attack was an error," *Ha'aretz,* (July 9, 2003); Hirsh Goodman and Zeev Schiff, "The Attack on the *Liberty," Atlantic Monthly,* (September 1984).

31. The Larry King Show" (radio), (February 5, 1987).

32. *Jerusalem Post,* (January 13, 2004); *Washington Times,* (January 12, 2004).

33. Quoted in Alfred Leroy Atherton, Jr., Foreign Affairs Oral History Collection of the Association for Diplomatic Studies and Training, (Summer 1990).

34. Walter Lacquer, *The Road to War,* (London: Weidenfeld and Nicolson, 1968), p. 297.

35. "Khartoum Resolutions," (September 1, 1967), www.JewishVirtualLibrary.org/jsource/Peace/three_noes.html.

36. Chaim Herzog, *The Arab-Israeli Wars,* (NY: Random House, 1982), p. 195.

37. Netanel Lorch, *One Long War,* (Jerusalem: Keter, 1976), pp. 139–146.

38. Some historians consider the starting date of the War of Attrition in 1968 or 1969. We are using Chaim Herzog's time frame. Chaim Herzog, *The Arab-Israeli Wars,* (NY: Random House, 1984), pp. 195–221; Nadav Safran, *Israel The Embattled Ally,* (MA: Harvard University Press, 1981), p. 266.

39. *Time,* (September 14, 1970); John Pimlott, *The Middle East Conflicts From 1945 to the Present,* (NY: Crescent Books, 1983), p. 99.

40. Cited in, Anwar Sadat, *The Public Diary of President Sadat, Vol 2.* (BRILL: 1978), pp. 33–34.

41. *Al-Ahram,* (February 25, 1971).

7. The 1973 War

MYTH

"Israel was responsible for the 1973 War."

FACT

Throughout 1972, and for much of 1973, Egyptian President Anwar Sadat threatened war unless the United States forced Israel to accept his interpretation of Resolution 242—total Israeli withdrawal from territories taken in 1967. In an April 1973 interview, Sadat again warned he would renew the war with Israel.[1] But it was the same threat he had made in 1971 and 1972, and most observers remained skeptical.

The U.S.-sponsored truce was three-years-old and Secretary of State Henry Kissinger had opened a new dialogue for peace at the UN. Almost everyone was confident the prospect of a new war was remote.

On October 6, 1973—Yom Kippur, the holiest day in the Jewish calendar—Egypt and Syria opened a coordinated surprise attack against Israel. The equivalent of the total forces of NATO in Europe was mobilized on Israel's borders.[2] On the Golan Heights, approximately 180 Israeli tanks faced an onslaught of 1,400 Syrian tanks. Along the Suez Canal, fewer than 500 Israeli defenders were attacked by 80,000 Egyptians.

Thrown onto the defensive during the first two days of fighting, Israel mobilized its reserves and eventually repulsed the invaders and carried the war deep into Syria and Egypt. The Arab states were swiftly resupplied by sea and air from the Soviet Union, which rejected United States efforts to work toward an immediate cease-fire. As a result, the United States belatedly began its own airlift to Israel. Two weeks later, Egypt was saved from a disastrous defeat by the UN Security Council, which had failed to act while the tide was in the Arabs' favor.

On October 22, the Security Council adopted Resolution 338 calling for "all parties to the present fighting to cease all firing and terminate all military activity immediately." The vote came on the day that Israeli forces cut off and isolated the Egyptian Third Army and were in a position to destroy it.[3]

Despite the Israel Defense Forces' ultimate success on the battlefield, the war was considered a diplomatic and military failure. A total of 2,688 Israeli soldiers were killed.

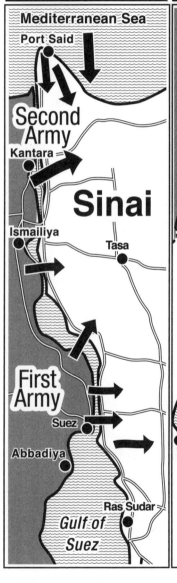

Map 13 Egyptian Attack Oct. 6 ,1973

Mediterranean Sea
Port Said
Second Army
Kantara
Sinai
Ismailiya
Tasa
First Army
Suez
Abbadiya
Ras Sudar
Gulf of Suez

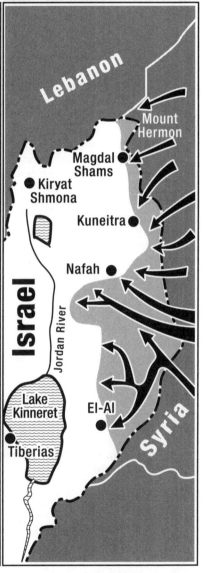

Syrian Attack Oct. 6 ,1973

Lebanon
Mount Hermon
Magdal Shams
Kiryat Shmona
Kuneitra
Nafah
Israel
Jordan River
Lake Kinneret
El-Al
Tiberias
Syria

MYTH

"Israel missed the opportunity for peace by rejecting Sadat's 1971 peace proposal."

FACT

In 1971, Egyptian President Anwar Sadat raised the possibility of signing an agreement with Israel, provided that *all* the disputed territories were returned by the Israelis.

Contrary to revisionist histories suggesting that Israel missed a chance to make peace and avoid the 1973 war by failing to respond favorably to Sadat's initiatives, Sadat did not sound like a leader interested in peace. He threatened to go to war if a political solution was not achieved and demanded Israel's complete withdrawal from the Sinai and a resolution of the Palestinian refugee problem, while at the same time declaring he would never establish diplomatic relations with Israel. He was also unwilling to negotiate because of fears he would anger his financial patrons in Libya and Saudi Arabia and possibly lose power. Furthermore, Sadat could not have made peace in 1971 because it would have been from a point of weakness and dishonor.[4]

In 1972, after Israel rejected his offer, Sadat said war was inevitable and he was prepared to sacrifice one million soldiers in the showdown with Israel.[5] He carried out his threat a year later.

> *"All countries should wage war against the Zionists, who are there to destroy all human organizations and to destroy civilization and the work which good people are trying to do."*
>
> **—King Faisal of Saudi Arabia[6]**

MYTH

"Egypt and Syria were the only Arab states involved in the 1973 war."

FACT

At least nine Arab states, including four non-Middle Eastern nations, actively aided the Egyptian-Syrian war effort.

A few months before the Yom Kippur War, Iraq transferred a squadron of Hunter jets to Egypt. During the war, an Iraqi division of some 18,000 men and several hundred tanks was deployed in the central Golan and participated in the October 16 attack against Israeli positions.[7] Iraqi MiGs began operating over the Golan Heights as early as October 8, the third day of the war.

Besides serving as financial underwriters, Saudi Arabia and Kuwait committed men to battle. A Saudi brigade of approximately 3,000 troops was dispatched to Syria, where it participated in fighting along the approaches to Damascus. Also, violating Paris's ban on the transfer of French-made weapons, Libya sent Mirage fighters to Egypt.[8]

Syrian Minister of Defense Mustafa Tlas told the Syrian National Assembly in December 1973 of the following example of "supreme valor" by Syrian troops:

"There is the outstanding case of a recruit from Aleppo who murdered 28 Jewish soldiers all by himself, slaughtering them like sheep. All of his comrades in arms witnessed this. He butchered three of them with an ax and decapitated them. . . . He struggled face to face with one of them and throwing down his ax managed to break his neck and devour his flesh in front of his comrades. This is a special case. Need I single it out to award him the Medal of the Republic. I will grant this medal to any soldier who succeeds in killing 28 Jews, and I will cover him with appreciation and honor his bravery."[9]

Other North African countries responded to Arab and Soviet calls to aid the frontline states. Algeria sent three aircraft squadrons of fighters and bombers, an armored brigade and 150 tanks. Approximately 1,000–2,000 Tunisian soldiers were positioned in the Nile Delta. The Sudan stationed 3,500 troops in southern Egypt, and Morocco sent three brigades to the front lines, including 2,500 men to Syria.

Lebanese radar units were used by Syrian air defense forces. Lebanon also allowed Palestinian terrorists to shell Israeli civilian settlements from its territory. Palestinians fought on the southern front with the Egyptians and Kuwaitis.[10]

The least enthusiastic participant in the October fighting was probably Jordan's King Hussein, who apparently had been kept uninformed of Egyptian and Syrian war plans. But Hussein did send two of his best units—the 40th and 60th Armored Brigades—to Syria. This force took positions in the southern sector, defending the main Amman-Damascus route and attacking Israeli positions along the Kuneitra-Sassa road on October 16. Three Jordanian artillery batteries also participated in the assault, carried out by nearly 100 tanks.[11]

Notes

1. *Newsweek,* (April 9, 1973).
2. Chaim Herzog, *The Arab-Israeli Wars,* (NY: Random House, 1984), p. 230.
3. Herzog, p. 280.
4. Shlomo Aronson, "On Sadat's Peace Initiatives in the Wake of the Yom Kippur War"; Mitchell Bard, *Will Israel Survive,* (NY: Palgrave, 2007), pp. 8–9.

5. Howard Sachar, *A History of Israel: From the Rise of Zionism to Our Time,* (NY: Alfred A. Knopf, 1979), p. 747.
6. *Beirut Daily Star,* (November 17, 1972).
7. Trevor Dupuy, *Elusive Victory: The Arab-Israeli Wars, 1947-1974,* (NY: Harper & Row, 1978), p. 462.
8. Dupuy, p. 376; Herzog, p. 278; Nadav Safran, *Israel The Embattled Ally,* (MA: Harvard University Press, 1981), p. 499.
9. Official Gazette of Syria, (July 11, 1974).
10. Herzog, pp. 278, 285, 293; Dupuy, p. 534.
11. Herzog, p. 300.

8. Boundaries

MYTH

"The creation of Israel in 1948 changed political and border arrangements between independent states that had existed for centuries."

FACT

The boundaries of Middle East countries were arbitrarily fixed by the Western powers after Turkey was defeated in World War I and the French and British mandates were set up. The areas allotted to Israel under the UN partition plan had all been under the control of the Ottomans, who had ruled Palestine from 1517 until 1917.

When Turkey was defeated in World War I, the French took over the area now known as Lebanon and Syria. The British assumed control of Palestine and Iraq. In 1926, the borders were redrawn and Lebanon was separated from Syria.

Britain installed the Emir Faisal, who had been deposed by the French in Syria, as ruler of the new kingdom of Iraq. In 1922, the British created the emirate of Transjordan, which incorporated all of Palestine east of the Jordan River. This was done so that the Emir Abdullah, whose family had been defeated in tribal warfare in the Arabian peninsula, would have a Kingdom to rule. None of the countries that border Israel became independent until the Twentieth Century. Many other Arab nations became independent after Israel.[1]

MYTH

"Israel has been an expansionist state since its creation."

FACT

Israel's boundaries were determined by the United Nations when it adopted the partition resolution in 1947. In a series of defensive wars, Israel captured additional territory. On numerous occasions, Israel has withdrawn from these areas.

As part of the 1974 disengagement agreement, Israel returned territories captured in the 1967 and 1973 wars to Syria.

Under the terms of the 1979 Israeli-Egyptian peace treaty, Israel withdrew from the Sinai peninsula for the third time. It had already withdrawn from large parts of the desert area it captured in its War of

Map 14 Missile and Artillery Ranges From West Bank Positions

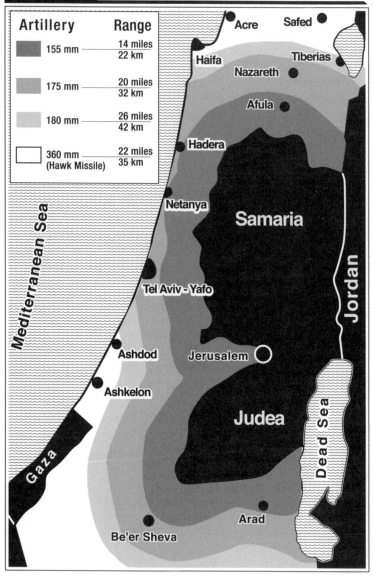

Independence. After capturing the entire Sinai in the 1956 Suez conflict, Israel relinquished the peninsula to Egypt a year later.

In September 1983, Israel withdrew from large areas of Lebanon to positions south of the Awali River. In 1985, it completed its withdrawal from Lebanon, except for a narrow security zone just north of the Israeli border. That too was abandoned, unilaterally, in 2000.

After signing peace agreements with the Palestinians, and a treaty with Jordan, Israel agreed to withdraw from most of the territory in the West Bank captured from Jordan in 1967. A small area was returned to Jordan, and more than 40 percent was ceded to the Palestinian Authority. The agreement with the Palestinians also involved Israel's withdrawal in 1994 from most of the Gaza Strip, which had been captured from Egypt in 1973.

Israeli Prime Minister Ehud Barak offered to withdraw from 95 percent of the West Bank and 100 percent of the Gaza Strip in a final settlement. In addition, Prime Minister Yitzhak Rabin and his successors offered to withdraw from virtually all of the Golan Heights in exchange for peace with Syria.

In August 2005, all Israeli troops and civilians were evacuated from the Gaza Strip and the territory was turned over to the control of the Palestinian Authority. In addition, four communities in Northern Samaria that covered an area larger than the entire Gaza Strip were also evacuated as part of the disengagement plan. As a result, Israel has now withdrawn from approximately 94 percent of the territory it captured in 1967.

Negotiations continue regarding the final disposition of the remaining 6 percent (about 1,600 square miles) of the disputed territories in Israel's possession. Israel's willingness to make territorial concessions in exchange for security proves its goal is peace, not expansion.

MYTH

"Israel seized the Golan Heights in a war of aggression."

FACT

Between 1948 and 1967, Syria controlled the Golan Heights and used it as a military stronghold from which its troops randomly sniped at Israeli civilians in the Hula Valley below, forcing children living on kibbutzim to sleep in bomb shelters. In addition, many roads in northern Israel could be crossed only after being cleared by mine-detection vehicles. In late 1966, a youth was blown to pieces by a mine while playing soccer near the Lebanon border. In some cases, attacks were carried out by Yasser Arafat's Fatah, which Syria allowed to operate from its territory.[2]

Israel repeatedly, and unsuccessfully, protested the Syrian bombardments to the UN Mixed Armistice Commission, which was charged with enforcing the cease-fire. For example, Israel went to the UN in October 1966 to demand a halt to the Fatah attacks. The response from the Syrian ambassador was defiant: "It is not our duty to stop them, but to encourage and strengthen them."[3]

Nothing was done to stop Syria's aggression. A mild Security Council resolution expressing "regret" for such incidents was vetoed by the Soviet Union. Meanwhile, Israel was condemned by the UN when it retaliated. "As far as the Security Council was officially concerned," historian Netanel Lorch wrote, "there was an open season for killing Israelis on their own territory."[4]

After the Six-Day War began, the Syrian air force attempted to bomb oil refineries in Haifa. While Israel was fighting in the Sinai and West Bank, Syrian artillery bombarded Israeli forces in the eastern Galilee, and armored units fired on villages in the Hula Valley below the Golan Heights.

On June 9, 1967, Israel moved against Syrian forces on the Golan. By late afternoon, June 10, Israel was in complete control of the plateau. Israel's seizure of the strategic heights occurred only after 19 years of provocation from Syria, and after unsuccessful efforts to get the international community to act against the aggressors.

MYTH

"The Golan has no strategic significance for Israel."

FACT

Syria—deterred by an IDF presence within artillery range of Damascus—has kept the Golan quiet since 1974. But during this time, Syria has supported and provided a haven for numerous terrorist groups that attack Israel from Lebanon and other countries. These include the Democratic Front for the Liberation of Palestine (DFLP), the Popular Front for the Liberation of Palestine (PFLP), Hezbollah and the Popular Front for the Liberation of Palestine-General Command (PFLP-GC). In addition, Syria still deploys hundreds of thousands of troops—as much as 75 percent of its army—on the Israeli front near the Heights.

From the western Golan, it is only about 60 miles—without major terrain obstacles—to Haifa and Acre, Israel's industrial heartland. The Golan—rising from 400 to 1700 feet in the western section bordering on pre-1967 Israel—overlooks the Hula Valley, Israel's richest agricultural area. In the hands of a friendly neighbor, the escarpment has little military importance. If controlled by a hostile country, however, the Golan has the potential to again become a strategic nightmare for Israel.

Before the Six-Day War, when Israeli agricultural settlements in the Galilee came under fire from the Golan, Israel's options for countering the Syrian attacks were constrained by the geography of the Heights.

Map 15 The Golan Heights Ridge Line

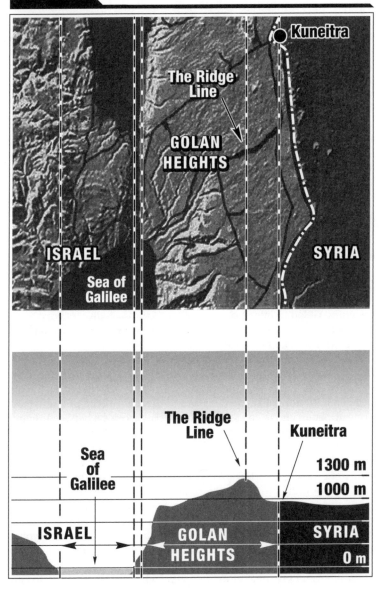

"Counterbattery fire was limited by the lack of observation from the Hula Valley; air attacks were degraded by well-dug-in Syrian positions with strong overhead cover, and a ground attack against the positions ... would require major forces with the attendant risks of heavy casualties and severe political repercussions," U.S. Army Col. (Ret.) Irving Heymont observed.[5]

When Israel eventually took these risks and stormed the Syrian positions in 1967, it suffered 115 dead—roughly the number of Americans killed during Operation Desert Storm.

Relinquishing the Golan to Syria without adequate security arrangements could jeopardize Israel's early-warning system against surprise attack. Israel has built radar systems on Mt. Hermon, the highest point in the region. If Israel withdrew from the Golan and had to relocate these facilities to the lowlands of the Galilee, they would lose much of their strategic effectiveness.

MYTH

"Syria is willing to make peace if Israel withdraws from the Golan Heights."

FACT

Syria's position has not wavered: Israel must completely withdraw from the entire Golan Heights before President Assad will discuss what Syria might do in return. Assad has never expressed any willingness to make peace even if Israel met his demand.

Israel has been equally adamant that it would not give up any territory without knowing what Syria was prepared to concede. Israel's willingness to trade some or all of the Golan is dependent on Syria's agreement to normalize relations and to sign an agreement that would bring about an end to the state of war Syria says exists between them.

The topographical concerns associated with withdrawing from the Golan Heights could be offset by demilitarization, but Israel needs to have a defensible border from which the nation can be defended with minimum losses. The deeper the demilitarization, and the better the early warning, the more flexible Israel can be regarding that border.

In addition to military security, Israelis seek the normalization of relations between the two countries. At a minimum, ties with Syria should be on a par with those Israel has with Egypt; ideally, they would be closer to the type of peace Israel enjoys with Jordan. This means going beyond a bare minimum of an exchange of ambassadors and flight links and creating an environment whereby Israelis and Syrians will feel comfortable visiting each other's country, engaging in trade, and pursuing other forms of cooperation typical of friendly nations.

In past negotiations, Israel has expressed a willingness to make substantial concessions, and the outline of an agreement has been essentially sitting on the table waiting for Syria to agree to the exchange of peace and security for land. In the meantime, substantial opposition exists within Israel to withdrawing from the Golan Heights. The expectation of many is that public opinion will shift if and when the Syrians sign an agreement and take measures, such as ending support for Hezbollah and closing the headquarters of terrorist organizations in Damascus, that demonstrate a genuine interest in peace. And public opinion will determine whether a treaty is concluded because of a law adopted during Prime Minister Netanyahu's term that requires any agreement to be approved in a national referendum.

Meanwhile, Syria has continued to build up its military forces, attempted to establish a nuclear weapons program, smuggled arms to Hezbollah in Lebanon and allowed terrorist groups to retain headquarters in Damascus, all of which have increased Israel's concerns about Assad's intentions. Upheaval in Syria has raised the possibility of a change in regime; nevertheless, absent dramatic changes in Syria's government and its attitude toward Israel, the Jewish State's security will depend on its retention of military control over the Golan Heights.

"From a strictly military point of view, Israel would require the retention of some captured territory in order to provide militarily defensible borders."

—Memorandum for the Secretary of Defense from the Joint Chiefs of Staff, June 29, 1967

MYTH

"Israel illegally annexed the Golan Heights in 1981."

FACT

On December 14, 1981, the Knesset voted to annex the Golan Heights. The statute extended Israeli civilian law and administration to the residents of the Golan, replacing the military authority that had ruled the area since 1967. The law does not foreclose the option of negotiations on a final settlement of the status of the territory.

Following the Knesset's approval of the law, Professor Julius Stone of Hastings College of the Law wrote: "There is no rule of international law which requires a lawful military occupant, in this situation, to wait forever before [making] control and government of the territory permanent.... Many international lawyers have wondered, indeed, at the patience which led Israel to wait as long as she did."[6]

Map 16   Relative Size of the Golan Heights

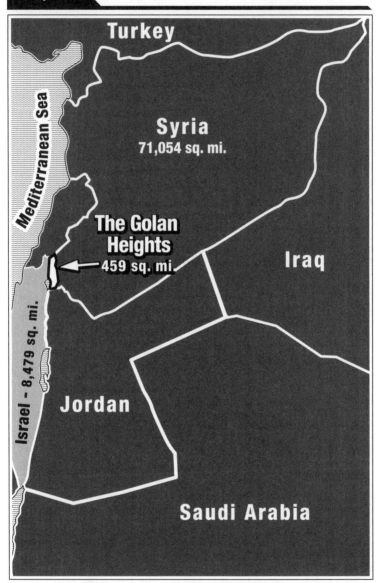

> *"It is impossible to defend Jerusalem unless you hold the high ground. . . .*
> *An aircraft that takes off from an airport in Amman is going to be over*
> *Jerusalem in two-and-a-half minutes, so it's utterly impossible for me to*
> *defend the whole country unless I hold that land."*
>
> **—Lieutenant General (Ret.) Thomas Kelly, director of operations**
> **for the Joint Chiefs of Staff during the Gulf War[7]**

MYTH

"Israel can withdraw from the West Bank with little
more difficulty than was the case in Sinai."

FACT

Several pages of Israel's peace treaty with Egypt are devoted to security arrangements. For example, Article III of the treaty's annex concerns the areas where reconnaissance flights are permitted, and Article V allows the establishment of early-warning systems in specific zones.

The security guarantees, which were required to give Israel the confidence to withdraw, were only possible because the Sinai was demilitarized. They provide Israel a large buffer zone of more than 100 miles of sparsely populated desert. Today, the Egyptian border is 60 miles from Tel Aviv and 70 from Jerusalem, the nearest major Israeli cities.

The situation in the territories is entirely different. More than two million Arabs live in the West Bank, many in crowded cities and refugee camps. Most of them are located close to Israeli cities such as Tel Aviv and Jerusalem. The Palestinians have rockets capable of threatening these cities as well as Ben-Gurion Airport.

It is important for Israel that the West Bank not fall into the hands of hostile neighbors. The infiltration in recent years of terrorists from the Palestinian Authority, who have committed horrific acts such as suicide bombings, illustrate the danger. The 2011 uprisings in Egypt are a reminder of the risk involved in making permanent territorial concessions to leaders whose tenure is only temporary. Israel must consider the possibility of a hostile regime coming to power in the future and account for the likelihood that the Palestinians will have even more sophisticated weapons at their disposal in the future.

Despite the risks, Israel has withdrawn from more than 40 percent of the West Bank since Oslo. In past negotiations, Israel has offered to give up 97 percent of it in return for a final settlement with the Palestinians. Israel will not, however, return to the pre-1967 borders as demanded by the Palestinians and the Arab states.

Map 17 Flying Times to Israel

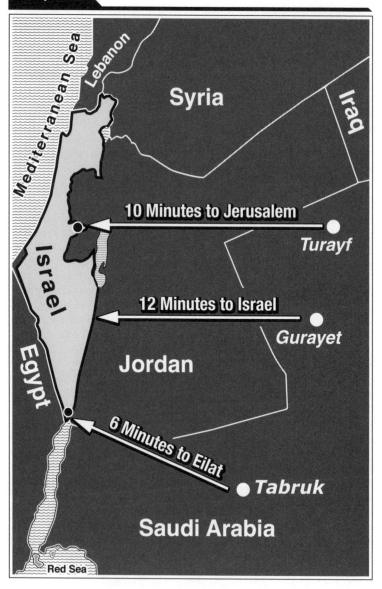

MYTH

"Defensible borders are unrealistic in an era of ballistic missiles and long-range bombers."

FACT

History shows that aerial attacks have never defeated a nation. Countries are only conquered by troops occupying land. One example of this was Iraq's invasion of Kuwait, in which the latter nation was overrun and occupied in a matter of hours. Though the multinational force bombed Iraq for close to six weeks, Kuwait was not liberated until the Allied troops marched into that country in the war's final days. Defensible borders are those that would prevent or impede such a ground assault.

Israel's return to its pre-1967 borders, which the Arab states want to reimpose, would sorely tempt potential aggressors to launch attacks on the Jewish State—as they did routinely before 1967. Israel would lose the extensive system of early-warning radars it has set up in the hills of Judea and Samaria. Were a hostile neighbor then to seize control of these mountains, its army could split Israel in two: From there, it is only about 15 miles—without any major geographic obstacles—to the Mediterranean.

At their narrowest point, these 1967 lines are within 9 miles of the Israeli coast, 11 miles from Tel Aviv, 10 from Be'er Sheva, 21 from Haifa and one foot from Jerusalem.

To defend Jerusalem, the U.S. Joint Chiefs concluded in a 1967 report to the Secretary of Defense, Israel would need to have its border "positioned to the east of the city."[8]

Control over the Jordan River Valley is also critical to Israeli security because it "forms a natural security barrier between Israel and Jordan, and effectively acts as an anti-tank ditch," military analyst Anthony Cordesman noted. "This defensive line sharply increases the amount of time Israel has to mobilize and its ability to ensure control over the West Bank in the event of a war." He added that sacrificing control over the routes up to the heights above the West Bank makes it more difficult for the IDF to deploy and increases the risk of Jordanian, Syrian, or Palestinian forces deploying on the heights.[9]

Even in the era of ballistic missiles, strategic depth matters. The Jaffee Center for Strategic Studies, an Israeli think tank considered dovish, concluded: "Early-warning stations and the deployment of surface-to-air missile batteries can provide the time needed to sound an air-raid alert, and warn the population to take shelter from a missile attack. They might even allow enemy missiles to be intercepted in mid-flight. . . . As long as such missiles are armed with conventional warheads, they may cause painful losses and damage, but they cannot decide the outcome of a war."[10]

Map 18 — Distances Between Israeli Population Centers and Pre-1967 Armistice Lines

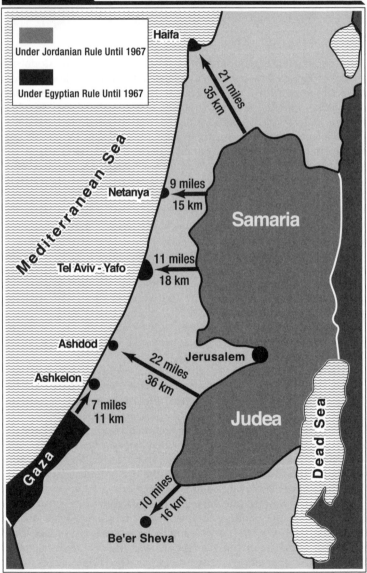

Haifa

Under Jordanian Rule Until 1967

Under Egyptian Rule Until 1967

21 miles
35 km

Mediterranean Sea

Netanya — 9 miles / 15 km

Samaria

Tel Aviv - Yafo — 11 miles / 18 km

Ashdod — 22 miles / 36 km — Jerusalem

Ashkelon

7 miles
11 km

Judea

Gaza

Dead Sea

10 miles / 16 km

Be'er Sheva

MYTH

"Israel 'occupies' the West Bank."

FACT

In politics words matter and, unfortunately, the misuse of words applying to the Arab-Israeli conflict has shaped perceptions to Israel's disadvantage. As in the case of the term "West Bank," the word "occupation" has been hijacked by those who wish to paint Israel in the harshest possible light. It also gives apologists a way to try to explain away terrorism as "resistance to occupation," as if the women and children killed by suicide bombers in buses, pizzerias, and shopping malls were responsible for the plight of the Arabs.

Given the negative connotation of an "occupier," it is not surprising that Arab spokespersons use the word, or some variation, as many times as possible when interviewed by the press. The more accurate description of the territories in Judea and Samaria, however, is "disputed" territories.

> *"For a Texan, a first visit to Israel is an eye-opener. At the narrowest point, it's only 8 miles from the Mediterranean to the old Armistice line: That's less than from the top to the bottom of Dallas-Ft. Worth Airport. The whole of pre-1967 Israel is only about six times the size of the King Ranch near Corpus Christi."*
>
> **—President George W. Bush**[11]

In fact, most other disputed territories around the world are not referred to as being occupied by the party that controls them. This is true, for example, of the hotly contested region of Kashmir.[12]

Occupation typically refers to foreign control of an area that was under the previous sovereignty of another state. In the case of the West Bank, there was no legitimate sovereign because the territory had been illegally occupied by Jordan from 1948 to 1967. Only two countries— Britain and Pakistan—recognized Jordan's action. The Palestinians never demanded an end to Jordanian occupation and the creation of a Palestinian state.

It is also important to distinguish the acquisition of territory in a war of conquest as opposed to a war of self-defense. A nation that attacks another and then retains the territory it conquers is an occupier. One that gains territory in the course of defending itself is not in the same category. This is the situation with Israel, which specifically told King Hussein that if Jordan stayed out of the 1967 war, Israel would not fight against him. Hussein ignored the warning and attacked Israel. While fending off the assault and driving out the invading Jordanian troops, Israel came to control the West Bank.

By rejecting Arab demands that Israel be required to withdraw from all the territories won in 1967, UN Security Council Resolution 242 acknowledged that Israel was entitled to claim at least part of these lands for new defensible borders.

Since Oslo, the case for tagging Israel as an occupying power has been further weakened by the fact that Israel transferred virtually all civilian authority in the West Bank to the Palestinian Authority. Israel retained the power to control its own external security and that of its citizens, but 98 percent of the Palestinian population in the West Bank and 100 percent in Gaza came under the PA's authority. The extent to which Israel has been forced to maintain a military presence in the territories has been governed by the Palestinians' unwillingness to end violence against Israel. The best way to end the dispute over the territories is for the Palestinians to negotiate a final settlement.

MYTH

"Israel's security fence is meant to create a Palestinian ghetto."

FACT

Israel did not want to build a fence, and resisted doing so for more than 35 years. If anyone is to blame for the construction, it is Hamas, Islamic Jihad and the other Palestinian terrorists.

Following the 1967 war, the frontier separating Israel from the West Bank had no physical obstacles to prevent the infiltration of terrorists. In response to dozens of suicide bombings, and daily terrorist attacks against its civilians, Israel decided to construct a security fence near the "Green Line" (the 1949 armistice line) to prevent Palestinian terrorists from crossing the border.

A large majority of Israelis support the construction of the security fence. Israelis living along the Green Line, both Jews and Arabs, favor the fence to prevent penetration by thieves and vandals as well as terrorists. In fact, the fence caused a revolution in the daily life of some Israeli Arab towns because it has brought quiet, which allowed a significant upsurge in economic activity.[13]

The fence is not impregnable. It is possible that some terrorists will manage to get past the barrier; nevertheless, the obstacle makes it far more difficult for incursions and thereby minimizes the number of attacks. During the 34 months from the beginning of the violence in September 2000 until the construction of the first continuous segment of the security fence at the end of July 2003, Samaria-based terrorists carried out 73 attacks in which 293 Israelis were killed and 1,950 wounded. In the 11 months between the erection of the first segment at the beginning of August 2003 and the end of June 2004, only three attacks were successful, and all three occurred in the first half of 2003. The value of the fence in saving lives is evident from the data: In 2002, the year before construction started, 457 Israelis were murdered; in 2010, 8 Israelis were killed.

MYTH

"Israel is the only country that has a fence to secure its borders."

FACT

It is not unreasonable or unusual to build a fence for security purposes. Israel already has fences along the frontiers with Lebanon, Syria, and Jordan, so building a barrier to separate Israel from the Palestinian Authority is not revolutionary. Most nations have fences to protect their borders and several use barriers in political disputes:

- The United States is building a fence to keep out illegal Mexican immigrants.

- Spain built a fence to separate its enclaves of Ceuta and Melilla from Morocco to prevent people from sub-Saharan Africa from entering Europe.

- India constructed a 460-mile barrier in Kashmir to halt infiltrations supported by Pakistan.

- Saudi Arabia built a 60-mile barrier along an undefined border zone with Yemen to halt arms smuggling of weaponry and is constructing a 500-mile fence along its border with Iraq.

- Turkey built a barrier in the southern province of Alexandretta, which was formerly in Syria and is an area that Syria claims as its own.

- In Cyprus, the UN sponsored a security fence reinforcing the island's de facto partition.

- British-built barriers separate Catholic and Protestant neighborhoods in Belfast.[14]

Ironically, after condemning Israel's barrier, the UN announced plans to build its own fence to improve security around its New York headquarters.[15]

MYTH

"The security fence should be built along the pre-1967 border."

FACT

Critics have complained that the fence is being built beyond Israel's pre-1967 border, but the so-called "Green Line" was not an internationally recognized border, it was an armistice line between Israel and Jordan pending the negotiation of a final border. As Israel's Supreme Court noted in its ruling on the route of the barrier, building the fence along that line would have been a political statement and would not accomplish the principal goal of the barrier, namely, the prevention of terror.

The route of the fence must take into account topography, population density, and threat assessment of each area. To be effective in protecting the maximum number of Israelis, it also must incorporate some of the settlements in the West Bank.

Most of the fence runs roughly along the "Green Line." In some places, the fence is *inside* this line. One of the most controversial questions has been whether to build the fence around Ariel, a town of approximately 20,000 people. To incorporate Ariel, the fence would have to extend approximately 12 miles into the West Bank. In the short-run, Israel decided to build a separate fence around Ariel.

Palestinians complain that the fence creates "facts on the ground," but most of the area incorporated within the fence is expected to be part of Israel in any peace agreement with the Palestinians. Israeli negotiators have always envisioned the future border to be the 1967 frontier with modifications to minimize the security risk to Israel and maximize the number of Jews living within the State, and a growing number of Israelis have come to the conclusion that the best solution to the conflict with the Palestinians is separation.

The original route has been repeatedly modified. As a result of the June 2004 Supreme Court decision, the route was altered to move the barrier closer to the 1967 cease-fire line and to make it less burdensome to the Palestinians. The fence is now expected to cover approximately 500 miles and incorporate just 7 percent of the West Bank—less than 160 square miles—on its "Israeli side," while 2,100 square miles will be on the "Palestinian side." To date, more than 320 miles of the fence has been completed.

Approximately 99 percent of West Bank Palestinians are on the Palestinian side of the fence. Every effort is being made to exclude Palestinian villages from the area within the fence and no territories are being annexed. The land used in building the security fence is seized for military purposes, not confiscated, and it remains the property of the owner. Legal procedures are already in place to allow every owner to file an objection to the seizure of their land. In addition, Israel budgeted $22 million to compensate Palestinians for the use of their land.

Israel is doing its best to minimize the negative impact on Palestinians in the area of construction and is providing agricultural passageways to allow farmers to continue to cultivate their lands, and crossing points to allow the movement of people and the transfer of goods. Moreover, property owners are offered compensation for the use of their land and for any damage to their trees. Contractors are responsible for carefully uprooting and replanting the trees. So far, more than 60,000 olive trees have been relocated in accordance with this procedure.

Despite Israel's best efforts, the fence has caused some injury to residents near the fence. Israel's Supreme Court took up the grievances of Palestinians (who are allowed to petition the court without being Israeli citizens) and ruled the government had to reduce the infringement upon local inhabitants by altering the path of the fence in an area near Jerusalem. Though the Court's decision made the government's job of securing the population from terrorist threats more difficult, costly, and time-consuming, the Prime Minister immediately accepted the ruling.

If and when the Palestinians decide to negotiate an end to the conflict, the fence may be torn down or moved (as occurred after Israel's withdrawal from Lebanon). Even without any change, a Palestinian state could now theoretically be created in 93 percent of the West Bank (the PA now controls 100 percent of the Gaza Strip). This is very close to the 97 percent Israel offered to the Palestinians at Camp David in 2000, which means that while other difficult issues remain to be resolved, the territorial aspect of the dispute will be reduced to a negotiation over roughly 90 square miles.

MYTH

"Israel's security fence is comparable to the Berlin Wall."

FACT

Although critics have sought to portray the security fence as a kind of "Berlin Wall," it is nothing of the sort. First, unlike the Berlin Wall, the fence does not separate one people, Germans from Germans, or deny freedom to those on one side. Israel's security fence separates two peoples, Israelis and Palestinians, and offers freedom and security for both. Second, while Israelis are fully prepared to live with Palestinians, and 20 percent of the Israeli population is already Arab, it is the Palestinians who say they do not want to live with any Jews and call for the West Bank to be *judenrein*. Third, the fence is not being constructed to prevent the citizens of one state from escaping; it is designed solely to keep terrorists out of Israel.

Finally, most of the barrier will be a chain-link type fence, similar to those used all over the United States, combined with underground and long-range sensors, unmanned aerial vehicles, trenches, landmines and guard paths. Less than 3 percent (about 15 miles) is a 30-foot-high concrete wall, built in areas where it will prevent Palestinian snipers from shooting at Israeli cars, as they did for three years along the Trans-Israel Highway, one of the country's main roads.

Notes

1. Egypt didn't achieve independence until 1922; Lebanon, 1946; Jordan, 1946; and Syria, 1946. Many of the Gulf states became independent after Israel: Kuwait, 1961; Bahrain, 1970; the United Arab Emirates, 1971; and Qatar, 1971.
2. Netanel Lorch, *One Long War,* (Jerusalem: Keter, 1976), pp. 106-110.
3. Anne Sinai and Allen Pollack, *The Syrian Arab Republic,* (NY: American Academic Association for Peace in the Middle East, 1976), p. 117.
4. Lorch, p. 111.
5. Sinai and Pollack, pp. 130-31.
6. *Near East Report,* (January 29, 1982).
7. *Jerusalem Post,* (November 7, 1991).
8. Memorandum for the Secretary of Defense, June 29, 1967, cited in "Israel's Requirements for Defensible Borders," Major General (Res) Yaakov Amidror, pp. 25-26.
9. Anthony Cordesman, "Escalating to Nowhere: The Israeli-Palestinian War—The Final Settlement Issues," (DC: CSIS, January 13, 2005), p. 15.
10. *Israel's Options for Peace,* (Tel Aviv: The Jaffee Center for Strategic Studies, 1989), pp. 171-72.
11. Speech to the American Jewish Committee, (May 3, 2001).
12. U.S. Department of State, Consular Information Sheet: India, (February 2011).
13. Yair Ettinger, "Highway, fence spur growth in Wadi Ara," *Haaretz,* (July 14, 2004).
14. Ben Thein, "Is Israel's Security Barrier Unique?" *Middle East Quarterly,* (Fall 2004), pp. 25-32.
15. United Nations, (May 6, 2004).

9. Israel and Lebanon

MYTH

"The PLO posed no threat to Israel in 1982
when Israel attacked Lebanon."

FACT

The PLO repeatedly violated the July 1981 cease-fire agreement. By June 1982, when the IDF went into Lebanon, the PLO had made life in northern Israel intolerable through its repeated shelling of Israeli towns.

In the ensuing 11 months, the PLO staged 270 terrorist actions in Israel, the West Bank and Gaza, and along the Lebanese and Jordanian borders. Twenty-nine Israelis died, and more than 300 were injured in the attacks.[1] The frequency of attacks in the Galilee forced thousands of residents to flee their homes or to spend large amounts of time in bomb shelters.

A force of some 15-18,000 PLO members was encamped in scores of locations in Lebanon. About 5,000-6,000 were foreign mercenaries, coming from such countries as Libya, Iraq, India, Sri Lanka, Chad and Mozambique.[2] The PLO had an arsenal that included mortars, Katyusha rockets, and an extensive anti-aircraft network Israel later discovered enough light arms and other weapons in Lebanon to equip five brigades.[3] The PLO also brought hundreds of T-34 tanks into the area.[4] Syria, which permitted Lebanon to become a haven for the PLO and other terrorist groups, brought surface-to-air missiles into that country, creating yet another danger for Israel.

Israeli strikes and commando raids were unable to stem the growth of this PLO army. Israel was not prepared to wait for more deadly attacks to be launched against its civilian population before acting against the terrorists.

After Israel launched one such assault on June 4-5, 1982, the PLO responded with a massive artillery and mortar attack on the Israeli population of the Galilee. On June 6, the IDF moved into Lebanon to drive out the terrorists.

Former Secretary of State Henry Kissinger defended the Israeli operation: "No sovereign state can tolerate indefinitely the buildup along its borders of a military force dedicated to its destruction and implementing its objectives by periodic shellings and raids."[5]

MYTH

"Israel was responsible for the massacre of Palestinian refugees at Sabra and Shatila."

FACT

The Lebanese Christian Phalangist militia was responsible for the massacres that occurred at the two Beirut-area refugee camps on September 16–17, 1982. Israeli troops allowed the Phalangists to enter Sabra and Shatila to root out terrorist cells believed to be located there. It had been estimated that there may have been up to 200 armed men in the camps working out of the countless bunkers built by the PLO over the years, and stocked with generous reserves of ammunition.[6]

When Israeli soldiers ordered the Phalangists out, they found hundreds dead (estimates range from 460 according to the Lebanese police, to 700–800 calculated by Israeli intelligence). The dead, according to the Lebanese account, included 35 women and children. The rest were men: Palestinians, Lebanese, Pakistanis, Iranians, Syrians and Algerians.[7] The killings were perpetrated to avenge the murders of Lebanese President Bashir Gemayel and 25 of his followers, killed in a bomb attack earlier that week.[8]

Israel had allowed the Phalange to enter the camps as part of a plan to transfer authority to the Lebanese, and accepted responsibility for that decision. The Kahan Commission of Inquiry, formed by the Israeli government in response to public outrage and grief, found that Israel was indirectly responsible for not anticipating the possibility of Phalangist violence. Subsequently, Defense Minister Ariel Sharon resigned and the Army Chief of Staff, Gen. Raful Eitan, was dismissed.

The Kahan Commission, declared former Secretary of State Henry Kissinger, was "a great tribute to Israeli democracy.... There are very few governments in the world that one can imagine making such a public investigation of such a difficult and shameful episode."[9]

Ironically, while 300,000 Israelis protested the killings, little or no reaction occurred in the Arab world. Outside the Middle East, a major international outcry against Israel erupted over the massacres. The Phalangists, who perpetrated the crime, were spared the brunt of the condemnations for it.

By contrast, few voices were raised in May 1985, when Muslim militiamen attacked the Shatila and Burj-el Barajneh Palestinian refugee camps. According to UN officials, 635 were killed and 2,500 wounded. During a two-year battle between the Syrian-backed Shiite Amal militia and the PLO, more than 2,000 people, including many civilians, were reportedly killed. No outcry was directed at the PLO or the Syrians and their allies over the slaughter. International reaction was also muted in

October 1990 when Syrian forces overran Christian-controlled areas of Lebanon. In the eight-hour clash, 700 Christians were killed—the worst single battle of Lebanon's Civil War.[10] These killings came on top of an estimated 95,000 deaths that had occurred during the civil war in Lebanon from 1975–1982.[11]

MYTH

"Israel has not withdrawn completely from Lebanon."

FACT

Despite the UN ruling that Israel completed its withdrawal from southern Lebanon, Hezbollah and the Lebanese government insist that Israel still holds a largely uninhabited patch of Lebanese territory called Shebaa Farms.[12]

Israel, which has built a series of observation posts on strategic hilltops in the area, maintains that the land was captured from Syria; nevertheless, the Syrians have supported Hezbollah's claim. The controversy benefits each of the Arab parties. "For Syria, it means Hezbollah can still be used to keep the Israelis off balance; for Lebanon, it provides a way to apply pressure over issues, like the return of Lebanese prisoners still held in Israeli jails. For Hezbollah, it is a reason to keep its militia armed and active, providing a ready new goal for a resistance movement that otherwise had nothing left to resist."[13]

> *"If they go from Shebaa, we will not stop fighting them. Our goal is to liberate the 1948 borders of Palestine... [Jews] can go back to Germany or wherever they came from."*
>
> **—Hezbollah spokesperson Hassan Ezzedin**[14]

In January 2005, the UN Security Council adopted a resolution condemning the violence along the Israel-Lebanon border and reasserted that the Lebanese claim to the Shebaa Farms area is "not compatible with Security Council resolutions" affirming that Israel completely withdrew from Lebanon.

In November 2008, Nawaf Musawi, Hezbollah's head of international relations, told Norway's ambassador to Lebanon that portions of northern Israel belong to Lebanon. He referred to the Blue Line, the border demarcation accepted by the United Nations in 2000 after Israeli forces withdrew from southern Lebanon, as merely a "withdrawal line." Musawi's comments have been interpreted to mean that Hezbollah has territorial demands that extend beyond the Shebaa Farms and into northern Israel.[15]

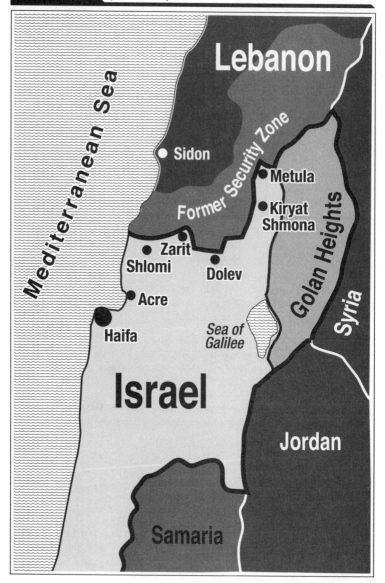

Map 19 — Israel's Border with Lebanon (in 2000)

MYTH

*"Lebanon has abided by UN Resolution 1701
and poses no direct threat to Israel."*

FACT

On August 11, 2006, the UN Security Council adopted Resolution 1701 in response to the Israel-Hezbollah war. The resolution called upon the Lebanese government "to secure its borders and other entry points to prevent the entry in Lebanon without its consent of arms and related materials."

In May 2007, United Nations Secretary General Ban Ki-moon established the Lebanon Independent Border Assessment Team (LIBAT) to evaluate Lebanon's compliance with Resolution 1701. The committee concluded that "the performance of the (Lebanese inspection) agencies in stopping ongoing arms smuggling, which is generally accepted as a fact, can only be described as not up to what can be expected."[16]

The committee discovered widespread corruption amongst Lebanese border police and described the ease by which missiles and militants move across the Syrian-Lebanese border. The report illustrated the United Nations' skepticism of Lebanese attempts to end the flow of illegal arms into Lebanon when it said "one would have expected that an occasional seizure of arms . . . would have taken place. If by nothing else, then by pure chance. This lack of performance is worrying."[17]

Lebanon's failure to implement Resolution 1701 poses a direct threat to Israel and to Lebanese stability. Since the war in 2006, large quantities of weapons (including rockets capable of striking as far south as Tel Aviv and southern Israel), have been smuggled into Lebanon from Syria and Iran. Hezbollah leader Hassan Nasrallah has declared openly that Hezbollah will not disarm so long as Israel remains a threat. He also claims to have tens of thousands of rockets ready to fire at Israel (Israeli military estimates place the number at 20,000).[18] The smuggling and stockpiling of weapons by Hebollah, with the complicity of Lebanese border officials, also threatens the pro-Western Lebanese government. If the UN does not take steps to ensure the implementation of its resolution, the risk of renewed violence between Israel and Hezbollah will grow, as will the possibility of a takeover of Lebanon by Hezbollah.

MYTH

*"Israeli forces deliberately targeted civilians
during the war instigated by Hezbollah."*

FACT

Three weeks after the beginning of the war initiated by Hezbollah on July 12, 2006, Human Rights Watch (HRW) issued a report that charged

Israel with indiscriminate attacks against civilians in Lebanon."[19] Nothing in the report was based on first-hand knowledge of HRW; rather, it was gathered from interviews with "eye-witnesses and survivors" of Israeli strikes who "told HRW that neither Hezbollah fighters nor other legitimate military targets were in the area that the IDF attacked."

If the investigators did not find evidence of Hezbollah's presence at bomb sites, it does not necessarily follow that the terrorists had not been there since it is possible that any weapons, documents or bodies were removed before HRW arrived on the scene. As analyst Joshua Muravchik observed, "There was no dependable method by which HRW could assess the veracity of what it was told by the 'witnesses,' many of whom were in areas where the population was sympathetic to, or intimidated by Hezbollah. Indeed, there was no means by which it could be sure that they were not Hezbollah cadres, since members of the group do not ordinarily wear uniforms or display identity badges."[20]

HRW also has no evidence for the scurrilous accusation that civilians were "deliberately" killed. On the contrary, a great deal of evidence was available showing the efforts Israel made to avoid harming noncombatants, such as dropping leaflets to warn civilians to evacuate locations before they were attacked, the pinpoint attacks of buildings in neighborhoods that could more easily have been carpet-bombed, and the reports of Israeli pilots and others who withheld fire because of the presence of civilians in target areas.

Anyone watching television saw the images of rockets being fired from civilian areas, and the photos of weapons and armed men in what should have been peaceful neighborhoods. Numerous witnesses told reporters very different stories than those reported by HRW, giving examples of weapons caches in mosques and fighters using UN troops as shields.[21] HRW had no trouble accepting the word of the Lebanese people it interviewed, but gave no credence to evidence presented by Israel, such as weapons captured in fighting in civilian areas or videos showing the deployment and launching of rockets from areas that were attacked.

HRW ignored basic moral and legal distinctions. The group did not differentiate between Hezbollah's action in initiating the conflict and Israel's reaction in self-defense, or between Hezbollah's deliberate targeting of civilians and Israel's efforts to avoid civilian casualties. Most remarkably, HRW did not take note of the contrasting goals of the combatants. One of Hezbollah's declared aims is to destroy Israel, while Israel's goal was to survive and to protect its citizens.

The spurious allegations made by HRW, as well as similar ones published by Amnesty International, were further undermined by a report issued in November 2006 by the Intelligence and Terrorism Center at the Israeli Center for Special Studies. This publication provided extensive documentation and photographic evidence of "Hezbollah's consistent pattern of intentionally placing its fighters and weapons among civilians." It also shows that Hezbollah was "well aware of the civilian casualties that would ensue" from this activity.[22]

MYTH

"The overwhelming majority of casualties in the war with Hezbollah were civilians."

FACT

Throughout the 2006 war with Hezbollah, the media reported casualty totals offered by Lebanese officials as facts with no apparent effort to verify them. When the number of Hezbollah terrorists killed was mentioned at all, it was invariably with a qualifier such as "Israel says" or "Israel claims." The evidence suggests, however, that it is likely that half or more of the casualties were not innocent civilians, but Hezbollah fighters.

According to Lebanon's Higher Relief Council, the total number of Lebanese who died in the war was 1,191.[23] No distinctions were made between civilians and terrorists. Press reports usually ignored the fact that it was in Hezbollah and the Lebanese government's interest to exaggerate the number of civilian casualties to blacken the image of Israel and support their contention that Israeli attacks were disproportionate and indiscriminate. Simultaneously, Hezbollah sought to conceal its casualties to enhance its prestige and make propagandistic claims about the damage it was inflicting on Israel while suffering few losses of its own.

The truth did dribble out, though it was largely ignored. For example, the *Daily Telegraph* reported:

> Lebanese officials estimate that up to 500 fighters have been killed in the past three weeks of hostilities with Israel, and another 1,500 injured. Lebanese officials have also disclosed that many of Hezbollah's wounded are being treated in hospitals in Syria to conceal the true extent of the casualties. "Hezbollah is desperate to conceal its casualties because it wants to give the impression that it is winning its war," said a senior security official. "People might reach a very different conclusion if they knew the true extent of Hezbollah's casualties."[24]

The *Kuwait Times* quoted a report that said Hezbollah "buried more than 700 fighters so far, with many more to go."[25] Military expert John Keegan said Hezbollah losses might have been as high as 1,000 out of a total strength of 5,000.[26]

These sources are consistent with information provided by Israel.

Maj. Gen. Yaakov Amidror, a former senior officer in Israeli military intelligence, said "Israel identified 440 dead guerillas by name and address, and experience shows that Israeli figures are half to two-thirds of the enemy's real casualties. Therefore, Amidror estimated, "Hezbollah's real death toll might be as high as 700."[27] A subsequent report three weeks later said that Israel had identified the names of 532 dead Hezbollah terrorists and estimated at least 200 others had been killed.[28]

These reports suggest that at a minimum, roughly half the casualties in the war were combatants. It is more likely the figure approaches 60 percent, which would mean the majority of dead were terrorists. This reinforces the Israeli position that it did indeed inflict heavy losses on Hezbollah and that the civilian casualties were not a result of deliberate or indiscriminate attacks.

Tragically, many civilians were killed, often because they were used as human shields. Of course, there would have been zero casualties if Hezbollah had not attacked Israel and kidnapped and murdered its soldiers.

MYTH

"The media fairly and accurately covered the second war in Lebanon."

FACT

Reporters covering the war from Lebanon were particularly egregious in revealing their own biases based, it seems, on living in the country and developing sympathies for their subjects. More serious, however, was the way some of these correspondents allowed themselves to be used by Hezbollah. In the first Lebanon war, the PLO threatened reporters and made favorable coverage the price of access. Hezbollah learned from their example and now influences much of what reporters can see and say.

CNN's Nic Robertson, for example, was taken to an area of Beirut and told that the rubble of buildings was a result of Israeli air strikes on civilian targets. He repeated the allegation as fact. He had no way of knowing what was in the buildings, whether it was a rocket workshop, a hiding place for Katyushas, the home of a Hezbollah leader, or a command center. In fact, he didn't even know if Israel was responsible for the destruction that he was shown.

Robertson later admitted that his report had been influenced by his Hezbollah guide. He acknowledged that he had been told what to film and where. "They designated the places that we went to, and we certainly didn't have time to go into the houses or lift up the rubble to see what was underneath." Robertson said Hezbollah controls south

Beirut."You don't get in there without their permission. We didn't have enough time to see if perhaps there was somebody there who was, you know, a taxi driver by day, and a Hezbollah fighter by night." Unlike what he said on air during his guided reports, Robertson told CNN's *Reliable Sources,* "there's no doubt that the bombs there are hitting Hezbollah facilities."[29]

Robertson's CNN colleague, Anderson Cooper, one of the journalists who was consistently fair and balanced, highlighted Hezbollah's mendacity. He said the group was "just making things up," and gave as one example a tour he was given in which Hezbollah had lined up some ambulances. They were told to turn on their sirens and then the ambulances drove off as if they were picking up wounded civilians when, in fact, they were simply going back and forth.[30]

Time Magazine contributor Christopher Albritton made clear that reporters understand the rules of the game. "To the south, along the curve of the coast, Hezbollah is launching Katyushas, but I'm loath to say too much about them. The Party of God has a copy of every journalist's passport, and they've already hassled a number of us and threatened one."[31]

Under no duress whatsoever, the *Washington Post's* Thomas Ricks made perhaps the most outrageous charge of the war when he claimed that Israel intentionally left Hezbollah launchers intact because having Israeli civilians killed helps Israel in the public relations war.[32]

Israel's image was tarred by suggestions that it targeted Lebanese Christian areas, intimating that Israel was killing innocent Christians rather than restricting its attacks to the Shiite Muslims of Hezbollah. CNN reported, for example, an Israeli strike "on the edge of the city's mostly *Christian* eastern district" that killed 10 people. In the next paragraph, however, the report says Israel hit "a building *near a mosque.*"[33]

Photographs can be especially powerful, but they can also be misleading or outright fakes. A photo of a baby pulled from the rubble of a building in Qana that appeared on front pages around the world, for example was exposed as a fake.[34] One of the photographers involved, Adnan Hajj, was discovered to have doctored at least two photographs, one of which was changed to show more and darker smoke rising from buildings in Beirut bombed by Israel, and the other changed the image of an Israeli jet so it showed three flares being discharged instead of one. Reuters admitted the photos had been changed, suspended the photographer, and removed all of his photographs from its database.[35]

Reporters in Lebanon exaggerated the destruction in Beirut and elsewhere by showing tight shots of buildings hit in Israeli air strikes and rebroadcasting the same images repeatedly. "You would think Beirut has begun to resemble Dresden and Hamburg in the aftermath of Second World War air raids," observed former *Sunday Telegraph* correspondent Tom Gross. But, Gross notes, "a careful look at aerial satellite photos of the areas targeted by Israel in Beirut shows that certain specific buildings housing Hezbollah command centers in the city's southern suburbs have been singled out. Most of the rest of Beirut, apart from strategic sites such as airport runways used to ferry Hezbollah weapons in and out of Lebanon, has been left pretty much untouched."[36]

While an Israeli strike that killed UN observers drew headlines, little attention was given to reports that Hezbollah was using the UN posts as shields. A Canadian soldier with UNIFIL, for example, reported that his team could observe "most of the Hezbollah static positions in and around our patrol base" and noted that Israeli ordnance that fell near the base was not a result of deliberate targeting, but "has rather been due to tactical necessity."[37]

Over the years, Arab propagandists have learned one sure-fire way to get media attention is to scream "massacre" when Israelis are in the neighborhood. On August 7, news outlets repeated Lebanese Prime Minister Fouad Siniora's claim that Israel had committed a "massacre" by killing 40 people in an air raid on the village of Houla. Later, it was learned that one person had died.[38]

Here are some facts the media neglected during the war:

- Two million Israelis lived under threat of rockets, including approximately 700,000 Israeli Arabs.

- More than 300,000 Israelis were displaced from their homes.

- Fifteen percent of the entire Israeli population lived in bomb shelters.

- Approximately 5,500 homes were damaged by Hezbollah rockets.

- Israel's tourist industry, which had finally started to recover from the Palestinian War, was again devastated.

- Towns that are home to important sites of the three major religions came under fire, including Tiberias, Nazareth and Safed.

- Fires sparked by rockets destroyed 16,500 acres of forests and grazing fields in Israel.

Wars are never easy to cover, and each side of a conflict wants to make its case through the media. A responsible press, however, does not repeat whatever it hears, it first makes every effort to ensure the accuracy of its reporting.

Notes

1. Jillian Becker, *The PLO,* (London: Weidenfeld and Nicolson, 1984), p. 205.
2. Becker, p. 205.
3. *Jerusalem Post,* (June 28, 1982).
4. Quoted in Raphael Israeli ed., *PLO in Lebanon,* (London: Weidenfeld and Nicolson, 1983), p. 7.

5. Henry Kissinger, "From Lebanon to the West Bank to the Gulf," *Washington Post,* (June 16, 1982).
6. Zeev Schiff and Ehud Yaari, *Israel's Lebanon War,* (NY: Simon and Schuster, 1984), p. 70.
7. Becker, p. 212.
8. Schiff and Yaari, p. 257.
9. *Washington Post,* (February 8, 1983).
10. *New York Times,* (October 19, 1990).
11. Becker, p. 212.
12. "Security Council Endorses Secretary-General's Conclusion on Israeli Withdrawal from Lebanon as of 16 June," UN Press Release, (June 18, 2000).
13. *Washington Post,* (January 30, 2001).
14. Jeffrey Goldberg, "In the Party of God," *New Yorker,* (October 14, 2002).
15. Yoav Stern, "Hezbollah: Large Swaths of North Israel Belong to Lebanon," *Haaretz,* (November 4, 2008).
16. Lebanonwire, Independent Border Assesment Team Report, (June 2007).
17. Lebanonwire, Independent Border Assesment Team Report, (June 2007).
18. Uzi Mahnaimi Zarit, "Hezbollah 'has stockpiled rockets' on Israeli border," Timesonline. *The Sunday Times.* (June 10, 2007).
19. Human Rights Watch, "Fatal Strikes: Israel's Indiscriminate Attacks Against Civilians in Lebanon," Vol. 18, No. 3, (August 2006), p. 3.
20. Joshua Muravchik, "Human Rights Watch vs. Human Rights: The cynical manipulation of a worthy cause has a history," *The Weekly Standard,* (September 11, 2006).
21. Alan Dershowitz, "What Are They Watching?" *New York Sun,* (August 23, 2006).
22. Dr. Reuven Erlich (Col. Ret.), "Hezbollah's use of Lebanese civilians as human shields: the extensive military infrastructure positioned and hidden in populated areas. From within the Lebanese towns and villages deliberate rocket attacks were directed against civilian targets in Israel." Intelligence and Terrorism Information Centerat the Center for Special Studies (C.S.S), (November 2006).
23. Lebanese Higher Relief Council, (December 6, 2006).
24. Con Coughlin, "Teheran fund pays war compensation to Hezbollah families," *Daily Telegraph,* (August 4, 2006).
25. *Kuwait Times,* (August 30, 2006).
26. John Keegan, "Why Israel will go to war again—soon," *Daily Telegraph,* (November 3, 2006).
27. UPI, (September 7, 2006).
28. *Washington Times,* (September 27, 2006); Steven Stotsky, "Questioning the Number of Civilian Casualties in Lebanon," CAMERA, (September 7, 2006); Wikipedia.
29. CNN, (July 23, 2006). Also, corrected transcripts from broadcast.
30. Anderson Cooper, "Our Very Strange Day With Hezbollah," AC 360 (CNN), (July 23, 2006).
31. Tom Gross, "The media war against Israel: The Jewish state is fighting not one enemy but two: Hezbollah, and those who peddle its propaganda," *National Post,* (August 2, 2006).
32. CNN, (August 6, 2006).
33. CNN, (August 7, 2006).
34. Reuven Koret, Hezbollywood Horror: "Civil Defense Worker" doubles as Traveling Mortician," Israelinsider.com, (August 3, 2006) and "Hezbollywood? Evidence mounts that Qana collapse and deaths were staged," Israelinsider.com, (July 31, 2006); EU Referendum, (July 31, August. 1, August 5, 2006).
35. Ricki Hollander, "A Reprise: Media Photo Manipulation," CAMERA, (August 9, 2006).

36. Tom Gross, "The media war against Israel: The Jewish state is fighting not one enemy but two: Hezbollah, and those who peddle its propaganda," *National Post,* (August 2, 2006).

37. "A Canadian soldier's report from South Lebanon," CTV.ca, (July 26, 2006).

38. AP, (August 7, 2006) and Amos Harel, "One Dead in IDF Strike in Beirut Southern Suburb," *Haaretz,* (August 7, 2006).

10. The Gulf Wars

MYTH

"The 1991 Gulf War was fought for Israel."

FACT

Prior to President George Bush's announcement of Operation Desert Storm, critics of Israel were claiming the Jewish State and its supporters were pushing Washington to start a war with Iraq to eliminate it as a military threat. President Bush made the U.S. position clear, however, in his speech on August 2, 1990, saying that the United States has "longstanding vital interests" in the Persian Gulf. Moreover, Iraq's "naked aggression" violated the UN charter.[1]

Over the course of the Gulf crisis, the President and other top Administration officials made clear that U.S. interests—primarily oil supplies—were threatened by the Iraqi invasion of Kuwait.

Most Americans agreed with the President's decision to go to war. For example, the *Washington Post*/ABC News Poll on January 16, 1991, found that 76 percent of Americans approved of the U.S. going to war with Iraq and 22 percent disapproved.[2]

It is true that Israel viewed Iraq as a serious threat to its security given its leadership of the rejectionist camp. Israeli concerns proved justified after the war began and Iraq fired 39 Scud missiles at its civilian population centers.

Israel has never asked American troops to fight its battles. Although Israeli forces were prepared to participate in the Gulf War, they did not because the United States asked them not to. Even after the provocation of the Scud missile attacks, Israel assented to U.S. appeals not to respond.

MYTH

"Israel's low profile in the Gulf War proved it has no strategic value to the United States."

FACT

Israel was never expected to play a major role in hostilities in the Gulf. American officials knew the Arabs would not allow Israel to help defend them; they also knew U.S. troops would have to intervene because the Gulf States could not protect themselves.

Israel's posture reflected a deliberate political decision in response to American requests. Nevertheless, it did aid the United States' successful campaign to roll back Iraq's aggression. For example:

- By warning that it would take military measures if any Iraqi troops entered Jordan, Israel, in effect, guaranteed its neighbor's territorial integrity against Iraqi aggression.

- The United States benefited from the use of Israeli-made Have Nap air-launched missiles on its B52 bombers. The Navy, meanwhile, used Israeli Pioneer pilotless drones for reconnaissance in the Gulf.

- Israel provided mine plows that were used to clear paths for allied forces through Iraqi minefields.

- Mobile bridges flown directly from Israel to Saudi Arabia were employed by the U.S. Marine Corps.

- Israeli recommendations, based upon system performance observations, led to several software changes that made the Patriot a more capable missile defense system.

- Israel Aircraft Industries developed conformal fuel tanks that enhanced the range of F-15 aircraft. These were used in the Gulf.

- General Dynamics, a U.S. military contractor, has implemented a variety of Israeli modifications to improve the worldwide F16 aircraft fleet, including structural enhancements, software changes, increased capability landing gear, radio improvements and avionic modifications.

- An Israeli-produced targeting system was used to increase the Cobra helicopter's night-fighting capabilities.

- Israel manufactured the canister for the highly successful Tomahawk missile.

- Night-vision goggles used by U.S. forces were supplied by Israel.

- A low-altitude warning system produced and developed in Israel was utilized on Blackhawk helicopters.

- Israel offered the United States the use of military and hospital facilities. U.S. ships utilized Haifa port shipyard maintenance and support on their way to the Gulf.

- Israel destroyed Iraq's nuclear reactor in 1981. Consequently, U.S. troops did not face a nuclear-armed Iraq. Even in its low-profile mode, Israeli cooperation was extremely valuable: Israel's military intelligence had focused on Iraq much more carefully over the years than had the U.S. intelligence community. Thus, the Israelis were able to provide Washington with detailed tactical intelligence on Iraqi military activities. Defense Secretary Richard Cheney said, for example, that the U.S. utilized Israeli information about western Iraq in its search for Scud missile launchers.

MYTH

"Israel benefited from the 1991 Gulf War without paying any price."

FACT

It is true that Israel benefited from the destruction of Iraq's military capability by the United States-led coalition, but the cost was enormous. Even before hostilities broke out, Israel had to augment its defense budget to maintain its forces at a heightened state of alert. The Iraqi missile attacks justified Israel's prudence in keeping its air force flying round the clock. The war required the defense budget to be increased by more than $500 million. Another $100 million boost was needed for civil defense.

The damage caused by the 39 Iraqi Scud missiles that landed in Tel Aviv and Haifa was extensive. Approximately 3,300 apartments and other buildings were affected in the greater Tel Aviv area. Some 1,150 people who were evacuated had to be housed at a dozen hotels at a cost of $20,000 per night.

Beyond the direct costs of military preparedness and damage to property, the Israeli economy was also hurt by the inability of many Israelis to work under the emergency conditions. The economy functioned at no more than 75 percent of normal capacity during the war, resulting in a net loss to the country of $3.2 billion.[3]

The biggest cost was in human lives. A total of 74 people died as a consequence of Scud attacks. Two died in direct hits, four from suffocation in gas masks and the rest from heart attacks.[4]

A UN committee dealing with reparation claims against Iraq dating to the 1991 Gulf War approved more than $31 million to be paid to Israeli businesses and individuals. The 1999 decision stemmed from a 1992 Security Council decision calling on Iraq to compensate victims of the Gulf War.[5] In 2001, the United Nations Compensation Commission awarded $74 million to Israel for the costs it incurred from Iraqi Scud missile attacks during the Gulf War. The Commission rejected most of the $1 billion that Israel had requested.[6]

MYTH

"Iraq was never a threat to Israel."

FACT

Iraqi President Saddam Hussein was a leader of the rejectionist Arab states and one of the most belligerent foes of Israel. On April 2, 1990, Saddam's rhetoric became more threatening: "I swear to God we will let our fire eat half of Israel if it tries to wage anything against Iraq." Saddam said his nation's chemical weapons capability was matched only by that of the United States and the Soviet Union, and that he would annihilate anyone who threatened Iraq with an atomic bomb by the "double chemical."[7]

Several days later, Saddam said that war with Israel would not end until all Israeli-held territory was restored to Arab hands. He added that Iraq could launch chemical weapons at Israel from several different sites.[8] The Iraqi leader also made the alarming disclosure that his commanders had the freedom to launch attacks against Israel without consulting the high command if Israel attacked Iraq. The head of the Iraqi Air Force subsequently said he had orders to strike Israel if the Jewish State launched a raid against Iraq or any other Arab country.[9]

On June 18, 1990, Saddam told an Islamic Conference meeting in Baghdad: "We will strike at [the Israelis] with all the arms in our possession if they attack Iraq or the Arabs." He declared "Palestine has been stolen," and exhorted the Arab world to "recover the usurped rights in Palestine and free Jerusalem from Zionist captivity."[10]

Saddam's threat came in the wake of revelations that Britain and the United States foiled an attempt to smuggle American-made "krytron" nuclear triggers to Iraq.[11] Britain's MI6 intelligence service prepared a secret assessment three years earlier that Hussein had ordered an all-out effort to develop nuclear weapons.[12] After Saddam used chemical weapons against his own Kurdish population in Halabja in 1988, few people doubted his willingness to use nuclear weapons against Jews in Israel if he had the opportunity.

In April 1990, British customs officers found tubes about to be loaded onto an Iraqi-chartered ship that were believed to be part of a giant cannon that would enable Baghdad to lob nuclear or chemical missiles into Israel or Iran.[13] Iraq denied it was building a "supergun," but, after the war, it was learned that Iraq had built such a weapon.[14]

Iraq emerged from its war with Iran with one of the largest and best-equipped military forces in the world. In fact, Iraq had one million battle-tested troops, more than 700 combat aircraft, 6,000 tanks, ballistic missiles and chemical weapons. Although the U.S. and its allies won a quick victory, the magnitude of Hussein's arsenal only became clear after the war when UN investigators found evidence of a vast program to build chemical and nuclear weapons.[15]

Iraq also served as a base for several terrorist groups that menaced Israel, including the PLO and Abu Nidal's Fatah Revolutionary Council.

After the Iraqi invasion of Kuwait, Saddam Hussein consistently threatened to strike Israel if his country was attacked. If the U.S. moves against Iraq, he said in December 1990, "then Tel Aviv will receive the next attack, whether or not Israel takes part."[16] At a press conference, following his January 9, 1991, meeting with Secretary of State James

Baker, Iraqi Foreign Minister Tariq Aziz was asked if the war starts, would Iraq attack Israel. He replied bluntly: "Yes. Absolutely, yes."[17]

Ultimately, Saddam carried out his threat.

MYTH

"Saddam Hussein was never interested in acquiring nuclear weapons."

FACT

In 1981, Israel became convinced Iraq was approaching the capability to produce a nuclear weapon. To preempt the building of a weapon they believed would undoubtedly be directed against them, the Israelis launched a surprise attack that destroyed the Osirak nuclear complex. At the time, Israel was widely criticized. On June 19, the UN Security Council unanimously condemned the raid. Critics minimized the danger of Iraq's nuclear program, claiming that because Baghdad had signed the Nuclear Non-Proliferation Treaty and permitted its facilities to be inspected, Israeli fears were baseless.

It was not until after Iraq invaded Kuwait that U.S. officials began to acknowledge publicly that Baghdad was developing nuclear weapons and that it was far closer to reaching its goal than previously thought. Again, many critics argued the Administration was only seeking a justification for a war with Iraq.

Months later, after allied forces had announced the destruction of Iraq's nuclear facilities, UN inspectors found Saddam's program to develop weapons was far more extensive than even the Israelis believed. Analysts had thought Iraq was incapable of enriching uranium for bombs, but Saddam's researchers used several methods (including one thought to be obsolete) that were believed to have made it possible for Iraq to build at least one bomb.

MYTH

"American Jews goaded the United States to go to war against Iraq in 2003 to help Israel."

FACT

Some opponents of the U.S.-led war against Iraq in 2003 claimed that American Jews somehow were responsible for persuading President George W. Bush to launch the military campaign on Israel's behalf. In fact, President Bush decided that Iraq posed a threat to the United States because it was believed to possess weapons of mass destruction and was pursuing a nuclear capability that could have been used directly against Americans or could have been transferred to terrorists who would use them against U.S. targets. The removal of Saddam Hussein was also designed to eliminate one of the principal sponsors of terrorism.

The war in Iraq liberated the Iraqi people from one of the world's most oppressive regimes. Even in the Arab world, where many people objected to the U.S. action, no Arab leader rose to Saddam Hussein's defense.

It is true that Israel will benefit from the elimination of a regime that launched 39 missiles against it in 1991, paid Palestinians to encourage them to attack Israelis, and led a coalition of Arab states committed to Israel's destruction. It is also true, however, that many Arab states benefited from the removal of Saddam Hussein, in particular, Saudi Arabia and Kuwait. This is why these nations allowed Allied forces to use their countries as bases for operations.

As for the role of American Jews, it is important to remember that Jews comprise less than three percent of the U.S. population and were hardly the most vocal advocates of the war. On the contrary, the Jewish community had divisions similar to those in the country as a whole, and most major Jewish organizations purposely avoided taking any position on the war. Meanwhile, public opinion polls showed that a significant majority of all Americans initially supported the President's policy toward Iraq.[18]

Some critics have suggested that prominent Jewish officials in the Bush Administration pushed for the war; however, only a handful of officials in the Administration were Jewish, and not one of the President's top advisers at the time—the Secretary of Defense, Secretary of State, Vice President, or National Security Adviser—was Jewish. These opponents of the war chose the age-old approach of blaming the Jews for a policy they disagreed with rather than addressing the substantive arguments in the debate.

Notes

1. *Washington Post,* (August 3, 1990).
2. *Washington Post,* (January 17, 1991).
3. *Near East Report,* (February 4, 1991).
4. *Jerusalem Post,* (January 17, 1992).
5. Jewish Telegraphic Agency, (April 15, 1999).
6. Jewish Telegraphic Agency, (June 22, 2001).
7. Nick Williams, "Iraq Threatens Israel With Use of Nerve Gas," *Los Angeles Times,* (April 13, 1990).
8. "Iraq Said to Have Standing Orders for Attack on Israel," *Los Angeles Times* (April 18, 1990).
9. UPI, (April 22, 1990).
10. Baghdad Domestic Service, (June 18, 1990).
11. *Washington Post,* (March 29, 1990).
12. *Washington Times,* (April 3, 1990).

13. Reuters, (April 12, 1990).

14. "Iraq's 165-ft-long Supergun Examined by UN Inspectors," *Houston Chronicle,* (August 13, 1991).

15. *Washington Post,* (August 8, 1991).

16. AP, "Iraq: First Target Tel Aviv," *Los Angeles Times,* (December 24, 1990).

17. U.S. Department of State, "Memorandum of Conversation including Press Conference Transcript," (January 9, 1991), p. 6.

18. "Public Attitudes Towards the War in Iraq: 2003-2008," Pew Research Center, (March 19, 2008).

11. The Palestinian War, 2000–2005*

MYTH

"Ariel Sharon's visit to the Temple Mount in
September 2000 caused the Palestinian War."

FACT

To believe Palestinian spokesmen, the five-year "al-Aqsa intifada," was caused by the desecration of a Muslim holy place—*Haram al-Sharif* (the Temple Mount)—by Likud leader Ariel Sharon and the "thousands of Israeli soldiers" who accompanied him. The violence was carried out through unprovoked attacks by Israeli forces, which invaded Palestinian-controlled territories and "massacred" defenseless Palestinian civilians, who merely threw stones in self-defense. The only way to stop the violence, then, was for Israel to cease-fire and remove its troops from the Palestinian areas.

The truth is dramatically different.

Imad Faluji, the Palestinian Authority Communications Minister, admitted months after Sharon's visit that the violence had been planned in July, far in advance of Sharon's "provocation." "It [the violence] had been planned since Chairman Arafat's return from Camp David, when he turned the tables on the former U.S. president and rejected the American conditions."[1] Similarly, in 2010, Mahmoud Zahar of Hamas said that Arafat instructed his organization to launch terror attacks against Israel after the failure of peace negotiations.[2]

> *"The Sharon visit did not cause the 'Al-Aqsa Intifada.'"*
>
> **—Conclusion of the Mitchell Report, (May 4, 2001)[3]**

The violence started before Sharon's September 28, 2000, visit to the Temple Mount. The day before, for example, an Israeli soldier was killed at the Netzarim Junction. The next day, in the West Bank city of Kalkilya,

---

*Sometimes referred to as the second, or al-Aqsa intifida, the war was never formally declared, but began in September 2000 with a surge of Palestinian terrorist attacks in Israel. The war also had no formal ending resulting in a cease-fire or peace agreement. The Israeli Defense Forces succeeded in suppressing the violence to the point where the war had petered out by the end of September 2005.

a Palestinian police officer working with Israeli police on a joint patrol opened fire and killed his Israeli counterpart.

Official Palestinian Authority media exhorted the Palestinians to violence. On September 29, the Voice of Palestine, the PA's official radio station sent out calls "to all Palestinians to come and defend the al-Aqsa mosque." The PA closed its schools and bused Palestinian students to the Temple Mount to participate in the organized riots.

Just prior to Rosh Hashanah (September 30), the Jewish New Year, when hundreds of Israelis were worshipping at the Western Wall, thousands of Arabs began throwing bricks and rocks at Israeli police and Jewish worshippers. Rioting then spread to towns and villages throughout Israel, the West Bank and Gaza Strip.

Internal Security Minister Shlomo Ben-Ami permitted Sharon to go to the Temple Mount—Judaism's holiest place—only after calling Palestinian security chief Jabril Rajoub and receiving his assurance that if Sharon did not enter the mosques, no problems would arise. The need to protect Sharon arose when Rajoub later said that the Palestinian police would do nothing to prevent violence during the visit.[4]

Sharon did not attempt to enter any mosques and his 34 minute visit to the Temple Mount was conducted during normal hours when the area is open to tourists. Palestinian youths—eventually numbering around 1,500—shouted slogans in an attempt to inflame the situation. Some 1,500 Israeli police were present at the scene to forestall violence.

There were limited disturbances during Sharon's visit, mostly involving stone throwing. During the remainder of the day, outbreaks of stone throwing continued on the Temple Mount and in the vicinity, leaving 28 Israeli policemen injured. There are no accounts of Palestinian injuries on that day. Significant and orchestrated violence was initiated by Palestinians the next day following Friday prayers.

> *"Philosophically, the difference between me and the terrorist is that he wants to hurt me and my children and my wife, while I want to hit him and spare his children and his wife ... because even the killing of one innocent person is unfortunate and should be avoided."*
>
> **—Senior Israeli Air Force pilot[5]**

MYTH

"A handful of Israelis were murdered in the war while thousands of innocent Palestinians were killed by Israeli troops."

FACT

During the Palestinian War, the number of Palestinian casualties was higher than the figure for Israelis; however, the gap narrowed as Palestinian suicide bombers used increasingly powerful bombs to kill larger numbers of Israelis in their terror attacks. When the war unofficially concluded at the end of September 2005, more than 2,100 Palestinians and 1,061 Israelis had been killed. The disproportionate number of Palestinian casualties was primarily a result of the number of Palestinians involved in violence and was the inevitable result of an irregular, ill-trained group of terrorists attacking a well-trained regular army. The unfortunate death of noncombatants was largely due to the habit of Palestinian terrorists using civilians as shields.

What is more revealing than the tragic totals, however, is the specific breakdown of the casualties. According to one study, Palestinian noncombatants were mostly teenage boys and young men. "This completely contradicts accusations that Israel has 'indiscriminately targeted women and children,'" according to the study. "There appears to be only one reasonable explanation for this pattern: that Palestinian men and boys engaged in behavior that brought them into conflict with Israeli armed forces."[6]

By contrast, the number of women and older people among the noncombatant Israeli casualties illustrates the randomness of Palestinian attacks, and the degree to which terrorists have killed Israelis for the "crime" of being Israeli. Israeli troops do not target innocent Palestinians, but Palestinian terrorists do target Israeli civilians.

> "It is not a mistake that the Koran warns us of the hatred of the Jews and put them at the top of the list of the enemies of Islam.... The Muslims are ready to sacrifice their lives and blood to protect the Islamic nature of Jerusalem and al- Aksa!"
>
> **—Sheik Hian Al-Adrisi**[7]

MYTH

"Israel created Hamas."

FACT

Israel had nothing to do with the creation of Hamas. The organization grew out of the ideology and practice of the Islamic fundamentalist Muslim Brotherhood movement that arose in Egypt in the 1920s.

Hamas was legally registered in Israel in 1978 as an Islamic Association by Sheik Ahmad Yassin. Initially, the organization engaged primarily in social welfare activities and soon developed a reputation for improving the lives of Palestinians, particularly the refugees in the Gaza Strip.

Though Hamas was committed from the outset to destroying Israel, it took the position that this was a goal for the future, and that the more immediate focus should be on winning the hearts and minds of the people through its charitable and educational activities. Its funding came primarily from Jordan and Saudi Arabia.

The PLO was convinced that Israel was helping Hamas in the hope of triggering a civil war. Since Hamas did not engage in terror at first, Israel did not see it as a serious short-term threat, and some Israelis believed the rise of fundamentalism in Gaza would have the beneficial impact of weakening the PLO, and this is what ultimately happened.

Hamas certainly didn't believe it was being supported by Israel. As early as February 1988, the group put out a primer on how its members should behave if confronted by the Shin Bet. Several more instructional documents were distributed by Hamas to teach followers how to confront the Israelis and maintain secrecy.

Israel's assistance was more passive than active, that is, it did not interfere with Hamas activities or prevent funds from flowing into the organization from abroad. Israel also may have provided some funding to allow its security forces to infiltrate the organization.[8] Meanwhile, Jordan was actively helping Hamas, with the aim of undermining the PLO and strengthening Jordanian influence in the territories.

Though some Israelis were very concerned about Hamas before rioting began in December 1987, Israel was reluctant to interfere with an Islamic organization, fearing that it might trigger charges of violating the Palestinians' freedom of religion. It was not until early in the intifada, when Hamas became actively involved in the violence, that the group began to be viewed as a potentially greater threat than the PLO. The turning point occurred in the summer of 1988 when Israel learned that Hamas was stockpiling arms to build an underground force and Hamas issued its covenant calling for the destruction of Israel. At this point it became clear that Hamas was not going to put off its *jihad* to liberate Palestine and was shifting its emphasis from charitable and educational activity to terrorism. Hamas has been waging a terror war against Israel ever since.[9]

MYTH

"Palestinians do not encourage children to engage in terror."

FACT

Most Palestinians who adopt terror in the hope of either "ending the occupation" or destroying Israel do so because they freely choose murder over any other option. Palestinian terrorists also use children, however, to do their dirty work.

On March 15, 2004, Israeli security forces caught an 11-year-old boy attempting to smuggle a bomb through a roadblock. The boy was promised a large sum of money by Tanzim activists in Nablus if he delivered a bag containing a bomb stuffed with bolts to a woman on the other side of the checkpoint. If the boy was stopped and searched, the terrorists who sent him planned to use a cell phone to immediately detonate the explosives he was carrying, murdering nearby soldiers as well as the boy. The plan was foiled by an alert Israeli soldier, and the bomb apparently malfunctioned when the terrorists tried to remotely detonate it. A week later, on March 24, 2004, a 14-year-old Palestinian child was found to be carrying explosives when attempting to pass through the Israeli army checkpoint at Hawara, at the entrance of the town of Nablus.[10]

Just over a year later, on May 22, 2005, a 14-year-old boy was again arrested at the Hawara checkpoint with two pipe bombs strapped to a belt he was wearing. A few days later, a 15-year-old tried to get through the checkpoint with two more pipe bombs. Yet another teen, a 16-year-old, was caught on July 4, 2005, attempting to smuggle a bomb and homemade handgun. In August, another 14-year-old boy was caught carrying three pipe bombs packed with explosives, shrapnel and glass balls.[11]

These are a few examples of the cynical use of children by Palestinians waging war on Israel. Young Palestinians are routinely indoctrinated and coerced into the cult of martyrdom.

"Using children to carry out or assist in armed attacks of any kind is an abomination. We call on the Palestinian leadership to publicly denounce these practices."

—Amnesty International[12]

Despite occasional claims that terror is only promoted by "extremists," the truth is the Palestinian Authority has consistently incited its youth to violence. Children are taught that the greatest glory is to die for Allah in battle as a *shahid*. The PA regularly broadcast television shows that encouraged children to embrace this concept. One film used the death of Muhammad Al-Dura, the child killed in the crossfire of a shootout between Palestinian gunmen and Israeli forces, to show that life after death is paradise. An actor playing Al-Dura was shown in an amusement park, playing on the beach, and flying a kite. The Al-Dura in the film invited viewers to follow his example. Similar messages extolling the virtue of the *shahid* can be found in school textbooks and sermons by Muslim clergy.[13]

The indoctrination is having an impact. According to one Palestinian newspaper, 79–80% of children told pollsters they were willing to be *shahids*.[14]

Palestinian children now play death games, competing to see who will be the *shahid*. They also collect "terrorist cards" the way American kids collect baseball cards. The maker of the Palestinian cards sold 6 million in just over two years. "I take hundreds of these pictures from children every day and burn them," said Saher Hindi, a teacher at a Nablus elementary school. "They turn children into extremists."[15]

> *"As one of the Islamic fanatics who inspired al-Qaida said: 'We are not trying to negotiate with you. We are trying to destroy you.' . . . They wish to destroy the whole basis of Western society—secular democracy, individual liberty, equality before the law, toleration and pluralism—and replace it with a theocracy based on a perverted and dogmatic interpretation of the Koran. . . . The idea that we should try to appease the terrorists is wrong in every respect. It would not protect us, for nothing acts as a greater incentive to terrorists than the realization that their target is weak and frightened. And it would only weaken the institutions we are trying to protect, and demonstrate to the terrorists that we are—as they frequently allege—too decadent and craven to defend the way of life to which we claim to be attached."*
>
> **—London Daily Telegraph**[16]

Many Palestinian youngsters have gone from pretending to carrying out actual terrorist attacks. More than two dozen suicide bombers have been under the age of 18. Between 2001 and March 2004, more than 40 minors involved in planning suicide bombings were arrested. In those years, 22 shootings and bombings were carried out by minors. For example, teens ages 11–14 attempted to smuggle munitions from Egypt into the Gaza Strip; three teenagers, ages 13–15, were arrested on their way to carry out a shooting attack in Afula; and a 17-year-old blew himself up in an attempted suicide attack. In just the first five months of 2005, 52 more Palestinian minors were caught wearing explosive belts or attempting to smuggle weapons through checkpoints in the West Bank.[17]

The situation finally became so serious Palestinian families protested. The mother of one of the three teenagers sent to carry out the Afula attack said of the letter he had left behind, "My son doesn't know how to write a letter like that and has never belonged to one of the organizations. Some grownup wrote the letter for him." The boy's father added, "Nobody can accept to send his children to be slaughtered. I am sure that whoever recruits children in this kind of unlawful activity will not recruit his own children."[18]

Martin Fletcher interviewed the parents of the 15-year-old stopped at the Hawara checkpoint. His parents expressed their anger at the Al-Aqsa Martyrs' Brigades, calling its operatives criminals and saying that Allah would punish them. The correspondent spoke with the boy and read him a letter from his mother asking him to confess and to give Israel all the information in his possession about the men who had sent him.[19]

MYTH

"Palestinian women become suicide bombers because of their commitment to 'liberate' Palestine."

FACT

It may be that some Palestinian women share the ideology of the terrorists who believe that blowing up innocent men, women, and children will achieve their political objective, but many others are blackmailed into carrying out suicide attacks by sadistic and manipulative Palestinian men.

More than 20 Palestinian women have engaged in suicide attacks. The terrorist organizations that recruit them do so in part because they believe women will generate less suspicion, and that Israeli soldiers will be more reticent to search them.

Some of the women have been convinced to engage in terrorist attacks to rehabilitate their reputations in their community if they have acquired a bad name or done something to bring shame upon their family. Shame is a powerful force in Arab society, and women who are promiscuous, engage in adultery, become pregnant out of wedlock, or behave in other ways deemed improper may be ostracized or severely punished (e.g., husbands may kill wives who shamed them in so-called "honor crimes").

Terrorist organizations have used emotional blackmail against these often vulnerable women to convince them that by carrying out a suicide attack against Jews, they may restore their honor or that of their family. Israeli intelligence declassified a report that said Fatah operatives went so far as to seduce women and then, after they became pregnant, used their condition to blackmail them into committing heinous crimes. The report cited two specific cases, one involved a 21-year-old from Bethlehem who blew herself up in the Mahane Yehuda market in Jerusalem, killing six and wounding more than 60, and the other was an

18-year-old from the Dehaishe refugee camp who blew up a Jerusalem supermarket and killed two people and wounded 22 others.[20]

These examples show the merciless way Palestinian terrorists treat not only their victims, but their own people.

MYTH

"Palestinians interested in peace are allowed freedom of speech by the Palestinian Authority."

FACT

One of the principal deterrents to speaking out against Palestinian irredentism and terror in the Palestinian Authority is the threat of being murdered. By the end of the first intifada in the early 1990s, more Palestinians were killed by their fellow Palestinians than died in clashes with Israeli security forces. During the Palestinian War, intimidation and murder were used to muzzle dissent. Usually those seeking peace or an end to terror are labeled "collaborators" and, if they are lucky, arrested by the Palestinian Authority. The unlucky ones are murdered, often in grisly and public ways, such as stringing them up from lamp posts in public squares to send the message that a similar fate awaits anyone who dares cross those seeking Israel's destruction.

> *"If Muslims claim that we are against violence, why aren't we demonstrating in the streets against suicide bombings? Why is it so much easier to draw us into protest against a French ban on the **hijab**, but next to impossible to exorcise ourselves about slavery, stonings and suicide killings? Where's our collective conscience?"*
>
> **—Muslim author Irshad Manji**[21]

A Palestinian need not be interested in peace to become a target of violence; one need only express opposition or offer a challenge to the ruling Fatah party. For example, after student elections at Bir Zeit University in Ramallah resulted in the Islamic Bloc of Hamas and Islamic Jihad receiving more votes than Fatah, Palestinian security forces and members of Fatah attacked members of the Islamic groups and their supporters. Security forces opened fire on the crowd and wounded more than 100 students.[22] When the president of the Gaza-based National Institute of Strategic Studies, Riad al-Agha, criticized the Palestinian security forces on Palestine TV for failing to impose law and order after Israel's disengagement, he was arrested.[23]

There are no exact figures for the number of Palestinians killed in the internecine war; however, Amnesty International reported that "scores of Palestinians" had been unlawfully killed and that the PA "consistently failed to investigate these killings and none of the perpetrators was brought to justice."[24] The Independent Commission for Human Rights (ICHR), a Palestinian organization that monitors slayings of Palestinians by Palestinians, recorded 43 such murders in 2002; 56 in 2003, and 93 in 2004. By October, 151 Palestinians had already been killed in 2005, more than had died in clashes with Israeli troops.[25]

The killings continued after the Palestinian War. Between January 2006 and June 2007, Palestinian factions killed an estimated 616 Palestinians during the civil war between Fatah and Hamas, according to the ICHR. From January 2008 to March 2011, ICHR reports at least 570 Palestinians were killed as a result of murder, tribal fighting, gang violence, tunnel collapses (Egypt to Gaza), weapons misuse, torture, executions, revenge actions and public safety.[26]

MYTH

"The shooting of a child being protected by his father shown on TV proves Israel does not hesitate to kill innocent Palestinian children."

FACT

Perhaps the most vivid image of the Palestinian War was the film of a Palestinian father trying unsuccessfully to shield his son from gunfire. Israel was universally blamed for the death of 12-year-old Mohammed al-Dura, but subsequent investigations found that the boy was most likely killed by Palestinian bullets.

The father and son took cover adjacent to a Palestinian shooting position at the Netzarim junction in the Gaza Strip. After Palestinian policemen fired from this location and around it toward an IDF position, soldiers returned fire toward the sources of the shooting. During the exchanges of fire, the Palestinian child was hit and killed.

Contrary to the conventional belief that the footage of the incident was live, it was actually edited before it was broadcast around the world. Though a number of cameramen were in the area, only one, a Palestinian working for France 2, recorded the shooting.

An IDF investigation of the incident released November 27, 2000, found that al-Dura was most likely killed by a Palestinian policeman and not by IDF fire. This report was confirmed by an independent investigation by German ARD Television, which said the footage of al-Dura's death was censored by the Palestinians to look as if he had been killed by the Israelis when, in fact, his death was caused by Palestinian gunfire.[27]

James Fallows revisited the story and found that "the physical evidence of the shooting was in all ways inconsistent with shots coming from the IDF outpost." In addition, he cites a number of unanswered questions, which have led some to conclude the whole incident was staged. For example, Fallows asks, "Why is there no footage of the boy after he was shot? Why does he appear to move in his father's lap, and to clasp a hand over his eyes after he is supposedly dead? Why is one Palestinian policeman wearing a Secret Service-style earpiece in one ear? Why is another Palestinian man shown waving his arms and yelling at others, as if 'directing' a dramatic scene? Why does the funeral appear—based on the length of shadows—to have occurred before the apparent time of the shooting? Why is there no blood on the father's shirt just after they are shot? Why did a voice that seems to be that of the France 2 cameraman yell, in Arabic, 'The boy is dead' before he had been hit? Why do ambulances appear instantly for seemingly everyone else and not for al-Dura?"[28]

Denis Jeambar, editor-in-chief of the French news weekly *l'Express,* and filmmaker Daniel Leconte, a producer and owner of the film company Doc en Stock, saw raw, unedited video of the shooting and said the boy could not have been shot by Israeli soldiers. "The only ones who could hit the child were the Palestinians from their position. If they had been Israeli bullets, they would be very strange bullets because they would have needed to go around the corner."[29]

Despite the evidence that the report was inaccurate, France 2 has refused to retract the story.

"I think when you are attacked by a terrorist and you know who the terrorist is and you can fingerprint back to the cause of the terror, you should respond."

—U.S. Secretary of State Colin Powell[30]

MYTH

"Israel's policy of targeted killings is immoral and counterproductive."

FACT

Israel is faced with a nearly impossible situation in attempting to protect its civilian population from Palestinians who are prepared to blow themselves up to murder innocent Jews. One strategy for dealing with the problem has been to pursue negotiations to resolve all of the conflicts with the Palestinians and offer to trade land for peace and security. After Israel gave back much of the West Bank and Gaza Strip, and offered virtually all of the remainder, however, the Palestinians chose to use violence to try to force Israel to capitulate to all their demands.

A second strategy is for Israel to "exercise restraint," that is, not respond to Palestinian terror. The international community lauds Israel when it turns the other cheek after heinous attacks. While this restraint might win praise from world leaders, it does nothing to assuage the pain of the victims or to prevent further attacks.

> *"The assassination of Hamas head Sheik Ahmed Yassin in 2004 played in the world as the killing of a crippled holy man by Israeli rockets as he was leaving the mosque in a wheelchair after morning prayers. Because of secrecy surrounding the operation, no file was prepared to explain why he was being killed, that he was an arch-terrorist who had, two days previously, sent two Gaza suicide bombers into Ashdod Port in an attempt to cause a mega-blast of the fuel and nitrates stored there. Or that he had been directly responsible for the deaths of scores, if not hundreds of Israelis."*
>
> **—Columnist Hirsh Goodman**[31]

Moreover, the same nations that urge Israel to exercise control have often reacted forcefully when put in similar situations. For example, the British assassinated Nazis after World War II and targeted IRA terrorists in Northern Ireland. In April 1986, after the U.S. determined that Libya had directed the terrorist bombing of a West Berlin discotheque that killed one American and injured 200 others, it launched a raid on a series of Libyan targets, including President Muammar Qaddafi's home. Qaddafi escaped, but his infant daughter was killed and two of his other children were wounded. President Reagan justified the action as self-defense against Libya's state-sponsored terrorism. "As a matter of self-defense, any nation victimized by terrorism has an inherent right to respond with force to deter new acts of terror. I felt we must show Qaddafi that there was a price he would have to pay for that kind of behavior and that we wouldn't let him get away with it."[32] The Clinton Administration attempted to assassinate Osama bin Laden in 1998 in retaliation for his role in the bombings of the United States embassies in Tanzania and Kenya. George W. Bush ordered "hits" on the Iraqi political leadership during the 2003 war in Iraq and his Administration said it would not hesitate to kill bin Laden while targeting a number of other al-Qaeda operatives.[33] Similarly, the Obama Administration has used drones to kill Taliban fighters and terrorists and found and killed bin Laden in 2011.[34]

More recently, Israel has chosen a third option—eliminating the masterminds of terror attacks. It is a policy that is supported by a vast majority of the public (70 percent in an August 2001 *Haaretz* poll supported the general policy and a similar percentage in 2003 specifically backed the attempt to kill the leader of Hamas). The policy is also supported by the American public according to an August 2001 poll by the America Middle East Information Network. The survey found that 73 percent of respondents felt Israel was justified in killing terrorists if it had proof they were planning bombings or other attacks that could kill Israelis.[35]

Then Deputy Chief of Staff Major-General Moshe Ya'alon explained the policy this way:

> There are no executions without a trial. There is no avenging someone who had carried out an attack a month ago. We are acting against those who are waging terror against us. We prefer to arrest them and have detained over 1,000. But if we can't, and the Palestinians won't, then we have no other choice but to defend ourselves.[36]

The Israeli government also went through a legal process before adopting the policy of targeted killings. Israel's attorney general reviewed the policy and determined that it is legal under Israeli and international law.[37]

Targeting the terrorists has a number of benefits. First, it places a price on terror: Israelis can't be attacked with impunity anymore, for terrorists know that if they target others, they will become targets themselves. Second, it is a method of self-defense: pre-emptive strikes eliminate the people who would otherwise murder Israelis. While it is true that there are others to take their place, they can do so only with the knowledge they too will become targets, and leaders are not easily replaceable. Third, it throws the terrorists off balance. Extremists can no longer nonchalantly plan an operation; rather, they must stay on the move, look over their shoulders at all times, and work much harder to carry out their goals.

Of course, the policy also has costs. Besides international condemnation, Israel risks revealing informers who often provide the information needed to find the terrorists. Soldiers also must engage in sometimes high-risk operations that occasionally cause tragic collateral damage to property and persons.

The most common criticism of "targeted killings" is that they do no good because they perpetuate a cycle of violence whereby the terrorists seek revenge. This is probably the least compelling argument against the policy, because the people who blow themselves up to become martyrs could always find a justification for their actions. They are determined to bomb the Jews out of the Middle East and will not stop until their goal is achieved.

Case Study

In August 2002, we had all the leadership of Hamas—Sheik Yassin and all his military commanders . . . in one room in a three-story house and we knew we needed a 2,000-pound bomb to eliminate all of them—the whole leadership, 16 people, all the worst terrorists. Think about having Osama bin Laden and all the top leadership of al-Qaeda in one house. However, due to the criticism in Israeli society and in the media, and due to the consequences of innocent Palestinians being killed, a 2,000-pound bomb was not approved and we hit the building with a much smaller bomb. There was a lot of dust, a lot of noise, but they all got up and ran away and we missed the opportunity. So the ethical dilemmas are always there.[38]

MYTH

"Israel indiscriminately murders terrorists and Palestinian civilians."

FACT

It is always a tragedy when innocent civilians are killed in a counterterrorism operation. Civilians would not be at risk, however, if the Palestinian Authority arrested the terrorists, the murderers did not choose to hide among noncombatants and the civilians refused to protect the killers.

Israel does not attack Palestinian areas indiscriminately. On the contrary, the IDF takes great care to target people who are planning terrorist attacks against Israeli civilians. Israeli forces have a history of accuracy in such assaults, nevertheless, mistakes are sometimes made. Whereas the terrorists make no apology for their attacks on civilians, and purposely target them, Israel always investigates the reasons for any errors and takes steps to prevent them from reoccurring.

Israel is not alone in using military force against terrorists or in sometimes inadvertently harming people who are not targets. For example, on the same day that American officials were condemning Israel because a number of civilians died when Israel assassinated a leader of Hamas, news reports disclosed that the United States bombed a village in Afghanistan in an operation directed at a Taliban leader that instead killed 48 Afghan civilians at a wedding party. In both cases, flawed intelligence played a role in the tragic mistakes.

"In Gaza last week, crowds of children reveled and sang while adults showered them with candies. The cause for celebration: the cold-blooded murder of at least seven people—five of them Americans—and the maiming of 80 more by a terrorist bomb on the campus of Jersualem's Hebrew University."

—Historian Michael Oren[39]

The terrorists themselves do not care about the lives of innocent Palestinians and are ultimately responsible for any harm that comes to them. The terrorists' behavior is a violation of international law, specifically Article 51 of the 1977 amendment to the 1949 Geneva Conventions, which prohibits the use of civilians to "shield, favor or impede military operations."[40]

Notes

1. *Jerusalem Post,* (March 4, 2001).
2. Khaled Abu Toameh, "Arafat ordered Hamas attacks against Israel in 2000," *Jerusalem Post,* (September 28, 2010).
3. Conclusion of the Mitchell Report, (May 4, 2001).
4. Israel Radio, (October 3, 2000), cited by Independent Media Review & Analysis, http://www.imra.org.il/story.php3?id=4750.
5. Christian Lowe and Barbara Opall-Rome, "Israel Air Force Seeks Expanded Anti-Terror Role," *Defense News,* (March 28, 2005).
6. "An Engineered Tragedy: Statistical Analysis of Casualties in the Palestinian-Israeli Conflict, September 2000-June 2002," International Policy Institute for Counter-Terrorism, (June 2002).
7. Quoted in Sharm El-Sheikh Fact-Finding Committee First Statement of the Government of Israel, Israeli Foreign Ministry, (December 28, 2000).
8. Richard Sale, "Hamas history tied to Israel," UPI, (June 18, 2002).
9. Ze'ev Schiff and Ehud Ya''ari, *Intifada: The Palestinian Uprising—Israel's Third Front.* NY: Simon and Schuster, 1990), pp. 227-239.
10. Associated Press; *Jerusalem Post; New York Post,* (March 16, 2004); CNN.com (March 24, 2004).
11. *Jerusalem Post,* (May 25, July 5, August, 29, 2005).
12. Amnesty International, Press Release, (March 24, 2004).
13. Itamar Marcus, "Ask for Death," *The Review,* (March 2003).
14. *Al-Hayat Al-Jadida,* (June 18, 2002).
15. *Jerusalem Post,* (December 25, 2003).
16. London *Daily Telegraph,* (March 14, 2004).
17. *Jerusalem Post,* (March 15, 2004, May 25, 2005).
18. Associated Press, (February 29, 2004).
19. MSNBC, (May 27, 2005).
20. "Blackmailing Young Women into Suicide Terrorism," Israeli Foreign Ministry, (February 12, 2003).
21. Pearl Sheffy Gefen, "Irshad Manji, Muslim Refusenik," *Lifestyles Magazine,* (Summer 2004), p. 29.

22. NewsFirstClass, (December 12, 2003).

23. Khaled Abu Toameh, "PA arrests academic voicing criticism," *Jerusalem Post*, (July 5, 2005).

24. *Country Reports on Human Rights Practices—2002*, The State Department, March 31, 2003; B'tselem, Amnesty International, January-December 2002; *Jerusalem Post*, (August 25, 2002).

25. Mohammed Daraghmeh, "Palestinian Vigilante Killings on the Rise," Associated Press, (October 6, 2005).

26. "Over 600 Palestinians killed in internal clashes since 2006," Reuters, (June 6, 2007); "Monthly Reports on Violations of HR," The Independent Commission for Human Rights, http://www.ichr.ps/etemplate.php?id=12, accessed March 28, 2011.

27. CNN, Israel Defense Forces, *Jerusalem Post*, (November 27, 2000); Jewish Telegraphic Agency, (March 21, 2002).

28. James Fallows, "Who Shot Mohammed al-Dura?" *The Atlantic Monthly*, (June 2003).

29. Eva Cahen, "French TV Sticks by Story That Fueled Palestinian Intifada," CNSNews. com, (February 15, 2005).

30. News Conference, (September 12, 2001).

31. Hirsh Goodman, "A Lesson Learned," *Jerusalem Report*, (September 19, 2005).

32. Ronald Reagan, "Ronald Reagan on Libya," Ronald Reagan.com, Posted (June 5, 2004).

33. *Washington Post*, (September 14 and 18, 2001).

34. "Drones are Lynchpin of Obama's War on Terror," *Der Spiegel*, (March 12, 2010).

35. Jewish Telegraphic Agency, (August 31, 2001).

36. *Jerusalem Post*, (August 10, 2001).

37. Jewish Telegraphic Agency, (December 3, 2001).

38. Amos Yadlin, "Ethical Dilemma's in Fighting Terrorism," Vol. 4, No. 8, *JCPA*, (November 25, 2004).

39. Michael Oren, "Palestinians Cheer Carnage," Wall Street Journal, (August 7, 2002).

40. Customary International Humanitarian Law, "Practice Relating to Rule 97—Human Shields," ICRC, Additional Protocal #1.

12. The United Nations

MYTH

"According to Security Council Resolution 242, Israel's acquisition of territory through the 1967 war is 'inadmissible.'"

FACT

On November 22, 1967, the UN Security Council unanimously adopted Resolution 242, establishing the principles that were to guide the negotiations for an Arab-Israeli peace settlement.

The first point addressed by the resolution is the "inadmissibility of the acquisition of territory by war." Some people take this to mean that Israel is required to withdraw from all the territories it captured. On the contrary, the reference clearly applies only to an offensive war. If not, the resolution would provide an incentive for aggression. If one country attacks another, and the defender repels the attack and acquires territory in the process, the former interpretation would require the defender to return all the land it took. Thus, aggressors would have little to lose because they would be ensured against the main consequence of defeat.

> *"This is the first war in history which has ended with the victors suing for peace and the vanquished calling for unconditional surrender."*
>
> **—Abba Eban**[1]

The ultimate goal of 242, as expressed in paragraph 3, is the achievement of a "peaceful and accepted settlement." This means a negotiated agreement based on the resolution's principles rather than one imposed upon the parties. This is also the implication of Resolution 338, according to Arthur Goldberg, the American ambassador who led the delegation to the UN in 1967.[2] That resolution, adopted after the 1973 war, called for negotiations between the parties to start immediately and concurrently with the cease-fire.

MYTH

"Resolution 242 requires Israel to return to its pre-1967 boundaries."

FACT

The most controversial clause in Resolution 242 is the call for the "Withdrawal of Israeli armed forces from territories occupied in the recent conflict." This is linked to the second unambiguous clause calling for "termination of all claims or states of belligerency" and the recognition that "every State in the area" has the "right to live in peace within secure and recognized boundaries free from threats or acts of force."

The resolution does not make Israeli withdrawal a prerequisite for Arab action. Moreover, it does not specify how much territory Israel is required to give up. The Security Council did not say Israel must withdraw from "all the" territories occupied after the Six-Day War. This was quite deliberate. The Soviet delegate wanted the inclusion of those words and said that their exclusion meant "that part of these territories can remain in Israeli hands." The Arab states pushed for the word "all" to be added; when the Council rejected their idea, they read the resolution as if it was included. The British Ambassador who drafted the approved resolution, Lord Caradon, declared after the vote: "It is only the resolution that will bind us, and we regard its wording as clear."[3]

This literal interpretation, without the implied "all," was repeatedly declared to be the correct one by those involved in drafting the resolution. On October 29, 1969, for example, the British Foreign Secretary told the House of Commons the withdrawal envisaged by the resolution would *not* be from "all the territories."[4] When asked to explain the British position later, Lord Caradon said: "It would have been wrong to demand that Israel return to its positions of June 4, 1967, because those positions were undesirable and artificial."[5]

Similarly, U.S. Ambassador Arthur Goldberg explained: "The notable omissions—which were not accidental—in regard to withdrawal are the words 'the' or 'all' and the 'June 5, 1967 lines'...the resolution speaks of withdrawal from occupied territories without defining the extent of withdrawal."[6]

The resolutions clearly call on the Arab states to make peace with Israel. The principal condition is that Israel withdraw from "territories occupied" in 1967. Since Israel withdrew from approximately 94 percent of the territories when it gave up the Sinai, the Gaza Strip and portions of the West Bank, it has already partially, if not wholly, fulfilled its obligation under 242.

The Arab states also objected to the call for "secure and recognized boundaries" because they feared this implied negotiations with Israel. The Arab League explicitly ruled this out at Khartoum in August 1967, when it proclaimed the three "noes." Amb. Goldberg explained that this phrase was specifically included because the parties were expected to make "territorial adjustments in their peace settlement encompassing less than a complete withdrawal of Israeli forces from occupied territories, inasmuch as Israel's prior frontiers had proved to be notably insecure." The question, then, is whether Israel has to give up any additional territory. Now that peace agreements have been signed with Egypt and Jordan, and Israel has withdrawn to the international border with Lebanon, the only remaining territorial disputes are with the Palestinians (who are not even mentioned in 242) and Syria.

The dispute with Syria is over the Golan Heights. Israel has repeatedly expressed a willingness to negotiate a compromise in exchange for peace; however, Syria has refused to consider even a limited peace treaty unless Israel first agrees to a complete withdrawal. Under 242, Israel has no obligation to withdraw from any part of the Golan in the absence of a peace accord with Syria.

Meanwhile, other Arab states—such as Saudi Arabia, Lebanon, and Libya—continue to maintain a state of war with Israel, or have refused to grant Israel diplomatic recognition, even though they have no territorial disputes with Israel. These states have nevertheless conditioned their relations (at least rhetorically) on an Israeli withdrawal to the pre-1967 borders.

> *"There are some who have urged, as a single, simple solution, an immediate return to the situation as it was on June 4. . . . this is not a prescription for peace but for renewed hostilities."*
>
> **—President Lyndon Johnson, speech on June 19, 1967[7]**

MYTH

"Resolution 242 recognizes a Palestinian right to self-determination."

FACT

The Palestinians are not mentioned anywhere in Resolution 242. They are only alluded to in the second clause of the second article of 242, which calls for "a just settlement of the refugee problem." Nowhere does it require that Palestinians be given any political rights or territory.

MYTH

"The Arab states and the PLO accepted Resolution 242 whereas Israel rejected it."

FACT

The Arab states have traditionally said they accept 242—as defined by them—that is, requiring Israel's unconditional withdrawal from all the disputed territories.

The Palestinians, angered by the exclusion of any mention of them in the text, rejected the resolution.[8]

By contrast, Ambassador Abba Eban expressed Israel's position to the Security Council on May 1, 1968: "My government has indicated its acceptance of the Security Council resolution for the promotion of agreement on the establishment of a just and lasting peace. I am also authorized to reaffirm that we are willing to seek agreement with each Arab State on all matters included in that resolution."

It took nearly a quarter century, but the PLO finally agreed that Resolutions 242 and 338 should be the basis for negotiations with Israel when it signed the Declaration of Principles in September 1993.

MYTH

"The United Nations plays a constructive role in Middle East affairs."

FACT

Starting in the mid-1970s, an Arab-Soviet-Third World bloc joined to form what amounted to a pro-Palestinian lobby at the United Nations. This was particularly true in the General Assembly where these countries—nearly all dictatorships or autocracies—frequently voted together to pass resolutions attacking Israel and supporting the PLO.

In 1975, at the instigation of the Arab states and the Soviet Bloc, the Assembly approved Resolution 3379, which slandered Zionism by branding it a form of racism.

U.S. Ambassador Daniel Moynihan called the resolution an "obscene act." Israeli Ambassador Chaim Herzog told his fellow delegates the resolution was "based on hatred, falsehood and arrogance." Hitler, he declared, would have felt at home listening to the UN debate on the measure.[9]

On December 16, 1991, the General Assembly voted 111–25 (with 13 abstentions and 17 delegations absent or not voting) to repeal Resolution 3379. No Arab country voted for repeal. The PLO denounced the vote and the U.S. role.

Israel is the object of more investigative committees, special representatives and rapporteurs than any other state in the UN system. The Commission on Human Rights routinely adopts disproportionate resolutions concerning Israel. Of all condemnations of this agency, nearly 49 percent refer to Israel alone (38 total resolutions), while rogue states such as Iran and Libya have only been criticized once each and Syria was never mentioned until Syrian troops began slaughtering its citizens in the summer of 2011.[10]

In March 2005, the Security Council issued an unprecedented condemnation of a suicide bombing in Tel Aviv carried out by Islamic Jihad. Unlike Israeli actions that provoke resolutions, the Security Council issued only a "policy statement" urging the Palestinian Authority to "take immediate, credible steps to find those responsible for this terrorist attack" and bring them to justice. It also encouraged "further and sustained action to prevent other acts of terror." The statement required the consent of all 15 members of the Security Council. The one Arab member, Algeria, signed on after a reference to Islamic Jihad was deleted.[11] The Council has never adopted a resolution condemning a terrorist atrocity committed against Israel.

In August 2005, just as Israel was prepared to implement its disengagement from the Gaza Strip, the Palestinian Authority produced materials to celebrate the Israeli withdrawal. These included banners that read, "Gaza Today. The West Bank and Jerusalem Tomorrow." News agencies reported that the banners were produced with funds from the UN Development Program and were printed with the UNDP's logo.[12]

History has proven that the path to peace is through direct negotiations between the parties; however, the UN constantly undercuts this principle. The General Assembly routinely adopts resolutions that attempt to impose solutions disadvantageous to Israel on critical issues such as Jerusalem, the Golan Heights and settlements. Ironically, UN Security Council Resolutions 242 and 338 proposed the bilateral negotiations that are consistently undermined by the General Assembly resolutions.

Thus, the record to date indicates the UN has not played a useful role in resolving the Arab-Israeli conflict.

"What takes place in the Security Council more closely resembles a mugging than either a political debate or an effort at problem-solving."

—former UN Ambassador Jeane Kirkpatrick[13]

MYTH

"The Palestinians have been denied a voice at the UN."

FACT

Besides the support the Palestinians have received from the Arab and Islamic world, and most other UN members, the Palestinians have been afforded special treatment at the UN since 1975. That year, the General Assembly awarded permanent representative status to the PLO and established the pro-PLO "Committee on the Inalienable Rights of the Palestinian People." The panel became, in effect, part of the PLO propaganda apparatus, issuing stamps, organizing meetings, and preparing films and draft resolutions in support of Palestinian "rights."

In 1976, the committee recommended "full implementation of the inalienable rights of the Palestinian people, including their return to the Israeli part of Palestine." It also recommended that November 29—the day the UN voted to partition Palestine in 1947—be declared an "International Day of Solidarity with the Palestinian People." Since then, it has been observed at the UN with anti-Israel speeches, films and exhibits. Over the objections of the United States, a special unit on Palestine was established as part of the UN Secretariat.

In 1988, the PLO's status was upgraded when the General Assembly designated the PLO as "Palestine." Ten years later, the General Assembly voted to give the Palestinians a unique status as a non-voting member of the 185 member Assembly.

Palestinian representatives can now raise the issue of the peace process in the General Assembly, cosponsor draft resolutions on Middle East peace and have the right of reply. They still do not have voting power and cannot put forward candidates for UN bodies such as the Security Council.

In 2011, Palestinian leaders went to the UN to seek recognition of a state of Palestine based on the 1967 borders with East Jerusalem as its capital. By using the international body to circumvent negotiations, the Palestinians sought to avoid the necessity of recognizing Israel and ending the conflict, and to convince the UN to force Israel to capitulate to their demands.

MYTH

"Israel enjoys the same rights as any other member of the United Nations."

FACT

Israel had been the only UN member excluded from a regional group. Geographically, it belongs in the Asian Group; however, the Arab states have barred its membership. Without membership in a regional group, Israel cannot sit on the Security Council or other key UN bodies. For 40 years, Israel was the only UN member excluded from a regional group.

A breakthrough in Israel's exclusion from UN bodies occurred in 2000, when Israel accepted temporary membership in the Western

European and Others (WEOG) regional group. The WEOG is the only regional group that is geopolitical rather than purely geographical. WEOG's 27 members—the West European states, Australia, Canada, New Zealand and the United States—share a Western-Democratic common denominator. This historic step opened the door to Israeli participation in the Security Council. Israel formally applied for membership to the Council in 2005, but the next seat will not be available until 2019.

MYTH

"The United States has always supported Israel at the UN."

FACT

Many people believe the United States can always be relied upon to support Israel with its veto in the UN Security Council. The historical record, however, shows that the U.S. has often opposed Israel in the Council.

The United States did not cast its first veto until 1972, on a Syrian-Lebanese complaint against Israel. From 1967–72, the U.S. supported or abstained on 24 resolutions, most critical of Israel. From 1973–2010, the Security Council adopted approximately 130 resolutions on the Middle East, most of which were critical of Israel. The U.S. vetoed a total of 43 resolutions and, hence, supported the Council's criticism of Israel by its vote of support, or by abstaining, roughly two-thirds of the time.[14]

American officials also often try to convince sponsors to change the language of a resolution to allow them to either vote for, or abstain from a resolution. These resolutions are still critical of Israel, but may not be so one-sided that the United States feels obligated to cast a veto. In 2011, for example, the Palestinians called on the Security Council to label Israeli settlements illegal and to call for a construction freeze. The U.S. ambassador to the UN tried to convince the Palestinians to change the wording, but they refused. After vetoing the resolution, U.S. Ambassador Susan Rice still criticized Israeli policy.[15]

In July 2002, the United States shifted its policy and announced that it would veto any Security Council resolution on the Middle East that did not condemn Palestinian terror and name Hamas, Islamic Jihad and the Al-Aqsa Martyrs Brigade as the groups responsible for the attacks. The U.S. also said that resolutions must note that any Israeli withdrawal is linked to the security situation, and that both parties must be called upon to pursue a negotiated settlement.[16] The Arabs can still get around the United States by taking issues to the General Assembly, where non-binding resolutions pass by majority vote, and support for almost any anti-Israel resolution is assured.

MYTH

"America's Arab allies routinely support U.S. positions at the UN."

FACT

In 2010, Morocco was the Arab nation that voted with the United States most often, and that was on only 35 percent of the resolutions. U.S. allies Saudi Arabia, Kuwait, and Egypt, voted with the United States only 32 percent of the time. As a group, in 2010, the Arab states voted against the United States on nearly 70 percent of the resolutions. Syria was at the bottom of the list, opposing the U.S. 84 percent of the time. By contrast, Israel has consistently been America's top UN ally. Israel voted with the U.S. 92 percent of the time in 2010, outpacing the support levels of major U.S. allies such as Great Britain, and France, which voted with the United States on only 73 percent of the resolutions.[17]

> *"The UN has the image of a world organization based on universal principles of justice and equality. In reality, when the chips are down, it is nothing other than the executive committee of the Third World dictatorships."*
>
> **—former UN Ambassador Jeane Kirkpatrick[18]**

MYTH

"Israel's failure to implement UN resolutions is a violation of international law."

FACT

UN resolutions are documents issued by political bodies and need to be interpreted in light of the constitution of those bodies. Votes at the UN are not based on legal principles, but the self-interest of the member states; therefore, UN resolutions represent political rather than legal viewpoints. Resolutions can have moral and political force when they are perceived as expressing the agreed view of the international community, or the views of leading, powerful and respected nations.

The UN Charter (Articles 10 and 14) specifically empowers the General Assembly to make only nonbinding "recommendations." Assembly resolutions are only considered binding in relation to budgetary and internal procedural matters.

The legality of Security Council resolutions is more ambiguous. It is not clear if all Security Council resolutions are binding or only those adopted under Chapter 7 of the Charter.[19] Under Article 25 of the Charter, UN member states are obligated to carry out "decisions of the Security

Council in accordance with the present Charter," but it is unclear which kinds of resolutions are covered by the term "decisions." These resolutions remain political statements by nation states and not legal determinations by international jurists.

Israel has not violated any Security Council resolutions and the Council has never sanctioned Israel for noncompliance.

Notes

1. Abba Eban, *Abba Eban,* (NY: Random House, 1977), p. 446.
2. "Middle East Peace Prospects," *Christian Science Monitor,* (July 9, 1985).
3. Security Council Official Records, 1382nd Meeting (S/PV 1382), United Nations, (November 22, 1967).
4. Eban, p. 452.
5. *Beirut Daily Star,* (June 12, 1974).
6. Speech to AIPAC Policy Conference, (May 8, 1973).
7. "Address by President Johnson at National Foreign Policy Conference of Educators," (June 19, 1967).
8. Joel Beinin, "The Palestine Liberation Organization," Middle East Research and Information Project, http://www.merip.org/palestine-israel_primer/intro-pal-israel-primer.html.
9. Chaim Herzog, *Who Stands Accused?,* (NY: Random House, 1978), pp. 4–5.
10. "Human Rights Actions," Eye on the UN, accessed on April 27, 2011, at http://www.eyeontheun.org/browse-un.asp?ya=1&sa=1&u=344&un_s=0&ul=1&tp=1&tpn=Resolution&hc=1&av=19&mn=1&mx=38&ta=78; "Anti-Israel Resolutions at the HRC," UN Watch, accessed on April 27, 2011, at http://www.unwatch.org/site/c.bdKKISNqEmG/b.3820041/.
11. "Policy Statement by Security Council on Terrorist Attack in Israel," Press Release SC/8325, United Nations, (February 28, 2005).
12. "U.N. Funds Palestinian Campaign," Fox News, (August 17, 2005).
13. *New York Times,* (March 31, 1983).
14. U.S. State Department.
15. Richard Grenell, "Susan Rice Fails to Convince the Palestinians, and Offers a Rebuke to Israel," Huffington Post, (February 17, 2011), accessed April 27, 2011, at http://www.huffingtonpost.com/richard-grenell/susan-rice-fails-to-convi_b_824897.html; "United States vetoes Security Council resolution on Israeli settlements," UN News Centre, (February 18, 2011).
16. *Washington Post,* (July 26, 2002).
17. *"Voting Practices at the United Nations—2010,"* U.S. State Department.
18. *Jerusalem Post,* (September 5, 2001).
19. Bruno Simma, ed., *The Charter of the United Nations: A Commentary,* (NY: Oxford University Press, 1994), pp. 237–241; 407–418.

13. The Refugees

MYTH

"One million Palestinians were expelled by Israel from 1947–49."

FACT

The Palestinians left their homes in 1947–49 for a variety of reasons. Thousands of wealthy Arabs left in anticipation of a war, thousands more responded to Arab leaders' calls to get out of the way of the advancing armies, a handful were expelled, but most simply fled to avoid being caught in the cross fire of a battle.

Many Arabs claim that 800,000 to 1,000,000 Palestinians became refugees in 1947–49. The last census taken by the British in 1945 found approximately 1.2 million permanent Arab residents in *all* of Palestine. A 1949 census conducted by the government of Israel counted 160,000 Arabs living in the new state after the war. In 1947, a total of 809,100 Arabs lived in the same area.[1] This meant no more than 650,000 Palestinian Arabs could have become refugees. A report by the UN Mediator on Palestine arrived at an even lower refugee figure—472,000.[2]

MYTH

"Palestinians were the only people who became refugees as a result of the Arab-Israeli conflict."

FACT

Although much is heard about the plight of the Palestinian refugees, little is said about the Jews who fled from Arab states. Their situation had long been precarious. During the 1947 UN debates, Arab leaders threatened them. For example, Egypt's delegate told the General Assembly: "The lives of one million Jews in Muslim countries would be jeopardized by partition."[3]

The number of Jews fleeing Arab countries for Israel in the years following Israel's independence was nearly double the number of Arabs leaving Palestine. Many Jews were allowed to take little more than the shirts on their backs. These refugees had no desire to be repatriated. Little is heard about them because they did not remain refugees for long. Of the 820,000 Jewish refugees between 1948 and 1972, 586,000 were resettled in Israel at great expense, and without any offer of compensation from the Arab governments who confiscated their possessions.[4]

Map 20

Jewish Refugees from Arab States
1948-1972

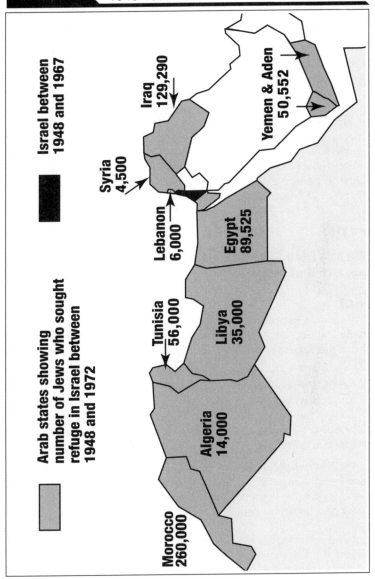

Arab states showing number of Jews who sought refuge in Israel between 1948 and 1972

Israel between 1948 and 1967

Morocco
260,000

Algeria
14,000

Libya
35,000

Tunisia
56,000

Egypt
89,525

Lebanon
6,000

Syria
4,500

Iraq
129,290

Yemen & Aden
50,552

Israel has consequently maintained that any agreement to compensate the Palestinian refugees must also include Arab reparations for Jewish refugees. To this day, the Arab states have refused to pay anything to the hundreds of thousands of Jews who were forced to abandon their property before fleeing those countries. Through 2010, at least 153 of the 914 UN General Assembly resolutions on the Middle East conflict (17 percent) referred directly to Palestinian refugees. Not one mentioned the Jewish refugees from Arab countries.[5]

The contrast between the reception of Jewish and Palestinian refugees is even starker when one considers the difference in cultural and geographic dislocation experienced by the two groups. Most Jewish refugees traveled hundreds—and some traveled thousands—of miles to a tiny country whose inhabitants spoke a different language. Most Arab refugees never left Palestine at all; they traveled a few miles to the other side of the truce line, remaining inside the vast Arab nation that they were part of linguistically, culturally and ethnically.

MYTH

"The Jews had no intention of living peacefully with their Arab neighbors."

FACT

In numerous instances, Jewish leaders urged the Arabs to remain in Palestine and become citizens of Israel. The Assembly of Palestine Jewry issued this appeal on October 2, 1947:

> We will do everything in our power to maintain peace, and establish a cooperation gainful to both [Jews and Arabs]. It is now, here and now, from Jerusalem itself, that a call must go out to the Arab nations to join forces with Jewry and the destined Jewish State and work shoulder to shoulder for our common good, for the peace and progress of sovereign equals.[6]

On November 30, the day after the UN partition vote, the Jewish Agency announced: "The main theme behind the spontaneous celebrations we are witnessing today is our community's desire to seek peace and its determination to achieve fruitful cooperation with the Arabs...."[7]

Israel's Proclamation of Independence, issued May 14, 1948, also invited the Palestinians to remain in their homes and become equal citizens in the new state:

> In the midst of wanton aggression, we yet call upon the Arab inhabitants of the State of Israel to preserve the ways of peace

and play their part in the development of the State, on the basis of full and equal citizenship and due representation in all its bodies and institutions. . . . We extend our hand in peace and neighborliness to all the neighboring states and their peoples, and invite them to cooperate with the independent Jewish nation for the common good of all.

MYTH

"The Jews created the refugee problem by expelling the Palestinians."

FACT

Had the Arabs accepted the 1947 UN resolution, not a single Palestinian would have become a refugee. An independent Arab state would now exist beside Israel. The responsibility for the refugee problem rests with the Arabs.

The beginning of the Arab exodus can be traced to the weeks immediately following the announcement of the UN partition resolution. The first to leave were roughly 30,000 wealthy Arabs who anticipated the upcoming war and fled to neighboring Arab countries to await its end. Less affluent Arabs from the mixed cities of Palestine moved to all-Arab towns to stay with relatives or friends.[8] By the end of January 1948, the exodus was so alarming the Palestine Arab Higher Committee asked neighboring Arab countries to refuse visas to these refugees and to seal their borders against them.[9]

On January 30, 1948, the Jaffa newspaper, *Ash Sha'ab,* reported: "The first of our fifth-column consists of those who abandon their houses and businesses and go to live elsewhere. . . . At the first signs of trouble they take to their heels to escape sharing the burden of struggle."[10]

Another Jaffa paper, *As Sarih* (March 30, 1948) excoriated Arab villagers near Tel Aviv for "bringing down disgrace on us all by 'abandoning the villages.'"[11]

Meanwhile, a leader of the Arab National Committee in Haifa, Hajj Nimer el-Khatib, said Arab soldiers in Jaffa were mistreating the residents. "They robbed individuals and homes. Life was of little value, and the honor of women was defiled. This state of affairs led many [Arab] residents to leave the city under the protection of British tanks."[12]

John Bagot Glubb, the commander of Jordan's Arab Legion, said: "Villages were frequently abandoned even before they were threatened by the progress of war."[13]

Contemporary press reports of major battles in which large numbers of Arabs fled conspicuously fail to mention any forcible expulsion by the Jewish forces. The Arabs are usually described as "fleeing" or "evacuating" their homes. While Zionists are accused of "expelling and dispossessing" the Arab inhabitants of such towns as Tiberias and Haifa, the truth is much different. Both of those cities were within the boundaries of the Jewish State under the UN partition scheme and both were fought for by Jews and Arabs alike.

Jewish forces seized Tiberias on April 19, 1948, and the entire Arab population of 6,000 was evacuated under British military supervision. The Jewish Community Council issued a statement afterward: "We did not dispossess them; they themselves chose this course.... Let no citizen touch their property."[14]

In early April, an estimated 25,000 Arabs left the Haifa area following an offensive by the irregular forces led by Fawzi al-Qawukji, and rumors that Arab air forces would soon bomb the Jewish areas around Mt. Carmel.[15] On April 23, the Haganah captured Haifa. A British police report from Haifa, dated April 26, explained that "every effort is being made by the Jews to persuade the Arab populace to stay and carry on with their normal lives, to get their shops and businesses open and to be assured that their lives and interests will be safe."[16] In fact, David Ben-Gurion sent Golda Meir to Haifa to try to persuade the Arabs to stay, but she was unable to convince them because of their fear of being judged traitors to the Arab cause.[17] By the end of the battle, more than 50,000 Palestinians had left.

> "Tens of thousands of Arab men, women and children fled toward the eastern outskirts of the city in cars, trucks, carts, and afoot in a desperate attempt to reach Arab territory until the Jews captured Rushmiya Bridge toward Samaria and Northern Palestine and cut them off. Thousands rushed every available craft, even rowboats, along the waterfront, to escape by sea toward Acre."
>
> **—New York Times, (April 23, 1948)**

Syria's UN delegate, Faris el-Khouri, interrupted the UN debate on Palestine to describe the seizure of Haifa as a "massacre" and said this action was "further evidence that the 'Zionist program' is to annihilate Arabs within the Jewish state if partition is effected."[18]

The following day, however, the British representative at the UN, Sir Alexander Cadogan, told the delegates that the fighting in Haifa had been provoked by the continuous attacks by Arabs against Jews a few days before and that reports of massacres and deportations were erroneous.[19]

The same day (April 23, 1948), Jamal Husseini, the chairman of the Palestine Higher Committee, told the UN Security Council that instead of accepting the Haganah"s truce offer, the Arabs "preferred to abandon their homes, their belongings, and everything they possessed in the world and leave the town."[20]

The U.S. Consul-General in Haifa, Aubrey Lippincott, wrote on April 22, 1948, for example, that "local mufti-dominated Arab leaders" were urging "all Arabs to leave the city, and large numbers did so."[21]

An army order issued July 6, 1948, made clear that Arab towns and villages were not to be demolished or burned, and that Arab inhabitants were not to be expelled from their homes.[22]

The Haganah did employ psychological warfare to encourage the Arabs to abandon a few villages. Yigal Allon, the commander of the *Palmach,* said he had Jews talk to the Arabs in neighboring villages and tell them a large Jewish force was in Galilee with the intention of burning all the Arab villages in the Lake Hula region. The Arabs were told to leave while they still had time and, according to Allon, they did exactly that.[23]

In the most dramatic example, in the Ramle-Lod area, Israeli troops seeking to protect their flanks and relieve the pressure on besieged Jerusalem, forced a portion of the Arab population to go to an area a few miles away that was occupied by the Arab Legion. "The two towns had served as bases for Arab irregular units, which had frequently attacked Jewish convoys and nearby settlements, effectively barring the main road to Jerusalem to Jewish traffic."[24]

As was clear from the descriptions of what took place in the cities with the largest Arab populations, these cases were clearly the exceptions, accounting for only a small fraction of the Palestinian refugees. The expulsions were not designed to force out the entire Arab population; the areas where they took place were strategically vital and meant to prevent the threat of any rearguard action against the Israeli forces, and to ensure clear lines of communication. Historian Benny Morris notes that "in general, Haganah and IDF commanders were not forced to confront the moral dilemma posed by expulsion; most Arabs fled before and during the battle, before the Israeli troops reached their homes and before the Israeli commanders were forced to confront the dilemma."[25]

MYTH

"The Arab invasion had little impact on the Palestinian Arabs."

FACT

Once the invasion began in May 1948, most Arabs remaining in Palestine left for neighboring countries. Surprisingly, rather than acting as a strategically valuable "fifth-column" that would fight the Jews from within the country, the Palestinians chose to flee to the safety of the other Arab states, still confident of being able to return. A leading Palestinian nationalist of the time, Musa Alami, revealed the attitude of the fleeing Arabs:

> The Arabs of Palestine left their homes, were scattered, and lost everything. But there remained one solid hope: The Arab armies were on the eve of their entry into Palestine to save the country and return things to their normal course, punish the aggressor, and throw oppressive Zionism with its dreams and dangers into the sea. On May 14, 1948, crowds of Arabs stood by the roads leading to the frontiers of Palestine, enthusiastically welcoming the advancing armies. Days and weeks passed, sufficient to accomplish the sacred mission, but the Arab armies did not save the country. They did nothing but let slip from their hands Acre, Sarafand, Lydda, Ramleh, Nazareth, most of the south and the rest of the north. Then hope fled.[26]

As the fighting spread into areas that had previously remained quiet, the Arabs began to see the possibility of defeat. As that possibility turned into reality, the flight of the Arabs increased—more than 300,000 departed after May 15—leaving approximately 160,000 Arabs in the State of Israel.[27]

Although most of the Arabs had left by November 1948, there were still those who chose to leave even after hostilities ceased. An interesting case was the evacuation of 3,000 Arabs from Faluja, a village between Tel Aviv and Beersheba:

> Observers feel that with proper counsel after the Israeli-Egyptian armistice, the Arab population might have advantageously remained. They state that the Israeli Government had given guarantees of security of person and property. However, no effort was made by Egypt, Transjordan or even the United Nations Palestine Conciliation Commission to advise the Faluja Arabs one way or the other.[28]

MYTH

"Arab leaders never encouraged the Palestinians to flee."

FACT

Despite revisionist historical attempts to deny that Palestinians were encouraged to leave their homes, a plethora of evidence demonstrates that the Palestinians who later became refugees were indeed told to leave their homes to make way for the invading Arab armies. In fact, in recent years, more Palestinians have come forward to candidly admit this truth.

The *Economist,* a frequent critic of the Zionists, reported on October 2, 1948: "Of the 62,000 Arabs who formerly lived in Haifa not more than 5,000 or 6,000 remained. Various factors influenced their decision to seek safety in flight. There is but little doubt that the most potent of the factors were the announcements made over the air by the Higher Arab Executive, urging the Arabs to quit.... It was clearly intimated that those Arabs who remained in Haifa and accepted Jewish protection would be regarded as renegades."

"The [refugee] problem was a direct consequence of the war that the Palestinians—and ... surrounding Arab states—had launched."

—Israeli historian Benny Morris[29]

Time's report of the battle for Haifa (May 3, 1948) was similar: "The mass evacuation, prompted partly by fear, partly by orders of Arab leaders, left the Arab quarter of Haifa a ghost city.... By withdrawing Arab workers their leaders hoped to paralyze Haifa."[30]

Starting in December 1947, historian Benny Morris said, "Arab officers ordered the complete evacuation of specific villages in certain areas, lest their inhabitants 'treacherously' acquiesce in Israeli rule or hamper Arab military deployments." He concluded, "There can be no exaggerating the importance of these early Arab-initiated evacuations in the demoralization, and eventual exodus, of the remaining rural and urban populations."[31]

The Arab National Committee in Jerusalem, following the March 8, 1948, instructions of the Arab Higher Committee, ordered women, children and the elderly in various parts of Jerusalem to leave their homes: "Any opposition to this order ... is an obstacle to the holy war ... and will hamper the operations of the fighters in these districts." The Arab Higher Committee also ordered the evacuation of "several dozen villages, as well as the removal of dependents from dozens more" in April-July 1948. "The invading Arab armies also occasionally ordered whole villages to depart, so as not to be in their way."[32]

Morris also said that in early May units of the Arab Legion ordered the evacuation of all women and children from the town of Beisan. The Arab Liberation Army was also reported to have ordered the evacuation of another village south of Haifa. The departure of the women and children, Morris says, "tended to sap the morale of the menfolk who were left behind to guard the homes and fields, contributing ultimately to the final evacuation of villages. Such two-tier evacuation—women and children first, the men following weeks later—occurred in Qumiya in the Jezreel Valley, among the Awarna bedouin in Haifa Bay and in various other places."

In his memoirs, Haled al Azm, the Syrian Prime Minister in 1948–49, also admitted the Arab role in persuading the refugees to leave:

"Since 1948 we have been demanding the return of the refugees to their homes. But we ourselves are the ones who encouraged them to leave. Only a few months separated our call to them to leave and our appeal to the United Nations to resolve on their return."[33]

Who gave such orders? Leaders such as Iraqi Prime Minister Nuri Said, who declared: "We will smash the country with our guns and obliterate every place the Jews seek shelter in. The Arabs should conduct their wives and children to safe areas until the fighting has died down."[34]

The Secretary of the Arab League Office in London, Edward Atiyah, wrote in his book, *The Arabs*: "This wholesale exodus was due partly to the belief of the Arabs, encouraged by the boastings of an unrealistic Arabic press and the irresponsible utterances of some of the Arab leaders that it could be only a matter of weeks before the Jews were defeated by the armies of the Arab States and the Palestinian Arabs enabled to reenter and retake possession of their country."[35]

"The refugees were confident their absence would not last long, and that they would return within a week or two," Monsignor George Hakim, a Greek Orthodox Catholic Bishop of Galilee told the Beirut newspaper, *Sada al-Janub* (August 16, 1948). "Their leaders had promised them that the Arab Armies would crush the 'Zionist gangs' very quickly and that there was no need for panic or fear of a long exile."

"The Arab States encouraged the Palestine Arabs to leave their homes temporarily in order to be out of the way of the Arab invasion armies," according to the Jordanian newspaper *Filastin*, (February 19, 1949).

One refugee quoted in the Jordan newspaper, *Ad Difaa* (September 6, 1954), said: "The Arab government told us: Get out so that we can get in. So we got out, but they did not get in."

"The Secretary-General of the Arab League, Azzam Pasha, assured the Arab peoples that the occupation of Palestine and Tel Aviv would be as simple as a military promenade," said Habib Issa in the New York Lebanese paper, *Al Hoda* (June 8, 1951). "He pointed out that they were already on the frontiers and that all the millions the Jews had spent on land and economic development would be easy booty, for it would be a simple matter to throw Jews into the Mediterranean. . . . Brotherly advice was given to the Arabs of Palestine to leave their land, homes and property and to stay temporarily in neighboring fraternal states, lest the guns of the invading Arab armies mow them down."

The Arabs' fear was exacerbated by stories of Jewish atrocities following the attack on Deir Yassin. The native population lacked leaders who could calm them; their spokesmen were operating from the safety of neighboring states and did more to arouse their fears than to pacify them. Local military leaders were of little or no comfort. In one instance the commander of Arab troops in Safed went to Damascus. The following day, his troops withdrew from the town. When the residents realized they were defenseless, they fled in panic.

"As Palestinian military power was swiftly and dramatically crushed, and the Haganah demonstrated almost unchallenged superiority in successive battles," Benny Morris noted, "Arab morale cracked, giving way to general, blind, panic, or a 'psychosis of flight,' as one IDF intelligence report put it."[36]

Dr. Walid al-Qamhawi, a former member of the Executive Committee of the PLO, agreed "it was collective fear, moral disintegration and chaos in every field that exiled the Arabs of Tiberias, Haifa and dozens of towns and villages."[37]

As panic spread throughout Palestine, the early trickle of refugees became a flood, numbering more than 200,000 by the time the provisional government declared the independence of the State of Israel.

Even Jordan's King Abdullah, writing in his memoirs, blamed Palestinian leaders for the refugee problem:

> The tragedy of the Palestinians was that most of their leaders had paralyzed them with false and unsubstantiated promises that they were not alone; that 80 million Arabs and 400 million Muslims would instantly and miraculously come to their rescue.[38]

These accounts have been bolstered by more recent statements by Palestinians who have become fed up with the phony narrative concocted by some Palestinian and Israeli academics. Asmaa Jabir Balasimah, for example, recalled her flight from Israel in 1948:

> We heard sounds of explosions and of gunfire at the beginning of the summer in the year of the "Catastrophe" [1948]. They told us: The Jews attacked our region and it is better to evacuate the village and return, after the battle is over. And indeed there were among us [who fled Israel] those who left a fire burning under the pot, those who left their flock [of sheep] and those who left their money and gold behind, based on the assumption that we would return after a few hours.[39]

An Arab resident of a Palestinian refugee camp explained why his family left Israel in 1948:

> The radio stations of the Arab regimes kept repeating to us: 'Get away from the battle lines. It's a matter of ten days or two weeks at the most, and we'll bring you back to Ein-Kerem [near Jerusalem].' And we said to ourselves, 'That's a very long

time. What is this? Two weeks? That's a lot!' That's what we thought [then]. And now 50 years have gone by.[40]

Mahmoud Al-Habbash, a Palestinian journalist wrote in the Palestinian Authority's official newspaper:

> ...The leaders and the elites promised us at the beginning of the "Catastrophe" in 1948, that the duration of the exile will not be long, and that it will not last more than a few days or months, and afterwards the refugees will return to their homes, which most of them did not leave only until they put their trust in those "Arkuvian" promises made by the leaders and the political elites. Afterwards, days passed, months, years and decades, and the promises were lost with the strain of the succession of events ... ["Arkuvian" is a reference to Arkuv, a figure from Arab tradition known for breaking promises and lying.][41]

Another Palestinian journalist, Jawad Al Bashiti, explained the cause of the "Catastrophe":

> The following happened: the first war between Arabs and Israel had started and the "Arab Salvation Army" came and told the Palestinians: 'We have come to you in order to liquidate the Zionists and their state. Leave your houses and villages, you will return to them in a few days safely. Leave them so we can fulfill our mission (destroy Israel) in the best way and so you won't be hurt.' It became clear already then, when it was too late, that the support of the Arab states (against Israel) was a big illusion. Arabs fought as if intending to cause the "Palestinian Catastrophe."[42]

"The Arab armies entered Palestine to protect the Palestinians from the Zionist tyranny but, instead, they abandoned them, forced them to emigrate and to leave their homeland, and threw them into prisons similar to the ghettos in which the Jews used to live."

—Palestinian Authority Prime Minister Mahmoud Abbas[43]

MYTH

"The Palestinian Arabs had to flee to avoid being massacred like the peaceful villagers in Deir Yassin."

FACT

The United Nations resolved that Jerusalem would be an international city apart from the Arab and Jewish states demarcated in the partition resolution. The 150,000 Jewish inhabitants were under constant military pressure; the 2,500 Jews living in the Old City were victims of an Arab blockade that lasted five months before they were forced to surrender on May 29, 1948. Prior to the surrender, and throughout the siege on Jerusalem, Jewish convoys tried to reach the city to alleviate the food shortage, which, by April, had become critical.

Meanwhile, the Arab forces, which had engaged in sporadic and unorganized ambushes since December 1947, began to make an organized attempt to cut off the highway linking Tel Aviv with —the city's only supply route. The Arabs controlled several strategic vantage points, which overlooked the highway and enabled them to fire on the convoys trying to reach the beleaguered city with supplies. Deir Yassin was situated on a hill, about 2,600 feet high, which commanded a wide view of the vicinity and was located less than a mile from the suburbs of Jerusalem.[44]

On April 6, Operation Nachshon was launched to open the road to Jerusalem. The village of Deir Yassin was included on the list of Arab villages to be occupied as part of the operation. The following day Haganah commander David Shaltiel wrote to the leaders of the Lehi and Irgun:

> I learn that you plan an attack on Deir Yassin. I wish to point out that the capture of Deir Yassin and its holding are one stage in our general plan. I have no objection to your carrying out the operation provided you are able to hold the village. If you are unable to do so I warn you against blowing up the village which will result in its inhabitants abandoning it and its ruins and deserted houses being occupied by foreign forces.... Furthermore, if foreign forces took over, this would upset our general plan for establishing an airfield.[45]

The Irgun decided to attack Deir Yassin on April 9, while the Haganah was still engaged in the battle for Kastel. This was the first major Irgun attack against the Arabs. Previously, the Irgun and Lehi had concentrated their attacks against the British.

According to Irgun leader Menachem Begin, the assault was carried out by 100 members of that organization; other authors say it was as many as 132 men from both groups. Begin stated that a small open truck fitted with a loudspeaker was driven to the entrance of the village before the attack and broadcast a warning for civilians to evacuate the area, which many did.[46] Most writers say the warning was never issued because the truck with the loudspeaker rolled into a ditch before it could broadcast the warning.[47] One of the fighters said, the ditch was filled in and the truck continued on to the village. "One of us called out on the loudspeaker in Arabic, telling the inhabitants to put down their weapons and flee. I don't know if they heard, and I know these appeals had no effect."[48]

Contrary to revisionist histories that say the town was filled with peaceful innocents, evidence shows that both residents and foreign troops opened fire on the attackers. One Irgun fighter described his experience:

> My unit stormed and passed the first row of houses. I was among the first to enter the village. There were a few other guys with me, each encouraging the other to advance. At the top of the street I saw a man in khaki clothing running ahead. I thought he was one of ours. I ran after him and told him, "advance to that house." Suddenly he turned around, aimed his rifle and shot. He was an Iraqi soldier. I was hit in the foot.[49]

The battle was ferocious and took several hours. The Irgun suffered 41 casualties, including four dead.

Surprisingly, after the "massacre," the Irgun escorted a representative of the Red Cross through the town and held a press conference. The *New York Times*' subsequent description of the battle was essentially the same as Begin's. The *Times* said more than 200 Arabs were killed, 40 captured and 70 women and children were released. No hint of a massacre appeared in the report.[50]

"Paradoxically, the Jews say about 250 out of 400 village inhabitants [were killed], while Arab survivors say only 110 of 1,000."[51] A study by Bir Zeit University, based on discussions with each family from the village, arrived at a figure of 107 Arab civilians dead and 12 wounded, in addition to 13 "fighters," evidence that the number of dead was smaller than claimed and that the village did have troops based there.[52] Other Arab sources have subsequently suggested the number may have been even lower.[53]

In fact, the attackers left open an escape corridor from the village and more than 200 residents left unharmed. For example, at 9:30 A.M., about five hours after the fighting started, the Lehi evacuated 40 old men, women and children on trucks and took them to a base in Sheik Bader. Later, the Arabs were taken to East Jerusalem. Seeing the Arabs in the hands of Jews also helped raise the morale of the people of Jerusalem who were despondent from the setbacks in the fighting to that point.[54] Another source says 70 women and children were taken away and turned over to the British.[55] If the intent was to massacre the inhabitants, no one would have been evacuated.

After the remaining Arabs feigned surrender and then fired on the Jewish troops, some Jews killed Arab soldiers and civilians indiscriminately. None of the sources specify how many women and children were killed (the *Times* report said it was about half the victims; their original casualty figure came from the Irgun source), but there were some among the casualties.

At least some of the women who were killed became targets because of men who tried to disguise themselves as women. The Irgun commander reported, for example, that the attackers "found men dressed as women and therefore they began to shoot at women who did not hasten to go down to the place designated for gathering the prisoners."[56] Another story was told by a member of the Haganah who overheard a group of Arabs from Deir Yassin who said "the Jews found out that Arab warriors had disguised themselves as women. The Jews searched the women too. One of the people being checked realized he had been caught, took out a pistol and shot the Jewish commander. His friends, crazed with anger, shot in all directions and killed the Arabs in the area."[57]

Contrary to claims from Arab propagandists at the time, and some since, no evidence has ever been produced that any women were raped. On the contrary, every villager ever interviewed has denied these allegations. Like many of the claims, this was a deliberate propaganda ploy, but one that backfired. Hazam Nusseibi, who worked for the Palestine Broadcasting Service in 1948, admitted being told by Hussein Khalidi, a Palestinian Arab leader, to fabricate the atrocity claims. Abu Mahmud, a Deir Yassin resident in 1948 told Khalidi "there was no rape," but Khalidi replied, "We have to say this, so the Arab armies will come to liberate Palestine from the Jews." Nusseibeh told the BBC 50 years later, "This was our biggest mistake. We did not realize how our people would react. As soon as they heard that women had been raped at Deir Yassin, Palestinians fled in terror."[58]

The Jewish Agency, upon learning of the attack, immediately expressed its "horror and disgust." It also sent a letter expressing the Agency's shock and disapproval to Transjordan's King Abdullah.

Arab radio stations broadcast accounts of what happened over the days and weeks that followed and the Arab Higher Committee hoped exaggerated reports about a "massacre" at Deir Yassin would shock the population of the Arab countries into bringing pressure on their governments to intervene in Palestine. Instead, the immediate impact was to stimulate a new Palestinian exodus.

Just four days after the reports from Deir Yassin were published, an Arab force ambushed a Jewish convoy on the way to Hadassah Hospital, killing 77 Jews, including doctors, nurses, patients, and the director of the hospital. Another 23 people were injured. This premeditated massacre attracted little attention and is never mentioned by those who are quick to bring up Deir Yassin. Moreover, despite attacks such as this against the Jewish community in Palestine, in which more than 500 Jews were killed in the first four months after the partition decision alone, Jews did not flee.

The Palestinians knew, despite their rhetoric to the contrary, the

Jews were not trying to annihilate them; otherwise, they would not have been allowed to evacuate Tiberias, Haifa or any of the other towns captured by the Jews. Moreover, the Palestinians could find sanctuary in nearby states. The Jews, however, had no place to run had they wanted to. They were willing to fight to the death for their country. It came to that for many, because the Arabs *were* interested in annihilating the Jews, as Secretary-General of the Arab League Abd Al-Rahman Azzam Pasha made clear in an interview with an Egyptian newspaper (October 11, 1947): "Personally, I hope that the Jews will not force this war upon us, because it will be a war of annihilation. It will be a momentous massacre in history that will be talked about like the massacres of the Mongols or the Crusades."[59]

References to Deir Yassin have remained a staple of anti-Israel propaganda for decades because the incident was unique.

MYTH

"Israel refused to allow Palestinians to return to their homes so Jews could steal their property."

FACT

Israel could not simply agree to allow all Palestinians to return, but consistently sought a solution to the refugee problem. Israel's position was expressed by David Ben-Gurion (August 1, 1948):

> When the Arab states are ready to conclude a peace treaty with Israel this question will come up for constructive solution as part of the general settlement, and with due regard to our counterclaims in respect of the destruction of Jewish life and property, the long-term interest of the Jewish and Arab populations, the stability of the State of Israel and the durability of the basis of peace between it and its neighbors, the actual position and fate of the Jewish communities in the Arab countries, the responsibilities of the Arab governments for their war of aggression and their liability for reparation, will all be relevant in the question whether, to what extent, and under what conditions, the former Arab residents of the territory of Israel should be allowed to return.[60]

The Israeli government was not indifferent to the plight of the refugees; an ordinance was passed creating a Custodian of Abandoned Property "to prevent unlawful occupation of empty houses and business premises, to administer ownerless property, and also to secure tilling of deserted fields, and save the crops...."[61]

The implied danger of repatriation did not prevent Israel from allowing some refugees to return and offering to take back a substantial number as a condition for signing a peace treaty. In 1949, Israel offered to allow families that had been separated during the war to return, to release refugee accounts frozen in Israeli banks (eventually released in 1953), to pay compensation for abandoned lands and to repatriate 100,000 refugees.[62]

The Arabs rejected all the Israeli compromises. They were unwilling to take any action that might be construed as recognition of Israel. They made repatriation a precondition for negotiations, something Israel rejected. The result was the confinement of the refugees in camps.

Despite the position taken by the Arab states, Israel did release the Arab refugees' blocked bank accounts, which totaled more than $10 million, paid thousands of claimants cash compensation and granted thousands of acres as alternative holdings.

MYTH

"UN resolutions call for Israel to repatriate all Palestinian refugees."

FACT

The United Nations took up the refugee issue and adopted Resolution 194 on December 11, 1948. This called upon the Arab states and Israel to resolve all outstanding issues through negotiations either directly, or with the help of the Palestine Conciliation Commission established by this resolution. Furthermore, Point 11 resolves:

> that refugees wishing to return to their homes *and live at peace* with their neighbors should be permitted to do so at the earliest practicable date, and that compensation should be paid for property of those choosing not to return and for loss of or damage to property which under principles of international law or in equity should be made good by Governments or authorities responsible. Instructs the Conciliation Commission to facilitate the repatriation, *resettlement* and economic and social rehabilitation of refugees and payment of compensation . . . (emphasis added).

The emphasized words demonstrate that the UN recognized that Israel could not be expected to repatriate a hostile population that might endanger its security. The solution to the problem, like all previous refugee problems, would require at least some Palestinians to be resettled in Arab lands. Furthermore, the resolution uses the word "should" instead of "shall," which, in legal terms, is not mandatory language.

The resolution met most of Israel's concerns regarding the refugees, whom they regarded as a potential fifth-column if allowed to return unconditionally. The Israelis considered the settlement of the refugee issue a negotiable part of an overall peace settlement. As President Chaim Weizmann explained:"We are anxious to help such resettlement provided that real peace is established and the Arab states do their part of the job. The solution of the Arab problem can be achieved only through an all-around Middle East development scheme, toward which the United Nations, the Arab states and Israel will make their respective contributions."[63]

> *"The Palestinian demand for the 'right of return' is totally unrealistic and would have to be solved by means of financial compensation and re-settlement in Arab countries."*
>
> **—Egyptian President Hosni Mubarak[64]**

At the time the Israelis did not expect the refugees to be a major issue; they thought the Arab states would resettle the majority and some compromise on the remainder could be worked out in the context of an overall settlement. The Arabs were no more willing to compromise in 1949, however, than they had been in 1947. In fact, they unanimously rejected the UN resolution.

The UN discussions on refugees had begun in the summer of 1948, before Israel had completed its military victory; consequently, the Arabs still believed they could win the war and allow the refugees to return triumphant. The Arab position was expressed by Emile Ghoury, the Secretary of the Arab Higher Committee:

It is inconceivable that the refugees should be sent back to their homes while they are occupied by the Jews, as the latter would hold them as hostages and maltreat them. The very proposal is an evasion of responsibility by those responsible. It will serve as a first step towards Arab recognition of the State of Israel and partition.[65]

The Arabs demanded that the United Nations assert the "right" of the Palestinians to return to their homes, and were unwilling to accept anything less until after their defeat had become obvious. The Arabs then reinterpreted Resolution 194 as granting the refugees the absolute right of repatriation and have demanded that Israel accept this interpretation ever since. Regardless of the interpretation, 194, like other General Assembly resolutions, is not legally binding.

MYTH

"Palestinians who wanted to return to their homes posed no danger to Israeli security."

FACT

When plans for setting up a state were made in early 1948, Jewish leaders in Palestine expected the new nation to include a significant Arab population. From the Israeli perspective, the refugees had been given an opportunity to stay in their homes and be a part of the new state. Approximately 160,000 Arabs had chosen to do so. To repatriate those who had fled would be, in the words of Foreign Minister Moshe Sharett, "suicidal folly."[66]

In the Arab world, the refugees were viewed as a potential fifth-column within Israel. As one Lebanese paper wrote:

> The return of the refugees should create a large Arab majority that would serve as the most effective means of reviving the Arab character of Palestine, while forming a powerful fifth-column for the day of revenge and reckoning.[67]

The Arabs believed the return of the refugees would virtually guarantee the destruction of Israel, a sentiment expressed by Egyptian Foreign Minister Muhammad Salah al-Din:

> It is well-known and understood that the Arabs, in demanding the return of the refugees to Palestine, mean their return as masters of the Homeland and not as slaves. With a greater clarity, they mean the liquidation of the State of Israel.[68]

The plight of the refugees remained unchanged after the Suez War. In fact, even the rhetoric stayed the same. In 1957, the Refugee Conference at Homs, Syria, passed a resolution stating:

> Any discussion aimed at a solution of the Palestine problem which will not be based on ensuring the refugees' right to annihilate Israel will be regarded as a desecration of the Arab people and an act of treason.[69]

A parallel can be drawn to the time of the American Revolution, during which many colonists who were loyal to England fled to Canada. The British wanted the newly formed republic to allow the loyalists to return to claim their property. Benjamin Franklin rejected this suggestion in a letter to Richard Oswald, the British negotiator, dated November 26, 1782:

> Your ministers require that we should receive again into our bosom those who have been our bitterest enemies and restore

their properties who have destroyed ours: and this while the wounds they have given us are still bleeding![70]

MYTH

"The Palestinian refugees were ignored by an uncaring world."

FACT

The General Assembly voted on November 19, 1948, to establish the United Nations Relief For Palestinian Refugees (UNRPR) to dispense aid to the refugees. Since then, more than 150 resolutions have been adopted that refer to Palestinian refugees, roughly 17 percent of all the resolutions on the conflict.[71]

The UNRPR was replaced by the United Nations Relief and Works Agency (UNRWA) on December 8, 1949. UNRWA was designed to continue the relief program initiated by the UNRPR, substitute public works for direct relief and promote economic development. The proponents of the plan envisioned that direct relief would be almost completely replaced by public works, with the remaining assistance provided by the Arab governments.

UNRWA had little chance of success, however, because it sought to solve a political problem using an economic approach. By the mid-1950s, it was evident neither the refugees nor the Arab states were prepared to cooperate on the large-scale development projects originally foreseen by the Agency as a means of alleviating the Palestinians' situation. The Arab governments, and the refugees themselves, were unwilling to contribute to any plan that could be interpreted as fostering resettlement. They preferred to cling to their interpretation of Resolution 194, which they believed would eventually result in repatriation.

Palestinian Refugees Registered by UNRWA[72]

Field of Operations	Official Camps	Registered Refugees	Registered Refugees in Camps
Jordan	10	1,999,466	350,899
Lebanon	12	455,373	227,718
Syria	9	495,970	149,822
West Bank	19	848,494	206,123
Gaza Strip	8	1,167,361	518,148
Agency Total	58	4,966,664	1,452,709

MYTH

"The Arab states have provided most of the funds for helping the Palestinian refugees."

FACT

While Jewish refugees from Arab countries received no international assistance, Palestinians received millions of dollars through UNRWA. Initially, the United States contributed $25 million and Israel nearly $3 million. The total Arab pledges amounted to approximately $600,000. For the first 20 years, the United States provided more than two-thirds of the funds, while the Arab states contributed a tiny fraction.

For many years, Israel donated more funds to UNRWA than most Arab states. The Saudis did not match Israel's contribution until 1973; Kuwait and Libya, not until 1980. After transferring responsibility for virtually the entire Palestinian population in the West Bank and Gaza Strip to the Palestinian Authority, Israel no longer controlled any refugee camps and in 1997 ceased contributing to UNRWA.

In 2010, the United States donated $228 million (approximately 20 percent) of UNRWA's more than $1.23 billion cash budget. Since 1950, the U.S. has contributed more than $4 billion, making it by far the largest donor. Despite their rhetorical support for the Palestinians, only two Arab countries are among UNRWA's top 10 donors, Nine other Arab states made nominal contributions. Interestingly, the total 2011 budget for the UN High Committee on Refugees (UNHCR), which handles all the world's non-Palestinian refugees, is only $2.78 billion.[73]

In addition to receiving annual funding from UNRWA for the refugees, the PA has received billions of dollars in international aid, most of which has come from Europe, the United States and other countries outside the region.

Given the amount of aid (approximately $1.45 billion in 2009) the PA has received from the international community, it is shocking that more than half a million Palestinians under PA control are being forced by their own leaders to remain in squalid camps. The PA has failed to build a single house to allow even one family to move out of a refugee camp into permanent housing. In the Gaza Strip, the Palestinians had insisted before the disengagement that Israel demolish all the homes of the Jewish settlers so they could build high-rise apartment buildings for refugees. Six years later, not a single brick had been laid.

MYTH

"The Arab states have always welcomed the Palestinians."

FACT

No one expected the refugee problem to persist after the 1948 war. John Blandford Jr., the Director of UNRWA, wrote in his report on November 29, 1951, that he expected the Arab governments to assume responsibility for relief by July 1952. Moreover, Blandford stressed the need to end relief operations: "Sustained relief operations inevitably contain the germ of human deterioration."[74] In 1952, the UNRWA set up a fund of $200 million to provide homes and jobs for the refugees, but it went untouched.

Meanwhile, Jordan was the only Arab country to welcome the Palestinians and grant some citizenship (Gazans were excluded). King Abdullah considered the Palestinian Arabs and Jordanians one people. By 1950, he annexed the West Bank and forbade the use of the term Palestine in official documents.[75] In 2004, Jordan began revoking the citizenship of Palestinians who do not have the Israeli permits that are necessary to reside in the West Bank.[76]

Although demographic figures indicated ample room for settlement existed in Syria, Damascus refused to consider accepting any refugees, except those who might refuse repatriation. Syria also declined to resettle 85,000 refugees in 1952–54, though it had been offered international funds to pay for the project. Iraq was also expected to accept a large number of refugees, but proved unwilling. Likewise, Lebanon insisted it had no room for the Palestinians.

After the 1948 war, Egypt controlled the Gaza Strip and its more than 200,000 inhabitants, but refused to allow the Palestinians into Egypt or permit them to move elsewhere. Saudi Arabian radio compared Egypt's treatment of Palestinians in Gaza to Hitler's rule in occupied Europe.[77]

> *"The Arab States do not want to solve the refugee problem. They want to keep it as an open sore, as an affront to the United Nations and as a weapon against Israel. Arab leaders don't give a damn whether the refugees live or die."*
>
> **—former head of UNRWA in Jordan,**
> **Sir Alexander Galloway, in April 1952[78]**

Little has changed in succeeding years. Arab governments have frequently offered jobs, housing, land and other benefits to Arabs and non-Arabs, *excluding* Palestinians. For example, Saudi Arabia chose not to

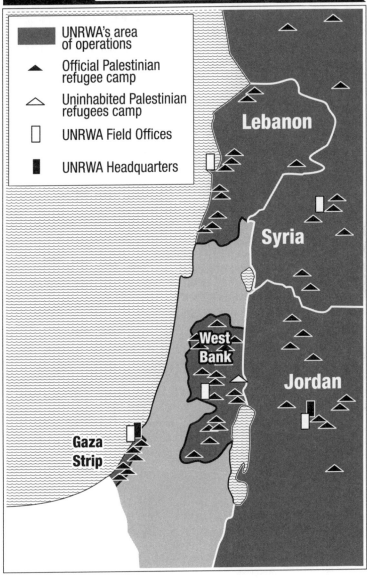

Map 21 UNRWA Refugee Camps (in 2000)

UNRWA's area of operations

▲ Official Palestinian refugee camp

△ Uninhabited Palestinian refugees camp

☐ UNRWA Field Offices

■ UNRWA Headquarters

Lebanon

Syria

West Bank

Jordan

Gaza Strip

use unemployed Palestinian refugees to alleviate its labor shortage in the late 1970's and early 1980's. Instead, thousands of South Koreans and other Asians were recruited to fill jobs.

The situation grew even worse in the wake of the 1991 Gulf War. Kuwait, which employed large numbers of Palestinians but denied them citizenship, expelled more than 300,000 Palestinians. "If people pose a security threat, as a sovereign country we have the right to exclude anyone we don't want," said Kuwaiti Ambassador to the United States, Saud Nasir Al-Sabah.[79]

Today, Palestinian refugees in Lebanon do not have social and civil rights, and have very limited access to public health or educational facilities. The majority relies entirely on UNRWA as the sole provider of education, health, and relief and social services. Considered foreigners, Palestinian refugees are prohibited by law from working in more than 70 trades and professions.[80]

The Palestinian refugees held the UN responsible for ameliorating their condition; nevertheless, many Palestinians were unhappy with the treatment they were receiving from their Arab brethren. Some, like Palestinian nationalist leader Musa Alami were incredulous: "It is shameful that the Arab governments should prevent the Arab refugees from working in their countries and shut the doors in their faces and imprison them in camps."[81] Most refugees, however, focused their discontentment on "the Zionists," whom they blamed for their predicament rather than the vanquished Arab armies.

---

*"I briefly visited the Balata refugee camp with its 20,000 residents. The camp is inside the West Bank city of Nablus—that is, within the jurisdiction of the Palestinian Authority (PA) . . . Balata's children, like the children in similar camps in Gaza and neighboring Arab countries, are nurtured on the myth that someday soon they will return in triumph to their ancestors' homes by the Mediterranean Sea. While awaiting redemption, Balata's residents are prohibited, **by the Palestinian Authority**, from building homes outside the camp's official boundaries."*

—Sol Stern[82]

MYTH

"Millions of Palestinians are confined by Israel to refugee camps."

FACT

By 2011, the number of Palestinian refugees on UNRWA rolls had risen to nearly five million, several times the number that left Palestine in

1948. One-third of the registered Palestine refugees, about 5 million, live in 58 recognized refugee camps in Jordan, Lebanon, Syria, the West Bank and Gaza Strip. The other two-thirds of the registered refugees live in and around the cities and towns of the host countries, and in the West Bank and the Gaza Strip, often in the environs of official camps.[83]

During the years that Israel controlled the Gaza Strip, a consistent effort was made to get the Palestinians into permanent housing. The Palestinians opposed the idea because the frustrated and bitter inhabitants of the camps provided the various terrorist factions with their manpower. Moreover, the Arab states routinely pushed for the adoption of UN resolutions demanding that Israel desist from the removal of Palestinian refugees from camps in Gaza and the West Bank.[84] They preferred to keep the Palestinians as symbols of Israeli "oppression."

Journalist Netty Gross visited Gaza and asked an official why the camps there hadn't been dismantled. She was told the Palestinian Authority had made a "political decision" not to do anything for the more than 650,000 Palestinians living in the camps until the final-status talks with Israel took place.[85]

The Palestinians have received billions of dollars in international aid since 1993, but have not moved the refugees into permanent housing. The refugees who remain in camps are there only because the host Arab governments and the Palestinian Authority keep them there.

"If refugees return to Israel, Israel will cease to exist."

—Gamal Nasser[86]

MYTH

"The Palestinians are the only refugee population barred from returning to their homes."

FACT

After World War II, 12.5 million Germans in Poland and Czechoslovakia were expelled and allowed to take only those possessions they could carry. They received no compensation for confiscated property. World War II's effects on Poland's boundaries and population were considered "accomplished facts" that could not be reversed after the war. No one in Germany petitions today for the right of these millions of deportees and their children to return to the countries they were expelled from despite the fact that they and their ancestors had lived in those places for hundreds of years.

Another country seriously affected by World War II was Finland, which was forced to give up almost one-eighth of its land and absorb more than 400,000 refugees (11 percent of the nation's population) from the Soviet Union. Unlike Israel, these were the *losers* of the war. There was no aid for their resettlement.

Perhaps an even better analogy can be seen in Turkey's integration of 150,000 Turkish refugees from Bulgaria in 1950. The difference between the Turks' handling of their refugees and the Arab states' treatment of the Palestinians was the attitude of the respective governments. As the *Des Moines Register* noted:

> Turkey has had a bigger refugee problem than either Syria or Lebanon and almost as big as Egypt has.... But you seldom hear about them because the Turks have done such a good job of resettling them.... The big difference is in spirit. The Turks, reluctant as they were to take on the burden, accepted it as a responsibility and set to work to clean it up as fast as possible.[87]

Had the Arab states wanted to alleviate the refugees' suffering, they could easily have adopted an attitude similar to Turkey's.

Another massive population transfer resulted from the partition of India and Pakistan in 1947. The eight *million* Hindus who fled Pakistan and the six *million* Muslims who left India were afraid of becoming a minority in their respective countries. Like the Palestinians, these people wanted to avoid being caught in the middle of the violence that engulfed their nations. In contrast to the Arab-Israeli conflict, however, the exchange of populations was considered the best solution to the problem of communal relations within the two states. Despite the enormous number of refugees and the relative poverty of the two nations involved, no special international relief organizations were established to aid them in resettlement.

"... if there were a Palestinian state, why would its leaders want their potential citizens to be repatriated to another state? From a nation-building perspective it makes no sense. In fact, the original discussions about repatriation took place at a time that there was no hope of a Palestinian state. With the possibility of that state emerging, the Palestinians must decide if they want to view themselves as a legitimate state or if it is more important for them to keep their self-defined status as oppressed, stateless refugees. They really can't be both."

—Fredelle Spiegel[88]

MYTH

"Israel expelled more Palestinians in 1967."

FACT

After ignoring Israeli warnings to stay out of the war, Jordan's King Hussein launched an attack on Jerusalem, Israel's capital. UNRWA estimated that during the fighting 175,000 of its registrants fled for a second time and approximately 350,000 fled for the first time. About 200,000 moved to Jordan, 115,000 to Syria and approximately 35,000 left Sinai for Egypt. Most of the Arabs who left came from the West Bank.

Israel allowed some West Bank Arabs to return. In 1967, more than 9,000 families were reunited and, by 1971, Israel had readmitted 40,000 refugees. By contrast, in July 1968, Jordan prohibited people intending to remain in the East Bank from emigrating from the West Bank and Gaza.[89]

When the Security Council empowered UN Secretary-General U Thant to send a representative to inquire into the welfare of civilians in the wake of the war, he instructed the mission to investigate the treatment of Jewish minorities in Arab countries, as well as Arabs in Israeli-occupied territory. Syria, Iraq and Egypt refused to permit the UN representative to carry out his investigation.[90]

> *"The demand that the refugees be returned to Israeli territory must be rejected, because if that were to happen, there would be two Palestinian states and no state at all for the Jewish people."*
>
> **—Amos Oz**[91]

MYTH

"All Palestinian refugees must be given the option to return to their homes."

FACT

According to UNRWA, as of 2011, there were nearly five million Palestinian refugees. Does Israel have any obligation to take in some or all of those people?

The current Israeli population is approximately 7.7 million, 5.8 million are Jews. If every Palestinian refugee was allowed to move to Israel, the population would exceed 12 million and the Jewish proportion would shrink from 75% to 46%. The Jews would be a minority in their own country, the very situation they fought to avoid in 1948, and which the UN expressly ruled out in deciding on a partition of Palestine.

Current peace talks are based on UN Resolution 242. The Palestinians are not mentioned anywhere in Resolution 242. They are only alluded to in the second clause of the second article of 242, which calls for "a just settlement of the refugee problem." The generic term "refugee" may also be applied to the Jewish refugees from Arab lands.

Furthermore, most Palestinians now live in historic Palestine, which is an area including the Palestinian Authority and Jordan. When Palestinians demand to return to Palestine they are referring not just to the area, but to the houses they lived in prior to 1948. These homes are either gone or inhabited now.

Even respected Palestinian leaders acknowledge that it is a mistake to insist that millions of refugees return to Israel. Palestinian intellectual Sari Nusseibeh, for example, said the refugees should be resettled in a future Palestinian state, "not in a way that would undermine the existence of the State of Israel as a predominantly Jewish state. Otherwise, what does a two-state solution mean?"[92] In leaked cables from the Palestinian negotiating team, PA President Mahmoud Abbas admitted this as well. "On numbers of refugees," he said, "it is illogical to ask Israel to take 5 million, or indeed 1 million—that would mean the end of Israel."[93]

In the context of a peace settlement, Israel has offered to accept some refugees, as Ben-Gurion said he would do more than 50 years ago. If and when a Palestinian state is created, most, if not all of the refugees should be allowed to move there, but the Palestinian leadership has expressed little interest in absorbing these people.

Notes

1. Arieh Avneri, *The Claim of Dispossesion*, (NJ: Transaction Books, 1984), p. 272; Benjamin Kedar, *The Changing Land Between the Jordan and the Sea*, (Israel: Yad Izhak Ben-Zvi Press, 1999), p. 206; Paul Johnson, *A History of the Jews*, (NY: Harper & Row, 1987), p. 529. Efraim Karsh analyzed rural and urban population statistics and concluded the total number of refugees was 583,000–609,000. Karsh, "How Many Palestinian Refugees Were There?" *Israel Affairs,* (April 2011).

2. Progress Report of the United Nations Mediator on Palestine, Submitted to the Secretary-General for Transmission to the Members of the United Nations, General Assembly Official Records: Third Session, Supplement No. 11 (A/648), Paris, 1948, p. 47 and Supplement No. 11A (A/689 and A/689/Add.1, p. 5; and "Conclusions from Progress Report of the United Nations Mediator on Palestine," (September 16, 1948), U.N. doc. A/648 (part 1, p. 29; part 2, p. 23; part 3, p. 11), (September 18, 1948).

3. "Ad Hoc Committee on Palestine - 30th Meeting," United Nations Press Release GA/PAL/84, (November 24, 1947).

4. Avneri, p. 276.

5. *Jerusalem Post,* (December 4, 2003).

6. David Ben-Gurion, *Rebirth and Destiny of Israel,* (NY: Philosophical Library, 1954), p. 220.

7. Atalia Ben Meir, "The Palestinian Refugee Issue and the Demographic Aspect," *Israel and A Palestinian State: Zero Sum Game?*, (ACPR Publishers: 2001), p. 215.

8. Joseph Schechtman, *The Refugee in the World,* (NY: A.S. Barnes and Co., 1963), p. 184.

9. I.F. Stone, *This is Israel,* (NY: Boni and Gaer, 1948), p. 27.

10. Shmuel Katz, *Battleground: Fact and Fantasy in Palestine,* (Taylor Publications Ltd: 2002), p. 10.

11. Ibid.

12. Avneri, p. 270

13. *London Daily Mail,* (August 12, 1948) cited in Shmuel Katz, *Battleground: Fact and Fantasy in Palestine,* (Taylor Publications Ltd: 2002), p. 13.

14. *New York Times,* (April 23, 1948).

15. Howard Sachar, *A History of Israel: From the Rise of Zionism to Our Time,* (NY: Alfred A. Knopf, 1979), p. 332; Avneri, p. 270.

16. Secret memo dated April 26, 1948, from the Superintendent of Police, regarding the general situation in Haifa, cited in Shmuel Katz, *Battleground: Fact and Fantasy in Palestine,* (Taylor Publications Ltd: 2002), p. 13.

17. Golda Meir, *My Life,* (NY: Dell, 1975), pp. 267-8.

18. *New York Times,* (April 23, 1948).

19. *London Times,* (April 24, 1948).

20. Schechtman, p. 190.

21. *Foreign Relations of the U.S. 1948,* Vol. V, (DC: GPO, 1976), p. 838.

22. Tom Segev, *1949: The First Israelis,* (NY: The Free Press, 1986), pp. 27-8.

23. Yigal Allon in *Sefer ha-Palmach,* quoted in Larry Collins and Dominique Lapierre, *O Jerusalem!,* (NY: Simon and Schuster, 1972), p. 337; Yigal Allon, *My Fathers House,* (NY: W.W. Norton and Company, Inc, 1976), p. 192.

24. Benny Morris, *The Birth of the Palestinian Refugee Problem Revisited,* (MA: Cambridge University Press, 2004), pp. 423-5.

25. Morris, p. 592.

26. *Middle East Journal,* (October 1949).

27. Terence Prittie, "Middle East Refugees," cited in Michael Curtis, et al, *The Palestinians,* (NJ: Transaction Books, 1975), p. 52.

28. *New York Times,* (March 4, 1949).

29. *The Guardian,* (February 21, 2002).

30. "International: On the Eve?," *Time Magazine,* (May 3, 1948).

31. Morris, p. 590.

32. *Middle East Studies,* (January 1986); See also, Morris, pp. 263, 590-2.

33. *The Memoirs of Haled al Azm,* (Beirut, 1973), Part 1, pp. 386-7.

34. Myron Kaufman, *The Coming Destruction of Israel,* (NY: The American Library Inc., 1970), pp. 26-7.

35. Edward Atiyah, *The Arabs,* (London: Penguin Books, 1955), p. 183.

36. Morris, p. 591.

37. Yehoshofat Harkabi, *Arab Attitudes to Israel,* (Jerusalem: Israel Universities Press, 1972), p. 364.

38. King Abdallah, *My Memoirs Completed,* (London: Longman Group, Ltd., 1978), p. xvi

39. *Al-Ayyam,* (May 16, 2006), quoted in Itamar Marcus and Barbara Cook, "The Evolving Palestinian Narrative: Arabs Caused the Refugee Problem," *Palestinian Media Watch,* (May 20, 2008).

40. Palestinian Authority TV, (July 7, 2009), quoted in *Palestinian Media Watch Bulletin,* (July 23, 2009).

41. *Al-Hayat al-Jadida,* (December 13, 2006), quoted in Itamar Marcus and Barbara Cook, "The Evolving Palestinian Narrative: Arabs Caused the Refugee Problem," *Palestinian Media Watch,* (May 20, 2008).

42. *Al-Ayyam,* (May 13, 2008), quoted in Itamar Marcus and Barbara Cook, "The Evolving

Palestinian Narrative: Arabs Caused the Refugee Problem," *Palestinian Media Watch,* (May 20, 2008).

43. *Falastin a-Thaura,* (March 1976).

44. Walid Khalidi, *Palestine Reborn,* (I.B. Tauris: 1992), p. 289.

45. Dan Kurzman, *Genesis 1948,* (OH: New American Library Inc., 1970), p. 141.

46. Menachem Begin, *The Revolt,* (NY: Nash Publishing, 1977), pp. xx-xxi, 162-3.

47. See, for example, Amos Perlmutter, *The Life and Times of Menachem Begin,* (NY: Doubleday, 1987), p. 214; J. Bowyer Bell, *Terror Out of Zion,* (NY: St. Martin's Press, 1977), pp. 292-6; Kurzman, p. 142.

48. Uri Milstein, *History of Israel's War of Independence, Vol IV,* (Lanham: University Press of America, 1999), p. 262.

49. Milstein, p. 262.

50. Dana Adams Schmidt, "200 Arabs Killed, Stronghold Taken," *New York Times,* (April 10, 1948).

51. Kurzman, p. 148.

52. Sharif Kanaana and Nihad Zitawi, "Deir Yassin," Monograph No. 4, Destroyed Palestinian Villages Documentation Project, (Bir Zeit: Documentation Center of Bir Zeit University, 1987), p. 55

53. Sharif Kanaana, "Reinterpreting Deir Yassin," *Bir Zeir University,* (April 1998).

54. Milstein, p. 267.

55. Rami Nashashibi, "Dayr Yasin," *Bir Zeit University,* (June 1996).

56. Yehoshua Gorodenchik testimony at Jabotinsky Archives.

57. Milstein, p. 276.

58. "Israel and the Arabs: The 50 Year Conflict," BBC Television Series, (1998).

59. "Interview with Abd al-Rahman Azzam Pasha," *Akhbar al-Yom (Egypt),* (October 11, 1947); translated by R. Green.

60. Sachar, p. 335.

61. Schechtman, p. 268.

62. Prittie in Curtis, pp. 66-7.

63. *New York Times,* (July 17, 1949).

64. *Jerusalem Post,* (January 26, 1989).

65. *Telegraph (*Beirut), (August 6, 1948), quoted in Schechtman, pp. 210-11.

66. Moshe Sharett,"Israels Position and Problems," *Middle Eastern Affairs, (*May 1952), p. 136.

67. *Al Said* (Lebanon), (April 6, 1950), cited in Prittie in Curtis, p. 69.

68. *Al-Misri,* (October 11, 1949), cited in Nathan Feinberg, *The Arab-Israeli Conflict in International Law,* (Jerusalem: Magnes Press, 1970), p. 109.

69. *Beirut al Massa,* (July 15, 1957), cited in Katz, p. 21.

70. Benjamin Franklin, *Memoirs of Benjamin Franklin, Vol 1,* (M'Carty & Davis: 1834), p. 463.

71. Melissa Radler, "UN Marks Partition Plan Anniversary with anti-Israel Fest," *Jerusalem Post,* (December 4, 2003).

72. UNRWA, (as of December 30, 2010).

73. UNRWA, http://www.unrwa.org/userfiles/file/fimnancial_updates/2009/Total_Contributions_to_UNRWA_2009_All_Donors.pdf; "Biennial Programme Budget 2010-2011 of the Office of the United Nations High Commissioner for Refugees," UN General Assembly, (September 17, 2009), http://www.unhcr.org/4abc7cc19.html

74. Schechtman, p. 220.

75. "Speech to Parliament - April 24, 1950," Abdallah, pp. 16-7; Aaron Miller, *The Arab States and the Palestine Question,* (DC: Center for Strategic and International Studies, 1986), p. 29.

76. Khaled Abu Toamed, "Amman Revoking Palestinians Citizenship," *Jerusalem Post,* (July 20, 2009).
77. Leibler, p. 48.
78. Alexander H. Joffe and Asaf Romirowsky, "A Tale of Two Galloways: Notes on the Early History of UNRWA and Zionist Historiography," *Middle Eastern Studies,* (September 2010).
79. *Jerusalem Report,* (June 27, 1991).
80. *UNRWA*
81. Musa Alami, "The Lesson of Palestine," *Middle East Journal,* (October 1949), p. 386.
82. Sol Stern, "Mr. Abbas, Tear Down This Wall!" *Jewish Ideas Daily,* (September 28, 2010).
83. *UNRWA*
84. Arlene Kushner, "the UN's Palestinian Refugee Problem," *Azure,* (Autumn 2005).
85. *Jerusalem Report,* (July 6, 1998).
86. Katz, p. 21.
87. Editorial, *Des Moines Register,* (January 16, 1952).
88. *Jerusalem Report,* (March 26, 2001).
89. UNRWA Annual Reports, (July 1, 1966-June 30, 1967), pp. 11-19; (July 1, 1967-June 30, 1968), pp. 4-10; (July 1, 1968-June 30, 1969), p. 6; (July 1, 1971-June 30, 1972), p. 3.
90. Maurice Roumani, *The Case of the Jews from Arab Countries: A Neglected Issue,* (Tel Aviv: World Organization of Jews from Arab Countries, 1977), p. 34.
91. *Associated Press,* (October 23, 2001).
92. "Meeting Minutes: President Abbas Meeting with the Negotiations Support Unit," (March 24, 2009).
93. Amos Oz, "Israel Partly at Fault," Ynetnews, (March 29, 2007).

14. Human Rights*

MYTH

"Arabs cannot possibly be anti-Semitic as they are themselves Semites."

FACT

The term "anti-Semite" was coined in Germany in 1879 by Wilhelm Marr to refer to the anti-Jewish manifestations of the period and to give Jew-hatred a more scientific sounding name.[1] "Anti-Semitism" has been accepted and understood to mean hatred of the Jewish people. Dictionaries define the term as: "Theory, action, or practice directed against the Jews" and "Hostility towards Jews as a religious or racial minority group, often accompanied by social, economic and political discrimination."[2]

The claim that Arabs cannot be anti-Semitic because they are themselves a Semitic people is a semantic distortion that ignores the reality of Arab discrimination and hostility toward Jews. Arabs, like any other people, can indeed be anti-Semitic.

> *"The Arab world is the last bastion of unbridled, unashamed, unhidden and unbelievable anti-Semitism. Hitlerian myths get published in the popular press as incontrovertible truths. The Holocaust either gets minimized or denied.... How the Arab world will ever come to terms with Israel when Israelis are portrayed as the devil incarnate is hard to figure out."*
>
> **—Columnist Richard Cohen[3]**

MYTH

"Jews who lived in Islamic countries during the days of the Islamic Empire were treated well by the Arabs."

---

*The situation of Jews in Arab/Islamic countries today can be found online in the Jewish Virtual Library at http://www.jewishvirtuallibrary.org/jsource/anti-semitism/arabjewtoc.html.

FACT

While Jewish communities in Islamic countries fared better overall than those in Christian lands in Europe during the nearly 1,300 years the Islamic Empire lasted, Jews were no strangers to persecution and humiliation among the Arabs. As Princeton University historian Bernard Lewis has written: "The Golden Age of equal rights was a myth, and belief in it was a result, more than a cause, of Jewish sympathy for Islam."[4]

Muhammad, the founder of Islam, traveled to Medina in 622 A.D. to attract followers to his new faith. When the Jews of Medina refused to recognize Muhammad as their Prophet, two of the major Jewish tribes were expelled. In 627, Muhammad's followers killed between 600 and 900 of the men, and divided the surviving Jewish women and children amongst themselves.[5]

The Muslim attitude toward Jews is reflected in various verses throughout the Koran, the holy book of the Islamic faith. "They [the Children of Israel] were consigned to humiliation and wretchedness. They brought the wrath of God upon themselves, and this because they used to deny God's signs and kill His Prophets unjustly and because they disobeyed and were transgressors" (Sura 2:61). According to the Koran, the Jews try to introduce corruption (5:64), have always been disobedient (5:78), and are enemies of Allah, the Prophet and the angels (2:97–98).

Jews were generally viewed with contempt by their Muslim neighbors; peaceful coexistence between the two groups involved the subordination and degradation of the Jews. In the ninth century, Baghdad's Caliph al-Mutawakkil designated a yellow badge for Jews, setting a precedent that would be followed centuries later in Nazi Germany.[6]

When Jews were perceived as having achieved too comfortable a position in Islamic society, anti-Semitism would surface, often with devastating results. On December 30, 1066, Joseph HaNagid, the Jewish vizier of Granada, Spain, was crucified by an Arab mob that proceeded to raze the Jewish quarter of the city and slaughter its 5,000 inhabitants. The riot was incited by Muslim preachers who had angrily objected to what they saw as inordinate Jewish political power.

Similarly, in 1465, Arab mobs in Fez slaughtered thousands of Jews, leaving only 11 alive, after a Jewish deputy vizier treated a Muslim woman in "an offensive manner." The killings touched off a wave of similar massacres throughout Morocco.[7]

Other mass murders of Jews in Arab lands occurred in Morocco in the 8th century, where whole communities were wiped out by the Muslim ruler Idris I; North Africa in the 12th century, where the Almohads either forcibly converted or decimated several communities; Libya in 1785, where Ali Burzi Pasha murdered hundreds of Jews; Algiers, where

Jews were massacred in 1805, 1815 and 1830; and Marrakesh, Morocco, where more than 300 Jews were murdered between 1864 and 1880.[8]

Decrees ordering the destruction of synagogues were enacted in Egypt and Syria (1014, 1293-4, 1301-2), Iraq (854-859, 1344) and Yemen (1676). Despite the Koran's prohibition, Jews were forced to convert to Islam or face death in Yemen (1165 and 1678), Morocco (1275, 1465 and 1790-92) and Baghdad (1333 and 1344).[9]

The situation of Jews in Arab lands reached a low point in the 19th century. Jews in most of North Africa (including Algeria, Tunisia, Egypt, Libya and Morocco) were forced to live in ghettos. In Morocco, which contained the largest Jewish community in the Islamic Diaspora, Jews were made to walk barefoot or wear shoes of straw when outside the ghetto. Even Muslim children participated in the degradation of Jews, by throwing stones at them or harassing them in other ways. The frequency of anti-Jewish violence increased, and many Jews were executed on charges of apostasy. Ritual murder accusations against the Jews became commonplace in the Ottoman Empire.[10]

As distinguished Orientalist G.E. von Grunebaum observed:

> It would not be difficult to put together the names of a very sizeable number Jewish subjects or citizens of the Islamic area who have attained to high rank, to power, to great financial influence, to significant and recognized intellectual attainment; and the same could be done for Christians. But it would again not be difficult to compile a lengthy list of persecutions, arbitrary confiscations, attempted forced conversions, or pogroms.[11]

MYTH

"As 'People of the Book,' Jews and Christians are protected under Islamic law."

FACT

This argument is rooted in the traditional concept of the "dhimma" ("writ of protection"), which was extended by Muslim conquerors to Christians and Jews in exchange for their subordination to the Muslims. Yet, as French authority Jacques Ellul has observed: "One must ask:'protected against whom?' When this 'stranger' lives in Islamic countries, the answer can only be: against the Muslims themselves."[12]

Peoples subjected to Muslim rule often faced a choice between death and conversion, but Jews and Christians, who adhered to the Scriptures, were usually allowed, as *dhimmis* (protected persons), to practice their faith. This "protection" did little, however, to ensure that

Jews and Christians were treated well by the Muslims. On the contrary, an integral aspect of the *dhimma* was that, being an infidel, he had to acknowledge openly the superiority of the true believer—the Muslim.

In the early years of the Islamic conquest, the "tribute" (or *jizya*), paid as a yearly poll tax, symbolized the subordination of the *dhimmi.*[13]

Later, the inferior status of Jews and Christians was reinforced through a series of regulations that governed the behavior of the *dhimmi. Dhimmis,* on pain of death, were forbidden to mock or criticize the Koran, Islam or Muhammad, to proselytize among Muslims, or to touch a Muslim woman (though a Muslim man could take a non-Muslim as a wife).

Dhimmis were excluded from public office and armed service, and were forbidden to bear arms. They were not allowed to ride horses or camels, to build synagogues or churches taller than mosques, to construct houses higher than those of Muslims or to drink wine in public. They were forced to wear distinctive clothing and were not allowed to pray or mourn in loud voices—as that might offend the Muslims. The *dhimmi* also had to show public deference toward Muslims; for example, always yielding them the center of the road. The *dhimmi* was not allowed to give evidence in court against a Muslim, and his oath was unacceptable in an Islamic court. To defend himself, the *dhimmi* would have to purchase Muslim witnesses at great expense. This left the *dhimmi* with little legal recourse when harmed by a Muslim.[14]

By the twentieth century, the status of the *dhimmi* in Muslim lands had not significantly improved. H.E.W. Young, British Vice Consul in Mosul, wrote in 1909:

> The attitude of the Muslims toward the Christians and the Jews is that of a master towards slaves, whom he treats with a certain lordly tolerance so long as they keep their place. Any sign of pretension to equality is promptly repressed.[15]

MYTH

"Modern Arab nations are only anti-Israel and have never been anti-Jewish."

FACT

Arab leaders have repeatedly made clear their animosity toward Jews and Judaism. For example, on November 23, 1937, Saudi Arabia's King Ibn Saud told British Colonel H.R.P. Dickson: "Our hatred for the Jews dates from God's condemnation of them for their persecution and rejection of Isa (Jesus) and their subsequent rejection of His chosen

Prophet." He added "that for a Muslim to kill a Jew, or for him to be killed by a Jew ensures him an immediate entry into Heaven and into the august presence of God Almighty."[16]

When Hitler introduced the Nuremberg racial laws in 1935, he received telegrams of congratulation from all corners of the Arab world.[17] Later, during the war, one of his most ardent supporters was the Mufti of Jerusalem.

Jews were never permitted to live in Jordan. Civil Law No. 6, which governed the Jordanian-occupied West Bank, states explicitly: "Any man will be a Jordanian subject if he is not Jewish."[18]

After the Six-Day War in 1967, the Israelis found public school textbooks that had been used to educate Arab children in the West Bank. They were replete with racist and hateful portrayals of Jews.[19]

According to a study of Syrian textbooks, "the Syrian educational system expands hatred of Israel and Zionism to anti-Semitism directed at all Jews. That anti-Semitism evokes ancient Islamic motifs to describe the unchangeable and treacherous nature of the Jews. Its inevitable conclusion is that all Jews must be annihilated."[20] An Arabic translation of Adolf Hitler's *Mein Kampf* was distributed in East Jerusalem and the territories controlled by the Palestinian Authority (PA) and became a bestseller. The official website of the Palestinian State Information Service also published an Arabic translation of the "Protocols of the Elders of Zion."[21]

Arab officials have also resorted to blood libels. King Faisal of Saudi Arabia, for example, said that Jews "have a certain day on which they mix the blood of non-Jews into their bread and eat it. It happened that two years ago, while I was in Paris on a visit, that the police discovered five murdered children. Their blood had been drained, and it turned out that some Jews had murdered them in order to take their blood and mix it with the bread that they eat on this day."[22]

"Syrian President Bashar Assad on Saturday [May 5] offered a vivid, if vile, demonstration of why he and his government are unworthy of respect or good relations with the United States or any other democratic country. Greeting Pope John Paul II in Damascus, Mr. Assad launched an attack on Jews that may rank as the most ignorant and crude speech delivered before the pope in his two decades of travel around the world. Comparing the suffering of the Palestinians to that of Jesus Christ, Mr. Assad said that the Jews 'tried to kill the principles of all religions with the same mentality in which they betrayed Jesus Christ and the same way they tried to betray and kill the Prophet Muhammad.' With that libel, the Syrian president stained both his country and the pope. . . ."

—Washington Post editorial[23]

Scurrilous allegations made by Palestinian officials include claims that Israel dumped toxic waste in the West Bank, marketed carcinogenic juice to Palestinians, released wild pigs to destroy crops in the West Bank, infected Palestinians with the AIDS virus, dropped poison candy for children in Gaza from airplanes, and used a "radial spy machine" at checkpoints that killed a Palestinian woman.[24]

The Arab/Muslim press, which is almost exclusively controlled by the governments in each Middle Eastern nation, regularly publish anti-Semitic articles and cartoons. Today, it remains common to find anti-Semitic publications in Egypt. For example, *Al-Ahram* published an article accusing Israel of using the blood of Palestinian children to bake matzos.[25]

Anti-Semitic articles also regularly appear in the press in Jordan and Syria. Many of the attacks deal with denial of the Holocaust, the "exploitation" of the Holocaust by Zionism, and the odious comparison of Zionism to Nazism.

In November 2001, a satirical skit aired on the second most popular television station in the Arab world, which depicted a character meant to be Ariel Sharon drinking the blood of Arab children as a grotesque-looking Orthodox Jew looked on. Abu Dhabi Television also aired a skit in which Dracula appears to take a bite out of Sharon, but dies because Sharon's blood is polluted.[26]

The Palestinian Authority's media have also contained inflammatory and anti-Semitic material. Here is an example of a sermon broadcast on Palestinian Authority television:

> "The loathsome occupation in Palestine—its land and its holy places—by these new Mongols and what they are perpetrating upon this holy, blessed and pure land—killing, assassination, destruction, confiscation, Judaization, harassment and splitting the homeland—are clear proof of . . . incomparable racism, and of Nazism of the 20th century. The Jews, the enemies of Allah and of His Messenger! Enemies of humanity in general, and of Palestinians in particular . . ."[27]

Even Palestinian crossword puzzles are used to delegitimize Israel and attack Jews, providing clues, for example, suggesting that a Jewish trait is "treachery."[28]

MYTH

"Israel discriminates against its Arab citizens."

FACT

Arabs in Israel have equal voting rights; in fact, it is one of the few places in the Middle East where Arab women may vote. Arabs in 2011 held 14 seats in the 120-seat Knesset. Israeli Arabs have also held various government posts, including one who served as Israel's ambassador to Finland and the deputy mayor of Tel Aviv. Oscar Abu Razaq was appointed Director General of the Ministry of Interior, the first Arab citizen to become chief executive of a key government ministry. Ariel Sharon's original cabinet included the first Arab minister, Salah Tarif, a Druze who served as a minister without portfolio. An Arab is also a Supreme Court justice. In October 2005, an Arab professor was named Vice President of Haifa University.

Arabic, like Hebrew, is an official language in Israel. More than 300,000 Arab children attend Israeli schools. At the time of Israel's founding, there was one Arab high school in the country. Today, there are hundreds of Arab schools.[29]

The sole legal distinction between Jewish and Arab citizens of Israel is that the latter are not required to serve in the Israeli army. This is to spare Arab citizens the need to take up arms against their brethren. Nevertheless, Bedouins have served in paratroop units and other Arabs have volunteered for military duty. Compulsory military service is applied to the Druze and Circassian communities at their own request.

Some economic and social gaps between Israeli Jews and Arabs result from the latter not serving in the military. Veterans qualify for many benefits not available to non-veterans. Moreover, the army aids in the socialization process.

On the other hand, Arabs do have an advantage in obtaining some jobs during the years Israelis are in the military. In addition, industries like construction and trucking have come to be dominated by Israeli Arabs.

Although Israeli Arabs have occasionally been involved in terrorist activities, they have generally behaved as loyal citizens. During the 1967, 1973 and 1982 wars, none engaged in any acts of sabotage or disloyalty. Sometimes, in fact, Arabs volunteered to take over civilian functions for reservists. During the Palestinian War that began in September 2000, Israeli Arabs for the first time engaged in widespread protests.

The United States has been independent for 235 years and still has not integrated all of its diverse communities. Even today, nearly half a century after civil rights legislation was adopted, discrimination has not been eradicated. It should not be surprising that Israel has not solved all of its social problems in only 63 years.

MYTH

"Israeli Arabs are barred from buying land in Israel."

FACT

In the early part of the century, the Jewish National Fund was established by the World Zionist Congress to purchase land in Palestine for Jewish settlement. This land, and that acquired after Israel's War of Independence, was taken over by the government. Of the total area of Israel, 92 percent belongs to the State and is managed by the Land Management Authority. It is not for sale to anyone, Jew or Arab. The remaining 8 percent of the territory is privately owned. The Arab Waqf (the Muslim charitable endowment), for example, owns land that is for the express use and benefit of Muslim Arabs. Government land can be leased by anyone, regardless of race, religion or sex. All Arab citizens of Israel are eligible to lease government land.

In 2002, the Israeli Supreme Court also ruled that the government cannot allocate land based on religion or ethnicity, and may not prevent Arab citizens from living wherever they choose.[30]

Meanwhile, in 1996, the Palestinian Authority (PA) Mufti, Ikremah Sabri, issued a *fatwa* (religious decree), banning the sale of Arab and Muslim property to Jews. Anyone who violated the order was to be killed. At least seven land dealers were killed that year.[31]

On May 5, 1997, Palestinian Authority Justice Minister Freih Abu Middein announced that the death penalty would be imposed on anyone convicted of ceding "one inch" to Israel. Later that month, two Arab land dealers were killed. A year later, another Palestinian suspected of selling land to Jews was murdered. The PA has also arrested suspected land dealers for violating the Jordanian law (in force in the West Bank), which prohibits the sale of land to foreigners.[32] An Islamic judge renewed the *fatwa* barring Palestinians from selling property to Jews in 2008 and, as recently as June 2010, a Palestinian was imprisoned for 10 years on charges of selling land to Israel.[33]

MYTH

"Arabs held in Israeli jails are tortured, beaten and killed."

FACT

Prison is not a pleasant place for anyone and complaints about the treatment of prisoners in American institutions abound. Israel's prisons are probably among the most closely scrutinized in the world. One reason is the government has allowed representatives of the Red Cross and other groups to inspect them regularly.

Israeli law prohibits the arbitrary arrest of citizens. In addition, defendants are considered innocent until proven guilty and have the right to writs of *habeas corpus* and other procedural safeguards. Israel holds no political prisoners and maintains an independent judiciary.

Years ago, some prisoners, particularly Arabs suspected of involvement in terrorism, were interrogated using severe methods that were criticized as excessive. Israel's Supreme Court issued a landmark ruling in 1999 prohibiting the use of a variety of practices that were considered abusive.[34]

The death penalty has been applied just once, in the case of Adolf Eichmann, the man largely responsible for the "Final Solution." No Arab has ever been given the death penalty, even after the most heinous acts of terrorism.

"The Israeli regime is not apartheid. It is a unique case of democracy."

—South African Interior Minister Chief Mangosuthu Buthelezi[35]

MYTH

"Israel's treatment of Palestinians is similar to the treatment of blacks in apartheid South Africa."

FACT

Even before the State of Israel was established, Jewish leaders consciously sought to avoid the situation that prevailed in South Africa. As David Ben-Gurion told Palestinian nationalist Musa Alami in 1934:

> We do not want to create a situation like that which exists in South Africa, where the whites are the owners and rulers, and the blacks are the workers. If we do not do all kinds of work, easy and hard, skilled and unskilled, if we become merely landlords, then this will not be our homeland.[36]

Today, within Israel, Jews are a majority, but the Arab minority are full citizens who enjoy equal rights and are represented in all the branches of government. Arabs are represented in the Knesset, and have served in the Cabinet, high-level foreign ministry posts (e.g., Ambassador to Finland) and on the Supreme Court.

Under apartheid, skin color determined every aspect of your life from birth until death. Black South Africans could not vote and were not citizens of the country in which they formed the overwhelming majority of the population. Laws dictated where they could live, work, go to school and travel. And, in South Africa, the government killed blacks who protested against its policies. By contrast, Israel allows freedom of movement, assembly and speech. Some of the government's harshest critics are Israeli Arabs who are members of the Knesset.

"The difference between the current Israeli situation and apartheid South Africa is emphasized at a very human level: Jewish and Arab babies are born in the same delivery room, with the same facilities, attended by the same doctors and nurses, with the mothers recovering in adjoining beds in a ward. Two years ago I had major surgery in a Jerusalem hospital: the surgeon was Jewish, the anaesthetist was Arab, the doctors and nurses who looked after me were Jews and Arabs. Jews and Arabs share meals in restaurants and travel on the same trains, buses and taxis, and visit each other's homes.

Could any of this possibly have happened under apartheid? Of course not."

—Benjamin Pogrund[37]

The situation of Palestinians in the territories is different. The security requirements of the nation, and a violent insurrection in the territories, forced Israel to impose restrictions on Arab residents of the West Bank and Gaza Strip that are not necessary inside Israel's pre-1967 borders. Israeli policy is not based on race, but is a result of Palestinian animosity. Palestinians in the territories dispute Israel's right to exist, whereas blacks did not seek the destruction of South Africa, only the apartheid regime.

If Israel were to give Palestinians full citizenship, it would mean the territories had been annexed. No Israeli government has been prepared to take that step. Instead, through negotiations, Israel agreed to give the Palestinians increasing authority over their own affairs. It is likely that a final settlement will allow most Palestinians to become citizens of their own state. The principal impediment to Palestinian independence is not Israeli policy, it is the unwillingness of the Palestinian leadership to give up terrorism and agree to live in peace beside Israel.

Despite all their criticism, when asked what governments they admire most, more than 80 percent of Palestinians consistently said Israel because they can see up close the thriving democracy in Israel, and the rights the Arab citizens enjoy there. By contrast, Palestinians place Arab regimes, including their own Palestinian Authority, at the bottom.[38]

In fact, growing numbers of Palestinians in East Jerusalem have been applying for Israeli citizenship and, given the choice, many say they would rather live in Israel than Palestine. A poll of Arabs living in East Jerusalem, for example, found that 35% would choose living in Israel, compared to 30% who preferred to live in a future Palestinian state. Forty percent said they would consider moving to another neighborhood to become a citizen of Israel rather than Palestine and 54% said that if they their neighborhood was part of Israel, they would not move to Palestine.[39]

"There is still one other question arising out of the disaster of nations which remains unsolved to this day, and whose profound tragedy, only a Jew can comprehend. This is the African question. Just call to mind all those terrible episodes of the slave trade, of human beings who, merely because they were black, were stolen like cattle, taken prisoner, captured and sold. Their children grew up in strange lands, the objects of contempt and hostility because their complexions were different. I am not ashamed to say, though I may expose myself to ridicule for saying so, that once I have witnessed the redemption of the Jews, my people, I wish also to assist in the redemption of the Africans."

—**Theodor Herzl**[40]

MYTH

"Israel is pursuing a policy of genocide toward the Palestinians that is comparable to the Nazis' treatment of the Jews."

FACT

This is perhaps the most odious claim made by Israel's detractors. The Nazis' objective was the systematic extermination of every Jew in Europe. Israel is seeking peace with its Palestinian neighbors. More than one million Arabs live as free and equal citizens in Israel. Of the Palestinians in the territories, 98 percent live under the civil administration of the Palestinian Authority. Israeli policies are designed to protect Israeli citizens—Jews and non-Jews—from the incessant campaign of terror. There has never been a plan to persecute, exterminate, or expel the Palestinian people.

In response to one such comparison, by a poet who referred to the "Zionist SS," *The New Republic's* literary editor Leon Wieseltier observed:

> The view that Zionism is Nazism—there is no other way to understand the phrase "Zionist SS"—is not different in kind from the view that the moon is cheese. It is not only spectacularly wrong, it is also spectacularly unintelligent. I will not offend myself (that would be self-hate speech!) by patiently explaining why the State of Israel is unlike the Third Reich, except to say that nothing that has befallen the Palestinians under Israel's control may responsibly be compared to what

befell the Jews under Germany's control, and that a considerable number of the people who have toiled diligently to find peace and justice for the Palestinians, and a solution to this savage conflict, have been Israeli, some of them even Israeli prime ministers. There is no support for the Palestinian cause this side of decency that can justify the locution "Zionist SS."[41]

The absurdity of the charge is also clear from the demography of the disputed territories. While detractors make outrageous claims about Israel committing genocide or ethnic cleansing, the Palestinian population has continued to grow exponentially. In Gaza, for example, the population increased from 731,000 in July 1994 to 1,657,155 in 2011, an increase of 127 percent. The growth rate was 3.2 percent, one of the highest in the world. The total Palestinian population in all the disputed territories (they include Gaza, the West Bank, and East Jerusalem) was 1,006,000 in 1950, 1,094,000 in 1970, and grew to 3,736,210 in 2011.[42]

MYTH

"Palestinians have the lowest standard of living in the Middle East."

FACT

When Israel captured the West Bank and Gaza Strip in 1967, officials took measures to improve the conditions that Palestinians had lived under during Jordan's 19-year occupation of the West Bank, and Egypt's occupation of Gaza. Universities were opened, Israeli agricultural innovations were shared, modern conveniences were introduced, and health care was significantly upgraded. More than 100,000 Palestinians were employed in Israel, and were paid the same wages as Israeli workers, which stimulated economic growth.

The rise in violence during the 1990s, and then the war instigated by Palestinian terrorists beginning in 2000, took a heavy toll on the Palestinian economy. To protect its citizens from suicide bombers and other terrorists, Israel was forced to take measures that had a deleterious impact on the economy in the Palestinian Authority. The most serious step was to limit the number of Palestinian laborers entering Israel to reduce the risk of terrorists pretending to be workers slipping into the country. This raised the level of unemployment, which, in turn, had a negative spillover effect on the rest of the Palestinian economy.

More recently, however, despite the global economic downturn, the West Bank economy grew by more than 7 percent, representing the 26th best growth rate in 2009 out of 212 countries and territories in the world, second in the Middle East, and double the rate of Israel. This remarkable growth was attributable to continued aid from the West, the implementation of economic reforms, and the easing of security restrictions on movement by Israel.[43]

Even when the economy was at a lowpoint, Palestinian Arabs were better off than many of their neighbors. The most recent Human Development Report from the United Nations ranks the PA 110 in terms of life expectancy, educational attainment and adjusted real income out of the 182 countries and territories in the world, placing it in the "medium human development" category along with most of the other Middle Eastern states (only the Gulf sheikdoms are ranked "high"). The PA is ranked just below Egypt (#101) and ahead of Syria (#111) and Morocco (#114).[44] Few Palestinians would trade places with Arabs in neighboring countries. Well, perhaps, with one exception. They might aspire to the standard of living in the country ranked 15th by the UN—Israel.

> *"I am a proud Israeli—along with many other non-Jewish Israelis such as Druze, Bahai, Bedouin, Christians and Muslims, who live in one of the most culturally diversified societies and the only true democracy in the Middle East. Like America, Israeli society is far from perfect, but... By any yardstick you choose—educational opportunity, economic development, women and gay's rights, freedom of speech and assembly, legislative representation—Israel's minorities fare far better than any other country in the Middle East."*
>
> **—Bedouin Diplomat Ishmael Khaldi**[45]

MYTH

"Israel uses checkpoints to deny Palestinians their rights and to humiliate them."

FACT

It is not unusual for nations to guard their borders and to establish checkpoints to prevent people from illegally entering their countries. The United States has checkpoints at its borders and airports and, as Americans saw on September 11, these are necessary but not foolproof security precautions.

In the case of Israel, the necessity for checkpoints has been created by the Palestinians. By pursuing a violent campaign of terror against Israel's citizens, they have forced Israel to set up barriers to make it as difficult as possible for terrorists to enter Israel or travel through the territories to carry out acts of violence. The checkpoints are an inconvenience to innocent Palestinians, but they also prevent terror and save lives.

For example, on October 5, 2008, two pipe bombs were found in a parcel carried by a Palestinian man at the Hawara checkpoint near Nablus. On June 8, 2008, an 18-year-old Palestinian was arrested at the same checkpoint carrying six pipe bombs, an ammunition cartridge, bullets, and a bag of gunpowder. "It's routine to find bombs at this checkpoint ... every day, we find knives and other weapons," said Cpl. Ron Bezalel of the military police. Just three weeks earlier, another Palestinian was arrested at Hawara carrying five pipe bombs, which he had attached and strapped to his chest to act as an explosives belt.[46]

> *"One does not judge a democracy by the way its soldiers immediately react, young men and women under tremendous provocation. One judges a democracy by the way its courts react, in the dispassionate cool of judicial chambers. And the Israeli Supreme Court and other courts have reacted magnificently. For the first time in Mideast history, there is an independent judiciary willing to listen to grievances of Arabs—that judiciary is called the Israeli Supreme Court."*
>
> **—Alan Dershowitz[47]**

On November 10, 2008, at the Taysir checkpoint outside of Jenin, Israeli soldiers caught a Palestinian attempting to smuggle through a pipe bomb.[48]

On January 9, 2011, a Palestinian was killed at the Bekaot checkpoint after charging at the soldiers. He was carrying a pipe bomb and another explosive device.[49]

On March 9, 2011, five pipe bombs and 3 Molotov cocktails were found in a Palestinian's bag at Tapuach junction.[50]

Hyperbolic media reports and anti-Israel propaganda have suggested Israel is harassing Palestinian women at checkpoints. It is unfortunate that women cannot be ignored as potential security threats. Border policemen at a checkpoint north of Jerusalem, for example, arrested a Palestinian woman pushing a baby stroller that concealed a pistol, two ammunition clips and a knife.[51]

Commercial goods, food, medicine, ambulances and medical crews continue to circulate freely, hampered only by continuing attacks. Palestinian workers going to jobs in Israel also may pass through the checkpoints with the proper identification; restrictions are only imposed when necessitated by the security situation.

Barriers are not set up to humiliate Palestinians, but to ensure the safety of Israeli citizens. Frequently, when Israel has relaxed its policy and withdrawn checkpoints, Palestinian terrorists have taken advantage of the opportunity to launch new attacks on innocent Israelis. Still, Israel has dismantled more than 120 unmanned checkpoints and reduced the number of manned checkpoints from 41 to 14 in the last two years.[52]

MYTH

*"Israeli checkpoints prevent Palestinians
from receiving medical attention."*

FACT

Israel has instituted checkpoints for one reason—to prevent Palestinian terrorists from infiltrating Israel. If the Palestinian Authority was fulfilling its Road Map obligations to dismantle the terrorist networks and disarm the terrorists, and its security forces were taking adequate measures to prevent Palestinians from planning and launching attacks, the checkpoints would be dismantled.

Israel tries to balance its security concerns with the welfare of the Palestinians, and is especially sensitive to the medical needs of Palestinians. According to IDF guidelines, any Palestinian in need of urgent medical care is allowed passage through checkpoints. The severity of the medical condition is determined by the checkpoint commander, who is to make decisions in favor of the Palestinian if there is any doubt. Palestinians are also allowed to enter Israel for routine medical care unless there is a security problem. Even then, Palestinians can appeal decisions and are also offered other options, such as transfer to neighboring states.

Ambulances are still stopped and searched at Israeli checkpoints because they have frequently been used as a means to transport terrorist bombs, and many of the murderers who have triggered suicide bombings in Israel gained access by driving or riding in Red Crescent ambulances. For example:

- In October 2001, Nidal Nazal, a Hamas operative in Kalkilya, was arrested by the IDF. He was an ambulance driver for the Palestinian Red Crescent who served as a messenger between the Hamas headquarters in several West Bank towns.[53]

- In January 2002, Wafa Idris blew herself up on the crowded Jaffa Street in Jerusalem, becoming one of the first female suicide bombers. She was an ambulance driver for the Palestinian Red Crescent, as was Mohammed Hababa, the Tanzim operative who sent her on her mission. She left the West Bank by way of an ambulance.[54]

- On March 27, 2002, a Tanzim member who worked as a Red Crescent ambulance driver was captured with explosives in his ambulance. A child disguised as a patient was riding in the ambulance along with the child's family. The explosives were found under the stretcher the "sick" child was laying on.[55]

■ On May 17, 2002, an explosive belt was found in a Red Crescent ambulance at a checkpoint near Ramallah. The bomb, the same type generally used in suicide bombings, was hidden under a gurney on which a sick child was lying. The driver, Islam Jibril, was already wanted by the IDF, and admitted that this was not the first time that an ambulance had been used to transport explosives or terrorists. In a statement issued the same day, the International Committee of the Red Cross said that it "understands the security concerns of the Israeli authorities, and has always acknowledged their right to check ambulances, provided it does not unduly delay medical evacuations." The sick passengers in the ambulance were escorted by soldiers to a nearby hospital.[56]

■ On June 30, 2002, Israeli troops found 10 suspected Palestinian terrorists hiding in two ambulances in Ramallah. They were caught when soldiers stopped the vehicles for routine checks.[57]

■ In December 2003, Rashed Tarek al-Nimr, who worked as a chemist in hospitals in Nablus and Bethlehem, supplied chemicals from the hospitals to Hamas for use in making bombs and admitted he used ambulances to transport the chemicals. He also said the Hamas commanders would hide in hospitals to avoid arrest.[58]

■ In December 2004, a Hamas agent with forged documents claiming that he was a cancer patient in need of medical treatment from an Israeli hospital was arrested by security forces. Hamed A-Karim Hamed Abu Lihiya was to meet up with another terrorist, obtain weapons from allies inside Israel, and carry out an attack. That same month, a man recruited by the al-Aqsa Martyrs Brigade to plant a bomb on the railway tracks near Netanya tried to use false papers indicating he needed hospital treatment to enter Israel. Another Hamas terrorist planning a suicide bombing was arrested in March 2005 after pretending to be a kidney donor.[59]

"Israeli hospitals extend humanitarian treatment to Palestinians from the Gaza Strip and West Bank. These efforts continued when all other cooperation between Palestinians and Israelis came to a halt during the most recent intifada."

—Palestinian obstetrician and gynecologist Dr. Izzeldin Abuelaish[60]

On June 20, 2005, Wafa Samir Ibrahim Bas was arrested attempting to smuggle an explosives belt through the Erez crossing. Bas aroused the suspicion of soldiers at the checkpoint when a biometric scanner revealed she was hiding explosives. When she realized they had discovered the explosive belt, she attempted unsuccessfully to detonate it.[61]

Bas had been admitted on humanitarian grounds to Soroka Medical Center in Be'er Sheva several months earlier for treatment of massive burns she received as a result of a cooking accident. After her arrest, she admitted that the Fatah al-Aqsa Martyrs Brigade had instructed her to use her personal medical authorization documents to enter into Israel to carry out a suicide attack. In an interview shown on Israeli television, Bas said her "dream was to be a martyr" and that her intent was to kill 40 or 50 people—as many young people as possible.

Since its founding in 1996, Save a Child's Heart, an Israeli humanitarian group that treats children suffering from heart problems, has treated more than 900 children from Gaza.[62]

Dr. Izzeldin Abuelaish, a Palestinian obstetrician and gynecologist from the Jabalya refugee camp in the Gaza Strip, who has worked at the Soroka Hospital, wrote that he was "outraged at the cynical and potentially deadly suicide bombing attempt." Dr. Abuelaish said he does research at the hospital's Genetic Institute and has warm relations with his colleagues. "I make a point, whenever I'm at the hospital, of visiting Palestinian patients," he said. "I also schedule appointments for other Gaza residents, and even bring medication from Soroka to needy patients in the Strip. . . . On the very day that she planned to detonate her bomb, two Palestinians in critical condition were waiting in Gaza to be taken for urgent treatment at Soroka."

Dr. Abuelaish added, "Wafa was sent to kill the very people in Israel who are healing Palestinians from the Gaza Strip and West Bank. What if Israeli hospitals now decide to bar Palestinians seeking treatment? How would those who sent Bas feel if their own relatives, in need of medical care in Israel, are refused treatment?"[63]

By using this tactic, the Palestinians have reinforced the necessity of retaining the checkpoints and forced Israel to carry out more stringent inspections, yet another example of how terrorists are making life unnecessarily difficult for innocent Palestinians.

Despite a number of other cases where Palestinian terrorists tried to take advantage of the "medical route" to infiltrate Israel, more than 18,000 Palestinians from Gaza, and 175,000 from the West Bank, were allowed to travel to hospitals in Israel in 2010 to receive treatment from some of the finest medical facilities in the world. This includes approximately 7,500 children. Many of these patients receive life-saving treatments that are not available in the Palestinian territories.[64]

> ### Case Study
>
> Picture a 19-year-old soldier commanding a checkpoint. An ambulance arrives, and inside is a woman who is seemingly pregnant. The woman appears to be in pain and her husband is also highly anxious. But the soldier has been warned about an ambulance bearing a pregnant woman who is not really pregnant. The intelligence said that underneath the stretcher in the ambulance a wanted terrorist is hiding with an explosive belt for a suicide attack. It is a hot day and there is a long line of cars. His commanders are yelling at him on the two-way radio, "Do not let ambulances go through because there is a terrorist in an ambulance!" To complicate the picture, a news video crew is present.
>
> The soldier has to make an incredible number of decisions in a very short time. He is only 19 and has no medical training. He knows that if he lets the ambulance go through and it contains a terrorist, then innocent people will die and he will have failed in his mission. On the other hand, if there is not a terrorist in this particular ambulance, and he delays a truly pregnant woman from reaching a hospital, the lives of the mother and baby could be endangered.
>
> What would you do?

MYTH

"Israeli textbooks are just as hateful as those in the Palestinian Authority."

FACT

The best hope for the future is that Israeli and Arab children will grow up with a greater understanding and tolerance of one another. Unfortunately, the textbooks in Arab countries, and the Palestinian Authority, in particular, do not promote coexistence. By contrast, Israeli textbooks are oriented toward peace and tolerance. The Palestinians are accepted as Palestinians. Islam and Arab culture are referred to with respect. Islamic holy places are discussed along with Jewish ones. Stereotypes are avoided to educate against prejudice.

More than 20 years ago, it was true that some Israeli textbooks used stereotyped images of Arabs; however, the books in use in public schools today are very different. Israeli texts go out of their way to avoid prejudices and to guard against generalizations. In one seventh grade lesson, students are given the following problem:

> Many people think: The dove is a bird that pursues peace. This belief is incorrect; it is a prejudice: people believe it without checking it. There are a lot of prejudices. For example:

1. The Jews control the world and exploit all those who live in it.

2. The blacks are inferior; they are incapable of being scientists.

3. The Arabs only understand the language of force ...
Be ready to explain orally why these are prejudices.[65]

In an elementary textbook on reading comprehension, students read how a Jewish girl was saved by an Arab woman. The book notes, "The Arabs are like the Jews.... There are nasty people among them and there are decent people and ... they should not be labeled."[66]

Contrary to suggestions that Israelis do not accept the idea that Palestinians are a people, Israeli textbooks explain the origins of Palestinian nationalism. For example, a ninth grade text observes that "during the 1930's, Arab nationalist movements evolved all over the Middle East. Many of the Arabs of Eretz Yisrael also began formulating a national consciousness—in other words, the perception that they are not just part of the larger Arab nation, but are also Palestinians."[67]

While Palestinian texts omit references to Jewish contributions to the world, the Israeli books recognize the achievements of Arabs and Muslims. One text highlights the Arab role as creators of culture: " ... they were the first to discover the existence of infectious diseases. They were also the first to build public hospitals. Because of their considerable contribution to various scientific fields, there are disciplines that to this day are called by their Arabic names, such as algebra." Islam's contributions are also acknowledged in the same passage: "The Islamic religion also influenced the development of culture. The obligation to pray in the direction of Mecca led to the development of astronomy, which helped identify the direction according to the heavenly bodies. The duty to make a pilgrimage developed geography and gave a push to the writing of travel books. These books, and the Arabs' high capability in map drawing, helped develop trade. To this day, merchants use Arabic words, such as bazaar, check and tariff."[68]

Palestinian textbooks also negate the Jewish connection to the Holy Land while Israeli texts show respect for the Arab/Muslim attachment to the land. "The Land of Israel in general, and Jerusalem in particular, have been sanctified more and more in Islamic thought—as Islam has developed and spread, both religiously and geographically. As Islam absorbed more and more of the world conquered by it, so it adapted and Islamized the values that it absorbed, including the holiness of the Land of Israel, its flora and its water, living in it, the sanctity of being buried in it and the like. All these became from that time onwards part of orthodox Islam." [69]

Israeli textbooks contain a plurality of views, including those that conflict with conventional research and are critical of Israeli policies.

Controversial topics, such as the disputed territories, the refugee issue, and the status of Israeli Arabs are covered from multiple viewpoints.[70]

The content of the peace treaties between Israel and Egypt and Jordan is detailed, along with the implications of those agreements. Agreements with the Palestinians are discussed as well, and the atlas used in Israeli schools shows the Palestinian Authority.[71]

Israeli texts also use simulation games to help students understand different perspectives on an issue. In one, students are told to divide into groups representing Jewish and Palestinian journalists and prepare a report on the discussion in the United Nations leading to the partition resolution. Students are then asked to discuss the differences between the reports of the Jewish and Palestinian journalists.[72]

Israel is not perfect and exceptions do exist. Some generalizations and patronizing terminology are found in textbooks used in the ultra-Orthodox schools. These schools comprise less than 10 percent of the Israeli educational system, and the same Israeli watchdog organizations that have pointed out problems in Palestinian textbooks have also publicized the need to remove inappropriate references from school books in this system.[73]

MYTH

"Israel is a theocracy and should not be a Jewish State."

FACT

It often makes people uncomfortable to refer to Israel as "the Jewish State" because it suggests a theocracy and, therefore, the demise of Israel as a Jewish state is viewed by some people as a positive development. Israel is not a theocracy; it is governed by the rule of law as drafted by a democratically elected parliament. It is informed by Jewish values and adheres to many Jewish religious customs (such as holidays), but this is similar to the United States and other nations that are shaped by the Judeo-Christian heritage and also have expressly religious elements (e.g., church-state separation in the U.S. does not preclude the recognition of Christmas as a holiday). Israel has no state religion, and all faiths enjoy freedom of worship; yet, it is attacked for its Jewish character, whereas the Arab states that all have Islam as their official religion are regarded as legitimate.

Why shouldn't the Jews have a state? The Jewish people are a nation with a shared origin, religion, culture, language, and history. No one suggests that Arabs are not entitled to a nation of their own (and they have not one, but twenty-one) or Swedes or Germans, or that Catholics are not entitled to a state (Vatican City) headed by a theocrat (the Pope). To suggest that Zionism, the nationalist movement of the Jewish people, is the only form of nationalism that is illegitimate is pure bigotry. It is especially ironic that the Jewish nation should be challenged given that Jewish statehood preceded the emergence of most modern nation-states by thousands of years.

It is also not unusual that one community should be the majority within a nation and seek to maintain that status. In fact, this is true in nearly every country in the world. Moreover, societies usually reflect the cultural identity of the majority. India and Pakistan were established at the same time as Israel through a violent partition, but no one believes these nations are illegitimate because one is predominantly Hindu and the other has a Muslim majority, or that these nations shouldn't be influenced by those communities (e.g., that cows in India should not be treated as sacred).

In the United States, a vigorous debate persists over the boundaries between church and state. Similar discussions regarding "synagogue and state" are ongoing in Israel, with philosophical disagreements over whether Israel can be a Jewish and a democratic state, and practical arguments over Sabbath observance, marriage and divorce laws, and budgets for religious institutions. Nevertheless, most Jews take for granted that Israel is, and must remain, a Jewish state. Arab citizens also understand that Israel is a Jewish state and, while they might prefer that it was not, they have still chosen to live there (nothing prevents Arabs from moving to any of the 190-odd non-Jewish states in the world). Both Jews and Arabs realize that if Jews cease to be a majority in Israel, Israel will no longer have a Jewish character or serve as a haven for persecuted Jews, and that is one of the elements underlying peace negotiations between Israel and the Palestinians.

MYTH

"Israel is persecuting Christians."

FACT

While Christians are unwelcome in Islamic states such as Saudi Arabia, and most have been driven out of their longtime homes in Lebanon, Christians continue to be welcome in Israel. Christians have always been a minority in Israel, but it is the only Middle East nation where the Christian population has grown in the last half century (from 34,000 in 1948 to 150,000 today), in large measure because of the freedom to practice their religion.

By their own volition, the Christian communities have remained the most autonomous of the various religious communities in Israel, though they have increasingly chosen to integrate their social welfare, medical and educational institutions into state structures. The ecclesiastical courts of the Christian communities maintain jurisdiction in matters of personal status, such as marriage and divorce. The Ministry of Religious Affairs deliberately refrains from interfering in their religious life, but maintains a Department for Christian Communities to address problems and requests that may arise.

In Jerusalem, the rights of the various Christian churches to custody of the Christian holy places were established during the Ottoman Empire. Known as the "status quo arrangement for the Christian holy places in Jerusalem," these rights remain in force today in Israel.

It was during Jordan's control of the Old City from 1948 until 1967 that Christian rights were infringed and Israeli Christians were barred from their holy places. The Christian population declined by nearly half, from 25,000 to 12,646. Since then, the population has slowly been growing.

Some Christians have been among those inconvenienced by Israel's construction of the security fence, but they have not been harmed because of their religious beliefs. They simply live in areas where the fence is being built. Like others who can show they have suffered some injury, Christians are entitled to compensation. Meanwhile, Israel has taken measures to minimize the impact of the fence on Christians. For example, a special terminal was built to facilitate security checks for those traveling between Bethlehem and Jerusalem. Special gates were built in other areas allowing pilgrims to visit religious sites on the Palestinian side of the fence. Israel often moved the fence route to accommodate requests of Christians, as in the case of the Rosary School that was moved to the Israeli side in response to requests from the Mother Superior. Ultimately, 19 of 22 Christian sites in and around Jerusalem were brought inside the fence, with the exceptions primarily due to the desire to avoid moving the fence deep into the West Bank or compromising Muslim property rights.[74]

Meanwhile, Israel's detractors ignore the precarious plight of Christians under Arab rule, especially under the Palestinian Authority, where approximately 50,000 Christians live among 3 million Muslims. The total number of Christians in the Palestinian territories has remained stable since 1967, however, the proportion has dropped from 15 percent of the Arab population in 1950 to just over 1 percent today. Three-fourths of all Bethlehem Christians now live abroad, and the overwhelming majority of the city's population is Muslim. By contrast, Israel's Christian population *grew* by approximately 114 percent since 1967.[75]

Jonathan Adelman and Agota Kuperman noted that Yasser Arafat "tried to erase the historic Jesus by depicting him as the first radical Palestinian armed *fedayeen* (guerrilla). Meanwhile, the Palestinian Authority has adopted Islam as its official religion, used *shari'a* Islamic codes, and allowed even officially appointed clerics to brand Christians (and Jews) as infidels in their mosques." The authors add that the "militantly

Islamic rhetoric and terrorist acts of Hamas, Islamic Jihad . . . offer little comfort to Christians."

David Raab observed that "Palestinian Christians are perceived by many Muslims—as were Lebanon's Christians—as a potential fifth column for Israel. In fact, at the start of the Palestinian War in 2000, Muslim Palestinians attacked Christians in Gaza." Raab also wrote that "anti-Christian graffiti is not uncommon in Bethlehem and neighboring Beit Sahur, proclaiming: 'First the Saturday people (the Jews), then the Sunday people (the Christians),'" and that "Christian cemeteries have been defaced, monasteries have had their telephone lines cut, and there have been break-ins at convents." In 2002, Palestinian terrorists holed up in the Church of the Nativity in Bethlehem, endangering the shrine and provoking a tense standoff with Israeli troops.

When Arafat died, Vatican Radio correspondent Graziano Motta said, "The death of the president of the Palestinian National Authority has come at a time when the political, administrative and police structures often discriminate against [Christians]." Motta added that Christians "have been continually exposed to pressures by Muslim activists, and have been forced to profess fidelity to the intifada." In addition, he reported, "Frequently, there are cases in which the Muslims expropriate houses and lands belonging to Catholics, and often the intervention of the authorities has been lacking in addressing acts of violence against young women, or offenses against the Christian faith."[76]

It certainly wouldn't be difficult for critics to find evidence of mistreatment of Christians in the PA if they were interested, but unlike Christians who enjoy freedom of speech as well as religion in Israel, beleaguered Palestinian Christians are afraid to speak out. "Out of fear for their safety, Christian spokesmen aren't happy to be identified by name when they complain about the Muslims' treatment of them . . . off the record they talk of harassment and terror tactics, mainly from the gangs of thugs who looted and plundered Christians and their property, under the protection of Palestinian security personnel."[77]

"Christian Arabs," Adam Garfinkle noted, "see Israel as protection against the rising sea of Islam in which they live." Christians also rarely publicly complain, Garfinkle says, "because Arab Christians are somewhat marginalized in majority Islamic culture, they have often gone out of their way to act more Arab than the Arabs, and that has sometimes meant taking the lead in anti-Western and anti-Israel advocacy."[78]

One Christian who has gone public is Samir Qumsiyeh, a journalist from Beit Sahur who told the Italian newspaper *Corriere della Sera* that Christians were being subjected to rape, kidnapping, extortion and expropriation of land and property. Qumsiyeh compiled a list of 93 cases of anti-Christian violence between 2000 and 2004 and specifically mentioned the case of a 17-year-old girl from his town who was raped by members of Fatah. "Even though the family protested," he said, "none of the four was ever arrested. Because of the shame her family was forced to move to Jordan." He added that "almost all 140 cases of expropriation of land in the last three years were committed by militant Islamic groups and members of the Palestinian police" and that the Christian population of Bethlehem has dropped from 75 percent in 1950 to 12 percent today. "If the situation continues," Qumsiyeh warned, "we won't be here any more in 20 years."[79]

MYTH

"Hamas respects the rights of Palestinian Christians."

FACT

In Gaza only about 2,000 Christians live among more than one million Muslims. The population has declined as Hamas persecution has intensified.

On June 14, 2007, the Rosary Sisters School and Latin Church in the Gaza Strip were ransacked, burned and looted by Hamas gunmen who used rocket-propelled grenades to storm the buildings. Father Manuel Musalam, leader of the Latin community in Gaza, expressed outrage that copies of the Bible were burned, crosses destroyed and computers and other equipment stolen. The same year, the owner of Gaza's only Christian bookstore was murdered.[80]

"I expect our Christian neighbors to understand the new Hamas rule means real changes. They must be ready for Islamic rule if they want to live in peace in Gaza," said Sheik Abu Saqer, leader of Jihadia Salafiya, an Islamic outreach movement that opened a "military wing" to enforce Muslim law in Gaza. The application of Islamic law, he said, includes a prohibition on alcohol and a requirement that women be covered at all times while in public.[81]

Critics of Israel who express concern for Christians, such as Jimmy Carter, have consistently ignored the persistent discrimination and abuse of Christians by Muslims throughout the Middle East. It is therefore not surprising that they have remained silent while Palestinian Muslims persecute Christians.

The Christian position throughout the territories has always been precarious, which is why many have fled the Palestinian Authority.

MYTH

"Israel denies Palestinians basic rights and freedoms"

FACT

Palestinians are deprived of the freedoms Americans and Israelis take for granted, namely, freedom of religion, freedom of the press, freedom of speech, gay rights and women's rights. Israel has nothing to do with the denial of these rights, however, they are all blocked by the Palestinian Authority.

As documented elsewhere in this book, non-Muslims regularly face discrimination and Christians have been driven out of Gaza by Hamas. Journalists are not allowed to report freely and critics of the leadership are harassed, jailed or prevented from reporting. In a December 2010 poll, only 27 percent of Palestinians in the West Bank and 19 percent in Gaza said they can criticize officials without fear.[82] Gays are not tolerated and many have fled to Israel for sanctuary. Women are routinely discriminated against and honor killings are still practiced.

While human rights groups obsessively focus on Israel's treatment of Palestinians, they routinely ignore abuses by Palestinians against their own people. While Israel may be blamed for hardships faced by Palestinians, the denial of these basic civil and human rights in the territories has been the sole responsibility of the Palestinian leadership.

MYTH

"The Goldstone Report proves Israel is guilty of war crimes in Gaza."

FACT

Following the report's release, Susan Rice, the U.S. Ambassador to the United Nations, said, "The mandate was unbalanced, one-sided and unacceptable ... The weight of the report is something like 85% oriented towards very specific and harsh condemnation and conclusions related to Israel and very lightly treats without great specificity Hamas' terrorism and its own atrocities."[83]

The Goldstone Commission was created to conduct a fact-finding mission and to investigate whether any violations of international humanitarian law took place during the conflict between Israel and Hamas during Israel's Operation Cast Lead in Gaza in December 2008/January 2009. No one was surprised when the Commission issued a report highly critical of Israel given that it was created by the UN Human Rights Council, an organization long ago discredited for its obsessive and biased focus on Israel, and that one of the Commission members, Christine Chinkin, had previously accused Israel of war crimes.[84]

The four-person panel, led by Judge Richard Goldstone, based virtually all of its 575-page report on unverified accounts by Palestinians and NGOs. The Goldstone Commission fixated on Israel's incursion into Gaza while failing to adequately address the provocation—three years of Hamas rocket bombardment of Israeli towns and villages—that led to the Israeli operation. The Israeli government did not cooperate with the Commission because of its one-sided mandate that presumed Israel was guilty of war crimes.[85]

While ignoring journalistic accounts of the activities of Hamas, the Commission relied on critical reports of Israeli actions by groups such as Human Rights Watch (HRW), which had already been disputed. HRW, in particular, has been discredited by revelations that it has tried to raise money from Saudi Arabia by touting its history of anti-Israel reportage and that its "senior military expert," Marc Garlasco, is a collector of Nazi memorabilia.[86]

When interviewing Gazans, the Commission was chaperoned by Hamas officials.[87] Hence, it was not surprising that investigators made little effort to investigate Hamas activities before or during Operation Cast Lead. It was equally unremarkable for the commission to then report that it found no evidence that Hamas fired rockets from civilian homes, that terrorists hid among the civilian population, fired mortars, anti-tank missiles and machine guns into Palestinian villages when IDF forces were in proximity, or that they seized and booby-trapped Palestinian civilian houses to ambush IDF soldiers. In fact, the report refers to Hamas "police" as civilians, absolving them of terrorist rocket attacks against Israeli civilians and their illegal actions in Gaza during the conflict.[88] This directly contradicts the ample photos, video and reports by journalists that depict Hamas militants participating in all of these illegal activities.[89]

One postwar study rebutting Goldstone's conclusions found that many Hamas fighters were dressed as civilians; some were seen in videos firing mortars and rocket-propelled grenades at troops. The report also documented the use by Hamas of dozens of mosques as armories, command centers and launching areas for rockets. Evidence was also found of Hamas fighters using civilians as shields.[90]

Ironically, Hamas undermined claims by Goldstone and other critics of Israel who insisted the victims of the war were mostly innocent civilians when Hamas Interior Minister Fathi Hammad admitted in 2010 that it lost more than 600 men during the war. This is consistent with the figure of 709 calculated by the Israel Defense Forces after it released an official list of the 1,166 names of Palestinians killed during the war.[91]

Even the UN's Humanitarian Affairs chief, John Holmes, had criticized Hamas for "the reckless and cynical use of civilian installations ... and indiscriminate firing of rockets against civilian populations," which he characterized as "clear violations of international law."[92]

By not holding Hamas accountable for targeting Israeli civilians, the report essentially legitimizes terrorism and criminalizes self-defense.

"For the Palestinian people, death has become an industry at which women excel, and so do all the people living on this land. The elderly excel at this, and so do the mujahideen and the children. This is why they have formed human shields of the women, the children, the elderly, and the mujahideen, in order to challenge the Zionist bombing machine. It is as if they are saying to the Zionist enemy: We desire death like you desire life."

—Hamas parliamentarian Fathi Hammad[93]

Israel does not need outsiders to tell it how to defend itself or how to investigate the actions of its military. The people of Israel expect their soldiers to uphold the highest moral standards and they demand that allegations of misconduct be promptly and thoroughly probed even when the results may be embarrassing. The war in Gaza was no exception. Israel has already examined various charges, and taken action against soldiers who acted inappropriately, and will continue to do so without intervention by parties with political agendas who start with the premise that Israelis are guilty and then set out to prove it.

MYTH

"Justice Goldstone remains convinced that Israel committed war crimes documented in the Goldstone Report."

FACT

In an April 1, 2011, editorial published by the *Washington Post,* Justice Richard Goldstone retracted his accusations that Israel intentionally targeted civilians and was guilty of war crimes during its conflict with Hamas in Gaza in December 2008.[94] The principal author of the 575 page report bearing his name, commissioned by the UN Human Rights Council to investigate allegations of criminal misconduct during the Gaza conflict, Goldstone now admits the work used by Israel's detractors to vilify Israel was based on incomplete information and falsely accused Israel of wrongdoing. Goldstone conceded that "if I had known then what I know now, the Goldstone Report would have been a different document."[95]

The report, which erroneously claimed that Israel led a "deliberately disproportionate attack designed to punish, humiliate and terrorize a civilian population," became a tool for Israel's detractors to demonize the Jewish state and denigrate its right to self-defense.[96] Goldstone now accepts that "civilians were not intentionally targeted [by Israel] as a matter of policy" and that in the aftermath of having thousands of rockets and missiles fired at its cities, Israel had the "right and obligation to defend itself and its citizens against such attacks."[97] In fact, as Colonel Richard Kemp, former Commander British Forces in Afghanistan, testified to the Goldstone committee in 2009, "The IDF did more to safeguard the rights of civilians in a combat zone than any other army in the history of warfare."[98]

Israel's claims regarding casualties also have proved correct, Goldstone acknowledges. "The Israeli military's numbers have turned out to be similar to those recently furnished by Hamas." He is referring to the recent Hamas admission that, as Israel maintained, most of the Palestinians who were killed in the fighting were terrorists and not bystanders.[99]

Goldstone also takes the UN Human Rights Council to task, noting that its original mandate was "skewed against Israel." He said he "hoped that our inquiry into all aspects of the Gaza conflict would begin a new era of evenhandedness at the UN Human Rights Council, whose history of bias against Israel cannot be doubted."[100]

> *"Everything that we said proved to be true. Israel did not intentionally target civilians and it has proper investigatory bodies. In contrast, Hamas intentionally directed strikes towards innocent civilians and did not conduct any kind of probe … The fact that Goldstone changed his mind must lead to the shelving of [the Goldstone Report] once and for all."*
>
> **—Benjamin Netanyahu, Israeli Prime Minister**[101]

Goldstone also now rightfully focuses his criticism on Hamas. "That comparatively few Israelis have been killed by the unlawful rocket and mortar attacks from Gaza," Goldstone writes, "in no way minimizes their criminality."[102] He added that Hamas' actions during the conflict were intentional and "purposefully indiscriminate" and he excoriates them for failing to investigate any of the war crimes accusations. By contrast, Goldstone acknowledged that Israel has "dedicated significant resources to investigate" allegations of misconduct.

Though long overdue, Goldstone's retraction is timely because Hamas has resumed rocket attacks on Israeli civilians and Israel may again be forced to reengage Hamas to defend its citizens. Nevertheless, the damage caused to Israel by the Goldstone Report is incalculable. Public protests, university forums and official declarations have used the "evidence" released in the report to smear Israel and its brave soldiers. Unfortunately, renouncing his report will not stem the tide of anti-Israel propaganda based on its mendacious claims. Goldstone nevertheless has an obligation to go to all the forums where his report was misused and set the record straight. As a member of the UN Human Rights Council, the United States should demand that the Goldstone Report be denounced as a sham and erased from the record.

MYTH

"Israel's blockade of Gaza is collective punishment."

FACT

International law requires that Israel permit passage of food, clothing and medicines intended for children under fifteen, expectant mothers and maternity cases. If Israel has reason to believe Hamas will intercept these goods and the enemy will benefit, even these provisions may be prohibited. Israel also need not provide these supplies; it is obligated only to allow others to transfer provisions.

Furthermore, the law does not prohibit Israel from cutting off fuel supplies and electricity to Gaza, withholding commercial items or sealing its border. Israel also is not obligated to provide any minimum supplies to prevent a "humanitarian crisis."

Some critics of labeled Israel's actions "collective punishment"; however, this refers to the "imposition of criminal-type penalties to individuals or groups on the basis of another's guilt." Israel has done no such thing. Israel has no obligation to maintain open borders with a hostile territory. The suspension of trade relations or embargoes is a frequent tool of international diplomacy and has never been regarded as "collective punishment."[103]

Israel has complied with international law and gone beyond it by delivering humanitarian supplies it was not required to provide.

Notes

1. Vamberto Morais, *A Short History of Anti-Semitism,* (NY: W.W Norton and Co., 1976), p. 11; Bernard Lewis, *Semites & Anti-Semites,* (NY: WW Norton &Co., 1986), p. 81.
2. *Oxford English Dictionary; Webster''s Third International Dictionary.*
3. *Washington Post,* (October 30, 2001).
4. Bernard Lewis, *Islam in History: Ideas, People and Events in the Middle East,* (IL: Open Court, 2001), p. 148.
5. Bat Ye'or, *The Dhimmi,* (NJ: Fairleigh Dickinson University Press, 1985), pp. 43-44.
6. Bat Ye'or, pp. 185-86, 191, 194.
7. Norman Stillman, *The Jews of Arab Lands,* (PA: The Jewish Publication Society of America, 1979), p. 81; Maurice Roumani, *The Case of the Jews from Arab Countries: A Neglected Issue,* (Tel Aviv: World Organization of Jews from Arab Countries, 1977), pp. 26-27; Bat Ye'or, p. 72.
8. Stillman, pp. 59, 284.
9. Roumani, pp. 26-27.
10. Bernard Lewis, *The Jews of Islam,* (NJ: Princeton University Press, 1984), p. 158.
11. G.E. Von Grunebaum, "Eastern Jewry Under Islam," *Viator,* (1971), p. 369.
12. Bat Ye'or, p. 30.
13. Bat Ye'or, p. 14.
14. Bat Ye'or, pp. 56-57.
15. Bat Ye'or, *Islam and Dhimmitude: Where Civilizations Collide,* (NJ: Farleigh Dickinson University Press, 2002), p. 107.

16. Official British document, Foreign Office File No. 371/20822 E 7201/22/31; Elie Kedourie, *Islam in the Modern World,* (London: Mansell, 1980), pp. 69–72.

17. Howard Sachar, *A History of Israel: From the Rise of Zionism to Our Time,* (NY: Alfred A. Knopf, 1979), p. 196.

18. Jordanian Nationality Law, Official Gazette, No. 1171, Article 3(3) of Law No. 6, 1954, (February 16, 1954), p. 105.

19. Modern World History, Jordanian Ministry of Education, 1966, p. 150.

20. Meyrav Wurmser, *The Schools of Ba'athism: A Study of Syrian Schoolbooks,* (Washington, D.C.: Middle East Media and Research Institute (MEMRI), 2000), p. xiii.

21. Aaron Klein, "Official PA site publishes 'Protocols' in Arabic," *WorldNetDaily,* (May 21, 2005).

22. *Al-Mussawar,* (August 4, 1972).

23. *Washington Post,* (May 8, 2001).

24. Middle East Media and Research Institute (MEMRI); *Al-Hayat Al-Jadeeda,* (May 15, 1997); *Jerusalem Post,* (May 23, 2001); Palestine News Agency WAFA, (April 28, 2005).

25. *Al-Ahram,* (October 28, 2000).

26. *Jerusalem Post,* (November 19, 2001).

27. Palestinian Authority television, (January 29, 2010), cited in "PATV Sermon: Jew are Enemies," *Palestinian Media Watch,* (February 1, 2010).

28. Jonathan Krashinsky, "Even Palestinian Crosswords Reject Israel," *Palestinian Media Watch,* (March 15, 2001).

29. Israeli Central Bureau of Statistics.

30. Alan Dershowitz, *The Case for Israel,* (NY: John Wiley & Sons, 2003), p. 157.

31. *Jerusalem Post,* (August 19, 2002).

32. U.S. State Department, Human Rights Report for the Occupied Territories, 1997, 1998.

33. Khaled Abu Toameh, "Islamic judge issues fatwa against Arabs voting in Jerusalem," *Jerusalem Post,* (October 26, 2008); *Ma'an News Agency,* (June 30, 2010).

34. "Torture and Ill Treatment as Perceived by Israel's High Court of Justice," *B'Tselem,* (May 6, 2010).

35. *Haaretz,* (September 23, 2003). *Newsview,* (March 23, 1982).

36. Shabtai Teveth, *Ben-Gurion and the Palestinian Arabs: From Peace to War,* (London: Oxford University Press, 1985), p. 140; *Haaretz,* (September 23, 2003).

37. Benjamin Pogrund, "Apartheid? Israel is a democracy in which Arabs vote," *Focus 40,* (December 2005).

38. James Bennet, "Letter from the Middle East; Arab Showplace? Could It Be the West Bank?" *New York Times,* (April 2, 2003). The last time the question was asked was in 2002.

39. Daniel Estrin, "Jerusalem Palestinians taking Israeli citizenship," Associated Press, (January 12, 2011); Jackson Diehl, "Why Palestinians want to be Israeli citizens," *Washington Post,* (January 12, 2011).

40. Golda Meir, *My Life,* (NY: Dell Publishing Co., 1975), pp. 308–309.

41. *The New Republic,* (December 30, 2002).

42. July 2011 estimates, *The World Factbook* 2011. Washington, DC: Central Intelligence Agency, 2011. Accessed March 11, 2010, at https://www.cia.gov/library/publications/the-world-factbook/geos/gz.html; https://www.cia.gov/library/publications/the-world-factbook/geos/we.html.

43. *The World Factbook* 2011. Washington, DC: Central Intelligence Agency, 2011. Accessed March 11, 2010, at https://www.cia.gov/library/publications/the-world-factbook/geos/we.html.

44. "Human Development Report 2009/10,"UN, (January 2010). Accessed March 11, 2010,

at http://arabstates.undp.org/contents/file/PHDR2010/PHDR_Book_Eng.pdf; http://hdr.undp.org/en/data/profiles/.

45. Ishmael Khaldi, "Lost in the blur of slogans," SFGate.com, (March 4, 2009).

46. Efrat Weiss, "IDF thwarts smuggling of pipe bombs," Ynetnews, (October 5, 2008); Yaakov Katz and jpost.com Staff, "Palestinian bomber arrested near Nablus," *Jerusalem Post,* (June 8, 2008).

47. Speech to AIPAC Policy Conference, (May 23, 1989), cited in *Near East Report,* (October 16, 1989).

48. Efrat Weiss, "Palestinian Caught with Pipe Bomb near Jenin," Ynetnews, (November 10, 2008).

49. "IDF Thwarts Terror Attack at Bekaot Crossing," *IDF Spokesperson,* (January 9, 2011).

50. "Explosives and Molotov Cocktails Discovered at Tapuach Junction," *Ministry of Foreign Affairs,* (March 9, 2011).

51. *Maariv,* (October 14, 2003); Efrat Weiss, "Palestinian girl hides gun in undies," Ynetnews, (April 15, 2005); Ali Daraghmeh, "Woman Found Hiding Grenade Under Baby," Associated Press, (October 22, 2005); Center for Monitoring the Impact on Peace, Newsletter, (February 2004).

52. "UN: Israel has dismantled 20 percent of West Bank checkpoint," Associated Press, (June 16, 2010); "Israel, the Conflict and Peace: Answers to frequently asked questions," Israel Ministry of Foreign Affairs, (December 30, 2009).

53. Israeli Foreign Ministry, "Use of Ambulances by Palestinian Terrorists," (February 14, 2002).

54. *Washington Post,* (January 31, 2002).

55. Israeli Foreign Ministry.

56. "Bomb found in Red Crescent Ambulance," *Ha'aretz,* (March 29, 2002).

57. Jewish Telegraphic Agency, (June 30, 2002).

58. "Palestinian Use of Ambulances for Terror," *Ministry of Foreign Affairs,* (December 22, 2003).

59. "Attack by Female Suicide Bomber Thwarted at Erez Crossing," *Ministry of Foreign Affairs,* (June 20, 2005).

60. *Jerusalem Post,* (July 1, 2005).

61. *Jerusalem Post,* (July 1, 2005); BBC, (June 21, 2005).

62. "Developments in Policy Towards the West Bank and Gaza in 2010," *IDF Spokesperson,* (March 2011).

63. *Jerusalem Post,* (July 1, 2005).

64. Yaakov Katz, "Gaza plan: Fill tankers, cut supplies," *Jerusalem Post,* (January 14, 2008).

65. *I Understand,* 1993, p. 259.

66. What is the Interpretation? Comprehension B, pp. 184-188.

67. *The Twentieth Century—On the Threshold of Tomorrow,* Grade 9, 1999, p. 44.

68. *From Generation to Generation,* Vol. b, 1994, p. 220.

69. H. Peleg, G. Zohar, *This is the Land—Introduction to Land of Israel Studies for the Upper Grades, 2000,* pp. 161-162.

70. *From Exile to Independence—The History of the Jewish People in Recent Generations,* vol. 2, 1990, p. 312.

71. *Center for the Monitoring of Peace,* "Newsletter," (December 2003).

72. K. Tabibian, *Journey To The Past—The Twentieth Century, By Dint of Freedom,* 1999, p. 294.

73. Center for Monitoring the Impact on Peace, Newsletter, (February 2004).

74. Danny Tirza, "The Influence of Christian Interests in Setting the Route of the Security Fence in Jerusalem," *Jerusalem* Viewpoints, Jerusalem Center for Public Affairs, (November-December 2008).

75. Alex Safian, "New York Times Omits Major Reason Christians are Leaving Bethlehem,"

(December 24, 2004), CAMERA; "The Palestinian Christian Population," JCPA Background Paper, (2011).

76. "Christians in Palestine Concerned About their future Zenit," Zenit News Agency, (November 14, 2004).

77. *Maariv,* (December 24, 2001).

78. Adam Garfinkle, *Politics and Society in Modern Israel: Myths and Realities,* (NY: M.E. Sharpe, 1997), pp. 108 & 110.

79. *Jerusalem Post,* (October 28, 2005); Harry de Quetteville, "'Islamic mafia' accused of persecuting Holy Land Christians," *Telegraph,* (September 9, 2005).

80. Khaled Abu Toameh, "Gaza's Christians fear for their lives," *Jerusalem Post,* (June 18, 2007); "Catholic compound ransacked in Gaza," Associated Press, (June 19, 2007)

81. Aaron Klein, " 'Christians must accept Islamic rule,'" WorldNetDaily, (June 19, 2007); Daniel Schwammenthal, "The Forgotten Palestinian Refugees," *Wall Street Journal* (December 28, 2009).

82. Palestinian Center for Policy and Survey Research, December 16–18, 2010; see also "Palestinian Public Opinion Poll #38."

83. "Excerpts from Interview with U.N. Ambassador Susan E. Rice," *Washington Post,* (September 22, 2009) and "Israel's Bombardment of Gaza is Not Self-Defence—It's a War Crime," *The Sunday Times,* (January 11, 2009).

84. Bernard Josephs, "Dispute Over 'Biased' Gaza Inquiry Professor," *thejc.com,* (August 27, 2009).

85. "Israel's Initial Reaction to the Report of the Goldstone Fact Finding Mission," Israel Ministry of Foreign Affairs, (September 15, 2009).

86. "UN Smears Israeli Self-Defense as War Crimes," Gerald M. Steinberg, *Wall Street Journal,* (September 16, 2009).

87. "Israel's Analysis and Comments on the Gaza Fact-Finding Mission Report," Israel Ministry of Foreign Affairs, (September 15, 2009).

88. "Israel's Analysis and Comments on the Gaza Fact-Finding Mission Report," Israel Ministry of Foreign Affairs, (September 15, 2009).

89. "Analysis: Blocking the Truth Behind the Gaza War," Jonathan D. Halevi, *Jerusalem Post,* September 21, 2009.

90. "Hamas and the Terrorist Threat from the Gaza Strip: The Main Findings of the Goldstone Report Versus the Factual Findings," Intelligence & Terrorism Information Center," (March 2010).

91. "IDF releases Cast Lead casualty numbers," *Jerusalem Post,* (March 28, 2009).

92. "Top UN official blasts Hamas for 'cynical' use of civilian facilities," *Haaretz,* (January 28, 2009).

93. "Hamas MP Fathi Hammad: We Used Women and Children as Human Shields," *Al-Aqsa TV,* cited in Dispatch #1710, MEMRI (February 29, 2008).

94. Richard Goldstone, "Reconsidering the Goldstone Report on Israel and War Crimes", *Washington Post,* (April 1, 2011).

95. Ibid.

96. Editorial, "Mr. Goldstone Recants", *Wall Street Journal,* (April 5, 2011).

97. Richard Goldstone, "Reconsidering the Goldstone Report on Israel and War Crimes", *Washington Post,* (April 1, 2011).

98. Colonel Richard Kemp, "Goldstone Gaza Report", *UN Watch,* (October 16, 2009).

99. David Harris, "Hamas Admits Up to 700 Fighters Killed in Operation Cast Lead", *The Israel Project,* (November 1, 2010).

100. Richard Goldstone, "Reconsidering the Goldstone Report on Israel and War Crimes", *Washington Post,* (April 1, 2011).

101. Barak Ravid, "Netanyahu to UN: Retract Gaza War Report in wake of Goldstone's Comments", *Haaretz,* (April 2, 2011).

102. Ibid.
103. Abraham Bell, "International Law and Gaza: The Assault on Israel's Right to Self-Defense," (January 28, 2008) and "Is Israel Bound by International Law to Supply Utilities, Goods, and Services to Gaza?", (February 28, 2008), Jerusalem: Institute of Contemporary Affairs.

15. Jerusalem

MYTH

"Jerusalem is an Arab City."

FACT

Jews have been living in Jerusalem continuously for three millennia. They have constituted the largest single group of inhabitants there since the 1840's. Jerusalem contains the Western Wall of the Temple Mount, the holiest site in Judaism.

Jerusalem was never the capital of any Arab entity. In fact, it was a backwater for most of Arab history. Jerusalem never served as a provincial capital under Muslim rule nor was it ever a Muslim cultural center. For Jews, the entire city is sacred, but Muslims revere only one site—the Dome of the Rock—not the city. "To a Muslim," observed British writer Christopher Sykes, "there is a profound difference between Jerusalem and Mecca or Medina. The latter are holy places containing holy sites." Besides the Dome of the Rock, he noted, Jerusalem has no major Islamic significance.[1]

Jerusalem's Population[2]

Year	Jews	Muslims	Christians	Total
1844	7,120	5,000	3,390	15,510
1876	12,000	7,560	5,470	25,030
1896	28,112	8,560	8,748	45,420
1922	33,971	13,411	4,699	52,081
1931	51,222	19,894	19,335	90,451
1948	100,000	40,000	25,000	165,000
1967	195,700	54,963	12,646	263,309
1987	340,000	121,000	14,000	475,000
1990	378,200	131,800	14,400	524,400
2009	476,000	247,800	15,200	760,800

MYTH

"The Temple Mount has always been a Muslim holy place and Judaism has no connection to the site."

FACT

During the 2000 Camp David Summit, Yasser Arafat said that no Jewish Temple ever existed on the Temple Mount.[3] A year later, the Palestinian Authority-appointed Mufti of Jerusalem, Ikrima Sabri, told the German publication *Die Welt*, "There is not [even] the smallest indication of the existence of a Jewish temple on this place in the past. In the whole city, there is not even a single stone indicating Jewish history."[4]

These views are contradicted by a book entitled *A Brief Guide to al-Haram al-Sharif*, published by the Supreme Moslem Council in 1930. The Council, the principal Muslim authority in Jerusalem during the British Mandate, wrote in the guide that the Temple Mount site "is one of the oldest in the world. Its sanctity dates from the earliest times. Its identity with the site of Solomon's Temple is beyond dispute. This, too, is the spot, according to universal belief, on which David built there an altar unto the Lord, and offered burnt offerings and peace offerings."

> *"The Zionist movement has invented that this was the site of Solomon's Temple. But this is all a lie."*
>
> **—Sheik Raed Salah, a leader of the Islamic Movement in Israel[5]**

In a description of the area of Solomon's Stables, which Islamic Waqf officials converted into a new mosque in 1996, the guide states:" ... little is known for certain about the early history of the chamber itself. It dates probably as far back as the construction of Solomon's Temple ... According to Josephus, it was in existence and was used as a place of refuge by the Jews at the time of the conquest of Jerusalem by Titus in the year 70 A.D."[6]

More authoritatively, the Koran—the holy book of Islam—describes Solomon's construction of the First Temple (34:13) and recounts the destruction of the First and Second Temples (17:7).

The Jewish connection to the Temple Mount dates back more than 3,000 years and is rooted in tradition and history. When Abraham bound his son Isaac upon an altar as a sacrifice to God, he is believed to have done so atop Mount Moriah, today's Temple Mount. The First Temple's Holy of Holies contained the original Ark of the Covenant, and both the First and Second Temples were the centers of Jewish religious and social life until the Second Temple's destruction by the Romans. After the destruction of the Second Temple, control of the Temple Mount passed through several conquering powers. It was during the early period of Muslim control, in the Seventh Century, that the Dome of the Rock was built on the site of the ancient temples.

MYTH

"Jerusalem need not be the capital of Israel."

FACT

Ever since King David made Jerusalem the capital of Israel more than 3,000 years ago, the city has played a central role in Jewish existence. The Temple Mount in the Old City is the object of Jewish veneration and the focus of Jewish prayer. Three times a day, for thousands of years, Jews have prayed "To Jerusalem, thy city, shall we return with joy," and have repeated the Psalmist's oath: "If I forget thee, O Jerusalem, let my right hand forget her cunning."

> *"For three thousand years, Jerusalem has been the center of Jewish hope and longing. No other city has played such a dominant role in the history, culture, religion and consciousness of a people as has Jerusalem in the life of Jewry and Judaism. Throughout centuries of exile, Jerusalem remained alive in the hearts of Jews everywhere as the focal point of Jewish history, the symbol of ancient glory, spiritual fulfillment and modern renewal. This heart and soul of the Jewish people engenders the thought that if you want one simple word to symbolize all of Jewish history, that word would be 'Jerusalem.'"*
>
> **—Teddy Kollek[7]**

MYTH

"Unlike the Jews, the Arabs were willing to accept the internationalization of Jerusalem."

FACT

When the United Nations took up the Palestine question in 1947, it recommended that all of Jerusalem be internationalized. The Vatican and many predominantly Catholic delegations pushed for this status, but a key reason for the UN decision was the Soviet Bloc's desire to embarrass Transjordan's King Abdullah and his British patrons by denying Abdullah control of the city.

The Jewish Agency, after much soul-searching, agreed to accept internationalization in the hope that in the short-run it would protect the city from bloodshed and the new state from conflict. Since the partition resolution called for a referendum on the city's status after 10 years, and Jews comprised a substantial majority, the expectation was that the city would later be incorporated into Israel. The Arab states were as bitterly opposed to the internationalization of Jerusalem as they were to the rest of the partition plan.

In May 1948, Jordan invaded and occupied East Jerusalem, dividing the city for the first time in its history, and driving thousands of Jews—whose families had lived in the city for centuries—into exile. The UN partition plan, including its proposal that Jerusalem be internationalized, was overtaken by events.

"You ought to let the Jews have Jerusalem; it was they who made it famous."

—Winston Churchill[8]

MYTH

"Internationalization is the best solution to resolve the conflicting claims over Jerusalem."

FACT

The seeming intractability of resolving the conflicting claims to Jerusalem has led some people to resurrect the idea of internationalizing the city. Curiously, the idea had little support during the 19 years Jordan controlled the Old City and barred Jews and Israeli Muslims from their holy sites.

The fact that Jerusalem is disputed, or that it is of importance to people other than Israeli Jews, does not mean the city belongs to others or should be ruled by some international regime. There is no precedent for such a setup. The closest thing to an international city was post-war Berlin when the four powers shared control of the city, and that experiment proved to be a disaster.

Even if Israel were amenable to such an idea, what conceivable international group could be entrusted to protect the freedoms Israel already guarantees? Surely not the United Nations, which has shown no understanding of Israeli concerns since partition. Israel can count only on the support of the United States, and it is only in the UN Security Council that an American veto can protect Israel from political mischief by other nations.

MYTH

While in control of Jerusalem, Jordan ensured freedom of worship for all religions."

FACT

From 1948-67, Jerusalem was divided between Israel and Jordan. Israel made western Jerusalem its capital; Jordan occupied the eastern section. Because Jordan maintained a state of war with Israel, the city became, in essence, two armed camps, replete with concrete walls and bunkers, barbed-wire fences, minefields and other military fortifications.

Under paragraph eight of the 1949 Armistice Agreement, Jordan and Israel were to establish committees to arrange the resumption of the normal functioning of cultural and humanitarian institutions on Mt. Scopus, use of the cemetery on the Mount of Olives, and free access to holy places and cultural institutions. Jordan violated the agreement, however, and denied Israelis access to the Western Wall and to the cemetery on the Mount of Olives, where Jews have buried their dead for more than 2,500 years.

Under Jordanian rule, "Israeli Christians were subjected to various restrictions during their seasonal pilgrimages to their holy places" in Jerusalem, noted Teddy Kollek. "Only limited numbers were grudgingly permitted to briefly visit the Old City and Bethlehem at Christmas and Easter."[9]

In 1955 and 1964, Jordan passed laws imposing strict government control on Christian schools, including restrictions on the opening of new schools, state control over school finances and appointment of teachers and the requirements that the Koran be taught. In 1953 and 1965, Jordan adopted laws abrogating the right of Christian religious and charitable institutions to acquire real estate in Jerusalem.

In 1958, police seized the Armenian Patriarch-elect and deported him from Jordan, paving the way for the election of a patriarch supported by King Hussein's government. Because of these repressive policies, many Christians emigrated from Jerusalem. Their numbers declined from 25,000 in 1949 to fewer than 13,000 in June 1967.[10]

These discriminatory laws were abolished by Israel after the city was reunited in 1967.

MYTH

"Jordan safeguarded Jewish holy places."

FACT

Jordan desecrated Jewish holy places during its occupation in 1948-67. King Hussein permitted the construction of a road to the Intercontinental Hotel across the Mount of Olives cemetery. Hundreds of Jewish graves were destroyed by a highway that could have easily been built elsewhere. The gravestones, honoring the memory of rabbis and sages, were used by the engineer corps of the Jordanian Arab Legion as pavement and latrines in army camps (inscriptions on the stones were still visible when Israel liberated the city).

The ancient Jewish Quarter of the Old City was ravaged, 58 Jerusalem synagogues—some centuries old—were destroyed or ruined, others were turned into stables and chicken coops. Slum dwellings were built abutting the Western Wall.[11]

MYTH

"Under Israeli rule, religious freedom has been curbed in Jerusalem."

FACT

After the 1967 war, Israel abolished all the discriminatory laws promulgated by Jordan and adopted its own tough standard for safeguarding access to religious shrines. "Whoever does anything that is likely to violate the freedom of access of the members of the various religions to the places sacred to them," Israeli law stipulates, is "liable to imprisonment for a term of five years." Israel also entrusted administration of the holy places to their respective religious authorities. Thus, for example, the Muslim Waqf has responsibility for the mosques on the Temple Mount.

The State Department notes that Israeli law provides for freedom of worship, and the Government respects this right.[12]

"I also respect the fact that Israel allows for a multifaith climate in which every Friday a thousand Muslims pray openly on the Temple Mount in Jerusalem. When I saw that, I had to ask myself, where in the Islamic world can 1,000 Jews get together and pray in full public view?"

—Muslim author Irshad Manji[13]

MYTH

"Israel denies Muslims and Christians free access to their holy sites."

FACT

Since 1967, hundreds of thousands of Muslims and Christians—many from Arab countries that remain in a state of war with Israel—have come to Jerusalem to see their holy places.

According to Islam, the prophet Muhammad was miraculously transported from Mecca to Jerusalem, and it was from there that he made his ascent to heaven. The Dome of the Rock and the al-Aqsa Mosque, both built in the seventh century, made definitive the identification of Jerusalem as the "Remote Place" that is mentioned in the Koran, and thus a holy place after Mecca and Medina. Muslim rights on the Temple Mount, the site of the two shrines, have not been infringed.

"There is only one Jerusalem. From our perspective, Jerusalem is not a subject for compromise. Jerusalem was ours, will be ours, is ours and will remain as such forever."

—Prime Minister Yitzhak Rabin[14]

After reuniting Jerusalem during the Six-Day War, Defense Minister Moshe Dayan permitted the Islamic authority, the Waqf, to continue its civil authority on the Temple Mount even though it is part of the holiest site in Judaism. The Waqf oversees all day-to-day activity there. An Israeli presence is in place at the entrance to the Temple Mount to ensure access for people of all religions.

Arab leaders are free to visit Jerusalem to pray, just as Egyptian President Anwar Sadat did at the al-Aqsa mosque in 1977. For security reasons, restrictions are sometimes temporarily imposed on the Temple Mount, but the right to worship has never been abridged, and other mosques remain accessible even in times of high tension.

For Christians, Jerusalem is the place where Jesus lived, preached, died and was resurrected. While it is the heavenly rather than the earthly Jerusalem that is emphasized by the Church, places mentioned in the New Testament as the sites of Jesus' ministry have drawn pilgrims and devoted worshipers for centuries. Among these sites are the Church of the Holy Sepulcher, the Garden of Gethsemane, the site of the Last Supper, and the Via Dolorosa with the fourteen Stations of the Cross.

The rights of the various Christian churches to custody of the Christian holy places in Jerusalem were defined in the course of the nineteenth century, when Jerusalem was part of the Ottoman Empire. Known as the "status quo arrangement for the Christian holy places in Jerusalem," these rights remained in force during the period of the British Mandate and are still upheld today in Israel.

MYTH

"Israel has refused to discuss a compromise on the future of Jerusalem."

FACT

Jerusalem was never the capital of any Arab entity. Palestinians have no special claim to the city; they simply demand it as their capital. Nevertheless, Israel has recognized that the city has a large Palestinian population, that the city is important to Muslims, and that making concessions on the sovereignty of the city might help minimize the conflict with the Palestinians. The Palestinians, however, have shown no reciprocal appreciation for the Jewish majority in the city, the significance of Jerusalem to the Jewish people or the fact that it is already the nation's capital.

The Israeli-Palestinian Declaration of Principles (DoP) signed in 1993 left open the status of Jerusalem. Article V said only that Jerusalem is one of the issues to be discussed in the permanent status negotiations.

> *"Anyone who relinquishes a single inch of Jerusalem is neither an Arab nor a Muslim."*
>
> **—Yasser Arafat**[15]

Most Israelis oppose dividing Jerusalem; still, efforts have been made to find some compromise that could satisfy Palestinian interests. For example, while the Labor Party was in power, Knesset Member Yossi Beilin reportedly reached a tentative agreement that would allow the Palestinians to claim the city as their capital without Israel sacrificing sovereignty over its capital. Beilin's idea was to allow the Palestinians to set up their capital in a West Bank suburb of Jerusalem—Abu Dis. The PA subsequently constructed a building for its parliament in the city.

Prime Minister Ehud Barak offered dramatic concessions that would have allowed the Arab neighborhoods of East Jerusalem to become the capital of a Palestinian state, and given the Palestinians control over the Muslim holy places on the Temple Mount. These ideas were discussed at the White House Summit in December 2000, but rejected by Yasser Arafat.

In 2008, Prime Minister Ehud Olmert offered a peace plan that included the partitioning of Jerusalem on a demographic basis. Abbas rejected the offer.

MYTH

"Israel has restricted the political rights of Palestinian Arabs in Jerusalem."

FACT

Along with religious freedom, Palestinian Arabs in Jerusalem have unprecedented political rights. Arab residents were given the choice of whether to become Israeli citizens. Most chose to retain their Jordanian citizenship. Moreover, regardless of whether they are citizens, Jerusalem Arabs are permitted to vote in municipal elections and play a role in the administration of the city.

> *"I'll urge the Muslims to launch jihad and to use all their capabilities to restore Muslim Palestine and the holy al-Aqsa mosque from the Zionist usurpers and aggressors. The Muslims must be united in the confrontation of the Jews and those who support them."*
>
> **—Saudi King Fahd**[16]

MYTH

"Under UN Resolution 242, East Jerusalem is considered 'occupied territory.'"

FACT

One drafter of the UN Resolution was then-U.S. Ambassador to the UN Arthur Goldberg. According to Goldberg, "Resolution 242 in no way refers to Jerusalem, and this omission was deliberate.... Jerusalem was a discrete matter, not linked to the West Bank." In several speeches at the UN in 1967, Goldberg said: "I repeatedly stated that the armistice lines of 1948 were intended to be temporary. This, of course, was particularly true of Jerusalem. At no time in these many speeches did I refer to East Jerusalem as occupied territory."[17]

Because Israel was defending itself from aggression in the 1948 and 1967 wars, former President of the International Court of Justice Steven Schwebel wrote, it has a better claim to sovereignty over Jerusalem than its Arab neighbors.[18]

MYTH

"East Jerusalem should be part of a Palestinian state because all its residents are Palestinian Arabs and no Jews have ever lived there."

FACT

Before 1865, the entire population of Jerusalem lived behind the Old City walls (what today would be considered part of the eastern part of the city). Later, the city began to expand beyond the walls because of population growth, and both Jews and Arabs began to build in new areas of the city.

By the time of partition, a thriving Jewish community was living in the eastern part of Jerusalem, an area that included the Jewish Quarter of the Old City. This area of the city also contains many sites of importance to the Jewish religion, including the City of David, the Temple Mount and the Western Wall. In addition, major institutions such as Hebrew University and the original Hadassah Hospital are on Mount Scopus—in eastern Jerusalem.

The only time that the eastern part of Jerusalem was exclusively Arab was between 1949 and 1967, and that was because Jordan occupied the area and forcibly expelled all the Jews.

> *"The basis of our position remains that Jerusalem must never again be a divided city. We did not approve of the status quo before 1967; in no way do we advocate a return to it now."*
>
> **—President George Bush**[19]

MYTH

"The United States does not recognize Jerusalem as Israel's capital."

FACT

Of the 190 nations with which America has diplomatic relations, Israel is the only one whose capital is not recognized by the U.S. government. The U.S. embassy, like most others, is in Tel Aviv, 40 miles from Jerusalem. The United States does maintain a consulate in East Jerusalem, however, that deals with Palestinians in the territories and works independently of the embassy, reporting directly to Washington. Today, then, we have the anomaly that American diplomats refuse to meet with Israelis in their capital because Jerusalem's status is negotiable, but make their contacts with Palestinians in the city.

In 1990, Congress passed a resolution declaring that "Jerusalem is and should remain the capital of the State of Israel" and "must remain an undivided city in which the rights of every ethnic and religious group are protected." During the 1992 presidential campaign, Bill Clinton said: "I recognize Jerusalem as an undivided city, the eternal capital of Israel, and I believe in the principle of moving our embassy to Jerusalem." He never reiterated this view as president; consequently, official U.S. policy remained that the status of Jerusalem is a matter for negotiations.

In an effort to change this policy, Congress overwhelmingly passed The Jerusalem Embassy Act of 1995. This landmark bill declared that, as a statement of official U.S. policy, Jerusalem should be recognized as the undivided, eternal capital of Israel and required that the U.S. embassy in Israel be established in Jerusalem no later than May 1999. The law also included a waiver that allowed the president to essentially ignore the legislation if he deemed doing so to be in the best interest of the United States. President Clinton exercised that option.

"I would be blind to disclaim the Jewish connection to Jerusalem."

—Sari Nusseibeh, President of Al Quds University[20]

During the 2000 presidential campaign George W. Bush promised that as President he would immediately "begin the process of moving the United States ambassador to the city Israel has chosen as its capital."[21] As President, however, Bush followed Clinton's precedent and repeatedly used the presidential waiver to prevent the embassy from being moved. Since coming to office in 2008, President Obama has continued the policy of his predecessors.

While critics of congressional efforts to force the administration to recognize Jerusalem as Israel's capital insist that such a move would harm the peace process, supporters of the legislation argue the opposite is true. By making clear the United States position that Jerusalem should remain unified under Israeli sovereignty, unrealistic Palestinian expectations regarding the city can be moderated and thereby enhance the prospects for a final agreement.

MYTH

"Palestinians have been careful to preserve the archaeological relics of the Temple Mount."

FACT

Though it has refused to recognize Israeli sovereignty over the Temple Mount, the Waqf cooperated with Israeli inspectors when conducting work on the holy site. After the 1993 Oslo accords, however, the Jordanian-controlled Waqf was replaced with representatives beholden to the Palestinian Authority. Following the riots that accompanied Israel's decision to open an exit from the Western Wall tunnel, the Waqf ceased cooperating with Israel.

The Waqf has subsequently prevented Israeli inspectors from overseeing work done on the Mount that has caused irreparable damage to archaeological remains from the First and Second Temple periods.

Israeli archaeologists found that during extensive construction work, thousands of tons of gravel--which contained important relics--was removed from the Mount and discarded in the trash. Experts say that even the artifacts that were not destroyed were rendered archaeologically useless because the Palestinian construction workers mixed finds from diverse periods when they scooped up earth with bulldozers.[22]

"They should be using a toothbrush, not a bulldozer."

—Dr. Gabriel Barkan on Palestinian excavations on the Temple Mount[23]

In August 2007, Israeli archaeologists discovered the Muslim authorities had begun fresh excavations on the Temple Mount to create a 500-foot trench for water pipes and electricity cables. By indiscriminately piling up earth and stones, Israeli officials say the Palestinians are once again harming a sensitive area. Archaeologists from the nonpartisan Committee Against the Destruction of Antiquities on the Temple Mount say the digging has damaged a wall that dates back to Second-Temple times and was likely part of the Temple courts.[24]

While an international protest was mounted when Israel began to renovate a bridge to the Temple Mount that caused no harm, the same people who expressed such great concern about the integrity of the site have remained silent while the Palestinians destroy priceless relics.

Given the sensitivity of the Temple Mount, and the tensions already existing between Israelis and Palestinians over Jerusalem, the Israeli government has not interfered in the Waqf's activities. Meanwhile, the destruction of the past continues.

"There was never a Jewish temple on Al-Aqsa [the mosque compound] and there is no proof that there was ever a temple."

—Former mufti of Jerusalem, Ikrema Sabri[25]

Notes

1. *Encounter*, (February 1968).
2. John Oesterreicher and Anne Sinai, eds., *Jerusalem*, (NY: John Day, 1974), p. 1; Israel Central Bureau of Statistics; Jerusalem Foundation; Municipality of Jerusalem; JTA, (May 20, 2009). Totals include those classified as "other."
3. Interview with Dennis Ross, Fox News Sunday, (April 21, 2002).
4. Sheik 'Ikrima Sabri, PA-appointed Mufti of Jerusalem, Interviewed by German magazine *Die Welt*, (January 17, 2001), [Trans. MEMRI].
5. Leon and Jill Uris, *Jerusalem*, (New York: Doubleday and Company, 1981), p. 13.
6. "A Brief Guide to the Haram al-Sharif, Jerusalem," Supreme Muslim Council, (1925).

7. Teddy Kollek, *Jerusalem,* (DC: Washington Institute For Near East Policy, 1990), pp. 19-20.
8. Sir Eveyln Shuckburgh, *Descent to Suez; Diaries 1951-56,* (London, 1986).
9. Kollek, p. 15.
10. Kollek, p. 16.
11. Kollek, p. 15.
12. "2010 Report on International Religious Freedom," Released by the Bureau for Democracy, Human Rights, and Labor, U.S. Department of State, (Washington, D.C., November 17, 2010).
13. Pearl Sheffy Gefen, "Irshad Manji, Muslim Refusenik," *Lifestyles Magazine,* (Summer 2004), p. 29.
14. Jerusalem Day Address to Knesset, (May 29, 1995).
15. Voice of Palestine, Algiers, (September 2, 1993).
16. Saudi Press Agency, (July 15, 1986).
17. *New York Times,* (March 12, 1980).
18. *American Journal of International Law,* (April 1970), pp. 346-47.
19. Letter from President George Bush to Jerusalem Mayor Teddy Kollek, (March 13, 1990).
20. *Jerusalem Post,* (November 12, 2001).
21. Speech to AIPAC Policy Conference, (May 22, 2000).
22. Jewish Telegraphic Agency, (February 13, 2001).
23. Martin Asser, "Israeli anger over holy site work," BBC News, (August 28, 2007).
24. Martin Asser, "Israeli anger over holy site work," BBC News, (August 28, 2007); Etgar Lefkovits, "Archaeologists: Muslim dig damaged Temple wall," *Jerusalem Post,* (August 31, 2007).
25. Mike Seid, "Western Wall was never part of temple," *Jerusalem Post,* (October 25, 2007).

16. U.S. Middle East Policy

MYTH

"The creation of Israel resulted solely from U.S. pressure."

FACT

When the UN took up the question of Palestine, President Harry Truman explicitly said the United States should not "use threats or improper pressure of any kind on other delegations."[1] Some pressure was nevertheless exerted and the U.S. played a key role in securing support for the partition resolution. U.S. influence was limited, however, as became clear when American dependents such as Cuba and Greece voted against partition, and El Salvador and Honduras abstained.

Many members of the Truman Administration opposed partition, including Defense Secretary James Forrestal, who believed Zionist aims posed a threat to American oil supplies and its strategic position in the region. The Joint Chiefs of Staff worried that the Arabs might align themselves with the Soviets if they were alienated by the West. These internal opponents tried to undermine U.S. support for the establishment of a Jewish state.[2]

Meanwhile, the Soviet Union also supported partition, the first foreign policy issue on which the soon to be Cold War rivals agreed.

Although much has been written about the tactics of the supporters of partition, the behavior of the Arab lobby has been largely ignored. Arab states and their supporters were, in fact, actively engaged in arm-twisting of their own at the UN trying to scuttle partition.[3]

MYTH

"The United States favored Israel over the Arabs in 1948 because of the Jewish lobby."

FACT

Truman supported the Zionist movement because he believed the international community was obligated to fulfill the promise of the Balfour Declaration and because he believed that ameliorating the plight of the Jewish survivors of the Holocaust was the humanitarian thing to do. A sense of his attitude can be gleaned from a remark he made with regard to negotiations as to the boundaries of a Jewish state:

The whole region waits to be developed, and if it were handled the way we developed the Tennessee River basin, it could support from 20 to 30 million people more. To open the door to this kind of future would indeed be the constructive and humanitarian thing to do, and it would also redeem the pledges that were given at the time of World War I.[4]

The American public supported the President's policy. According to public opinion polls, 65 percent of Americans supported the creation of a Jewish state.[5] This public support was reflected in Congress where a resolution approving the Balfour Declaration was adopted in 1922. In 1944, both national parties called for the restoration of the Jewish Commonwealth and, in 1945, a similar resolution was adopted by Congress.

Rather than giving in to pressure, Truman tended to react negatively to the "Jewish lobby." He complained repeatedly about being pressured and talked about putting propaganda from the Jews in a pile and striking a match to it. In a letter to Rep. Claude Pepper, Truman wrote: "Had it not been for the unwarranted interference of the Zionists, we would have had the matter settled a year and a half ago."[6] This was hardly the attitude of a politician overly concerned with Jewish votes.

MYTH

"The United States and Israel have nothing in common."

FACT

The U.S.-Israel relationship is based on the twin pillars of shared values and mutual interests. Given this commonality of interests and beliefs, it should not be surprising that support for Israel is one of the most pronounced and consistent foreign policy values of the American people.

Although Israel is geographically located in a region that is relatively undeveloped and closer to the Third World than the West, Israel has emerged in less than 60 years as an advanced nation with the characteristics of Western society. This is partially attributable to the fact that a high percentage of the population came from Europe or North America and brought with them Western political and cultural norms. It is also a function of the common Judeo-Christian heritage.

Simultaneously, Israel is a multicultural society with people from more than 100 nations. Today, nearly half of all Israelis are Eastern or Oriental Jews who trace their origins to the ancient Jewish communities of the Islamic countries of North Africa and the Middle East.

While they live in a region characterized by autocracies, Israelis have a commitment to democracy no less passionate than that of Americans. All citizens of Israel, regardless of race, religion or sex, are guaranteed equality before the law and full democratic rights. Freedom of speech, assembly and press is embodied in the country's laws and traditions. Israel's independent judiciary vigorously upholds these rights.

The political system does differ from America's—Israel's is a parliamentary democracy—but it is still based on free elections with divergent parties. And though Israel does not have a formal constitution, it has adopted "Basic Laws" that establish similar legal guarantees.

Americans have long viewed Israelis with admiration, at least partly because they see much of themselves in their pioneering spirit and struggle for independence. Like the United States, Israel is a nation of immigrants. Despite the burden of spending nearly one-fifth of its budget on defense, it has had an extraordinary rate of economic growth for most of its history. It has also succeeded in putting most of the newcomers to work. Some immigrants come from relatively undeveloped societies, such as Ethiopia or Yemen, and arrive with virtually no possessions, education or training and become productive contributors to Israeli society.

In the beginning, Israel had a mixed economy, combining capitalism with socialism along the British model. After experiencing serious economic difficulties, created largely in the aftermath of the 1973 Yom Kippur War by increased oil prices and the need to spend a disproportionate share of its Gross National Product on defense, Israel gradually adopted reforms that reduced the role of the state and shifted the country closer to the free market system of the United States. America has been a partner in this evolution.

The special relationship is also reflected in a variety of *shared value initiatives,* which cover a broad range of common interests, such as the environment, energy, space, education, occupational safety and health. More than 400 American institutions in 47 states, the District of Columbia and Puerto Rico have received funds from binational programs with Israel. Little-known relationships like the Free Trade Agreement, the Cooperative Development Research Program, the Middle East Regional Cooperation Program and various memoranda of understanding with virtually every U.S. governmental agency demonstrate the depth of the special relationship. Even more important may be the broad ties between Israel and each of the individual 50 states and the District of Columbia.

In the 1980's, attention increasingly focused on one pillar of the relationship—shared interests. The Reagan Administration saw the Soviet Union as a threat to American Middle East interests and Israel as a bulwark of democracy in the region. Reagan formally recognized Israel's role through agreements for strategic cooperation. After the end of the Cold War, Israel has continued to play a role in joint efforts to protect American interests, including close cooperation in the war on terror. Strategic cooperation has progressed to the point where a de facto alliance now exists and the United States knows it can count on Israel.

MYTH

"Most Americans oppose a close U.S. relationship with Israel."

FACT

Support for Israel is not restricted to the Jewish community. Americans of all ages, races and religions sympathize with Israel. This support is also nonpartisan, with a majority of Democrats and Republicans consistently favoring Israel by large margins over the Arabs.

The best indication of Americans' attitude toward Israel is found in the response to the most consistently asked question about the Middle East: "In the Middle East situation, are your sympathies more with Israel or with the Arab nations?"

In 82 Gallup polls, going back to 1967, Israel has had the support of an average of 47 percent of the American people compared to 12 percent for the Arab states/Palestinians. Americans have slightly more sympathy for the Palestinians than for the Arab states, but the results of polls asking respondents to choose between Israel and the Palestinians have not differed significantly from the other surveys.

> *"The allied nations with the fullest concurrence of our government and people are agreed that in Palestine shall be laid the foundations of a Jewish Commonwealth."*
>
> **—President Woodrow Wilson**[7]

Some people have the misperception that sympathy for Israel was once much higher, but the truth is that before the Gulf War the peak had been 56 percent, reached just after the Six-Day War. In January 1991, sympathy for Israel reached a record high of 64 percent, according to Gallup. Meanwhile, support for the Arabs dropped to 8 percent and the margin was a record 56 points.

The most recent poll, reported by Gallup in February 2011, found that, for the second year in a row, sympathy for Israel was a near record 63 percent compared to only 17 percent for the Palestinians. Despite the violence of the preceding years, and a steady stream of negative media coverage, this is seven points higher than the level of support Israel enjoyed after the 1967 War, when many people mistakenly believe that Israel was overwhelmingly popular.

Polls also indicate the public views Israel as a reliable U.S. ally. In a May 2011 CNN poll, for example, 82 percent of Americans said Israel is "friendly" or an "ally."[8]

MYTH

"U.S. policy has always been hostile toward the Arabs."

FACT

Arabs rarely acknowledge the American role in helping the Arab states achieve independence. President Wilson's stand for self-determination for all nations, and the U.S. entry into World War I, helped cause the dissolution of the Ottoman Empire and stimulate the move toward independence in the Arab world.

Arab leaders assert that Middle East policy must be a zero-sum game whereby support for their enemy, Israel, necessarily puts them at a disadvantage. Thus, Arab states have tried to force the United States to choose between support for them or Israel. The U.S. has usually refused to fall into this trap. The fact that the U.S. has a close alliance with Israel while maintaining good relations with several Arab states is proof the two are not incompatible.

The U.S. has long sought friendly relations with Arab leaders and has, at one time or another, been on good terms with most Arab states. In the 1930s, the discovery of oil led U.S. companies to become closely involved with the Gulf Arabs. In the 1950s, U.S. strategic objectives stimulated an effort to form an alliance with pro-Western Arab states. Countries such as Iraq and Libya were friends of the U.S. before radical leaders took over those governments. Egypt, which was hostile toward the U.S. under Nasser, shifted to the pro-Western camp under Sadat.

Since World War II, the U.S. has poured economic and military assistance into the region and today is the principal backer of nations such as Jordan, Saudi Arabia, Morocco, Egypt and the Gulf sheikdoms. Although the Arab states blamed the U.S. for their defeats in wars they initiated with Israel, the truth is most of the belligerents had either been given or offered American assistance at some time.[9]

MYTH

"The United States always supports Israel."

FACT

The United States has been Israel's closest ally throughout its history; nevertheless, the U.S. has acted against the Jewish State's wishes many times.

The U.S. effort to balance support for Israel with placating the Arabs began in 1948 when President Truman showed signs of wavering on partition and advocating trusteeship. After the surrounding Arab states invaded Israel, the U.S. maintained an arms embargo that severely restricted the Jews' ability to defend themselves.

Ever since the 1948 war, the U.S. has been unwilling to insist on projects to resettle Arab refugees. The U.S. has also been reluctant to challenge Arab violations of the UN Charter and resolutions. Thus, for example, the Arabs were permitted to get away with blockading the Suez Canal, imposing a boycott on Israel and committing acts of terrorism. In fact, the U.S. has taken positions against Israel at the UN more often than not, and did not use its Security Council veto to block an anti-Israel resolution until 1972.

Perhaps the most dramatic example of American policy diverging from that of Israel came during the Suez War when President Eisenhower took a strong stand against Britain, France and Israel. After the war, U.S. pressure forced Israel to withdraw from the territory it conquered. David Ben-Gurion relied on dubious American guarantees that sowed the seeds of the 1967 conflict.

At various other times, American presidents have taken action against Israel. In 1981, for example, Ronald Reagan suspended a strategic cooperation agreement after Israel annexed the Golan Heights. On another occasion, he held up delivery of fighter planes because of unhappiness over an Israeli raid in Lebanon.

In 1991, President Bush held a press conference to ask for a delay in considering Israel's request for loan guarantees to help absorb Soviet and Ethiopian Jews because of his disagreement with Israel's settlement policy. In staking his prestige on the delay, Bush used intemperate language that inflamed passions and provoked concern in the Jewish community that anti-Semitism would be aroused.

Though often described as the most pro-Israel president in history, Bill Clinton also was critical of Israel on numerous occasions. George W. Bush's administration was considered equally sympathetic, but also criticized Israel. During the first year of the Palestinian War, the U.S. imposed an arms embargo on spare parts for helicopters because of anger over the use of U.S.-made helicopters in targeted killings. The Bush Administration also punished Israel for agreeing to sell military equipment to China in 2005.[10]

In his first two years in office, Barack Obama was very critical of Israeli policy and publicly demanded a freeze in settlement construction. A number of other confrontations took place publicly and privately, along with reported threats of punitive measures if Israel did not accede to the president's insistence that settlements be frozen. As a consequence of his approach to Israel and broader Middle East policy, polls in Israel found unprecedented distrust of the president's commitment to Israel.[11]

MYTH

"The U.S. has always ensured Israel would have a qualitative military edge over the Arabs."

FACT

The United States provided only a limited amount of arms to Israel, including ammunition and recoilless rifles, prior to 1962. In that year, President Kennedy sold Israel HAWK anti-aircraft missiles, but only after the Soviet Union provided Egypt with long-range bombers.

By 1965, the U.S. had become Israel's main arms supplier. This was partially necessitated by West Germany's acquiescence to Arab pressure, which led Germany to stop selling tanks to Israel. Throughout most of the Johnson Administration, however, the sale of arms to Israel was balanced by corresponding transfers to the Arabs. Thus, the first U.S. tank sale to Israel, in 1965, was offset by a similar sale to Jordan.[12]

The U.S. did not provide Israel with aircraft until 1966. Even then, secret agreements were made to provide the same planes to Morocco and Libya, and additional military equipment was sent to Lebanon, Saudi Arabia and Tunisia.[13]

As in 1948, the U.S. imposed an arms embargo on Israel during the Six-Day War, while the Arabs continued to receive Soviet arms. Israel's position was further undermined by the French decision to embargo arms transfers to the Jewish State, effectively ending their role as Israel's only other major supplier.

It was only after it became clear that Israel had no other sources of arms, and that the Soviet Union had no interest in limiting its sales to the region, that President Johnson agreed to sell Israel Phantom jets that gave the Jewish State its first qualitative advantage. "We will henceforth become the principal arms supplier to Israel," Assistant Secretary of Defense Paul Warnke told Israeli Ambassador Yitzhak Rabin, "involving us even more intimately with Israel's security situation and involving more directly the security of the United States."[14]

From that point on, the U.S. began to pursue a policy whereby Israel's qualitative edge was maintained. The U.S. has also remained committed, however, to arming Arab nations, providing sophisticated missiles, tanks and aircraft to Jordan, Morocco, Egypt, Saudi Arabia and the Gulf states. Thus, when Israel received F-15s in 1978, so did Saudi Arabia (and Egypt received F-5Es). In 1981, Saudi Arabia, for the first time, received a weapons system that gave it a qualitative advantage over Israel—AWACS radar planes

Today, Israel buys near top-of-the-line U.S. equipment, but many Arab states also receive some of America's best tanks, planes and missiles. In addition to the quality of U.S. weapons sold to Arab states, the quantity also endangers Israel. In 2010, for example, President Obama agreed to the largest arms sale in U.S. history, a $60 billion transaction with Saudi Arabia. The qualitative edge may be intact, but it is undoubtedly narrow.

> *"Our society is illuminated by the spiritual insights of the Hebrew prophets. America and Israel have a common love of human freedom, and they have a common faith in a democratic way of life."*
>
> **—President Lyndon Johnson**[15]

MYTH

"U.S. aid to the Middle East has always been one-sided in favor of Israel."

FACT

After Israel's victory in its War of Independence, the U.S. responded to an appeal for economic aid to help absorb immigrants by approving a $135 million Export-Import Bank loan and the sale of surplus commodities. In those early years of Israel's statehood (also today), U.S. aid was seen as a means of promoting peace.

In 1951, Congress voted to help Israel cope with the economic burdens imposed by the influx of Jewish refugees from the displaced persons camps in Europe and from the ghettos of the Arab countries. Arabs then complained the U.S. was neglecting them, though they had no interest in or use for American aid then. In 1951, Syria rejected offers of U.S. aid. Oil-rich Iraq and Saudi Arabia did not need U.S. economic assistance (yet the Saudis did get aid and continue to get assistance), and Jordan was, until the late 1950s, the ward of Great Britain. After 1957, when the United States assumed responsibility for supporting Jordan and resumed economic aid to Egypt, assistance to the Arab states soared. Also, the United States was by far the biggest contributor of aid to the Palestinians through UNRWA, a status that continues to the present day.

Prior to 1971, Israel received a total of only $277 million in military aid, all in the form of loans as credit sales. The bulk of the economic aid was also lent to Israel. By comparison, the Arab states received nearly three times as much aid before 1971, $4.4 billion, or $170 million per year. Moreover, unlike Israel, which receives nearly all its aid from the United States, Arab nations have gotten assistance from Asia, Eastern Europe, the Soviet Union and the European Community.

Israel did not begin to receive large amounts of assistance until 1974, following the 1973 war, and the sums increased dramatically after the

Camp David agreements. Altogether, since 1949, Israel has received more than $100 billion in assistance. In 1998, Israel offered to voluntarily reduce its dependence on U.S. aid and over the next ten years economic assistance was gradually phased out. Arab states that have signed agreements with Israel have also been rewarded. Since signing the peace treaty with Israel, Egypt has been the second largest recipient of U.S. foreign aid ($1.6 billion in 2010 compared to Israel's $2.7 billion). Jordan has also been the beneficiary of higher levels of aid since it signed a treaty with Israel (increasing from less than $40 million to $693 million in 2010). The multibillion dollar debts to the U.S. of both Arab nations were also forgiven.

> *"It is my responsibility to see that our policy in Israel fits in with our policy throughout the world; second, it is my desire to help build in Palestine a strong, prosperous, free and independent democratic state. It must be large enough, free enough, and strong enough to make its people self-supporting and secure."*
>
> **—President Harry Truman**[16]

After the Oslo agreements, the United States also began providing aid to the Palestinians.

Since 1994, Palestinians have received more than $2.9 billion in U.S. economic assistance via USAID projects—more than from any other donor country. In 2010, alone, financial aid exceeded $500 million.[17] More than 60 percent of the PA's GNP comes from U.S., European Union, UN, and World Bank funds. The PA receives an average of $1,000 per year for every Palestinian citizen from foreign sources.[18]

MYTH

"Israel doesn't need U.S. military assistance."

FACT

Israel has peace treaties with only two of its neighbors and the long-term policies of both toward Israel came into question during the "Arab spring" of 2011. The relationship with Egypt, in particular, is a matter of grave concern and will not be clarified until that country's political future is determined. Israel remains technically at war with the rest of the Arab/Islamic world, and several countries, notably Iran, are openly hostile. Given the potential threats, it is a necessity that Israel continue to maintain a strong defense.

As the arms balance chart in the Appendix indicates, Israel faces formidable enemies that could band together, as they have in the past, to threaten its security. It must, therefore, rely on its qualitative advantage to ensure it can defeat its enemies, and that can only be guaranteed by the continued purchase of the latest weapons. New tanks, missiles and planes carry high price tags, however, and Israel cannot afford what it needs on its own, so continued aid from the United States is vital to its security. Furthermore, Israel's enemies have numerous suppliers, but Israel must rely almost entirely on the United States for its hardware.

MYTH

"U.S. military aid subsidizes Israeli defense contractors at the expense of American industry."

FACT

Contrary to popular wisdom, the United States does not simply write billion dollar checks and hand them over to Israel to spend as they like. Only about 25 percent ($694 million of $2.775 billion in 2010) of what Israel receives in Foreign Military Financing (FMF) can be spent in Israel for military procurement. The remaining 75 percent is spent in the United States to generate profits and jobs. More than 1,000 companies in 47 states, the District of Columbia and Puerto Rico have signed contracts worth billions of dollars through this program over the last several years. The figures for 2010 are below:

The Value of Foreign Military Financing (FMF) Orders by State[19]

State	Value	State	Value
Alaska	$81,884.00	North Carolina	$8,143,528.02
Alabama	$2,241,523.00	North Dakota	$26,667.86
Arizona	$1,359,066.57	Nebraska	$26,667.86
California	$80,782,623.39	New Hampshire	$727,728.06
Colorado	$4,420,057.78	New Jersey	$44,176,250.96
Connecticut	$55,398,227.73	New York	$122,134,683.57
Delaware	$2,999,956.00	Ohio	$56,254,350.76
Florida	$75,217,283.80	Oklahoma	$2,033,022.52
Georgia	$22,848,592.34	Oregon	$1,011,213.04
Idaho	$3,952.00	Pennsylvania	$31,387,255.97
Iowa	$88,325.00	Puerto Rico	$33,431,580.00
Illinois	$123,136,963.87	Rhode Island	$2,130,542.00

Indiana	$596,482.95	South Carolina	$1,644,744.60
Kansas	$1,515,384.01	South Dakota	$1,929,860.00
Kentucky	$11,742,942.40	Tennessee	$2,101,734.17
Maine	$84,943.65	Texas	$43,485,376.89
Massachusetts	$23,490,440.12	Utah	$2,423,987.00
Maryland	$14,932,369.99	Virginia	$40,811,567.05
Michigan	$146,415,041.21	Vermont	$36,052.00
Minnesota	$6,384,437.05	Washington	$876,112.95
Missouri	$3,783,341.69	Wisconsin	$3,322,258.72
Mississippi	$170,526.91		

MYTH

"Israel has no strategic value to the United States."

FACT

In 1952, Gen. Omar Bradley, head of the Joint Chiefs of Staff, believed the West required 19 divisions to defend the Middle East and that Israel could supply two. He also expected only three states to provide the West air power in Middle Eastern defense by 1955: Great Britain, Turkey and Israel. Bradley's analysis was rejected because the political echelon decided it was more important for the United States to work with Egypt, and later Iraq. It was feared that integration of Israeli forces in Western strategy would alienate the Arabs.[20]

After trying unsuccessfully to build an alliance with Arab states, the National Security Council Planning Board concluded in 1958: "if we choose to combat radical Arab nationalism and to hold Persian Gulf oil by force if necessary, then a logical corollary would be to support Israel as the only pro-West power left in the Near East."[21]

Israel's crushing victory over the combined Arab forces in 1967 reinforced this view. The following year, the United States sold Israel sophisticated planes (Phantom jets) for the first time. Washington shifted its Middle East policy from seeking a balance of forces to ensuring that Israel enjoyed a qualitative edge over its enemies.

Israel proved its value in 1970 when the United States asked for help in bolstering King Hussein's regime. Israel's willingness to aid Amman, and movement of troops to the Jordanian border, persuaded Syria to withdraw the tanks it had sent into Jordan to support PLO forces challenging the king during "Black September."[22]

By the early 1970s it was clear that no Arab state could or would contribute to Western defense in the Middle East. The Baghdad Pact had long ago expired, and the regimes friendly to the United States were weak compared to the anti-Western forces in Egypt, Syria and Iraq. Even after Egypt's reorientation following the signing of its peace treaty with Israel, the United States did not count on any Arab governments for military assistance.

The Carter Administration began to implement a form of strategic cooperation (it was not referred to as such) by making Israel eligible to sell military equipment to the United States. The willingness to engage in limited, joint military endeavors was viewed by President Carter as a means of rewarding Israel for "good behavior" in peace talks with Egypt.

Though still reluctant to formalize the relationship, strategic cooperation became a major focus of the U.S.-Israel relationship when Ronald Reagan entered office. Before his election, Reagan had written: "Only by full appreciation of the critical role the State of Israel plays in our strategic calculus can we build the foundation for thwarting Moscow's designs on territories and resources vital to our security and our national well-being."[23]

Reagan's view culminated in the November 30, 1981, signing of a Memorandum of Understanding on "strategic cooperation." On November 29, 1983, a new agreement was signed creating the Joint Political-Military Group (JPMG) and a group to oversee security assistance, the Joint Security Assistance Planning Group (JSAP).

In 1987, Congress designated Israel as a major non-NATO ally. This law formally established Israel as an ally, and allowed its industries to compete equally with NATO countries and other close U.S. allies for contracts to produce a significant number of defense items.

"Since the rebirth of the State of Israel, there has been an ironclad bond between that democracy and this one."

—President Ronald Reagan[24]

In April 1988, President Reagan signed another MOU encompassing all prior agreements. This agreement institutionalized the strategic relationship.

By the end of Reagan's term, the U.S. had prepositioned equipment in Israel, regularly held joint training exercises, began co-development of the Arrow Anti-Tactical Ballistic Missile and was engaged in a host of other cooperative military endeavors. Since then, U.S.-Israel strategic cooperation has continued to evolve. Israel now regularly engages in joint training exercises with U.S. forces and, in 2005, for the first time, also trained and exercised with NATO forces.

In 2007, the United States and Israel signed a new MOU formalizing cooperation in the area of homeland security. Even before that, Israel routinely hosted U.S. law enforcement officers and first responders to share knowledge about prevention of terror attacks and response to emergencies.

Today, strategic ties are stronger than ever and Israel has become a de facto ally of the United States. America purchases innovative and advanced Israeli weapons systems, works together with Israeli companies on missile defense, and shares intelligence. Most important, Israel remains America's only reliable democratic ally in the region.

MYTH

"U.S. dependence on Arab oil has decreased over the years."

FACT

In 1973, the Arab oil embargo dealt the U.S. economy a major blow. This, combined with OPEC's subsequent price hikes and a growing American dependence on foreign oil, triggered the recession in the early seventies.

In 1973, foreign oil accounted for 35 percent of total U.S. oil demand. By 2010, the figure had risen to 63 percent, and Arab OPEC countries accounted for 22 percent of 2010 U.S. imports (with non-Arab OPEC countries Angola, Venezuela, Ecuador and Nigeria the figure is 42 percent). Saudi Arabia ranked number three and Algeria (#6), Iraq (#7), and Kuwait (#13) were among the top 15 suppliers of petroleum products to the United States in 2010. The Persian Gulf states alone supplied nearly 15 percent of U.S. petroleum imports in 2010.[25]

The growing reliance on imported oil has also made the U.S. economy even more vulnerable to price jumps, as occurred in 1979, 1981, 1982, 1990, 2000, 2005, 2007/8 and 2011. Oil price increases have also allowed Arab oil-producers to generate tremendous revenues at the expense of American consumers. These profits have subsidized large weapons purchases and nonconventional weapons programs such as Iran's.

America's dependence on Arab oil has occasionally raised the specter of a renewed attempt to blackmail the United States to abandon its support for Israel. The good news for Americans is that the top two suppliers of U.S. oil today—Canada and Mexico—are more reliable and better allies than the Persian Gulf nations.

MYTH

"The attacks on 9/11 were a consequence of U.S. support for Israel."

FACT

The heinous attacks against the United States were committed by Muslim fanatics who had a variety of motivations for these and other terrorist attacks. These Muslims have a perverted interpretation of Islam and believe they must attack infidels, particularly Americans and Jews, who do not share their beliefs. They oppose Western culture and democracy and object to any U.S. presence in Muslim nations. They are particularly angered by the existence of American military bases in Saudi Arabia and other areas of the Persian Gulf. This would be true regardless of U.S. policy toward the Israeli-Palestinian conflict. Nevertheless, an added excuse for their fanaticism is the fact that the United States is allied with Israel. Previous attacks on American targets, such as the *USS Cole* in 2000, and U.S. embassies in Kenya and Tanzania in 1998, were perpetrated by suicide bombers whose anger at the United States was unrelated to Israel.

> *"Osama bin Laden made his explosions and then started talking about the Palestinians. He never talked about them before."*
>
> **—Egyptian President Hosni Mubarak**[26]

Osama bin Laden claimed he was acting on behalf of the Palestinians, and that his anger toward the United States was shaped by American support for Israel. This was a new invention by bin Laden clearly intended to attract support from the Arab public and justify his terrorist acts. Bin Laden's antipathy toward the United States has never been related to the Arab-Israeli conflict. Though many Arabs were fooled by bin Laden's transparent effort to drag Israel into his war, Dr. Abd Al-Hamid Al-Ansari, dean of Shar'ia and Law at Qatar University was critical, "In their hypocrisy, many of the [Arab] intellectuals linked September 11 with the Palestinian problem—something that completely contradicts seven years of Al-Qaida literature. Al-Qaida never linked anything to Palestine."[27]

Even Yasser Arafat told the *Sunday Times* of London that bin Laden should stop hiding behind the Palestinian cause. Bin Laden "never helped us, he was working in another completely different area and against our interests," Arafat said.[28]

Though Al-Qaida's agenda did not include the Palestinian cause, the organization began to take a more active role in terror against Israeli targets, starting with the November 28, 2002, suicide bombing at an Israeli-owned hotel in Kenya that killed three Israelis and 11 Kenyans, and the attempt to shoot down an Israeli airliner with a missile as it was taking off from Kenya that same day.[29] In 2005, Al-Qaida also claimed responsibility for firing three rockets from Lebanon into the northern Israeli city of Kiryat Shmona.[30]

MYTH

"Groups such as Hezbollah, Islamic Jihad and Hamas are freedom fighters."

FACT

When the United States declared a war on terrorists and the nations that harbor them after September 11, Arab states and their sympathizers argued that many of the organizations that engage in violent actions against Americans and Israelis should not be targets of the new American war because they are "freedom fighters" rather than terrorists. This has been the mantra of the terrorists themselves, who claim that their actions are legitimate forms of resistance against the "Israeli occupation."

This argument is deeply flawed. First, the enemies of Israel rationalize any attacks as legitimate because of real and imagined sins committed by Jews since the beginning of the 20th century. Consequently, the Arab bloc and its supporters at the United Nations have succeeded in preventing the condemnation of any terrorist attack against Israel. Instead, they routinely sponsor resolutions criticizing Israel when it retaliates.

> *"You can't say there are good terrorists and there are bad terrorists."*
>
> **—U.S. National Security Adviser Condoleezza Rice**[31]

Second, nowhere else in the world is the murder of innocent men, women and children considered a "legitimate form of resistance." The long list of heinous crimes includes snipers shooting infants, suicide bombers blowing up pizzerias and discos, hijackers taking and killing hostages, and infiltrators murdering Olympic athletes. Hezbollah, Islamic Jihad, Hamas, and a number of other groups, mostly Palestinian, have engaged in these activities for decades and rarely been condemned or their members brought to justice. All of them qualify as terrorist groups according to the U.S. government's own definition—"Terrorism is the unlawful use of force or violence against persons or property to intimidate or coerce a government, the civilian population, or any segment thereof, in furtherance of political or social objectives"[32]—and therefore should be targets of U.S. efforts to cut off their funding, to root out their leaders and to bring them to justice.

In the case of the Palestinian groups, there is no mystery as to who the leaders are, where their funding comes from and which nations harbor them. American charitable organizations have been linked to funding some of these groups and Saudi Arabia, Syria, Lebanon, Iraq, Iran and the Palestinian Authority all shelter and/or financially and logistically support them.

MYTH

"The United States must be 'engaged' to advance the peace process."

FACT

The European Union, Russia, and the UN all have pursued largely one-sided policies in the Middle East detrimental to Israel, which has disqualified them as honest brokers. The United States is the only country that has the trust of both the Israelis and the Arabs and is therefore the only third party that can play a constructive role in the peace process. This has led many people to call for greater involvement by the Obama Administration in negotiations. While the United States can play a valuable role as a mediator, history shows that American peace initiatives have never succeeded, and that it is the parties themselves who must resolve their differences.

The Eisenhower Administration tried to ease tensions by proposing the joint Arab-Israeli use of the Jordan River. The plan would have helped the Arab refugees by producing more irrigated land and would have reduced Israel's need for more water resources. Israel cautiously accepted the plan, the Arab League rejected it.

President Johnson outlined five principles for peace. "The first and greatest principle," Johnson said, "is that every nation in the area has a fundamental right to live and to have this right respected by its neighbors." The Arab response came a few weeks later: "no peace with Israel, no recognition of Israel, no negotiations with it. . . ."

President Nixon's Secretary of State, William Rogers, offered a plan that sought to "balance" U.S. policy, but leaned on the Israelis to withdraw to the pre-1967 borders, to accept many Palestinian refugees, and to allow Jordan a role in Jerusalem. The plan was totally unacceptable to Israel and, even though it tilted toward the Arab position, was rejected by the Arabs as well.

President Ford's Secretary of State, Henry Kissinger, had a little more success in his shuttle diplomacy, arranging the disengagement of forces after the 1973 war, but he never put forward a peace plan, and failed to move the parties beyond the cessation of hostilities to the formalization of peace.

Jimmy Carter was the model for presidential engagement in the conflict. He wanted an international conference at Geneva to produce a comprehensive peace. While Carter spun his wheels trying to organize a conference, Egyptian President Anwar Sadat decided to bypass the Americans and go directly to the Israeli people and address the Knesset. Despite revisionist history by Carter's former advisers, the Israeli-Egyptian peace agreement was negotiated largely *despite* Carter. Menachem Begin and Sadat had carried on secret contacts long before Camp David and had reached the basis for an agreement before Carter's intervention. Carter's mediation helped seal the treaty, but Sadat's decision to go to Jerusalem was stimulated largely by his conviction that Carter's policies were misguided.

In 1982, President Reagan announced a surprise peace initiative that called for allowing the Palestinians self-rule in the territories in association with Jordan. The plan rejected both Israeli annexation and the creation of a Palestinian state. Israel denounced the plan as endangering Israeli security. The plan had been formulated largely to pacify the Arab states, which had been angered by the expulsion of the PLO from Beirut, but they also rejected the Reagan Plan.

George Bush's Administration succeeded in convening a historic regional conference in Madrid in 1991, but it ended without any agreements and the multilateral tracks that were supposed to settle some of the more contentious issues rarely met and failed to resolve anything. Moreover, Bush's perceived hostility toward Israel eroded trust and made it difficult to convince Israelis to take risks for peace.

> *"The United States was the first country to recognize Israel in 1948, minutes after its declaration of independence, and the deep bonds of friendship between the U.S. and Israel remain as strong and as unshakeable as ever."*
>
> **—President Barack Obama**[33]

President Clinton barely had time to get his vision of peace together when he discovered the Israelis had secretly negotiated an agreement with the Palestinians in Oslo. The United States had nothing to do with the breakthrough at Oslo and very little influence on the immediate aftermath. In fact, the peace process became increasingly muddled as the United States got more involved.

Peace with Jordan also required no real American involvement. The Israelis and Jordanians already were agreed on the main terms of peace, and the main obstacle had been King Hussein's unwillingness to sign a treaty before Israel had reached an agreement with the Palestinians. After Oslo, he felt safe to move forward and no American plan was needed.

In a last ditch effort to save his presidential legacy, Clinton put forward a peace plan to establish a Palestinian state. Again, it was Prime Minister Ehud Barak's willingness to offer dramatic concessions that raised the prospects for an agreement rather than the president's initiative. Even after Clinton was prepared to give the Palestinians a state in virtually all the West Bank and Gaza, and to make east Jerusalem their capital, the Palestinians rejected the deal.

President George W. Bush also offered a plan, but it was undercut by Yasser Arafat, who obstructed the required reforms of the Palestinian Authority, and refused to dismantle the terrorist infrastructure and stop the violence. Bush's plan morphed into the Road Map, which drew the support of Great Britain, France, Russia, and the United Nations, but was never implemented because of continuing Palestinian violence. The peace process only began to move again when Prime Minister Ariel Sharon made his disengagement proposal, a unilateral approach the State Department had long opposed. Rather than try to capitalize on the momentum created by Israel's evacuation of the Gaza Strip, however, the Bush Administration remained wedded to the Road Map.

President Barack Obama did not propose a peace plan, but focused instead on a demand for a settlement freeze in the West Bank and Jerusalem. This, combined with other public comments and policies, caused the Israeli government to doubt his commitment to Israeli security and created tension in the U.S.-Israel relationship. Simultaneously, because Israel agreed only to a temporary freeze in the West Bank, Arab leaders saw Obama as too weak to force Israel to make concessions and refused to respond positively to the administration's requests that they take steps to show their willingness to make peace with Israel if a Palestinian state were established. Meanwhile, the Palestinians, who had negotiated for years without insisting on a settlement freeze, refused to talk to the Israelis unless a total settlement freeze was imposed. After two years, Obama had succeeded in alienating all the parties and the Palestinians refused all Israeli invitations to restart peace talks.

History has shown that Middle East peace is not made in America. Only the parties can decide to end the conflict, and the terms that will be acceptable. No American plan has ever succeeded, and it is unlikely one will ever bring peace. The end to the Arab-Israeli conflict will not be achieved through American initiatives or intense involvement; it will be possible only when Arab leaders have the courage to follow the examples of Sadat and Hussein and resolve to live in peace with Israel.

Notes

1. *Foreign Relations of the United States 1947,* (DC: GPO, 1948), pp. 1173-4, 1198-9, 1248, 1284 [Henceforth FRUS 1947].
2. Mitchell Bard, *The Water's Edge And Beyond,* (NJ: Transaction Publishers, 1991), p. 132.
3. FRUS 1947, p. 1313; see also Mitchell Bard, *The Arab Lobby: The Invisible Alliance that Undermines America's Interest in the Middle East,* (NY: HarperCollins, 2010).
4. Harry Truman, *Years of Trial and Hope,* Vol. 2, (NY: Doubleday, 1956), p. 156.
5. John Snetsinger, *Truman, The Jewish Vote and the Creation of Israel,* (CA: Hoover Institution Press, 1974), pp. 9-10; David Schoenbaum, "The United States and the Birth of Israel," *Wiener Library Bulletin,* (1978), p. 144n.
6. Michael Cohen, *Truman and Israel,* (CA: University of California Press, 1990), p. 157.
7. Mitchell Bard, *U.S.-Israel Relations: Looking to the Year 2000,* AIPAC Papers on U.S.-Israeli Relations, (1991), p. 3.

8. CNN, (May 31, 2011).

9. See Bard, *The Arab Lobby.*

10. Nathan Guttman, "US Stopped parts sales during intifada," *Jerusalem Post,* (September 22, 2005); Ze'ev Schiff, "U.S. Sanctions still in place, despite deal over security exports," *Haaretz,* (August 28, 2005).

11. "The Obama Presidency–Pro Israel/Pro Palestinian," *Jerusalem Post,* (May 24, 2010).

12. Memorandum of conversation regarding Harriman-Eshkol talks, (February 25, 1965); Memorandum of conversation between Ambassador Avraham Harman and W. Averill Harriman, Ambassador-at-Large, (March 15, 1965), LBJ Library; Yitzhak Rabin, *The Rabin Memoirs,* (MA: Little Brown and Company, 1979), pp. 65-66.

13. Robert Trice, "Domestic Political Interests and American Policy in the Middle East: Pro-Israel, Pro-Arab and Corporate Non-Governmental Actors and the Making of American Foreign Policy, 1966-1971," (Unpublished Ph.D. Dissertation, University of Wisconsin-Madison, 1974), pp. 226-230.

14. Foreign Relations of the United States 1964-1968, Vol. xx, "Arab-Israeli Dispute 1967-8," Document 306, (DC: GPO, 1969), p. 605.

15. "Public Papers of the Presidents of the USA–Lyndon Johnson," (DC: GPO, 1970), p. 947.

16. "Public Papers of the President Harry Truman, 1945-1953," *Truman Library,* #262.

17. "U.S. Assistance to the Palestinian Authority," U.S. Department of State, (November 10, 2010).

18. "Gil Kol, "Research: PA highly dependent on aid," Ynetnews, (January 16, 2011).

19. Israeli Ministry of Defense.

20. Dore Gold, *America, the Gulf, and Israel,* (CO: Westview Press, 1988), p. 84.

21. "Issues Arising Out of the Situation in the Near East," July 29, 1958, Foreign Relations of the United States, 1958-1960, Vol. XII ("Near East Region; Iraq; Iran; Arabian Peninsula"), Washington: U.S. Government Printing Office, 1993, pp. 114-124 at p. 119.

22. Yitzhak Rabin, address to conference on "Strategy and Defense in the Eastern Mediterranean," sponsored by the Washington Institute for Near East Policy and Israel Military Correspondents Association, Jerusalem, (July 9-11, 1986).

23. Reagan Address to B'nai B'rith, cited in Mitchell Bard, *U.S.-Israel Relations: Looking to the Year 2000,* AIPAC Papers on U.S.-Israel Relations, p. 6.

24. Ibid.

25. U.S. Energy Administration "Petroleum and other Liquids," U.S. Department of Energy, 2010, accessed April 15, 2011, at http://www.eia.doe.gov/dnav/pet/pet_move_imp-cus_a2_nus_ep00_im0_mbbl_a.htm; Index Mundi, United States Oil Consumption, accessed April 15, 2011, at http://www.indexmundi.com/united_states/oil_consumption.html.

26. *Newsweek,* (October 29, 2001).

27. *Al-Raya* (Qatar), (January 6, 2002) cited in "Special Dispatch #337," MEMRI, (January 29, 2002).

28. *Washington Post,* (December 16, 2002).

29. CNN, (December 3, 2002).

30. CNN, (December 30, 2005).

31. "Definitions: Terrorism," Federal Bureau of Investigation.

32. *Jerusalem Post,* (October 17, 2001).

33. Statement on the 61st anniversary of Israel's independence, (April 28, 2009).

17. The Peace Process

FACT

The peace drive did not begin with President Anwar Sadat's November 1977 visit to Jerusalem. Sadat's visit was unquestionably a courageous act of statesmanship, but it came only after more than a half-century of efforts by early Zionist and Israeli leaders to negotiate peace with the Arabs.

"For Israel to equal the drama," said Simcha Dinitz, former Israeli Ambassador to the U.S., "we would have had to declare war on Egypt, maintain belligerent relations for years, refuse to talk to them, call for their annihilation, suggest throwing them into the sea, conduct military operations and terrorism against them, declare economic boycotts, close the Strait of Tiran to their ships, close the Suez Canal to their traffic, and say they are outcasts of humanity. Then Mr. Begin would go to Cairo, and his trip would be equally dramatic. Obviously, we could not do this, because it has been our policy to negotiate all along."[1]

Nonetheless, Israeli Prime Minister Menachem Begin proved that, like Sadat, he was willing to go the extra mile to achieve peace. Despite the Carter Administration's tilt toward Egypt during the talks, Begin remained determined to continue the peace process and froze Israeli settlements in the West Bank to facilitate the progress of negotiations.

In the end, Israel made tangible concessions to Egypt in exchange for only promises. Begin agreed to give the strategically critical Sinai—91 percent of the territory won by Israel during the Six-Day War—back to Egypt in exchange for Sadat's pledge to make peace.

In giving up the Sinai, Israel also lost electronic early-warning stations that provided intelligence on Egyptian military movements on the western side of the Suez Canal, as well as the areas near the Gulf of Suez and the Gulf of Eilat, which were vital to defending against an attack from the east. Additionally, Israel relocated more than 170 military installations, airfields and army bases after it withdrew.

The withdrawal may have also cost Israel its only chance to become energy-independent. The Alma oil field in the southern Sinai, discovered and developed by Israel, was transferred to Egypt in November

1979. When Israel gave up this field, it had become the country's largest single source of energy, supplying half the country's energy needs.

Israel also relinquished direct control of its shipping lanes to and from Eilat, as well as 1,000 miles of roadways, homes, factories, hotels, health facilities and agricultural villages.

Because Egypt insisted that Jewish civilians leave the Sinai, 7,000 Israelis were uprooted from the homes and businesses.

In 1988, Israel relinquished Taba—a resort town built by Israel in what had been a barren desert area near Eilat—to Egypt. Taba's status had not been resolved by the Camp David Accords. When an international arbitration panel ruled in Cairo's favor on September 29, 1988, Israel turned the town over to Egypt.

Sadat made a courageous decision to make peace with Israel, but Begin's decision was no less bold and the Israeli sacrifices far more substantial than those of the Egyptians.

"Israel wants to give the Palestinians what no one else gave them—a state. Not the Turks, the British, the Egyptians, or the Jordanians gave them this possibility.""

—Prime Minister Ariel Sharon[2]

MYTH

"The Palestinian question is the core of the Arab-Israeli conflict."

FACT

In reality, the Palestinian question is the result rather than the cause of the conflict, and stems from Arab unwillingness to accept a Jewish State in the Middle East.

Had Arab governments not gone to war in 1948 to block the UN partition plan, a Palestinian state would now be celebrating more than 60 years of independence. Had the Arab states not supported terrorism directed at Israeli civilians and provoked seven subsequent Arab-Israeli wars, the conflict could have been settled long ago, and the Palestinian problem resolved.

From 1948–67, the West Bank and Gaza were under Arab rule, and no Jewish settlements existed there, but the Arabs never set up a Palestinian state. Instead, Gaza was occupied by Egypt, and the West Bank by Jordan. No demands for a West Bank/Gaza independent state were heard until Israel took control of these areas in the Six-Day War.

MYTH

"If the Palestinian problem was solved, the Middle East would be at peace."

FACT

The Palestinian problem is but one of many simmering ethnic, religious and nationalistic feuds plaguing the region. Here is but a partial list of other conflicts the 1991 Gulf War; the Iran-Iraq War; the Lebanese Civil War; Libya's interference in Chad; the Sudanese Civil War; the Syria-Iraq conflict, the war between the Polisario Front and Morocco and, in 2011, the revolutions in Egypt, Tunisia, Libya, Syria and upheavals in several other Arab states.

"Almost every border in that part of the world, from Libya to Pakistan, from Turkey to Yemen, is either ill-defined or in dispute," scholar Daniel Pipes noted. "But Americans tend to know only about Israel's border problems, and do not realize that these fit into a pattern that recurs across the Middle East."[3]

If the Palestinian problem was solved, it would have negligible impact on the many inter-Arab rivalries that have spawned numerous wars in the region. The creation of a Palestinian state would also not eliminate Arab opposition to Israel. Syria and Lebanon, for example, have territorial disputes with Israel unrelated to the Palestinians. Other countries, such as Iran, whose president threatened to wipe Israel off the map, maintain a state of war with Israel despite having no territorial disputes.

"In the end we [Israel and the Palestinians] will reach a solution in which there will be a Palestinian state, but it has to be a Palestinian state by agreement and it has to be a demilitarized Palestinian state."

—Prime Minister Ariel Sharon[4]

MYTH

"A Palestinian state will pose no danger to Israel."

FACT

For many years, the consensus in Israel was that the creation of a Palestinian state would present a grave risk to Israeli security. These fears were well founded given the longstanding Palestinian commitment to the destruction of Israel, and the later adoption of the phased plan whereby the Palestinians expressed a reluctant willingness to start with a small state in the short-term and use it as a base from which to pursue the longer-term goal of replacing Israel.

Starting with the Oslo agreements in the early 1990s, a radical shift in opinion occurred and most Israelis became reconciled to the idea of living beside a peaceful demilitarized Palestinian state. The two-state solution is viewed as the best option for ending the conflict, but Israelis still believe it entails risks, a view reinforced by Palestinian actions since Oslo.

Even after returning much of the West Bank and all of Gaza, and allowing the Palestinians to govern themselves, terrorism and incitement against Israelis has continued. So far, no concessions by Israel have been sufficient to prompt the Palestinians to end the violence.

Israelis also fear that a Palestinian state will become dominated by Islamic extremists and serve as a staging area for terrorists, a concern grounded in the experience following the disengagement from Gaza. Another danger is that a Palestinian state could serve as a forward base for Arab nations that have refused to make peace with Israel in a future war.[5]

In an ideal world, a Palestinian state would pose no threat, but history and experience makes Israelis cautious. The level of support for the two-state solution is an indication, however, of the risks Israelis are prepared to take in the hope of peace.

MYTH

"If Israel ends the occupation, there will be peace."

FACT

The mantra of the Palestinians and their supporters since 1967 has been: "End the occupation." The assumption underlying this slogan is that peace will follow the end of Israel's "occupation." The equally popular slogan among critics of Israeli policy has been that it should "trade land for peace." Again, the premise being that it is simply Israel's presence on land claimed by the Palestinians that is the impediment to peace.

The experience in Gaza offered a stark case study of the disingenuousness of these slogans.

If the Palestinians' fervent desire was really to end Israeli control over their lives, they would have cheered Israel's plan to evacuate the Gaza Strip and done everything possible to make it a success. Instead, they denounced disengagement. Israel still withdrew from every inch of Gaza—not a single Israeli soldier or civilian remains—at great emotional and financial cost. And what has the end of "the occupation" brought Israel? Has Israel received peace in exchange for the land? No, to the contrary, the Palestinian answer to meeting their demands was a four-year barrage of rocket fire.[6]

Slogans are good for bumper stickers, but they are irrelevant to the future of Israel and its neighbors. Israelis have repeatedly shown a desire for peace, and a willingness to make painful sacrifices, but nothing they do will end the conflict. The escalation of violence occurred following Israel's evacuation of Gaza and after the Israeli Prime Minister expressed his intention to withdraw from virtually the entire West Bank. Rather than end the occupation, Palestinian actions have forced Israel to maintain it. Peace will be possible only when the Palestinians demonstrate through their actions a willingness to coexist in a state beside Israel.

> *"The responsibility for this escalation in the Israeli-Palestinian conflict rests with the Palestinians who have yet again turned their backs on peace. Rather than take the withdrawal of Israel from Gaza as an opportunity to build a future for their children, they instead refused to relinquish their embrace of a culture of hate and death."*
>
> **—Editorial, *Chicago Sun Times*[7]**

MYTH

"The Palestinians have never been offered a state of their own."

FACT

The Palestinians have actually had numerous opportunities to create an independent state, but have repeatedly rejected the offers:

- In 1937, the Peel Commission proposed the partition of Palestine and the creation of an Arab state.
- In 1939, the British White Paper proposed the creation of a unitary Arab state.
- In 1947, the UN would have created an even larger Arab state as part of its partition plan.
- The 1979 Egypt-Israel peace negotiations offered the Palestinians autonomy, which would almost certainly have led to full independence.
- The Oslo agreements of the 1990s laid out a path for Palestinian independence, but the process was derailed by terrorism.
- In 2000, Prime Minister Ehud Barak offered to create a Palestinian state in all of Gaza and 97 percent of the West Bank.
- In 2008, Prime Minister Ehud Olmert offered to withdraw from almost the entire West Bank and partition Jerusalem on a demographic basis.

In addition, from 1948 to 1967, Israel did not control the West Bank. The Palestinians could have demanded an independent state from the Jordanians.

The Palestinians have spurned each of these opportunities. A variety of reasons have been given for why the Palestinians have in Abba Eban's words, "never missed an opportunity to miss an opportunity." Historian Benny Morris has suggested that the Palestinians have religious, historical, and practical reasons for opposing an agreement with Israel. He says that "Arafat and his generation cannot give up the vision of the greater land of Israel for the Arabs. [This is true because] this is a holy land, *Dar al-Islam* [the world of Islam]. It was once in the hands of the Muslims, and it is inconceivable [to them] that infidels like us [the Israelis] would receive it."

The Palestinians also believe that time is on their side. "They feel that demographics will defeat the Jews in one hundred or two hundred years, just like the Crusaders." The Palestinians, Morris says, also hope the Arabs will acquire nuclear weapons in the future that will allow them to defeat Israel.[8]

"Barak made a proposal that was as forthcoming as anyone in the world could imagine, and Arafat turned it down. If you have a country that's a sliver and you can see three sides of it from a high hotel building, you've got to be careful what you give away and to whom you give it."

—U.S. Defense Secretary Donald Rumsfeld[9]

MYTH

"Yasser Arafat rejected Barak's proposals in 2000 because they did not offer the Palestinians a viable state."

FACT

In 2000, Israeli Prime Minister Ehud Barak offered to withdraw from 97 percent of the West Bank and 100 percent of the Gaza Strip. In addition, he agreed to dismantle 63 isolated settlements. In exchange for the 3 percent annexation of the West Bank, Israel said it would give up territory in the Negev that would increase the size of the Gaza territory by roughly a third.

Barak also made previously unthinkable concessions on Jerusalem, agreeing that Arab neighborhoods of East Jerusalem would become the capital of the new state. The Palestinians would maintain control over their holy places and have "religious sovereignty" over the Temple Mount.

According to U.S. peace negotiator Dennis Ross, Israel offered to create a Palestinian state that was contiguous, and not a series of cantons. Even in the case of the Gaza Strip, which must be physically separate from the West Bank unless Israel were to be cut into non-contiguous pieces, a solution was devised whereby an overland highway would connect the two parts of the Palestinian state without any Israeli checkpoints or interference. The proposal also addressed the Palestinian refugee issue, guaranteeing them the right of return to the Palestinian state and reparations from a $30 billion fund that would be collected from international donors to compensate them.

> *"In his last conversation with President Clinton, Arafat told the President that he was "a great man." Clinton responded, "The hell I am. I'm a colossal failure, and you made me one."*[10]

Arafat was asked to agree to Israeli sovereignty over the parts of the Western Wall religiously significant to Jews (i.e., not the entire Temple Mount), and three early warning stations in the Jordan Valley, which Israel would withdraw from after six years. Most important, however, Arafat was expected to agree that the conflict with Israel was over at the end of the negotiations. This was the true deal breaker. Arafat was not willing to end the conflict. "For him to end the conflict is to end himself," said Ross.[11]

The prevailing view of the Camp David/White House negotiations—that Israel offered generous concessions, and that Yasser Arafat rejected them to pursue the war that began in September 2000—was acknowledged for more than a year. To counter the perception that Arafat was the obstacle to peace, the Palestinians and their supporters then began to suggest a variety of excuses for why Arafat failed to say "yes" to a proposal that would have established a Palestinian state. The truth is that if the Palestinians were dissatisfied with any part of the Israeli proposal, all they had to do was offer a counterproposal. They never did.

MYTH

"The Palestinians are being asked to accept only 22 percent of Palestine for their state while Israel keeps 78 percent."

FACT

The government of Israel has agreed to a two-state solution to the conflict with the Palestinians. Once Israel agreed to give the Palestinians the independence they say they want, the Palestinians shifted their complaint to the *size* of the state they were being offered. Palestinians say Israel is doing them no favors by offering a state in the disputed territories because it is asking them to accept a state in only 22 percent of Palestine while Israel keeps 78 percent. This is a very convincing point to show the unfairness of the Palestinians' plight and to suggest Israel's peace overtures are inconsequential; that is, unless you know the history of Palestine and recognize that the truth is exactly the reverse.

Historic Palestine included not only Israel and the West Bank, but also all of modern Jordan. It is *Israel,* including the disputed territories, that is only 22 percent of "Palestine." If Israel were to withdraw completely from the West Bank and Gaza Strip, it would possess only about 18 percent. And from Israel's perspective, it is the Zionists who have made the real sacrifice by giving up 82 percent of the Land of Israel. In fact, by accepting the UN's partition resolution, they were prepared to accept only about 12 percent of historic Israel before the Arab states attacked and tried to destroy the nascent state of Israel.

Meanwhile, of the approximately 9 million Palestinians worldwide, three-fourths live in historic Palestine.

> *"To keep 3.5 million people under occupation is bad for us and them.... I want to say clearly that I have come to the conclusion that we have to reach a [peace] agreement."*
>
> **—Prime Minister Ariel Sharon**[12]

MYTH

"Israel should be replaced by a binational state."

FACT

The idea of a binational state is not new; it was first proposed by prominent Jews such as Judah Magnes in the 1920s. As is the case today, however, the suggestion enjoyed no popular support.

The utopian view of the advocates of binationalism was that the Jews and Arabs both had legitimate claims to the land and should live in peace together in one state. This idea negated the Jewish right to self-determination in their homeland; ignored the demographic concern that the rapidly growing Arab population would overwhelm that of the Jews, making them a minority in their homeland; and assumed the Arabs were prepared to coexist peacefully with the Jews within the same state. The idealists were proven wrong during two decades of violence by Arabs against Jews in Palestine, and by the Arab rejection of the British White Paper of 1939, which offered them the type of unitary state they proposed.

> *"A Palestinian state will never be built on a foundation of violence. Now is the time for every true friend of the Palestinian people, every leader in the Middle East, and the Palestinian people themselves, to cut off all money and support for terrorists and actively fight terror on all fronts. Only then can Israel be secure and the flag rise over an independent Palestine."*
>
> **—President George W. Bush**[13]

As early as 1937, it had become clear that the two peoples could not live together and needed to have states of their own. As a result, the Peel Commission proposed a partition in that year and the UN approved the same approach a decade later. Nothing has changed since that time to suggest any other solution can end the conflict.

Since Palestinian Arabs already constitute approximately 46 percent of the population living between the Mediterranean Sea and the Jordan River, and their birth rate is higher than that of Israeli Jews, they would soon become either a significant minority or the majority of the population in a binational state. The Jewish character of the nation would then erode and disappear, and Israeli Jews would lose political control over the one safe haven for Jews. Moreover, given the historical mistreatment of Jews in Arab lands, creation of a binational state would potentially lead to the persecution of Jews.

MYTH

"The Palestinian education system promotes peace with Israel."

FACT

Rather than use education to promote peace with their Jewish neighbors, the Palestinians have persistently indoctrinated their children with anti-Semitic stereotypes, anti-Israel propaganda and other materials designed more to promote hostility and intolerance rather than coexistence.

For example, a Palestinian children's television show called the "Children's Club" used a "Sesame Street" formula involving interaction between children, puppets and fictional characters to encourage a hatred for Jews and the perpetration of violence against them in a *jihad* (holy war). In one song, young children were shown singing about their desire to become "suicide warriors" and taking up machine guns against Israelis. Another song features young children singing a refrain, "When I wander into Jerusalem, I will become a suicide bomber."[14]

> *"We have found books with passages that are so anti-Semitic, that if they were published in Europe, their publishers would be brought up on anti-racism charges.""*
>
> **—French lawyer and European Parliament member Francois Zimeray**[15]

Another Palestinian TV show featured a Mickey Mouse-like character named Farfour who encouraged children to fight against Israel and to work for "a world led by Islamists." After attracting criticism, the show was cancelled, but not before a final episode aired in which Farfour is murdered by Israelis.[16]

Palestinian TV also called on their youth to drop their toys, pick up rocks, and do battle with Israel. In one commercial, actors recreated the incident where a child was killed in the crossfire of a confrontation between Israelis and Palestinians. The commercial shows the child in paradise urging other children to "follow him."[17]

PA-run TV also teaches children that all of Israel is "occupied Palestine," referring to Israeli cities such as Haifa and Jaffa, for example, as "occupied Palestinian cities."[18]

Similar messages are conveyed in Palestinian textbooks, many of which were prepared by the Palestinian Ministry of Education. The 5th grade textbook *Muqarar al-Tilawa Wa'ahkam Al-Tajwid* describes Jews as cowards for whom Allah has prepared fires of hell. In a text for 8th graders, *Al-Mutala'ah Wa'alnussus al-Adabia*, Israelis are referred to as the butchers in Jerusalem. Stories glorifying those who throw stones at soldiers are also found in various texts. A 9th grade text, *Al-Mutala'ah Wa'alnussus al-Adabia*, refers to the bacteria of Zionism that has to be uprooted out of the Arab nation.[19]

Newer textbooks are less strident, but still problematic. For example, they describe the Palestinian nation as one comprised of Muslims and Christians. No mention is made of Jews or the centuries-old Jewish communities of Palestine. The city of Jerusalem is described as exclusively Arab. Israel is not recognized as a sovereign nation and all maps are labeled "Palestine." Israel is held responsible for the 1948 war and refugee problem and a catalogue of abuses against the Palestinians are attributed to the "occupier." Zionism is depicted as racist and connected to Western imperialism. References to Jews are usually stereotypical and are often related in a negative way to their opposition to Muhammad and refusal to convert to Islam. A lesson on architecture describes prominent mosques and churches, but makes no mention of Jewish holy places.[20] One textbook analysis concludes:

> Despite the evident reduction in anti-Semitic references, compared to the old textbooks, the history of the relationship

between Muslims, Christians and Jews in the new textbooks strengthen classical stereotypes of Jews in both Islamic and Christian cultures. The linkage of present conflicts with ancient disputes of the time of Jesus or Muhammad implies that nothing has really changed.[21]

The lessons don't end in school. Summer camp teaches Palestinian children how to resist the Israelis and that the greatest glory is to be a martyr. Campers stage mock kidnappings and learn how to slit the throats of Israelis. Four "Paradise Camps" run by Islamic Jihad in the Gaza Strip offered 8–12 year-olds military training and encourage them to become suicide bombers.[22]

> *"We are teaching the children that suicide bombs make Israeli people frightened.... We teach them that after a person becomes a suicide bomber he reaches the highest level of paradise."*
>
> **—Palestinian "Paradise Camp" counselor speaking to BBC interviewer[23]**

In the summer of 2009, Hamas ran 700 camps for 100,000 children and teenagers. Included in the camps' curricula were lessons in shooting firearms and dismantling grenades. Two years earlier, some Palestinian parents were so upset about the military training and incitement of their children against Israel and Fatah they pulled them out of the camps.[24]

These teachings violate the letter and spirit of the peace agreements.

MYTH

"Palestinians no longer object to the creation of Israel."

FACT

One of the primary Palestinian obligations under the Road Map for peace is to affirm Israel's right to exist in peace and security. How then does one interpret Palestinian Authority Chairman Mahmoud Abbas's description of the decision to create a Jewish state in 1948 as a crime?[25]

While Israelis celebrate their independence, Abbas and other Palestinians mourn the establishment of Israel on what they call Nakba Day. Had the Palestinians and the Arab states accepted the partition resolution in 1947, the State of Palestine would also celebrate its birthday each year, and Palestinians would not be lamenting *Al Nakba* ("The Catastrophe").

Palestinians are understandably bitter about their history over these last six decades, but we are often told that what they object to today is the "occupation" of the territories Israel captured in 1967. If that is true, then why isn't their Nakba Day celebrated each June on the anniversary of the Arab defeat in the Six-Day War?

> *"Palestine means Palestine in its entirety—from the [Mediterranean] Sea to the [Jordan] River, from Ras Al-Naqura to Rafah. We cannot give up a single inch of it. Therefore, we will not recognize the Israeli enemy's [right] to a single inch."*
>
> **—Hamas leader Mahmoud Zahar**[26]

The reason is that the Palestinians consider the creation of Israel the original sin, and their focus on that event is indicative of a refusal, even today, to reconcile themselves with the Jewish State. Hamas has never left any doubt about its refusal to accept Israel's existence and unwavering commitment to the Hamas Covenant's call for the destruction of Israel.[27]

It may be that the current leadership does not truly represent the feelings of the Palestinian people. A March 2010 poll, for example, found that 58 percent of Palestinians support Israeli-Palestinian peace negotiations.[28] This is a hopeful sign; however, as long as the Palestinian Authority treats Israel's creation as a catastrophe on a par with the Holocaust, the prospects for coexistence will remain bleak.

MYTH

"The Palestinians have given up their dream of destroying Israel."

FACT

While Israelis have expressed a willingness to live in peace with a Palestinian state beside Israel, the Palestinian Authority continues to promote the maximalist vision in its school textbooks and, especially, its maps. The most dramatic expression of the goal is in the map of Palestine published on its official web site, which showed Palestine as encompassing not only the West Bank and Gaza Strip, but all of Israel as well. Similar maps appear in textbooks.[29] As the map vividly indicates, the Palestinians continue to dream of a Palestinian state that replaces Israel.

MYTH

"Palestinians are justified in using violence because Israel has not allowed them to achieve their national aspirations."

Map 22 The Palestinian Authority's Map of Palestine

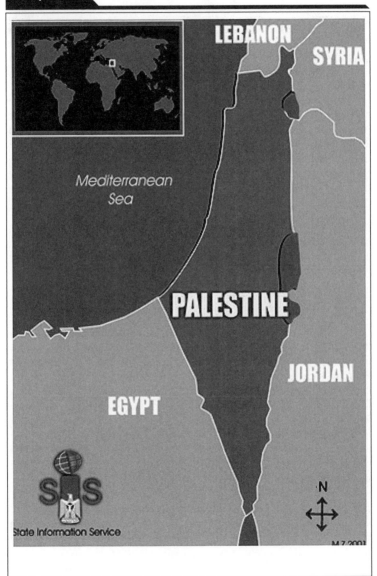

Mediterranean Sea

LEBANON

SYRIA

PALESTINE

JORDAN

EGYPT

N

State Information Service

M 7 2001

FACT

The premise from the beginning of the Oslo peace process was that disputes would be resolved by talking, not shooting. The Palestinian leadership has never accepted this most basic of principles for coexistence. The answer to complaints that Israel is not withdrawing far enough or fast enough should be more negotiations, more confidence-building measures and more demonstrations of a desire to live together without using violence.

To understand why the Oslo process failed, and why Palestinians and Israelis are not living peacefully beside each other, it is useful to look at the first Arab-Israeli peace process that did work, the Egyptian-Israeli negotiations. Though the peace agreement was hammered out in intensive negotiations at Camp David, the route to peace was a long, tortuous one that took years to navigate. What made it possible, however, was the commitment both nations made to peace and the actions they took to ensure it.

> *"If the Israelis can make compromises and you can't, I should go home. You have been here 14 days and said no to everything. These things will have consequences. Failure will end the peace process. . . ."*
>
> **—President Clinton to Yasser Arafat**[30]

Egypt maintained a state of war with Israel for more than 25 years before Anwar Sadat seriously talked about peace. Bloody conflicts were fought in 1948, 1956, 1967, 1968–70 and 1973. The anger, heartache and distrust of a quarter century did not dissipate overnight. The process began after the 1973 war when Henry Kissinger facilitated the negotiation of a disengagement agreement in which both sides made significant concessions.

Egypt had demanded that Israel make a substantial withdrawal from Sinai and commit to abandon all its territorial gains from 1967, but Israel gave up only a tiny area of the Sinai. Rather than resort to violence, the Egyptians engaged in more negotiations.

The first agreement was signed in January 1974. It took about a year and a half before a second agreement was reached. It wasn't easy. Israel was criticized for "inflexibility," and the Egyptians were no less difficult. Anwar Sadat agreed to limit anti-Israel propaganda in the Egyptian press and to end his country's participation in the Arab boycott. Yitzhak Rabin also made difficult territorial concessions, giving up oil fields and two critical Sinai passes.

After "Sinai II," Egypt still had not recovered all of its territory. Sadat was dissatisfied and was pilloried by the other Arabs for going as far as he did toward peace with Israel. Nevertheless, he did not resort to violence. There was no unleashing of *fedayeen,* as Nasser had done in the 1950s. Instead, he continued talking.

It took three more years before the Camp David Accords were signed and another six months after that before the final peace treaty was negotiated. It took five years to work out issues that were as complex as those in the current impasse.

In return for its tangible concessions, Israel received the promise of a new future of peaceful relations. Israel could take this risk because Egypt had demonstrated over the previous five years that it would resolve disputes with Israel peacefully, and that it no longer wished to destroy its neighbor.

Egypt still wasn't completely satisfied. Sadat demanded a small sliver of land that Israel retained in the Sinai. It took another nine years before international arbitration led Israel to give up Taba. Rather than using this dispute as a pretext for violating the peace treaty, Egypt negotiated.

The lesson for the Palestinians is that they can only achieve their objective through compromise during face-to-face negotiations.

MYTH

"Palestinian terrorists only attack Israelis; they never assault Americans."

FACT

The PLO has a long history of brutal violence against innocent civilians of many nations, including the United States. Palestinian Muslim terrorist groups are a more recent phenomenon, but they have not spared Americans either. Here are a few examples of Palestinian terrorist incidents involving American citizens.

- In September 1970, more than three dozen Americans were among the passengers who were held hostage when the Popular Front for the Liberation of Palestine (PFLP) hijacked four jets.

- In 1972, the PLO attempted to mail letter bombs to President Nixon, former Secretary of State William Rogers and Secretary of Defense Melvin Laird.

- On March 2, 1973, members of the PLO murdered U.S. Ambassador to the Sudan Cleo Noel and chargé d'affaires George Moore. The killers were captured by Sudan and admitted they had gotten orders directly from the PLO. U.S. intelligence officials were believed to also have evidence directly tying Yasser Arafat to the killings, but for unknown reasons suppressed it. All the terrorists were released.

- On March 11, 1978, PLO terrorists landed on Israel's coast and murdered an American photographer walking along the beach. The terrorists then commandeered a bus along the coastal road, shooting and lobbing grenades from the bus window at passersby. When Israeli troops stopped their deadly ride, 34 civilians were dead and another 82 wounded.

- In October 1985, a PLF terror squad commanded by Abul Abbas hijacked the ocean liner Achille Lauro. Leon Klinghoffer, a wheelchair-bound American passenger was murdered.

- In March 1988, Arafat's Fatah declared it had attempted to murder Secretary of State George Shultz by planting a car bomb near his Jerusalem hotel.[31]

- On April 9, 1995, an Islamic Jihad suicide bomber blew up an Israeli bus killing eight people, including 20-year-old Brandeis University student Alisa Flatow.

- August 9, 2001, Shoshana Yehudit Greenbaum, was among 15 people killed in a suicide bombing at the Sbarro pizzeria in downtown Jerusalem. Hamas and the Islamic Jihad claimed responsibility for the attack.

- July 31, 2002, a bomb exploded at the Hebrew University cafeteria killing seven and wounding 80. Five Americans were among the dead.

- June 11, 2003, a bus bombing in Jerusalem killed one American and injured the daughter of New Jersey State Senator Robert Singer.

- June 20, 2003, a shooting attack on a car driving through the West Bank killed Tzvi Goldstein, and injured his father, mother, and wife.

- August 19, 2003, a suicide bombing on a bus in Jerusalem killed five Americans, including children aged 9, 3, and 3 months; an 11-year-old American was injured.

- October 15, 2003, Palestinian terrorists ambushed an American convoy in the Gaza Strip killing three U.S. citizens on contract to the U.S. embassy in Tel Aviv.

- September 24, 2004, a mortar strike on a housing community killed dual citizen Tiferet Tratner.

- April 17, 2006, homicide bombing at the Rosh Ha'ir restaurant in Tel Aviv: Daniel Wultz, 16, of Weston, Florida, died one month after receiving his wounds in this bombing.

- December 20, 2010, an American tourist hiking in the foothills of Jerusalem was stabbed to death by a Palestinian terrorist.

"The bombing yesterday [August 9, 2001] of a crowded pizza restaurant in downtown Jerusalem, which killed at least 14 people and injured around 100, was an atrocity of the sort that must be distinguished from everything else that goes on in the Palestinian-Israeli conflict.... the deliberate targeting of civilians, including children ... is a simple savagery that no country can reasonably be expected to tolerate. Israel's determination last night to respond was entirely legitimate....

—*Washington Post* **Editorial**[32]

MYTH

"Palestinians never fabricate stories about Israeli atrocities."

FACT

Palestinian and other Arab leaders routinely use their media outlets to spread outrageous libels against Israel and the Jews to inflame their populations. Palestinians have become masters of the technique perfected by Adolf Hitler known as the "big lie." As Hitler explained in *Mein Kampf*:

> The size of a lie is a definite factor in causing it to be believed, for the vast masses of a nation are in the depths of their hearts more easily deceived than consciously and intentionally bad. The primitive simplicity of their minds renders them a more easy prey to a big lie than a small one, for they themselves often tell little lies but would be ashamed to tell big ones.

One example of the Palestinian big lie came on March 11, 1997, when the Palestinian representative to the UN Human Rights Commission claimed the Israeli government had injected 300 Palestinian children with the HIV virus.[33]

Palestinians claimed in 2002 that Israel was dropping poisoned candies from helicopters in front of schools to poison children. That lie was updated in 2003 with the fabrication that Israel is making "bombs and mines designed as toys" and dropping them into the Palestinian territories from airplanes so children will play with them and be blown up.[34] In 2005, the Palestinians announced that Israel was using a "radial spy machine" at checkpoints, and that the device had killed a 55-year-old Palestinian woman.[35]

The Palestinians also regularly try to inflame the Muslim world by falsely claiming the Jews are going to blow up the Temple Mount or the al-Aksa Mosque. For example, on September 29, 2000, the Voice of Palestine, the PA's official radio station, sent out calls "to all Palestinians to come and defend the al-Aksa mosque." This was the day *after* Ariel Sharon's visit to the Temple Mount, and the subsequent riots marked the unofficial beginning of the Palestinian War.

In the midst of that war, the Palestinian Authority TV "Message to the World" broadcast announced: "The Zionist criminals are planning to destroy the al-Aksa mosque on the ground that they are searching for the Holy Temple, which they falsely claim is under the mosque."[36]

One of the most outrageous lies circulated throughout the Middle East was that 4,000 Israelis did not report to work on September 11 because they knew an attack was coming. Israel and the Mossad are also said to be responsible for the atrocities. Of course, this was also a lie, but it is the type of conspiracy theory that is widely believed by Arabs who maintain the forgery, the Protocols of the Elders of Zion, is factual. "The problem is the same problem that has been there for the three years that I have been working in this account. And that is terrorism, terrorism that still emanates from Hamas, Palestinian Islamic Jihad, and other organizations that are not interested in peace, not interested in a state for the Palestinian people. They're interested in the destruction of Israel."

—Secretary of State Colin Powell[37]

MYTH

"Peace with Syria has been prevented only by Israel's refusal to withdraw from the Golan Heights."

FACT

Given past history, Israel is understandably reluctant to give away the strategic high ground and its early-warning system. Nevertheless, Israel repeatedly expressed a willingness to negotiate the future of the Golan Heights. One possible compromise might be a partial Israeli withdrawal, along the lines of its 1974 disengagement agreement with Syria. Another would be a complete withdrawal, with the Golan becoming a demilitarized zone.

After losing the 1999 election, Benjamin Netanyahu confirmed reports that he had engaged in secret talks with Syrian President Hafez Assad to withdraw from the Golan and maintain a strategic early-warning station on Mount Hermon. Publicly, Assad continued to insist on a total withdrawal with no compromises and indicated no willingness to go beyond agreeing to a far more limited "non-belligerency" deal with Israel than the full peace treaty Israel has demanded.

Intensive negotiations between Israeli and Syrian negotiators were held in 2000 and 2008, but the discussions did not result in any agreements.

Hafez Assad died in 2000 and was succeeded by his son, Bashar, who has publicly insisted on the same terms as his father—total Israeli withdrawal from the Golan Heights with no promise of peace in exchange. Israel has made clear it is prepared to compromise on the Golan and make significant territorial concessions. The only obstacle is Assad's unwillingness to say yes to peace with Israel.

MYTH

"Israel's occupation of Lebanese territory is the only impediment to the conclusion of a peace treaty with Lebanon."

FACT

Israel has never had any hostile intentions toward Lebanon, but has been forced to fight as a result of the chaotic conditions in southern Lebanon that have allowed terrorists, first the PLO, and now Hezbollah, to menace citizens living in northern Israel. In 1983, Israel did sign a peace treaty with Lebanon, but Syria forced President Amin Gemayel to renege on the agreement.

Israel pulled all its troops out of southern Lebanon on May 24, 2000. The Israeli withdrawal was conducted in coordination with the UN, and, according to the UN, constituted an Israeli fulfillment of its obligations under Security Council Resolution 425. Still, Hezbollah and the Lebanese government insist that Israel holds Lebanese territory in a largely uninhabited patch called Shebaa Farms. This claim provides Hezbollah with a pretext to continue its belligerency toward Israel. The Israelis maintain, however, that the land was captured from Syria.

Syria, meanwhile, has used its influence over Lebanon to discourage any peace negotiations until its claims on the Golan Heights are resolved. For some time it seemed possible a Lebanon-Israel agreement could be achieved once Israel and Syria reached an agreement, but the growing power in Lebanon of Iran's proxy, Hezbollah, has reduced the chance that Lebanon would make peace with Israel under any circumstances.

"Palestine is not only a part of our Arab homeland, but a basic part of southern Syria."

—Syrian President Hafez Assad[38]

MYTH

"Israel's refusal to share water with its neighbors could provoke the next war."

FACT

The supply of water is a matter of life and death for the peoples of the Middle East. A *Jerusalem Post* headline concisely stated the security threat for Israel: "The hand that controls the faucet rules the country."[39]

King Hussein said in 1990 the one issue that could bring Jordan to war again is water, so it is not surprising that an agreement on water supplies was critical to the negotiation of the peace treaty with Israel. Jordan now receives an annual allotment of water from Israel.[40]

Israel has had an ongoing water deficit for a number of years. Simply put, the amount of water consumed is greater than the amount of water collected from rainfall. In a drought year, the situation worsens, because the amount of water in reservoirs and the amount of water flowing in rivers and streams is significantly decreased.

The situation is growing more dangerous each year as the population of the region continues to grow exponentially, political disputes over existing water supplies become more pronounced, and Israel and the Palestinians negotiate rights to the water in the West Bank and Gaza Strip.

Israel has three main water sources: the coastal and mountain aquifers and Lake Kinneret (Sea of Galilee). Each supply approximately 25 percent of the total consumed. Roughly 20 percent is derived from smaller aquifers. The remaining 5 percent comes from the Shafdan project that recycles sewage in metropolitan Tel Aviv.

> *"In Old Testament times, there were two ways of solving disputes over water, which has always been scarce in our region. One was to fight over it. The other was to jointly place over the mouth of the well, a stone so large that five shepherds were needed to lift it, creating the need for cooperation."*
>
> **—Former Israeli Agriculture Minister Yaacov Tzur[41]**

The Palestinians maintain that Israel is stealing their water because the mountain aquifer is partially located in the West Bank. Most of the water extracted by Israel, however, is taken from the portion that is within the pre-1967 border of Israel. Nevertheless, the Palestinians argue the water should come under their control while Israel counters that it has a right to the water based on its prior use, its investment in development and because of the fact that the water naturally flows inside the Green Line.

The danger for Israel is that even if a future Palestinian state had peaceful intentions, it could significantly reduce the water available to Israel because of the need to satisfy the needs of its own population. As it is, unauthorized Palestinian drilling of wells in the West Bank has affected the quality of the aquifer. Without any other water source, the Palestinians will be tempted to pump more out of the aquifer to meet their growing needs and thereby could ultimately inundate it with seawater. There would be nothing Israel could do to stop them.

Also, the poor quality of PA water treatment facilities, mismanagement, neglect, and the low priority placed on environmental issues increases the likelihood that the aquifer will be polluted and its quality reduced perhaps to the point of being undrinkable. This has already occurred in the Gaza Strip where the sole aquifer is unusable because of contamination and salinity.

According to the Oslo accords, the Palestinians are entitled to 23.6 million cubic centimeters of water a year, but they actually pump, with Israeli consent, 70 million. Israel has also provided additional water to villages that suffer a water shortage.[42] In 2010 alone, 37 water projects in the West Bank were approved by Israel. Occasionally, Israel is accused of giving water to settlements at the expense of the Palestinians; however, most settlements get their water from inside Israel, not the West Bank.

If Israel gives up control of the mountain aquifer, as is implicit in the proposals made to date, it will depend on the goodwill of the Palestinians to protect the quality of the water and to ensure Israel continues to receive sufficient water to meet its needs.

"Israel has no right even to a single drop of water in this region."

—Syrian Foreign Minister Farouk al-Sharaa[43]

Water is also an issue in negotiations with the Syrians. Syria demands the full return of the Golan Heights in return for peace with Israel. This means that Israel would face problems regarding the quality and quantity of water that flows into the Kinneret from Syrian-controlled territory. According to water expert Joyce Starr, an Israeli government that concedes territory on the Golan without a guaranteed supply of Yarmuk waters, or some alternative source of water, would be putting the nation in "grave jeopardy."[44]

Israel is taking steps to ameliorate the water issue by constructing large desalination plants that are expected to satsify nearly one-fourth of Israel's needs. Israel offered to build a desalination plant in Hadera for the Palestinians in the West Bank, but they rejected the idea.

MYTH

"Saudi Arabia is a force for peace and moderation."

FACT

"The Saudis are active at every level of the terror chain, from planners to financiers, from cadre to foot-soldier, from ideologist to cheerleader," said Laurent Murawiec, a Rand Corporation analyst in a secret briefing

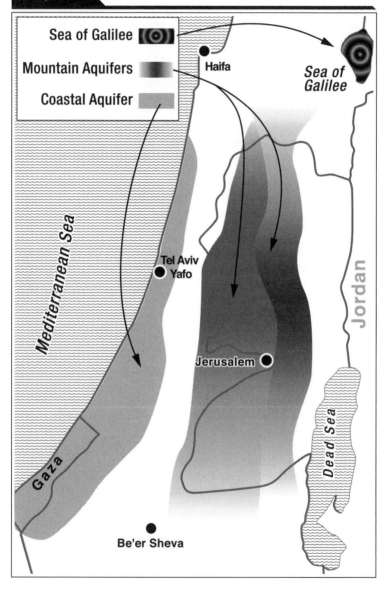

Map 23 Water Resources

Sea of Galilee
Mountain Aquifers
Coastal Aquifer

Haifa

Sea of Galilee

Mediterranean Sea

Jordan

Tel Aviv Yafo

Jerusalem

Dead Sea

Gaza

Be'er Sheva

to a top Pentagon advisory board. "Saudi Arabia," he added, "supports our enemies and attacks our allies."[45]

The most dramatic evidence of Saudi involvement in terror is the fact that 15 of the 19 September 11 terrorists were from Saudi Arabia. Despite this, the Saudi government refused to cooperate with the U.S. investigation of the attacks and rejected American requests to stop the flow of money through charitable organizations to terrorist groups. Many such charities are based in the United States and are being investigated by the Treasury Department.

Saudi support for terrorism and al-Qaida, in particular, is not restricted to extremists in the kingdom. A classified American intelligence report revealed that an October 2001 survey of educated Saudis between the ages of 25 and 41 found that 95 percent of the respondents supported Osama bin Laden's cause.[46] According to a UN report, "al-Qaida was able to receive between $300 and $500 million over the last 10 years from wealthy businessmen and bankers whose fortunes represent about 20 percent of the Saudi GNP, through a web of charities and companies acting as fronts."[47]

> "I thank Allah the exalted for His support in the Jihad of our people and for the liberation of the beloved Gaza Strip, and I ask him to help us to liberate Jerusalem and the West Bank, Acre, Haifa, Jaffa, Safed, Nazareth, Ashkelon, and all of Palestine."
>
> **—Muhammad Deif, Commander of the 'Izz Al-Din Al-Qassam Brigades[48]**

The Saudis have been heavily involved in supporting Palestinian terror. They were the largest financial backer of Hamas during the 1990s, providing perhaps as much as $10 million annually. At one point, Abu Mazen even complained to the governor of Riyadh that Saudi money wasn't reaching the "martyrs," but was going directly to Hamas.[49]

The Saudis held a terror telethon on April 11, 2002, which raised more than $100 million for families of Palestinian "martyrs," including the families of suicide bombers[50] and, during Operation Defensive Shield, the Israelis found numerous documents linking the Saudis to terror. One, for example, itemized their allocations line by line, detailing the circumstances of the death of Palestinians whose families received assistance, and making clear the allocation was for suicide attacks. The information came from the Saudi Committee for Aid to the Al-Quds Intifada, which is headed by Saudi Minister of the Interior, Prince Nayef bin 'Abd al-Aziz.

Israeli authorities arrested an Israeli-Arab Hamas activist in September 2005 who confessed to receiving instructions for Hamas field operatives and hundreds of thousands of dollars from the Hamas head-quarters in Saudi Arabia. Hamas leaders in Saudi Arabia provided funding to establish a "communications office" to report developments on the ground to Hamas operatives abroad. Money was also transferred, often under the cover of charity work, to the families of suicide bombers, imprisoned terrorists and Hamas institutions.[51]

On the sixth anniversary of the 9/11 attacks, Undersecretary of the Treasury for Terrorism and Financial Intelligence Stuart Levey said, "If I could somehow snap my fingers and cut off the funding from one country, it would be Saudi Arabia" and, in April 2008, he reiterated that Saudi Arabia remained the world's leading source of money for Al-Qaida and other extremist networks. In July 2009, Treasury Secretary Timothy Geithner praised more recent Saudi efforts to combat terrorist financing, but a leaked State Department cable dated December 2009 informed American diplomats: "Saudi Arabia remains a critical financial support base for al-Qa'ida, the Taliban, LeT [the group accused of the 2008 terror attacks in Mumbai], and other terrorist groups, including Hamas. . . .[52]

MYTH

"Arab states no longer boycott Israel."

FACT

The Arab League declared a boycott against the Jews in 1945, before Israel was established, and most of its members have pursued a diplomatic and economic embargo against the Jewish State since its establishment. The boycott's influence waned after Egypt and Jordan made peace with Israel, the Palestinians became engaged in peace negotiations, and several Gulf states started ignoring the blacklist, but it was never abandoned, and several nations, most notably Saudi Arabia, have energetically enforced it for decades.

In 2005, Saudi Arabia announced it would end its economic embargo of Israeli goods to win acceptance to the World Trade Organization.[53] After initially saying that it would do so, the government subsequently announced it would maintain its first-degree boycott of Israeli products. The government said it agreed to lift the second and third degree boycott in accordance with an earlier Gulf Cooperation Council decision rather than the demands of the WTO. In June 2006, the Saudi ambassador admitted his country still enforced the boycott in violation of promises made earlier to the Bush Administration and the Saudis participated in the 2007 boycott conference.

The continued effort to isolate Israel economically and diplomatically demonstrates that many Arab states are still unwilling to recognize Israel. Until the boycott is terminated, and the Arab League members accept the existence of Israel, the prospects for regional peace will remain dim.

MYTH

"The 2002 Arab peace initiative reflects the Arab states' acceptance of Israel."

FACT

In 2002, then Crown Prince Abdullah of Saudi Arabia told journalist Thomas Friedman his ideas for a comprehensive Mideast peace. Abdullah's ideas were revised and adopted by the Arab League as a peace initiative that offered Israel "normal relations" in exchange for a withdrawal to the 1967 borders and resolution of the Palestinian refugee issue.

The initiative amounts to nothing more than a restatement of the Arab interpretation of UN Resolution 242. The problem is that 242 does not say what the Saudi plan demands of Israel. The resolution calls on Israel to withdraw from territories occupied during the war, not "all" the territories in exchange for peace.

In addition, Resolution 242 also says that every state has the right to live within "secure and recognizable boundaries," which all military analysts have understood to mean the 1967 borders with modifications to satisfy Israel's security requirements. Moreover, Israel is under no obligation to withdraw before the Arabs agree to live in peace.

The Arab plan calls for Israel to withdraw from the Golan Heights. The Israeli government has offered to withdraw from most, if not all of the Golan in exchange for a peace agreement; however, Syrian President Bashar Assad has so far been unwilling to negotiate at all with Israel.

The demand that Israel withdraw from "the remaining occupied Lebanese territories in the south of Lebanon" is at odds with the UN conclusion that Israel has completely fulfilled its obligation to withdraw from Lebanese territory.

The Arab initiative calls for a just solution to the Palestinian refugee problem based on the nonbinding UN General Assembly Resolution 194. Under the Arab interpretation, the 4.7 million refugees should be allowed to live in Israel. This suicidal formula has been rejected by Israel since the end of the 1948 war and is totally unacceptable to all Israelis today. Israel does, however, recognize a right for all the refugees to live in a future Palestinian state and has agreed to allow some Palestinian refugees to live in Israel on a humanitarian basis, and as part of family reunification.

The refugee issue was not part of Abdullah's original proposal, but was added under pressure from other Arab states. Another change from Abdullah's original vision was a retreat from a promise of full normalization of relations with Israel to an even vaguer pledge of "normal relations."

The Arab demand that Israel accept the establishment of a Palestinian state in the West Bank and Gaza with East Jerusalem as its capital has been part of the negotiations since Oslo. Israel's leaders, including Prime Minister Ehud Olmert, have accepted the idea of creating a Palestinian state in part of those territories, and Israel has even offered compromises on the status of Jerusalem, but the Palestinians have rejected them all.

It is also worth noting that most of the Arab League nations have no reason not to be at peace with Israel now. Israel holds none of their territory and is more than willing to make peace with the members of the League. Several members of the League had already begun to normalize relations with Israel before the latest outbreak of violence, and their principal critic was Saudi Arabia.

If the Arab proponents of the plan were sincere, the response should be that they are prepared to sit down with Israel's leaders and discuss how to overcome the disagreements. But this has not been the Arab response. Rather than accept an Israeli invitation to come to Jerusalem to negotiate, the Arabs have told Israel it must accept the plan or face the threat of war. Here are a few examples:

- Saudi Foreign Minister Prince Saud al-Faisal, said: "If Israel refuses, that means it doesn't want peace and it places everything back into the hands of fate. They will be putting their future not in the hands of the peacemakers but in the hands of the lords of war."[54]

- The Syrian information minister, Muhsen Bilal, declared: "If Israel rejects the Arab League peace proposal, resistance will be the only way to liberate the Golan Heights."[55]

- The secretary general of the Gulf Cooperation Council, Abdulrahman al-Attiya, said that Israel should respond expeditiously to the Arab peace initiative because the Arabs are in no mood to wait interminably.[56]

Make peace on our terms or else. Is this the rhetoric you would expect from leaders who have moderated their views and want to seek an accommodation with Israel?

Peace plans are not worth the paper they are printed on if the proponents continue to talk about war and pursue policies such as supporting terrorists, arming radical Muslims, inciting their populations with anti-Semitic propaganda and enforcing boycotts that promote conflict. Progress toward real peace requires the Arab states to show by words and deeds that they are committed to finding a formula for coexisting with Israel. The only ultimatum should be that if the first efforts to reach an understanding do not succeed, they will try and try again.

MYTH

"Palestinians would prefer to live in a Palestinian state."

FACT

Most Palestinians currently living inside Israel's borders say they would prefer to live in Israel rather than a Palestinian state. One poll found that 62 percent of Israeli Arabs preferred to remain Israeli citizens rather than become citizens of a future Palestinian state. Another poll of East Jerusalemites found that only 30 percent of Palestinians would prefer Palestine over Israel and, if their neighborhood became an internationally recognized part of Israel, 54 percent said they would not move to Palestine.[57] Israeli Arabs know that, despite its faults, Israel is still a democratic state that offers them freedom of speech, assembly, religion, and the press, and respects human rights in general and women's rights and gay rights in particular. Palestinians are denied all these rights under Palestinian Authority rule.

> *"The major difficulty is that the Palestinians don't accept Israel's right to exist."*
>
> **—British Prime Minister Tony Blair[58]**

Residents of East Jerusalem began voting with their feet when politicians began discussing the possibility of dividing Jerusalem prior to the Annapolis Conference in 2007. Only about 12,000 East Jerusalemites had applied for citizenship since 1967 (out of some 250,000), but 3,000 new applications flooded Israel's Ministry of Interior in the four months prior to the meeting.[59]

For the Palestinians of the Ras Hamis and Shuafat refugee camps, which are a part of Jerusalem, but would most likely fall on the side of Jerusalem apportioned to the Palestinian Authority in any future peace agreement, the preference for staying in Israel is clear. They plan to take advantage of their status as Israeli permanent residents, which allows them freedom of movement, and move to a city well within Israel's borders and legal jurisdiction. "If they put a border here, we'll move to Haifa and Tel Aviv. You'll have fifty thousand people who live here leaving East Jerusalem in minutes," declared Jamil Sanduqa, head of the refugee camp's local council.[60]

Many of the 250,000 East Jerusalemites depend heavily on Israel for jobs, health care, and unemployment insurance. They do not foresee having the same opportunities or benefits under the Palestinian Authority. Palestinians living in Israel want to live normal lives and earn a living to help their family and don't want to be involved with extremists. "I don't want to raise my children on throwing stones, or on Hamas," Sanduqa said.[61]

One of the proposals for moving toward a two-state solution is a land swap. The idea is that Israel would evacuate most of the West Bank but keep the large settlement blocs that are home to approximately 200,000 Jews. This area is estimated to be 3–5 percent of the West Bank. Israel has proposed a land swap of a similar amount of territory now within Israel. One idea is to shift the border so the 45,000 residents of Umm el-Fahm, plus an additional 150,000 Israeli Arabs who sit on 200 square miles of land just northeast of the West Bank, would be a part of a future Palestinian state. The Palestinians swap citizenship; Israel exchanges land. In theory, it's a win-win situation where everyone gets to be citizens of their own nation. But the Israeli Arabs in these towns, especially Umm el-Fahm, the largest Muslim city in Israel, are vehemently opposed to being part of the deal.

> *"It's easy enough for global leaders to issue flowery appeals for action on the Middle East or to imply that progress would be possible if only the United States used its leverage with Israel. The stubborn reality is that there can be no movement toward peace until a Palestinian leadership appears that is ready to accept a two-state solution."*
>
> **—Editorial, Washington Post**[62]

"We wish to express our sharp opposition to any initiative taken by the State of Israel and the Palestinian Authority with regard to our civil, political and human rights," the heads of the Arab regional councils and cities wrote to Prime Minister Olmert and his cabinet members in response to the land swap proposal. " ...We wish to make it clear that as citizens of the State of Israel since 1948–1949 ... the proposed moving of borders will deprive us of these human rights and tear apart the social and economic ties that have been constructed on the basis of a long and difficult struggle."

One of the first to sign the letter to Prime Minister Olmert was Sheik Hasham Abed Elrahman, Umm el-Fahm Mayor and head of the Wadi Ara Forum of Arab and Jewish Mayors. He wrote, "I cannot argue with feelings. I can tell you that we want to work together with the Jewish majority for the betterment of all of Israel. Religiously, politically and socially, we want to remain part of the State of Israel."[63]

Not only do few Palestinians want to move to "Palestine," many Palestinians now living in the Palestinian Authority would emigrate if they could. According to a December 2007 survey, 34 percent of the residents would like to leave.[64]

MYTH

"Mahmoud Abbas is a moderate politician interested in compromise."

FACT

The definition of "moderate" is relative. Compared to Hamas, Hizbullah and Ahmadinejad, for example, Abbas can be viewed as a moderate since he explicitly negotiates with Israel. Abbas, however, has expressed no true willingness to compromise on any substantive issue, balks at true peace efforts and spews anti-Israel rhetoric that has significantly hampered the peace process.

In November 2010, Abbas spoke at the sixth annual memorial service for Yasser Arafat and definitively announced that he will continue to tow the hard line agenda of his mentor and predecessor.[65] Abbas is holding to Arafat's policies of declaring Jerusalem the capital of Palestine; requiring Israeli withdrawal from all settlements; demanding the full right of return for Palestinian refugees and their descendants; and refusing to acknowledge the Jewish character of the State of Israel. Abbas also publicly glorifies Palestinian martyrs and allows Holocaust denial to spread in official Palestinian sources.

On the issue of Jerusalem, Abbas said the city would be the capital of a future Palestinian state. "At the Camp David summit, the Palestinian leadership rejected an Israeli proposal to share sovereignty over the Aksa Mosque," he said. "They wanted to give the Muslims all what is above the mosque, while Israel would control what's under it. We continue to reject this offer. We cannot compromise on Jerusalem."[66] In an interview with the *Washington Post,* Abbas declared, "I say and have always said that East Jerusalem is an occupied territory. We have to restore it."[67] Again in 2010, he said that "the Arab city of Jerusalem, including its holy sites, is an integral part" of the future Palestinian state.[68]

On the subject of Israel's 2005 disengagement from Gaza, Abbas insisted that "The withdrawal from Gaza must only be part of other withdrawals.... Israel must pull out of all Palestinian lands occupied in 1967."[69] He reiterated again in a letter to Presidents Obama and Medvedev in 2010 that "the shortest way to peace is ending the Israeli occupation of all territory ... including Jerusalem, occupied Syrian Arab Golan Heights and the remaining Lebanese territories."[70] Abbas refuses to acknowledge Israeli security concerns that would stem from a complete withdrawal and is categorically opposed to land-swap deals to allay those fears.

In the same speech Abbas said that the refugee issue had to be solved on the basis of UN Resolution 194. According to Abbas, 4.7 million Palestinians are refugees. In a January 3, 2005, appearance, Abbas said Palestinian refugees and their descendants have the right to return to their original homes. "We will never forget the rights of the refugees, and we will never forget their suffering. They will eventually gain their rights, and the day will come when the refugees return home," Abbas told a cheering crowd.[71] In November 2010, the Fatah Revolutionary Council praised Abbas for standing up to pressure and maintaining his position on the Palestinian right of return.[72]

Though Abbas negotiates with Israel he rejects its raison d'etre as a Jewish state. Speaking to the Palestinian youth parliament in 2009, Abbas declared his refusal to recognize Israel's Jewish character saying, "Call yourselves what you want, but I will not accept it ...The 'Jewish State'...I will not accept it."[73] Abbas backed that statement again in September 2010, when he told members of the Hadash party it was an "unacceptable demand" that he recognize Israel as a Jewish state.[74]

In 2008, Israeli Prime Minister Ehud Olmert extended a peace proposal to Abbas that would have created two nation-states. Under the plan Israel would have withdrawn from almost the entire West Bank and partitioned Jerusalem on a demographic basis. Abbas rejected the offer.[75]

Abbas was supposed to have forsworn terror, but on February 28, 2008, he told the Jordanian newspaper *al-Dustur* that he did not rule out returning to the path of armed "resistance" against Israel. In fact, his reason for not engaging in "armed struggle" was not because he disavowed terror, but because he doesn't believe the Palestinians can achieve their objectives. "At this present juncture, I am opposed to armed struggle because we cannot succeed in it, but maybe in the future things will be different," he said.[76] Earlier, Abbas had launched his presidential election campaign by saying "the use of weapons is unacceptable because it has a negative impact on our image." The *Wall Street Journal* noted afterward that "Mr. Abbas does not reject terrorism because it is immoral, but because it no longer sells the cause abroad."[77]

Abbas was the number two person in the PLO under Arafat and a founder of the Fatah terrorist organization, which makes him responsible for decades of atrocities. In February 2008, he proudly claimed credit for initiating the terror campaign against Israel. "I had the honor of firing the first shot in 1965 and of being the one who taught resistance to many in the region and around the world," Abbas said. The PA president even takes credit for training the Lebanese Shiite terrorists. "We (Fatah) had the honor of leading the resistance and we taught resistance to everyone, including Hizbullah, who trained in our military camps."[78] In 2010, Abbas eulogized the mastermind behind the massacre at the 1972 Munich Olympics in which 11 Israeli athletes were murdered as "a leading figure in resistance" who "sacrificed for his people's just causes."[79]

Abbas is also a Holocaust denier. His Ph.D. dissertation suggested that six million Jews did not die at the hands of the Nazis and he denied that gas chambers were used to murder Jews.[80] Abbas also allows Holocaust denial to spread under his watch. The official PA media outlet airs programs where Palestinian academics teach that Auschwitz and Dachau "never existed" and the Palestinian Ministry of Education produces schoolbooks which teach the history of World War II yet completely ignores the Holocaust and the extermination of six million Jews.[81]

Abbas also clings to the hope that Israel will be forced to capitulate to his demands by outside powers, a fantasy that is fed by pressure exerted on Israel from the Europeans, UN, and the U.S. State Department. After refusing to negotiate with the Netanyahu government, Abbas announced plans to make an end-run around peace talks and seek UN recognition of a Palestinian state. He also agreed to reconcile with Hamas even as that organization insisted it remained committed to the destruction of Israel.

Israelis have no illusions about Abbas and remain skeptical that any agreements can be reached with a man who has shown neither the will nor the ability to carry out any of his promises. Nevertheless, Israeli leaders understand he is the only interlocutor they have for the moment and are willing to pursue negotiations in the hope that Abbas will genuinely moderate his views and compromise on the issues required to reach an agreement.

MYTH

"Palestinians are driven to terror by poverty and desperation."

FACT

The situation many Palestinians find themselves in is unfortunate and often quite severe. Many live in poverty, see the future as hopeless and are unhappy with the way they are treated by Israelis. None of these are excuses for engaging in terrorism. In fact, many of the terrorists are not poor, desperate people at all. Osama bin Laden, for example, was a Saudi millionaire.

On March 6, 2008, Ala Abu Dhaim murdered eight seminary students and wounded 15 more at the Merkaz Harav yeshiva in Jerusalem. Dhaim was not poor or desperate. He was engaged to be married, he came from a family that is financially comfortable, and was employed by the yeshiva as a driver. Dhaim also was not suffering under "occupation." In fact, as a resident of the East Jerusalem village of Jabel Mukaber, which lies within Jerusalem's municipal boundaries, he was entitled to all the same social and welfare benefits as Israeli citizens.

The stereotype that Palestinians turn to terrorism out of desperation is simply untrue. "There is no clear profile of someone who hates Israel and the Jewish people. They come in every shape and from every culture. Demonstrators, rioters and stone throwers do tend to be younger, unmarried males. But there's a big difference between the young men who participate in those types of disturbances and terrorists," remarked Aryeh Amit, former Jerusalem District Police Chief.[82]

> *"The use of suicide bombing is entirely unacceptable. Nothing can justify this. "*
>
> **—UN Special Representative for the protection of children in armed conflict, Under Secretary-General Olara Otunnu**[83]

A report by the National Bureau of Economic Research concluded, "economic conditions and education are largely unrelated to participation in, and support for, terrorism." The researchers said the outbreak of violence in the region that began in 2000 could not be blamed on deteriorating economic conditions because there is no connection between terrorism and economic depression. Furthermore, the authors found that support for violent action against Israel, including suicide bombing, does not vary much according to social background.[84]

For example, the cousin of one of the two Palestinian suicide bombers who blew themselves up on a pedestrian mall in Jerusalem in 2001, killing 10 people between the ages of 14 and 21, remarked candidly, "These two were not deprived of anything."[85]

Though some try to suggest the violence has nothing to do with radical Islam, the reality is that it is only Muslims who have engaged in suicide bombing. Palestinian Christians living in the same situation have not resorted to terror.

Terrorism is not Israel's fault. It is not the result of "occupation." And it certainly is not the only response available to the Palestinians' discontentment. Palestinians have an option for improving their situation, namely negotiations. But under the current Hamas regime, this is adamantly rejected. The Palestinians could also choose the nonviolent path emphasized by Martin Luther King or Gandhi. Unfortunately, they choose to pursue a war of terror instead of a process for peace. Israel has proven time and again a willingness to trade land for peace, but it can never concede land for terror.

MYTH

"Israel must negotiate with Hamas."

FACT

Hamas controls the Gaza Strip and, therefore, some people argue that Israel must negotiate with the terror group. Few Israelis seriously believe that Hamas is interested in any lasting peace with Israel, but the advocates for negotiations believe it may be possible to reach a long-term cease-fire agreement in which Hamas promises to stop firing rockets into Israel and Israel ceases its military operations against the group in Gaza.

Hamas cease-fires have resulted from fear that Israel was about to attack them or in response to targeted killings of their leaders. In 2007 and 2008, truces were used by Hamas to rearm and then were subsequently broken when terrorists resumed rocket attacks on southern Israel.

Meanwhile, its spokesmen continue to make belligerent statements. On August 2, 2010, for example, Hamas leader Khaled Mashal said, "We are not concerned about being called terrorists, since if our jihad is considered terrorism, then the detractors can say whatever they want. We are going to stick to jihad, resistance, and guns as the path towards liberation and return."[86] Hamas also remains committed to its covenant that calls for the destruction of Israel.

It is often said that you don't make peace with your friends, you make peace with your enemies, but this assumes the enemy you are negotiating with is not committed to your destruction. Golda Meir said it best when she explained the conflict had nothing to do with territory. "We're the only people in the world where our neighbors openly announce they just won't have us here," she observed. "And they will not give up fighting and they will not give up war as long as we remain alive ... They say we must be dead. And we say we want to be alive. Between life and death, I don't know of a compromise."

Notes

1. Speech to AIPAC Policy Conference, (May 8, 1978).
2. *Jerusalem Post*, (September 25, 2001).
3. Daniel Pipes, *The Long Shadow: Culture and Politics in the Middle East*, (NJ: Transaction Publishers, 1989), pp. 273-74.
4. Reuters, (November 11, 2001).
5. Michael Widlanski, *Can Israel Survive A Palestinian State?*, (Jerusalem: Institute for Advanced Strategic and Political Studies, 1990), pp. 10, 35.
6. Dore Gold, "Israel's War to Halt Palestinian Rocket Attacks," *JCPA*, (March 3, 2008).
7. Editorial, *Chicago Sun Times*, (June 27, 2006).
8. *Yediot Aharonot*, (November 23, 2001).
9. *Yediot Aharonot*, (August 7, 2002).
10. MSNBC, (June 27, 2002).
11. "Proceedings and Debates of the 107th Congress, 2nd Session, Vol. 148-Part 4," US Congressional Record, (April 11-24, 2002), p. 5174.
12. Associated Press, (May 26, 2003).
13. *New York Times*, (August 27, 2003).
14. Daniel Pipes, "[Suicide Bombers:] A father's pride and glory," *Jerusalem Post*, (August 15, 2001).
15. *Jerusalem Post*, (October 16, 2001).
16. "Hamas TV drops militant Mickey Mouse," *Jerusalem Post*, (May 9, 2007); Itamar Mar-

cus and Barbara Cook, "Hamas steals Mickey Mouse image to teach hate and Islamic supremacy," *Palestinian Media Watch Bulletin,* (May 6, 2007).

17. "Palestinian Children Taught Paradise Is Reward for Martyrdom," Palestinian Media Watch, (June 28, 2006).

18. Itamar Marcus and Nan Jacques Zilberdik, "PA TV to kids: Israeli cities, Haifa, Jaffa, Lod, Ramle, Acre are all 'occupied cities,' " Palestinian Media Watch, (August 29, 2010).

19. "Sharm el-Sheikh Fact-Finding Committee—First Statement of the Government of Israel," (December 28, 2000), http://www.mfa.gov.il/mfa/go.asp?MFAH0jcb0.

20. Lee Hockstader, "At Arab, Israeli Schools, Hatred Is Common Bond," *Washington Post,* (September 5, 2001).

21. Goetz Norbruch, *Narrating Palestinian Nationalism: A Study of the New Palestinian Textbooks,"* (DC: MEMRI, 2002).

22. *Near East Report,* (June 25, 2001); *Jerusalem Post,* (July 20, 2001).

23. Quoted in *Jerusalem Post,* (July 20, 2001).

24. Arnon Ben-Dror, "Welcome to Camp Hamas," *Israel Defense Forces,* (August 29, 2009).

25. *Jerusalem Post,* (May 15, 2005).

26. Al-Manar TV, (January 25, 2006).

27. For example, Hamas Foreign Minister Mahmoud Zahar, "I dream of hanging a huge map of the world on the wall at my Gaza home which does not show Israel on it," *Xinhua,* (April 1, 2006).

28. Jerusalem Media & Communication Center, (April, 2008).

29. "Map Erasing Israel on Palestinian Website," *Palestinian Media Watch,* (February 1, 2010).

30. *Washington Post,* (July 18, 2001), citing an article by Robert Malley and Hussein Agha in the *New York Review of Books* in which they quote the president at the Camp David summit in July 2000.

31. *Chicago Tribune,* (March 5, 1988).

32. *Washington Post,* (August 10, 2001).

33. Moshe Zak, "Did Israel Inject AIDS to Palestinian Children," Israel Behind the News, (March 30, 1998).

34. Palestinian Authority TV, (March 3, 2003).

35. Aaron Klein, "Palestinians Claim Israelis X-Rayed Woman to Death," WorldNet Daily, (May 2, 2005).

36. Palestinian Authority TV, (March 3, 2003).

37. VOA News, (February 12, 2004).

38. Radio Damascus, (March 8, 1974) cited in Daniel Pipes, "Palestine for the Syrians?," Commentary, (December 1986).

39. *Jerusalem Post,* (July 16, 1994).

40. "Main Points: Israel-Jordan Peace Treaty," *Ministry of Foreign Affairs,* (October 26, 1994).

41. "Averting the Middle East Water Crisis," *Link,* (May 1995).

42. Israel Harel, "Claims Israel deprives Palestinians of water are groundless," *Haaretz,* (October 29, 2009).

43. *Mideast Mirror,* (October 7, 1991).

44. *Washington Post,* (September 10, 1995).

45. *Washington Post,* (August 6, 2001); Matthew Levitt, "A Hamas Headquarters in Saudi Arabia?" Washington Institute for Near East Policy, (September 28, 2005).

46. *New York Times,* (January 27, 2002).

47. "Terrorism Financing—Report Prepared for the President of the Security Council," United Nations, (December 19, 2002).

48. Audiotape posted August 27, 2005, on the 'Izz Al-Din Al-Qassam Brigades website, translated by MEMRI.

49. Kenneth Timmerman, "Hamas' Friends," *Australia/Israel Review,* (June 2002), p. 13.
50. *Washington Post,* (April 2 and 12, 2002).
51. Matthew Levitt, "A Hamas Headquarters in Saudi Arabia?" Washington Institute for Near East Policy, (September 28, 2005).
52. Mitchell Bard, *The Arab Lobby.* (Harper Collins, 2010), p. 182; "Terrorist Finance: Action Request for Senior Level Engagement on Terrorism Finance," State Department cable, (December 30, 2009).
53. "Saudi Arabia lifts Israel embargo," *Jerusalem Post,* (November 15, 2005; June 22, 2006).
54. David Blair, "Accept peace plan or face war, Israel told," *Telegraph,* (March 28, 2007).
55. Roee Nahmias, "Syria: Without peace, resistance will liberate Golan Heights," Ynetnews, (April 16, 2007).
56. "Arabs won't wait decades for Israeli response to Arab Peace Initiative: GCC," Kuwait News Agency, (May 3, 2007).
57. KEEVOON Research, Strategy and Communications, (December 26, 2007); "The Palestinians of East Jerusalem: What Do They Really Want?" Pechter Middle East Polls/Council on Foreign Relations, (January 12, 2011).
58. Associated Press, (December 7, 2006).
59. Ronny Shaked, "Thousands of Palestinians apply for Israeli citizenship," Ynetnews, November 7, 2007).
60. Joshua Mitnick, "Better the Devil You Know," *The Jerusalem Report,* (November 11, 2007).
61. Ibid.
62. "Instransigent Hamas," *Washington Post,* (October 11, 2006).
63. Eetta Prince-Gibson, "Land (Swap) for Peace?" *The Jerusalem Report,* (November 26, 2007).
64. Near East Consulting, Bulletin # II-12, (December 2007).
65. "Abbas Talks Peace Process at Arafat Memorial," *Ma'an News Agency,* (November 11, 2010).
66. Tani Goldstein, "Rocket Hits Ashkelon House; Qassams Land in Sderot," Ynetnews, (March 3, 2008).
67. "A Conversation with Mahmoud Abbas," *Washington Post,* (September 30, 2007).
68. Khaled Abu Toameh, "Abbas Vows to Walk in Arafat's Footsteps in Palestine," *Jerusalem Post,* (November 12, 2010).
69. "Abbas Demands Israeli Pullout, Prisoner Release," *Daily Times,* (December 26, 2004).
70. "Erekat Delivers Message from President Abbas to Quarter," *Independent Media Review Analysis,* (August 22, 2010).
71. "Abbas: Refugees to Return to their Homes in Israel," *Haaretz,* (January 4, 2005).
72. Khaled Abu Toameh, "Fatah: No to Israel as Jewish State, No Land Swaps,' " *Jerusalem Post,* (November 28, 2010).
73. "Abbas Scorns 'Jewish State,' " *Palestinian Media Watch,* (April 27, 2009).
74. Ynet, "Abbas: We Won't Recognize Israel as Jewish State," Ynetnews, (October 15, 2010).
75. Ari Shavit, "The two nation-state solution," *Haaretz,* (April 23, 2009).
76. Roee Nahmias, "Report: Abbas Does Not Rule Out Resuming Armed Conflict with Israel," Ynetnews, (February 28, 2008).
77. Editorial, "The End of the Affair," *Wall Street Journal,* (December 31, 2004).
78. "Abbas: Armed Resistance Not Ruled Out," *Jerusalem Post,* (February 29, 2008).
79. Tzvi Ben Gedalyahu, "Abbas Eulogizes Munich Massacre Mastermind," Arutz Sheva, (July 4, 2010).
80. "Palestinian Authority Holocaust Denial and Distortion," *Palestinian Media Watch.*
81. Ibid.

82. Interview with Jerusalem District Police Chief Aryeh Amit by Eetta Prince Gibson, "The Back Page," *The Jerusalem Report,* (March 31, 2008).

83. *Jerusalem Post,* (January 15, 2003).

84. Jitka Maleckova and Alan Kreuger, "Education, Poverty, Political Violence and Terrorism: Is There a Causal Connection?" (July 2002), quoted in the *Daily Star* [Lebanon], (August 6, 2002).

85. *Washington Post,* (December 5, 2001).

86. Intelligence and Terrorism Information Center, (August 8, 2010).

18. Settlements

"Israeli settlements are illegal."

FACT

Jews have lived in Judea and Samaria—the West Bank—since ancient times. The only time Jews have been prohibited from living in the territories in recent decades was during Jordan's rule from 1948 to 1967.

Numerous legal authorities dispute the charge that settlements are "illegal." Stephen Schwebel, formerly President of the International Court of Justice, notes that a country acting in self-defense may seize and occupy territory when necessary to protect itself. Schwebel also observes that a state may require, as a condition for its withdrawal, security measures designed to ensure its citizens are not menaced again from that territory.[1]

According to Eugene Rostow, a former Undersecretary of State for Political Affairs in the Johnson Administration, Resolution 242 gives Israel a legal right to be in the West Bank. The resolution, Rostow noted, "Israel is entitled to administer the territories" it won in 1967 until "a just and lasting peace in the Middle East" is achieved.[2] Though critical of Israeli policy, the United States does not consider settlements illegal.

MYTH

"Settlements are an obstacle to peace."

FACT

Settlements have never been an obstacle to peace.

- From 1949-67, when Jews were forbidden to live on the West Bank, the Arabs refused to make peace with Israel.

- From 1967-77, the Labor Party established only a few strategic settlements in the territories, yet the Arabs were unwilling to negotiate peace with Israel.

- In 1977, months after a Likud government committed to greater settlement activity took power, Egyptian President Sadat went to Jerusalem and later signed a peace treaty with Israel. Incidentally, Israeli settlements existed in the Sinai and those were removed as part of the agreement with Egypt.

■ One year later, Israel froze settlement building for three months, hoping the gesture would entice other Arabs to join the Camp David peace process, but none would.

■ In 1994, Jordan signed a peace agreement with Israel and settlements were not an issue; if anything, the number of Jews living in the territories was growing.

■ Between June 1992 and June 1996, under Labor-led governments, the Jewish population in the territories grew by approximately 50 percent. This rapid growth did not prevent the Palestinians from signing the Oslo accords in September 1993 or the Oslo 2 agreement in September 1995.

■ In 2000, Prime Minister Ehud Barak offered to dismantle dozens of settlements, but the Palestinians still would not agree to end the conflict.

■ In August 2005, Israel evacuated all of the settlements in the Gaza Strip and four in Northern Samaria, but terror attacks continued.

■ In 2008, Prime Minister Ehud Olmert offered to withdraw from approximately 94 percent of the West Bank, but the deal was rejected.

■ In 2010, Prime Minister Benjamin Netanyahu froze settlement construction for 10 months and the Palestinians refused to engage in negotiations until the period was nearly over. After agreeing to talk, they walked out when Netanyahu refused to prolong the freeze.

Settlement activity may be a *stimulus* to peace because it forced the Palestinians and other Arabs to reconsider the view that time is on their side. References are frequently made in Arabic writings to how long it took to expel the Crusaders and how it might take a similar length of time to do the same to the Zionists. The growth in the Jewish population in the territories forced the Arabs to question this tenet. "The Palestinians now realize," said Bethlehem Mayor Elias Freij, "that time is now on the side of Israel, which can build settlements and create facts, and that the only way out of this dilemma is face-to-face negotiations."[3]

Even though settlements are not an obstacle to peace, many Israelis still have concerns about the expansion of settlements. Some consider them provocative, others worry that the settlers are particularly vulnerable, and note they have been targets of repeated Palestinian terrorist attacks. To defend them, large numbers of soldiers are deployed who would otherwise be training and preparing for a possible future conflict with an Arab army. Some Israelis also object to the amount of money that goes to communities beyond the Green Line, and special subsidies that have been provided to make housing there more affordable. Still others feel the settlers are providing a first line of defense and developing land that rightfully belongs to Israel.

The disposition of settlements is a matter for the final status negotiations. The question of where the final border will be between Israel and a Palestinian entity will likely be influenced by the distribution of these Jewish towns in Judea and Samaria (the border with Gaza was unofficially defined following Israel's withdrawal). Israel wants to incorporate as many settlers as possible within its borders while the Palestinians want to expel all Jews from the territory they control.

If Israel withdraws toward the 1949 armistice line unilaterally, or as part of a political settlement, many settlers will face one or more options: remain in the territories (the disengagement from Gaza suggests this may not be possible), expulsion from their homes, or voluntary resettlement in Israel (with financial compensation).

The impediment to peace is not the existence of Jewish communities in the disputed territories, it is the Palestinians' unwillingness to accept a state next to Israel instead of one replacing Israel.

MYTH

"The Geneva Convention prohibits the construction of Jewish settlements in occupied territories."

FACT

The Fourth Geneva Convention prohibits the *forcible* transfer of people of one state to the territory of another state that it has occupied as a result of a war. The intention was to insure that local populations who came under occupation would not be forced to move. This is in no way relevant to the settlement issue. Jews are not being forced to go to the West Bank; on the contrary, they are voluntarily moving back to places where they, or their ancestors, once lived before being expelled by others.

In addition, those territories never legally belonged to either Jordan or Egypt, and certainly not to the Palestinians, who were never the sovereign authority in any part of Palestine. "The Jewish right of settlement in the area is equivalent in every way to the right of the local population to live there," according to Professor Eugene Rostow, former Undersecretary of State for Political Affairs.[4]

As a matter of policy, moreover, Israel does not requisition private land for the establishment of settlements. Housing construction is allowed on private land only after determining that no private rights will be violated. The settlements also do not displace Arabs living in the territories. The media sometimes gives the impression that for every Jew who moves to the West Bank, several hundred Palestinians are forced to leave. The truth is that the vast majority of settlements have been built in uninhabited areas and even the handful established in or near Arab towns did not force any Palestinians to leave.

MYTH

"The size of the Jewish population in the West Bank precludes any territorial compromise."

FACT

Altogether, built-up settlement area is less than two percent of the disputed territories. An estimated 70 percent of the settlers live in what are in effect suburbs of major Israeli cities such as Jerusalem. These are areas that virtually the entire Jewish population believes Israel must retain to ensure its security, and presidents Clinton and Bush anticipated would remain under permanent Israeli sovereignty.[5]

Strategic concerns have led both Labor and Likud governments to establish settlements. The objective is to secure a Jewish majority in key strategic regions of the West Bank, such as the Tel Aviv-Jerusalem corridor, the scene of heavy fighting in several Arab-Israeli wars. Still, when Arab-Israeli peace talks began in late 1991, more than 80 percent of the West Bank contained no settlements or only sparsely populated ones.[6]

Today, approximately 300,000 Jews live in 122 communities in the West Bank. The overwhelming majority of these settlements have fewer than 1,000 citizens, 40 percent have fewer than 500 and several have only a few dozen residents. Contrary to Palestinian-inspired hysteria about settlement expansion, the truth is only five settlements have been built since 1990.[7] Analysts have noted that 70–80 percent of the Jews could be brought within Israel's borders with minor modifications of the "Green Line."

Ironically, while Palestinians complain about settlements, an estimated 35,000 work in them and support a population of more than 200,000.[8]

MYTH

"At Camp David, Begin promised to halt the construction of settlements for five years."

FACT

The five-year period agreed to at Camp David was the time allotted to Palestinian self-government in the territories. The Israeli moratorium on West Bank settlements agreed to by Prime Minister Menachem Begin was only for three months.

Israel's position on the matter received support from an unexpected source: Egyptian President Anwar Sadat, who said: "We agreed to put a freeze on the establishment of settlements for the coming three months, the time necessary in our estimation for signing the peace treaty."[9]

The Palestinians rejected the Camp David Accords and therefore the provisions related to them were never implemented. Had they accepted the terms offered by Begin, it is very likely the self-governing authority would have developed long before now into an independent Palestinian state.

> *"If settlement-building is now concentrated in areas that the Palestinians themselves acknowledge will remain part of Israel in any future peace agreement, why the obsessive focus on settlements as an 'obstacle to peace?'"*
>
> **—Yossi Klein Halevi[10]**

MYTH

"Israel must dismantle all the settlements or peace is impossible."

FACT

When serious negotiations begin over the final status of the West Bank, battle lines will be drawn over which settlements should be incorporated into Israel, and which must be evacuated. In August 2005, Prime Minister Ariel Sharon acknowledged that "not all the settlements that are today in Judea and Samaria will remain Israeli" while leaked Palestinian negotiating documents indicate the Palestinians are prepared to accept that some settlements will be incorporated into Israel.[11]

In Gaza, Israel's intent was to withdraw completely, and no settlements were viewed as vital to Israel for economic, security, or demographic reasons. The situation in the West Bank is completely different because Jews have strong historic and religious connections to the area stretching back centuries. Moreover, the West Bank is an area with strategic significance because of its proximity to Israel's heartland and the fact that roughly one-quarter of Israel's water resources are located there.

The disengagement from Gaza involved only 21 settlements and approximately 8,500 Jews; more than 100 settlements with a population of roughly 300,000 are located in Judea and Samaria. Any new evacuation from the West Bank will involve another gut-wrenching decision that most settlers and their supporters will oppose with even greater ferocity than the Gaza disengagement. Most Israelis, however, favor withdrawing from all but the largest communities.

Over two-thirds of the Jews in the West Bank live in five settlement "blocs" that are all near the 1967 border. Most Israelis believe these blocs should become part of Israel when final borders are drawn. The table below lists the "consensus" settlements:

Bloc	No. of Communities	Population	Approximate. Area (sq. miles)
Ma'ale Adumim	6	40,210	28
Modiin Illit	4	51,773	2
Ariel	15	41,720	47
Gush Etzion	18	54,939	10
Givat Ze'ev	5	12,916	3
Total	48	201,558	90

As the table shows, these are large communities with thousands of residents. Evacuating them would be the equivalent of dismantling major American cities such as Annapolis, Maryland, Olympia, Washington, or Carson City, Nevada.

Ma'ale Adumim is a suburb of Israel's capital, barely three miles outside Jerusalem's city limits, a ten-minute drive away. Ma'ale Adumim is not a recently constructed outpost on a hilltop; it is a 35-year-old community that is popular because it is clean, safe, and close to where many residents work. It is also the third-largest Jewish city in the territories, with a population of 34,324. Approximately 6,000 people live in surrounding settlements that are included in the Ma'ale bloc. Israel has long planned to fill in the empty gap between Jerusalem and this bedroom community (referred to as the E1 project). The corridor is approximately 3,250 acres and does not have any inhabitants, so no Palestinians would be displaced. According to the Clinton plan, Ma'ale was to be part of Israel.

The Gush Etzion Bloc consists of 18 communities with a population of nearly 55,000 just 10 minutes from Jerusalem. Jews lived in this area prior to 1948, but the Jordanian Legion destroyed the settlements and killed 240 women and children during Israel's War of Independence. After Israel recaptured the area in 1967, descendants of those early settlers reestablished the community. The largest of the settlements is the city of Betar Illit with nearly 35,000 residents.

The Givat Ze'ev bloc includes five communities just northwest of Jerusalem. Givat Ze'ev, with a population of just under 11,000, is the largest.

Modiin Illit is a bloc with four communities. The city of Modiin Illit is the largest in all the disputed territories, with nearly 46,000 people situated just over the Green Line, about 23 miles northwest of Jerusalem and the same distance east of Tel Aviv.

Ariel is now the heart of the third most populous bloc of settlements. The city is located just 25 miles east of Tel Aviv and 31 miles north of Jerusalem. Ariel and the surrounding communities expand Israel's narrow waist (which was just 9 miles wide prior to 1967) and ensure that Israel has a land route to the Jordan Valley in case Israel needs to fight a land war to the east. It is more controversial than the other consensus settlements because it is the furthest from the 1949 Armistice Line, extending approximately 12 miles into the West Bank. Nevertheless, Barak's proposal at Camp David included Ariel among the settlement blocs to be annexed to Israel; the Clinton plan also envisioned incorporating Ariel within the new borders of Israel.

> *"Clearly, in the permanent agreement we will have to give up some of the Jewish settlements."*
>
> **—Prime Minister Ariel Sharon**[12]

Most peace plans, including Clinton's, assumed that Israel would annex sufficient territory to incorporate 75–80% of the Jews currently living in the West Bank. Using the figures in the table above, however, it appears that Israel would fall short of that demographic goal even if these five blocs were annexed. The total population of these communities is approximately 202,000, which is roughly 66% of the estimated 304,000 Jews living in Judea and Samaria. The expectation, however, is that roughly one-third of the Jews living in other settlements will move into these blocs, which would bring the total close to 80%, but still require Israel to evacuate more than 60,000 people.

At Camp David, Israel insisted that 80 percent of the Jewish residents of Judea and Samaria would be in settlement blocs under Israeli sovereignty. President Clinton agreed and proposed that Israel annex 4–6 percent of the West Bank for three settlement blocs to accomplish this demographic objective and swap some territory within Israel in exchange.

Recognizing the demographics of the area, President Bush acknowledged the inevitability of some Israeli towns in the West Bank being annexed to Israel in his 2004 letter to Prime Minister Sharon. In his meeting a year later with Palestinian Authority President Abbas, however, he seemed to hedge his support by saying that any such decision would have to be mutually agreed to by Israelis and Palestinians. Nevertheless, the future border is likely to approximate the route of the security fence, given the Israeli prerequisite (with U.S. approval) of incorporating most settlers within Israel.

Ultimately, Israel may decide to unilaterally disengage from the West Bank and determine which settlements it will incorporate within the borders it delineates. Israel would prefer, however, to negotiate a peace treaty with the Palestinians that would specify which Jewish communities will remain intact within the mutually agreed border of Israel, and

Map 24 The Future Borders of Israel and Palestine?

Proposed Palestinian State

Israeli Settlement Blocs
Annexed to Israel

1967 "border"

*MEDITERRANEAN
SEA*

Haifa

*Sea of
Galilee*

Jenin

Tulkarm

Nablus

Qalqilya

Ariel
(est. bloc pop. 39,000)

Tel Aviv

Modiin Illit
(est. bloc pop. 31,000)

Ramallah

Jericho

ISRAEL

Jerusalem

Ma'aleh
Adumim
(est. bloc pop. 33,000)

Bethlehem

Gush Etzion
(est. bloc pop. 42,000)

Gaza

Hebron

**GAZA
STRIP**

*Dead
Sea*

Jordan River

JORDAN

ISRAEL

EGYPT

0   15
miles

N

which will need to be evacuated. Israel will undoubtedly insist that some or all of the "consensus" blocs become part of Israel.

MYTH

"If Israel annexes the settlement blocs, a Palestinian state will not be contiguous."

FACT

As Map 24 indicates, it is possible to create a contiguous Palestinian state in the West Bank even if Israel incorporates the major settlement blocs. The total area of these communities is only about 1.5 percent of the West Bank. A kidney-shaped state linked to the Gaza Strip by a secure passage would be contiguous. Some argue that the E1 project linking Ma'ale Adumim to Jerusalem would cutoff east Jerusalem, but even that is not necessarily true as Israel has proposed constructing a four-lane underpass to guarantee free passage between the West Bank and the Arab sections of Jerusalem.

Notes

1. *American Journal of International Law,* (April, 1970), pp. 345–46.
2. *New Republic,* (October 21, 1991), p. 14.
3. *Washington Post,* (November 1, 1991).
4. Eugene Rostow, "Bricks and Stones: Settling for Leverage," *The New Republic,* (April 23, 1990).
5. *Haaretz,* (September 13, 2001); President George W. Bush's Letter to Prime Minister Ariel Sharon, (April 14, 2004).
6. *Jerusalem Post,* (October 22, 1991).
7. Tovah Lazaroff, "Frontlines: Is settlement growth booming?" *Jerusalem Post,* (December 30, 2010).
8. Avi Issacharoff, "PA lightens ban on working in settlements to ease Palestinian unemployment," *Haaretz,* (December 28, 2010).
9. Middle East News Agency, (September 20, 1978).
10. *Los Angeles Times,* (June 20, 2001).
11. Greg Myre, "Middle East: Sharon Sees More West Bank Pullouts," *New York Times,* (August 30, 2005).
12. Prime Minister Ariel Sharon, Address to the Likud Central Committee, (January 5, 2004).

19. The Arms Balance

MYTH

"Israel is militarily superior to its neighbors and has nothing to fear from them."

FACT

Israel's qualitative military edge has declined as Arab and Muslim states acquire increasingly sophisticated conventional and unconventional arms. In fact, despite its pledges to the contrary, the United States is allowing Israel's qualitative edge to dissipate. In some cases, U.S. arms transfers to the Arabs are the reason for this erosion.

Israel's standing army is smaller than those of Egypt, Iran and Syria. Even with its reserves, Israel is outmanned by Egypt and Iran. In addition, Israel is likely to have to face a combination of enemies, as it has in each of its previous wars; together, virtually any combination of likely opponents would be superior in manpower, tanks and aircraft.

During the 1990's, the Arab states and Iran imported more than $180 billion worth of the most sophisticated weapons and military infrastructure available from both the Western and Eastern blocs. They added another $40 billion worth of materiel to their arsenals in the following decade.[1] In 2010, the U.S. alone (other countries also supply weapons to Arab states) planned to sell $60.1 billion worth of some of America's most sophisticated arms to Saudi Arabia (the largest arms sale in U.S. history). Other Arab states were also offered large packages, including the United Arab Emirates ($5.4 billion), Iraq ($4.9 billion), Oman ($3.6 billion), and Kuwait ($1.6 billion).[2]

Since 2009, Saudi Arabia has purchased nearly 200 combat aircraft, 100 combat helicopters and 550 tanks in addition to various air-to-surface missiles.[3] In 2010, Syria renewed its military purchases from Russia, obtaining hundreds of Grison SA-19 Surface-to-Air missiles and the promise of additional weapons. Despite being subjected to a UN arms embargo, Iran has procured hundreds of anti-aircraft, anti-tank and anti-ship missiles from China, Russia and North Korea.[4] Egypt purchased $6.8 billion worth of arms in the last decade. Additionally, transparency in arms transfers in the Middle East is extremely poor. Since 1998 only Israel, Jordan and Turkey have regularly submitted substantive reports to the UN Register of Conventional Arms, detailing their imports and exports of major conventional weapons.[5]

Israel allocates about $13 billion for defense annually, while Iran and the Arab states, many of which are in a state of war with Israel, spend more than $70 billion a year.[6] In addition to the quantity of weapons, Israel must also be concerned with the erosion of its qualitative edge as the Arab states acquire increasingly sophisticated systems.

In addition to the sheer quantity of arms, these states are also buying and producing increasing numbers of nonconventional weapons. The buildup of chemical and biological weapons, combined with the pursuit of a nuclear capability by Iran, Syria and possibly other Arab states (12 have either announced plans to explore atomic energy or signed nuclear cooperation agreements for "peaceful purposes"), makes Israel's strategic position more precarious.

The unrest in the Arab world has also increased the potential threats to Israel. The fall of the Mubarak regime in Egypt and uncertainty about that country's future could have a profound impact on Israel's security. If a future regime reneges on the peace treaty, Israel would have to dramatically reframe its strategy to prepare for the possibility of conflict with Egypt. If Egypt becomes more supportive of Hamas in the Gaza Strip or other terrorists, it will have to adapt to these threats. The takeover of Lebanon by Hezbollah and its rearmament by Iran and Syria has significantly increased the danger to northern Israel. If Jordan were to be destabilized, then Israel could find itself in the same position it was in prior to 1978 when it was surrounded by enemies.

Even before the "Arab Spring," Israel expressed concern about the sale of U.S. weapons to Arab states because of "the narrowing of the qualitative gap by potential adversaries." The U.S. provides cutting edge American weapons and technology as well as training to Arab armed forces, which significantly enhance their capabilities. Israel fears that erosion of its qualitative edge may influence the intentions of their enemies. Israel also worries "that some of the capabilities may, under certain circumstances, fall into the hands of terror elements."[7]

Beyond the security threat, the massive Arab arms build-up also requires Israel to spend about 7 percent of its GDP on defense, exacerbating the strain on Israel's economy. Moreover, even this high level of spending may be insufficient to meet the Arab/Iranian threat.

MYTH

"U.S. arms sales to Saudi Arabia enhance the kingdom's security and pose no threat to Israel."

FACT

The Saudi armed forces are structurally incapable of defending their country. They were helpless in the face of the Iraqi threat in 1990–91, despite the Saudi acquisition of more than $50 billion in U.S. arms and military services in the decade preceding the Gulf War.[8] If Saddam Hussein had continued his blitzkrieg into Saudi Arabia before American forces arrived in August 1990, much of the weaponry the United States sold to Riyadh over the years might have fallen into Saddam's hands.

The U.S. has no way to ensure that the vast quantities of aircraft and missiles it sells to Saudi Arabia will not be used against Israel. The possibility of these weapons falling into the hands of enemies of the United States cannot be ruled out either, given the Saudis' documented support for terrorists and the possibility that the monarchy could be overthrown by a more hostile regime. Moreover, it makes no sense to say that advanced American weapons can help the Saudis counter external threats but that those same arms pose no danger to Israel.

In past Arab-Israeli wars, the Saudis never had a modern arsenal of sufficient size to make their participation in an Arab coalition against Israel a serious concern. The Saudi buildup since the 1973 War changes this equation. The Kingdom could be pressured into offensive action against Israel by other eastern front partners precisely because of this buildup.

Israel has grown increasingly concerned with the Saudi buildup and aggressive activities. In addition to concerns over Saudi involvement in past wars, opposition to peace and ongoing involvement in terrorism, the Israelis complained to U.S. officials about the Saudis conducting "unusual and sometimes aggressive air activity from the Tabuq airfield." In particular, Israel said that Saudi interceptors had "repeatedly scrambled in response to routine Israeli air activity in the Eilat Gulf," actions that "could be interpreted as indicating hostile intentions."[9] Furthermore, the deployment to Tabuq constitutes a fundamental violation of promises given to Israel by the United States when it sold the planes to the Saudis.

MYTH

"Israel's refusal to sign the Nuclear Non-Proliferation Treaty allows it to conceal its nuclear arsenal and threaten its neighbors."

FACT

Though Israel does not formally acknowledge that it has a nuclear capability, it has been widely reported that Israel has been a member of the nuclear club for a number of years. During that time, Israel has never tested, used or threatened the use of nuclear weapons. Israel, has in fact, pledged never to be the first to introduce nuclear weapons into the region and proven through the wars since acquiring a bomb that it will use only conventional weapons to defend its security.

Like India, Israel has not signed the Non-Proliferation Treaty (NPT). Israel's decision is based largely on the grounds that the treaty has done little to stem nuclear proliferation in the region. Iraq is a signatory to the NPT and yet was able to amass a large amount of nuclear material without the knowledge of the International Atomic Energy Agency prior to the Israeli attack on its reactor in 1981.

Iran is also a signatory to the NPT and was discovered to have had a secret nuclear weapons program for more than a decade. Even after the disclosure, Iran has defied the international community and continued to enrich uranium for the purpose, most believe, of building a nuclear weapon.

Another signatory to the treaty, Syria, was accused of pursuing a nuclear weapon after Israel bombed a suspected weapons facility in 2007. The CIA subsequently said it was a plutonium reactor being built with the help of North Korea.[10]

> *"I wish Israel did not need defensive weapons of mass destruction or the region's most powerful defense forces. I wish the world had not driven the Jewish State into allocating its limited resources away from its universities and toward its military, but survival must come first, and Israel's military strength is the key to its survival. Anyone who believes that survival can be assured by moral superiority alone must remember the Warsaw Ghetto and the Treblinka gas chambers."*
>
> **—Alan Dershowitz[11]**

MYTH

"Iran has no ambition to become a nuclear power."

FACT

American and Israeli intelligence assessments suggest that the Islamic regime in Iran will have a nuclear weapon within a few years (estimates have changed but are typically 3–5 years) or possibly sooner if its current program is not slowed or stopped. Evidence of Iran's pursuit of nuclear weapons was revealed in 2002 with the discovery of two previously unknown nuclear facilities in Arak and Natanz. This was followed by the admission by Pakistan's top nuclear scientist, Abdul Qadeer Khan, that he provided nuclear weapons expertise and equipment to Iran.

Secretary of State Colin Powell said United States intelligence indicated Iran is trying to fit missiles to carry nuclear weapons. "There is no doubt in my mind—and it's fairly straightforward from what we've been saying for years—that they have been interested in a nuclear weapon that has utility, meaning that it is something they would be able to deliver, not just something that sits there," Powell said.[12]

Iranian President Mahmoud Ahmadinejad defended his country's right to produce nuclear fuel in a fiery speech to the UN General Assembly and later raised worldwide concern about nuclear proliferation when he said, "Iran is ready to transfer nuclear know-how to the Islamic countries due to their need."[13]

In fact, nuclear proliferation is one of the most serious dangers posed by Iran's program. In addition to what Iran might do, there is also the likelihood that its neighbors will feel the need to build their own weapons in the hope of creating a nuclear deterrent.

The international concensus opposing Iran's pursuit of nuclear weapons is reflected in the actions taken by the UN. On July 31, 2006, the Security Council approved Resolution 1696, giving Iran until August 31 to verifiably suspend its uranium enrichment and reprocessing-related activities and implement full transparency measures requested by the IAEA. Iran's top nuclear negotiator, Ali Larijani, responded to the resolution by insisting that Iran would expand uranium enrichment activities.[14]

On December 23, 2006, the Security Council unanimously passed Resolution 1737 "blocking the import or export of sensitive nuclear materiel and equipment and freezing the financial assets of persons or entities supporting its proliferation sensitive nuclear activities or the development of nuclear-weapon delivery systems." The resolution required Iran to suspend "all enrichment-related and reprocessing activities, including research and development; and work on all heavy-water related projects, including the construction of a research reactor moderated by heavy water." The Council also decided that "all States should prevent the supply, sale or transfer, for the use by or benefit of Iran, of related equipment and technology, if the State determined that such items would contribute to enrichment-related, reprocessing or heavy-water related activities, or to the development of nuclear weapon delivery systems." Iran again ignored the resolution.

On February 22, 2007, the IAEA found Iran in violation of a Security Council ultimatum to freeze uranium enrichment and other demands meant to dispel fears that it intends to build nuclear weapons. Iranian Foreign Minister Manouchehr Mottaki responded that Iran would never suspend uranium enrichment.[15]

In January 2010, President Obama's top advisers said they did not believe the governmewnt's earlier National Intelligence Estimate's conclusion that Iranian scientists ended all work on designing a nuclear warhead in late 2003. The following month, President Obama announced new unilateral sanctions by the United States. A day later, Iran announced it had begun enriching uranium to a higher level of purity, 20 percent, which is a step closer to producing weapons-grade uranium.[16]

The May 2010 IAEA report said Iran had produced a stockpile of nuclear fuel that, with further enrichment, would be sufficient to build two nuclear weapons.[17]

A lot of attention has focused on President Ahmadinejad because of his belligerent rhetoric, explicit threats against Israel and Holocaust denial. If he were to disappear tomorrow, however, the threat from Iran would remain because the desire to build nuclear weapons predated his regime and is considered a matter of national pride, even by Iranians who are considered pro-West.

The issue has also been falsely cast as one driven by Israeli fears, but, despite all the noise Iran makes about the "Zionist entity," and its patron, Iran's principal strategic interest is regional domination, and the countries that are most concerned are its immediate Arab neighbors. Iran wants to dominate the oil industry, to influence policy in the Middle East, and to become a major player in global politics. This would likely be the case whoever ran the country.

Given the unlikelihood of a counterrevolution in Iran, more active measures are required to prevent Iran from acquiring nuclear weapons. Everyone desires a political solution, but it is clear Iran has used diplomacy as a means to delay drastic measures by the international community while accelerating its work on uranium enrichment.

Economic sanctions are also being flouted by the Iranians and undermined by companies in Western countries that find ways to circumvent them, and by the governments of Russia and China, which have signed multibillion dollar business deals that undercut the impact of the sanctions. A military option exists, but it also poses serious risks to regional stability, future relations with Iran and the nation(s) that carries out the mission. It is in the interest of the international community, therefore, to do everything possible to prevent Iran from achieving a nuclear capability before it is too late.

MYTH

"Israel has nothing to fear from a nuclear Iran."

FACT

Jews have learned from painful history that when someone threatens to kill them, they should take it seriously. Therefore, no one should be surprised at the alarm expressed by Israel after hearing Iranian President Mahmoud Ahmadinejad proclaim, "This origin of corruption [Israel] will soon be wiped off the Earth's face!" and Ayatollah Ali Khamene'i, Iran's Supreme Leader, declaring, "Israel is a cancerous tumor. So what do you do with a cancerous tumor? What can be done to treat a tumor other than removing it?"

Some argue Iran would never launch a nuclear attack against Israel because no Muslim leader would risk an Israeli counterstrike that might destroy them. This theory doesn't hold up, however, if the Iranian leaders believe there will be destruction anyway at the end of time. What matters, Middle East expert Bernard Lewis observed, is that infidels go to hell and believers go to heaven. Lewis quotes a passage from Ayatollah Khomeini, cited in an 11th grade Iranian schoolbook, "I am decisively announcing to the whole world that if the world-devourers [the infidel powers] wish to stand against our religion, we will stand against the whole world and will not cease until the annihilation of all of them. Either we all become free, or we will go to the greater freedom, which is martyrdom. Either we shake one another's hands in joy at the victory of Islam in the world, or all of us will turn to eternal life and martyrdom. In both cases, victory and success are ours."[18]

Iranian President, Mahmoud Ahmadinejad, believes the most important task of the Iranian Revolution was to prepare the way for the return of the Twelfth Imam, who disappeared in 874, thus bringing an end to Muhammad's lineage. Shiites believe this imam, the Mahdi or "divinely guided one," will return in an apocalyptic battle in which the forces of righteousness will defeat the forces of evil and bring about a new era in which Shi'a Islam ultimately becomes the dominant religion throughout the world. The Shiites have been waiting patiently for the Twelfth Imam for more than a thousand years, but Ahmadinejad may believe he can now hasten the return through a nuclear war. It is this apocalyptic world view, Lewis notes, that distinguishes Iran from other governments with nuclear weapons.

There are those who think that Iran would never use such weapons against Israel because innocent Muslims would be killed as well; however, Ayatollah Ali Akbar Hashemi-Rafsanjani, Ahmadinejad's predecessor, explicitly said he wasn't concerned about fallout from an attack on Israel. "If a day comes when the world of Islam is duly equipped with the arms Israel has in its possession," he said, "the strategy of colonialism would face a stalemate because application of an atomic bomb would not leave anything in Israel but the same thing would just produce damages in the Muslim world." As one Iranian commentator noted, Rafsanjani apparently wasn't concerned that the destruction of the Jewish State would also result in the mass murder of Palestinians as well.[19]

Iran will not have to use nuclear weapons to influence events in the region. By possessing a nuclear capability, the Iranians can deter Israel or any other nation from attacking Iran or its allies. When Hezbollah attacked Israel in 2006, for example, a nuclear Iran could have threatened retaliation against Tel Aviv if Israeli forces bombed Beirut. The mere threat of using nuclear weapons would be sufficient to drive Israelis into shelters and could cripple the economy. Will immigrants want to come to a country that lives in the shadow of annihilation? Will companies want to do business under those conditions? Will Israelis be willing to live under a nuclear cloud?

If you were the prime minister of Israel, would you take seriously threats to destroy Israel by someone who might soon have the capability to carry them out? Could you afford to take the risk of allowing Iran to acquire nuclear weapons? How long would you wait for sanctions or other international measures to work before acting unilaterally to defend your country?

MYTH

"Iran's nuclear program threatens only Israel."

FACT

Israel is not alone in its concern about Iran's nuclear weapons program. In fact, the nations most worried about Iran are its immediate neighbors who have no doubts about the hegemonic ambitions of the radical Islamists in Tehran.

Iran's Arab neighbors have accused it of threatening the sovereignty and independence of the Kingdom of Bahrain and territories of the United Arab Emirates, "issuing provocative statements against Arab states," and interfering in the affairs of the Palestinians, Iraq and Morocco.[20]

In statements challenging Bahrain's sovereignty, Iranian officials renewed claims that the kingdom was actually a part of the Persian Empire. The effect of Iran's saber rattling, journalist Giles Whittell wrote, "is especially chilling in Bahrain as the only Sunni-led country with a Shia majority that is not at war or on the brink of war."[21] Arab League Deputy Secretary-General Ahmad Bin Hali angrily denounced Iran's claims to Bahrain while former Bahraini army chief of staff Sheik Maj.-Gen. Khalifa ibn Ahmad al-Khalifa said Iran stirs trouble in many Gulf nations. "[Iran] is like an octopus—it is rummaging around in Iraq, Kuwait, Lebanon, Gaza and Bahrain," al-Khalifa proclaimed.[22]

> *"The United States and the international community are determined to prevent Iran from acquiring nuclear weapons."*
>
> **—President Barrack Obama[23]**

The Crown Prince of Bahrain was the first Gulf leader to explicitly accuse Iran of lying about its weapons program. "While they don't have the bomb yet, they are developing it, or the capability for it," Salman bin Hamad bin Isa al-Khalifa said.[24]

Iran also reasserted its authority over three islands of the United Arab Emirates that it forcibly seized in the early 1970s and continues to occupy. While joint sovereignty was maintained between Iran and the UAE over the Abu Musa and Greater and Lesser Tunbs islands until 1994, Iran significantly increased its military capabilities on Abu Musa, stationed Islamic Revolutionary Guard Corps soldiers there, and expelled foreign workers in attempts to assert full control of the island. The United Nations General Assembly, the Arab League, and the Arab Parliamentary Union have all affirmed their support for the UAE and have made clear that Iran illegally occupies the islands.[25]

The Iranian threat is felt in Arab states beyond the Gulf as well. Morocco severed diplomatic relations with Iran in response to the inflammatory statements concerning Bahrain and hostile activity by Iranians inside Morocco. Morocco's foreign ministry accused the Iranian diplomatic mission in Rabat of interfering in the internal affairs of the kingdom and attempting to spread Shi'a Islam in the nation where 99 percent of the population are Sunni Muslims.[26]

Since 2006, at least 13 Arab countries have either announced new plans to explore atomic energy or revived pre-existing nuclear programs (including Saudi Arabia, Egypt, Jordan, Morocco, Turkey, and Syria) in response to Iran's nuclear program.[27] Many Middle Eastern countries sought to strengthen their nuclear cooperation with other nations, such as the United States, Russia and France. Both Saudi Arabia and the UAE signed nuclear cooperation accords with the United States, and Russia and Egypt have laid the groundwork for Russia to join a tender for Egypt's first civilian nuclear power station. Kuwait, Bahrain, Libya, Algeria, Morocco, and Jordan announced plans to build nuclear plants as well. Even Yemen, one of the poorest countries in the Arab world announced plans to purchase a nuclear reactor.

European leaders also see Iran as a threat to their interests. French President Nicolas Sarkozy has said, for example, "Iran is trying to acquire a nuclear bomb. I say to the French, it's unacceptable."

Similarly, German Chancellor Angela Merkel has stated, "I'm emphatically in favor of solving the problem through negotiations, but we also need to be ready to impose further sanctions if Iran does not give ground."[28]

"Iran is trying to get a nuclear weapon," British Prime Minister David Cameron said. "It's in the interests of everyone here and everyone in the world that we don't get a nuclear arms race."[29]

The international concern that has prompted a series of UN resolutions and ongoing condemnation of Iranian behavior has nothing to do with Israel. Most of the world understands that a nuclear Iran poses a direct threat to countries inside and outside the Middle East, raises the specter of nuclear terrorism, increases the prospects for regional instability, and promotes proliferation. Israel's detractors, such as professors Stephen Walt and John Mearsheimer, portray Israel and the "Israeli lobby" as campaigning for military action against Iran.[30] In fact, Israel and its supporters have been outspoken in their desire to see tough measures implemented to stop Iran's nuclear weapons program to avoid war. It is the Arab states that have aggressively lobbied the U.S. government to launch a military attack against Iran. The King of Saudi Arabia, for example, said the United States should put an end to its nuclear programs and "cut off the head of the snake."[31]

Notes

1. SIPRI Arms Transfers Database.
2. "Proposed U.S. Arms Export Agreements From January 1, 2010 to December 31, 2010," U.S. Department of Defense, (February 2011).

3. Carina Solmirano and Pieter D. Wezeman, "Military Spending and Arms Procurement in the Gulf States," SIPRI, (October 2010).

4. SIPRI

5. Sam Perlo-Freeman, "Arms Transfers to the Middle East," SIPRI, (July 2009).

6. "Military Expenditures," World Bank, http://data.worldbank.org/indicator/MS.MIL. XPND.GD.ZS, (accessed June 8, 2011).

7. "U.S.-Israel JPMG Follow-Up: Israeli Response To U.S. Proposed Defense Sales To Region," (March 13, 2006).

8. Arms Control and Disarmament Agency; Defense Security Assistance Agency Report; World Military Expenditures and Arms Transfers.

9. "U.S.-Israel JPMG Follow-Up: Israeli Response To U.S. Proposed Defense Sales To Region," (March 13, 2006).

10. Robert Siegel and Tom Gjelten, "CIA: North Korea Helping Syria Build Nuke Reactor," NPR, (April 24, 2008).

11. Alan Dershowitz, *Chutzpah*, (MA: Little Brown, and Co., 1991), p. 249.

12. *Washington Post*, (November 18, 2004).

13. Associated Press, (September 15, 2005).

14. *USA Today*, (August 6, 2006).

15. Associated Press, (February 27, 2007).

16. *New York Times*, (January 2, 2010); *Washington Post*, (February 11, 2010).

17. *New York Times*, (May 31, 2010).

18. "Does Iran have something in store?" *Wall Street Journal*, (August 8, 2006).

19. Iran Press Service, (December 14, 2001).

20. "AIP calls on Iran to respect int'l treaties relevant to Bahrain, UAE," Kuwait News Agency, (March 22, 2009).

21. Giles Whittell, "Bahrain accuses Iran of nuclear weapons lie," TimesOnline, (November 2, 2007).

22. *Al-Hayat* (London), May 16, 2008. "Arab League slams Iran's 'provocation,'" *The Jerusalem Post*, (March 22, 2009).

23. "Obama says new U.S. sanctions show international resolve in Iran issue, CNN, (July 1, 2010), accessed May 6, 2011, at http://articles.cnn.com/2010-07-01/politics/ obama.iran.sanctions_1_nuclear-program-nuclear-non-proliferation-treaty-iran-s-islamic-revolutionary-guard?_s=PM:POLITICS.

24. Giles Whittell, "Bahrain accuses Iran of nuclear weapons lie," TimesOnline, (November 2, 2007).

25. "AIP calls on Iran to respect int'l treaties relevant to Bahrain, UAE," Kuwait News Agency, (March 22, 2009); "Abu Musa Island," GlobalSecurity.org, (October 15, 2008).

26. "Morocco severs relations with Iran," aljazeera.net, (March 7, 2009).

27. Friedrich Steinhausler, "Infrastructure Security and Nuclear Power," *Strategic Insights*, Volume VIII, Issue 5 (December 2009), accessed May 6, 2011, at http://www.nps.edu/ Academics/centers/ccc/publications/OnlineJournal/2009/Dec/steinhauslerDec09.html.

28. David Jackson, "Iran, Iraq top agendas for meetings with allies," *USA Today*, (November 1, 2007).

29. "David Cameron threatens more Iran nuclear sanctions," BBC, (February 23, 2011), accessed May 6, 2011, at http://www.bbc.co.uk/news/uk-politics-12550216.

30. John J. Mearsheimer and Stephen M. Walt, *The Israel Lobby and U.S. Foreign Policy*, (NY: Farrar, Straus and Giroux, 2007), p. 298.

31. "Saudi King Abdullah And Senior Princes On Saudi Policy Toward Iraq," White House for OVP, Department For NEA/ARP AND S/I, (April 20, 2008).

20. The Media

MYTH

"Media coverage of the Arab world is objective."

FACT

When asked to comment on what many viewers regard as CNN's bias against Israel, Reese Schonfeld, the network's first president explained, "When I see them [reporters] on the air I see them being very careful about Arab sensibilities." Schonfeld suggested the coverage is slanted because CNN doesn't want to risk the special access it has in the Arab world.[1] Other networks engage in similar self-censorship.

In Arab countries, journalists are usually escorted to see what the dictator wants them to see or they are followed. Citizens are warned by security agencies, sometimes directly, sometimes more subtly, that they should be careful what they say to visitors.

In Lebanon during the 1980s, for example, the Palestine Liberation Organization (PLO) had reporters doing their bidding as the price for obtaining interviews and protection. During the Palestinian War, Israeli journalists were warned against going to the Palestinian Authority and some received telephone threats after publishing articles critical of the PA leadership.[2]

In the case of coverage of the PA, the Western media relies heavily on Palestinian assistants to escort correspondents in the territories. In addition, Palestinians often provide the news that is sent out around the world. For example, at least two journalists working for Agence France-Presse simultaneously worked for PA media outlets. An Associated Press correspondent also worked for the PA's official newspaper. One veteran journalist said, "It's like employing someone from the [Israeli] Government Press Office or one of the Israeli political parties to work as a journalist."[3]

"By my own estimate," journalist Ehud Ya'ari wrote, "over 95 percent of the TV pictures going out on satellite every evening to the various foreign and Israeli channels are supplied by Palestinian film crews. The two principle agencies in the video news market, Associated PressTN and Reuters TV, run a whole network of Palestinian stringers, freelancers and fixers all over the territories to provide instant footage of the events. These crews obviously identify emotionally and politically with the intifada and, in the 'best' case, they simply don't dare film anything that could embarrass the Palestinian Authority. So the cameras are angled to show a tainted view of the Israeli army's actions, never focus on the Palestinian gunmen and diligently produce a very specific kind of close-up of the situation on the ground."[4]

A particularly egregious incident occurred in October 2000 when two Israelis were lynched in Ramallah by a Palestinian mob. According to reporters on the scene, the Palestinian police tried to prevent foreign journalists from filming the incident. One Italian television crew managed to film parts of the attack and these shocking images ultimately made headlines around the world. A competing Italian news agency took a different tack, placing an advertisement in the PA's main newspaper, *Al Hayat-Al-Jadidah,* explaining that it had nothing to do with filming the incident.[5]

If a news organization strays from the pro-Palestinian line, it comes under immediate attack. In November 2000, for example, the Palestinian Journalist's Union complained that the Associated Press was presenting a false impression of the Palestinian War. The Union called Associated Press's coverage a conscious crime against the Palestinian people and said it served the Israeli position. The Union threatened to adopt all necessary measures against Associated Press staffers as well as against Associated Press bureaus located in the PA if the agency continued to harm Palestinian interests.[6]

> "We were filming the beginning of the demonstration. Suddenly, a van pulled in hurriedly. Inside, there were Fatah militants. They gave their orders and even distributed Molotov cocktails. We were filming. But these images, you will never see. In a few seconds, all those youngsters surrounded us, threatened us, and then took us away to the police station. There, we identified ourselves but we were compelled to delete the controversial pictures. The Palestinian Police calmed the situation but censored our pictures. We now have the proof that those riots are no longer spontaneous. All the orders came from the Palestinian hierarchy."
>
> **—Jean Pierre Martin**[7]

MYTH

"Journalists covering the Middle East are driven by the search for the truth."

FACT

It will come as no surprise to learn that journalists in the Middle East share an interest in sensationalism with their colleagues covering domestic issues. The most egregious examples come from television reporters whose emphasis on visuals over substance encourages facile treatment of the issues. For example, when NBC's correspondent in Israel was asked why reporters turned up at Palestinian demonstrations in the West Bank they knew were being staged, he said, "We play along because we need the pictures."[8] The networks can't get newsworthy pictures from closed societies such as Syria, Saudi Arabia, Iran or Libya, so events in Israel routinely make headlines while the Arab world is ignored.

Israel often faces an impossible situation of trying to counter images with words. "When a tank goes into Ramallah, it does not look good on TV," explains Gideon Meir of the Israeli Foreign Ministry. "Sure we can explain why we are there, and that's what we do. But it's words. We have to fight pictures with words."[9]

The magnitude of the problem Israel confronts is clear from Tami Allen-Frost, deputy chairman of the Foreign Press Association and a producer for Britain's ITN news, who says "the strongest picture that stays in the mind is of a tank in a city" and that "there are more incidents all together in the West Bank than there are suicide bombings. In the end, it's quantity that stays with you."[10]

One cause of misunderstanding about the Middle East and bias in media reporting is the ignorance of journalists about the region. Few reporters speak Hebrew or Arabic, so they have little or no access to primary resources. They frequently regurgitate stories they read in English language publications from the region rather than report independently. Media outlets also often rely on stringers—local Arabs who help them find stories—whose biases are often interjected into the coverage. When they do attempt to place events in historical context, they often get the facts wrong and create an inaccurate or misleading impression. To cite one example, during a recitation of the history of the holy sites in Jerusalem, CNN's Garrick Utley reported that Jews could pray at the Western Wall during Jordan's rule from 1948 to 1967.[11] In fact, Jews were prevented from visiting their holiest shrine. This is a critical historical point that helps explain Israel's position toward Jerusalem.

MYTH

"Arab officials tell Western journalists the same thing they tell their own people."

FACT

Arab officials often express their views differently in English than they do in Arabic. They express their true feelings and positions to their constituents in their native language. For external consumption, however, Arab officials have learned to speak in moderate tones and often relate very different views when speaking in English to Western audiences. Long ago, Arab propagandists became more sophisticated about how to make their case. They now routinely appear on American television news broadcasts and are quoted in the print media and come across as reasonable people with legitimate grievances. What many of these same people say in Arabic, however, is often far less moderate and reasonable. Since Israelis can readily translate what is said in Arabic they are well aware of the views of their enemies. Americans and other English-speakers, however, can easily be fooled by the slick presentation of an Arab propagandist.

To give just one example, Palestinian peace negotiator Saeb Erekat is frequently quoted by the Western media. After the brutal murder of two Israeli teenagers on May 9, 2001, he was asked for a reaction. The *Washington Post* reported his response:

> Saeb Erekat, a Palestinian official, said in English at a news conference that "killing civilians is a crime, whether on the Palestinian or the Israeli side." The comment was not reported in Arabic-language Palestinian media.[12]

The unusual aspect of this story was that the *Post* reported the fact that Erekat's comment was ignored by the Palestinian press.

In an interview with Israeli TV in March 2011, Palestinian Authority Chairman Mahmoud Abbas condemned the Palestinians' naming of a square after Dalal Mughrabi, the terrorist who led the most lethal terror attack in Israel's history. When speaking to Palestinians in 2010, however, Abbas said, "Of course we want to name a square after her . . . We carried out a military action; can I then later renounce all that we have done?"[13]

Case Study

A *Washington Post* story about the "cycle of death" in the West Bank included an interview with Raed Karmi, an official in Fatah, the dominant faction in Yasser Arafat's Palestine Liberation Organization. The report begins with the observation that Karmi is running out to join a battle against Israeli soldiers and grabs an M-16 assault rifle. What the story fails to mention is that only Palestinian police are supposed to be armed. The report implies that Israeli and Palestinian violence is equivalent in this "cycle" because Karmi said he was acting to avenge the death of a Palestinian who the Israelis assassinated for organizing terrorist attacks. Karmi admits that he participated in the kidnapping and execution-style murder of two Israelis who had been eating lunch in a Tulkarm restaurant. Karmi was jailed by the Palestinian Authority, but he was released after just four months and subsequently killed four more Israelis, including a man buying groceries and a driver who he ambushed. "I will continue attacking Israelis," he told the *Post*.[14]

Over the years Yasser Arafat was famous for saying one thing in English to the Western media and something completely different to the Arabic press in his native tongue. This is why the Bush Administration insisted that he repeat in Arabic what he said in English, in particular condemnations of terrorist attacks and calls to end violence.

It is more difficult for Arab leaders to get away with doubletalk today because their Arabic remarks are now translated by watchdog organizations and disseminated in English.

MYTH

"Israelis cannot deny the truth of pictures showing their abuses."

FACT

A picture may be worth a thousand words, but sometimes the picture and the words used to describe it are distorted and misleading. Photographers understandably seek the most dramatic pictures they can find, and those suggesting that brutal Israeli Goliaths are mistreating suffering Palestinian Davids are especially appealing, but the context is often missing.

In one classic example, the Associated Press circulated a dramatic photo of an angry baton-wielding Israeli soldier standing over a bloody young man. It appeared the soldier had just beaten the youth. The picture appeared in the *New York Times* and spurred international outrage because the caption, supplied by Associated Press, said, "An Israeli policeman and a Palestinian on the Temple Mount."[15] It turned out, however, the caption was inaccurate and the photo actually showed an incident that might have conveyed almost the exact opposite impression had it been reported correctly. The victim was not a Palestinian beaten by an Israeli soldier, it was a policeman protecting an American Jewish student, Tuvia Grossman, who had been riding in a taxi when it was stoned by Palestinians. Grossman was pulled out of the taxi, beaten and stabbed. He broke free and fled toward the Israeli policeman. At that point a photographer snapped the picture.

Besides getting the victim wrong, Associated Press also inaccurately reported that the photograph was taken on the Temple Mount. When Associated Press was alerted to the errors, it issued a series of corrections, several of which still did not get the story straight. As is usually the case when the media makes a mistake, the damage was already done. Many outlets that had used the photo did not print clarifications. Others issued corrections that did not receive anywhere near the prominence of the initial story.

Another example of how pictures can be both dramatic and misleading was a Reuters photo showing a young Palestinian being arrested by Israeli police on April 6, 2001. The boy was obviously frightened and wet his pants. The photo attracted worldwide publicity and reinforced the media image of brutal Israelis who abuse innocent children. In this instance it is the context that is misleading. Another Reuters photographer snapped another picture just before the first one was taken. It showed the same boy participating in a riot against Israeli soldiers. Few media outlets published this photo.

> *"By any logic, militants engaged in warfare don't blow up little babies."*
>
> **—Tom Fiedler, Executive Editor, *Miami Herald*[16]**

MYTH

"The press makes no apologies for terrorists."

FACT

The media routinely accepts and repeats the platitudes of terrorists and their spokespersons with regard to their agendas. The press gullibly treats claims that attacks against innocent civilians are acts of "freedom fighters." In recent years some news organizations have developed a resistance to the term "terrorist" and replaced it with euphemisms such as "militant" because they don't want to be seen as taking sides or making judgments about the perpetrators.

For example, after a Palestinian suicide bomber blew up a pizza restaurant in downtown Jerusalem on August 9, 2001, killing 15 people, the attacker was described as a "militant" (*Los Angeles Times, Chicago Tribune,* NBC Nightly News). When a Palestinian woman walked into a crowded beach restaurant in Haifa on October 4, 2003, and detonated a bomb that killed 21 people, including four children, the Reuters account said she had waged an "attack" in retaliation for previous Israeli army actions and that the bombing showed that Palestinian officials had failed to "rein in the militants."[17] The heinous attack on March 11, 2011, in which two Palestinian terrorists infiltrated the Israeli town of Itamar in the West Bank and brutally murdered a family of five, including a three-month-old infant, was described by the *Los Angeles Times* as part of a "continuing cycle of violence."[18] After terrorists killed eight Israelis and wounded more than 30 in multiple attacks near Eilat, the *New York Times* referred to the perpetrators only as "armed attackers" and reported that Israeli counterstrikes killed Palestinians from a "militant group."[19]

Clifford May of the Middle East Information Network pointed out the absurdity of the media coverage: "No newspaper would write, 'Militants struck the World Trade Center yesterday,' or say, 'They may think of themselves as freedom fighters, and who are we to judge, we're news people.'"[20]

One of the best examples of how the press sometimes distinguishes terrorist attacks against other nations was a list of "recent terror attacks around the world" disseminated by the Associated Press, probably the most influential news service in the world. The list cited 15 terrorist incidents during the five-year period between August 1998 and August 2003. During that period, more than 800 Israelis were murdered in terrorist attacks, but not one of the incidents in Israel made the list.[21] Similarly, when Associated Press released its Year in Photos 2003, six of the 130 photos chosen related to human suffering in the Israeli-Palestinian conflict. All six were of Palestinians.

In a memo to the *New York Times* foreign desk, former Jerusalem bureau chief James Bennet criticized his paper's reluctance to use the word "terrorism." He said, "The calculated bombing of students in a university cafeteria, or of families gathered in an ice cream parlor, cries out to be called what it is. . . . I wanted to avoid the political meaning that comes with 'terrorism,' but I couldn't pretend that the word had no usage at all in plain English." Bennett acknowledged that not using the term was "a political act in itself."[22]

Rather than apologize for terrorists, the media sometimes portrays the victims of terror as equivalent to the terrorists themselves. For example, photos are sometimes shown of Israeli victims on the same page with photos of Israelis capturing terrorists, giving the sense, for example, that the Palestinian held in handcuffs and blindfolded by a soldier is as much a victim as the shocked woman being helped from the scene of a suicide bombing.

In one of the most egregious examples, after a suicide bombing in Petah Tikva on May 27, 2002, CNN interviewed the mother of the bomber, Jihad Titi. The parents of a 15-month-old girl killed in the attack, Chen and Lior Keinan, were also interviewed. The interviews with the Keinans were not shown on CNN international in Israel or elsewhere around the world until hours after the interview with Titi's mother had been broadcast several times.

This was too much even for CNN, which subsequently announced a policy change whereby it would no longer "report on statements made by suicide bombers or their families unless there seemingly is an extraordinarily compelling reason to do so."[23]

MYTH

"The Palestinian Authority places no restrictions on reporters."

FACT

A case study of the Palestinian Authority's idea of freedom of the press occurred following the September 11 terrorist attacks against the

United States. An Associated Press cameraman filmed Palestinians at a rally in Nablus celebrating the terror attacks and was subsequently summoned to a Palestinian Authority security office and told that the material must not be aired.

Ahmed Abdel Rahman, Arafat's Cabinet secretary, said the Palestinian Authority "cannot guarantee the life" of the cameraman if the footage was broadcast.[24] The cameraman requested that the material not be aired and, Associated Press never released the footage.

More than a week later, the Palestinian Authority returned a videotape it confiscated from the Associated Press showing a Palestinian rally in the Gaza Strip in which some demonstrators carried posters supporting Osama bin Laden. Two separate parts of the six-minute tape involving "key elements"" were erased by the Palestinians, according to an Associated Press official.[25]

In October 2001, after the United States launched attacks against Afghanistan, Palestinians supporting Osama bin Laden staged rallies in the Gaza Strip that were ruthlessly suppressed by Palestinian police. The PA took measures to prevent any media coverage of the rallies or the subsequent riots. The Paris-based Reporters Without Frontiers issued a scathing protest to the PA and also objected to Palestinian orders not to broadcast calls for general strikes, nationalistic activities, demonstrations or other news without permission from the PA. The aim of the press blackout was expressed by an anonymous Palestinian official, "We don't want anything which could undermine our image."[26]

In August 2002, the Palestinian journalists' union banned journalists from photographing Palestinian children carrying weapons or taking part in activities by terrorist organizations because the pictures were hurting the Palestinians' image. The ban came after numerous photographs were published showing children carrying weapons and dressing up like suicide bombers. Another group, the Palestinian Journalists Syndicate, issued a similar ban that included photographing masked men. The Foreign Press Association expressed "deep concern" over the effort to censor coverage, and the threats of sanctions against journalists who disregarded the ban.[27]

In July 2004, as Gaza became increasingly unstable, and protests were being mounted against corruption in the Palestinian Authority and the leadership of Arafat, Palestinian journalists covering the crisis received death threats.[28] Numerous incidents have also been reported of physical attacks on journalists who offended PA officials. A reporter for a Saudi-owned news channel was wounded by gunfire when he was driving through the Gaza Strip. He was then dragged from his car and beaten because his station had allowed criticism of Yasser Arafat and other officials. A week later, 100 Palestinian journalists went to Arafat's headquarters in Ramallah to pledge allegiance to him.[29]

The Palestinian Authority and Hamas were accused of systematically abusing Palestinian journalists in a Human Rights Watch report released April 6, 2011. The report documents cases of torture, beatings and arbitrary detainment of journalists by security forces and says that "severe harassment by Palestinian Authority and Hamas security forces targeting Palestinian journalists in the West Bank and Gaza has had a pronounced chilling effect on freedom of expression."

For example, Hamas security forces detained an Al Quds radio reporter and attacked him "in a morgue where he had reported on a man, supposedly killed by Israeli military attack, who was discovered still to be alive."[30]

The Center for Development and Media Freedoms, a Palestinian rights group, said that the number of attacks by Palestinians on journalists, arrests and confiscations of equipment rose by 45 percent in 2010.[31]

In June 2011, the Palestinian Authority banned Palestinian journalists from reporting about the findings of the Ramallah-based Independent Commission for Human Rights concerning abuse of human rights by the PA and Hamas. "Assaults on journalists and censorship and restrictions on freedom of expression are still a dreadful nightmare for the journalists," said Palestinian reporter Mustafa Ibrahim. "Journalists avoid covering events out of fear of being targeted or arrested by [Palestinian] security forces in the West Bank."[32]

MYTH

"The media carefully investigates Palestinian claims before publicizing them."

FACT

Palestinians have learned that they can disseminate almost any information to the media and it will be published or broadcast somewhere. Once it is picked up by one media outlet, it is inevitably repeated by others. Quickly, misinformation can take on the appearance of fact, and while Israel can present evidence to correct the inaccuracies being reported, the damage is already done. Once an image or impression is in someone's mind, it is often difficult, if not impossible, to erase it.

For example, a Palestinian boy was stabbed to death in a village near a Jewish settlement. The media repeated Palestinian claims that the boy was attacked by settlers when in fact he had been killed in a brawl between rival Palestinian clans.[33] On another occasion, a 10-year-old Palestinian girl was allegedly killed by IDF tank fire. This time it turned out she died as a result of Palestinians shooting in the air to celebrate the return of Muslim worshipers from Mecca.[34]

One staple of Palestinian propaganda has been to distribute false statistics in an effort to make Israeli actions look monstrous. For example, if an incident involves some death or destruction, they can grossly exaggerate the figures and a gullible media will repeat the fabricated data until they become widely accepted as accurate. This occurred, for example, during the Lebanon War when Yasser Arafat's brother claimed that Israel's operations had left 600,000 Lebanese homeless. He made the number up, but it was repeated by the International Committee of the Red Cross and publicized in the media. By the time the ICRC repudiated the figure, it was too late to change the impression that Israel's military operation to defend itself from terrorist attacks on its northern border had created an unconscionable refugee problem.[35]

The Palestinians were caught lying again in April 2002 when Palestinian spokesman Saeb Erekat told CNN on April 17 that at least 500 people were massacred in Jenin and 1,600 people, including women and children, were missing. Erekat produced no evidence for his claim and the Palestinians' own review committee later reported a death toll of 56, of whom 34 were combatants. No women or children were reported missing.[36]

What is perhaps more outrageous than the repetition of Erekat's lie is that media outlets continue to treat him as a legitimate spokesperson, giving him access that allows him to disseminate misinformation.

MYTH

"Media coverage of Operation Cast Lead was fair and accurate."

FACT

Israel's enemies will do everything possible to manipulate the media to influence public opinion. Israel will be accused of massacres, fabricated casualty figures will be distributed, photographs will be doctored and journalists will be threatened. These and other ploys will be used to create sympathy for the Palestinians and cast aspersions on Israeli forces in the hope of turning world opinion against Israel.

Too often, irresponsible journalists have repeated unverified and often inaccurate information in their haste to be the first to report a story. In an effort to present an evenhanded account, some reporters have the mistaken belief that allowing an Arab spokesperson to lie and then giving an Israeli a chance to respond represents a balanced account. This is like allowing a spokesperson to accuse Israelis of beating their spouses and then inviting an Israeli to deny that they beat their husbands and wives.

One of the first examples of this in the Gaza war occurred after

Israeli forces fired near a UN-run school on January 6, 2009. The press immediately reported that more than 40 Palestinians seeking shelter in the building were killed, and the attack was portrayed as a deliberate assault on innocent people.[37] Hours later, Israeli investigators reported that they had fired after being attacked by Hamas terrorists launching mortars from the area. Witnesses supported the Israeli account, and the UN later claimed a "clerical error" led them to falsely accuse Israel of shelling the school.[38] Additionally, the original casualty figure was fabricated; the death toll was actually 12, nine of whom were Hamas combatants. The facts came too late, however, to offset the initial impression created and reinforced by repeated claims by UN officials discounting the Israeli version.[39]

France 2, the same television network that broadcast the notoriously inaccurate story about Mohammed al-Dura during the Palestinian War, aired an erroneous report showing dead children allegedly killed in the Gaza fighting. The amateur video of the dead toddlers being laid out on a white sheet was actually shot after they were killed by the explosion of a Hamas ammunition truck during a parade in Gaza in September 2005.[40]

CNN's Anderson Cooper described one way Hamas manipulated news coverage: "Inside Gaza, press controlled by Hamas is heavy-handed. There are few press freedoms inside Gaza and Hamas controls who reports from there and where they can go. While pictures of wounded children being brought to hospitals are clearly encouraged, we rarely see images of Hamas fighters or their rockets being fired into Israel."[41]

Even before Israel initiated Operation Cast Lead, many journalists were quick to report whatever they were told by Hamas. When Hamas staged blackouts in Gaza, the media incorrectly reported that Israel was preventing the Gazans from obtaining fuel and electricity. Israel was regularly blamed for a "humanitarian crisis" in Gaza while, at the same time, truckloads of goods were sent in from Israel each day. While Israel's air attacks on Gaza immediately made the front page of newspapers around the world, the rocket barrages on southern Israel, and the impact they had had on the population over the preceding three years, was rarely mentioned.

The media often turns conflicts into numbers games, keeping running tallies of casualties. Israel always is accused of disproportionality because fewer Israelis typically die in confrontations. Israelis, however, are under no obligation to take greater casualties for the sake of looking better in the media box score.

Notes

1. *New York Jewish Week*, (August 31, 2001).
2. *Jerusalem Report*, (May 7, 1991).

3. "Where the reporting stops," *Jerusalem Post,* (January 18, 2005).
4. *Jerusalem Report,* (May 7, 1991).
5. Judy Lash Balint, "Media Frightened into Self-Censorship," *WordNet Daily,* (March 5, 2001).
6. *Al Hayat-Al-Jadidab* (November 2, 2001).
7. Report filed by Jean Pierre Martin on October 5, 2000, a day after his Belgian television team from RTL-TV1 was filming in the area of Ramallah.
8. *Near East Report,* (August 5, 1991).
9. *Jerusalem Report,* (April 22, 2002).
10. *Jerusalem Report,* (April 22, 2002)
11. CNN, (October 10, 2000). Cited in Abraham Foxman, "Letter to Garrick Utley," *Anti-Defamation League,* (October 13, 2000).
12. *Washington Post,* (May 10, 2001).
13. *Al-Hayat Al-Jadida,* (January 17, 2010), cited in Itamar Marcus and Nan Jacques Zilberdik, "Abbas's duplicity about his support for honoring terrorist Dalal Mughrabi," Palestinian Media Watch, (May 27, 2011).
14. *Washington Post,* (September 7, 2001).
15. *New York Times,* (September 30, 2000).
16. Tom Fiedler, "Handle with care: words like 'conflict,' 'terrorist,' " *Miami Herald,* (January 4, 2004).
17. Ibid.
18. Editorial Staff, "A Fatal Israeli-Palestinian Flaw," *Los Angeles Times,* (March 14, 2011).
19. Isabel Kershner and David D. Kirkpatrick, "Attacks Near Israeli Resort Heighten Tensions with Egypt and Gaza," *New York Times,* (August 18, 2011).
20. *Washington Post,* (September 13, 2001).
21. *WorldnetDaily,* (November 24, 2003).
22. Daniel Okrent, "The War of the Words: A Dispatch From the Front Lines," *New York Times,* (March 6, 2005).
23. *Forward,* (June 28, 2002).
24. Associated Press, (September 12, 2001).
25. Jewish Telegraphic Agency, (September 18, 2001).
26. *Jerusalem Post,* (October 10, 2001).
27. *Jerusalem Post,* (August 26, 2002).
28. *Jerusalem Post,* (July 25, 2004).
29. *Jerusalem Post,* (January 12 & 14, 2004).
30. "West Bank/Gaza: Stop Harassing Journalists," Human Rights Watch, (April 6, 2011).
31. Lahav Harkov, "PA, Hamas systematically abuse Palestinian journalists," *Jerusalem Post,* (April 6, 2011).
32. Khaled Abu Toameh, "PA bans journalists from reporting human rights abuses," *Jerusalem Post,* (June 8, 2011).
33. Arnon Regular, "Palestinian boy likely stabbed to death in West Bank clan feud," *Haaretz,* (July 20, 2005).
34. Margot Dudkevitch, "PA arrests suspect in girl's murder," *Jerusalem Post,* (February 1, 2005).
35. "Toll of Lebanon Dead and Injured Still Uncertain in Chaos of War," *New York Times,* (July 14, 1982).
36. *New York Post,* (April 17, 2002). See also myths and facts related to coverage of the Lebanon wars, the Palestinian War and Operation Cast Lead.
37. Patrick Martin, "Account of Israeli Attack on Gaza School Doesn't Hold Up," *Scripps News* (January 29, 2009).
38. Yaakov Katz, "UN: IDF Did Not Shell Unrwa School," *Jerusalem Post* (February 1, 2009).

39. Steven Erlanger "Weighing Crimes and Ethics in the Fog of Urban Warfare," *New York Times,* (January 16, 2009).
40. Haviv Rettig Gur and Ehud Zion Waldoks, " 'Ask Egypt to let you into the Gaza Strip,' " *Jerusalem Post,* (January 7, 2009).
41. Anderson Cooper, "Covering the Gaza Crisis,"*CNN,* (January 6, 2009).

21. The Campaign to Delegitimize Israel

MYTH

"Anti-Semitism is a result of Israeli policies."

FACT

Anti-Semitism has existed for centuries, well before the rise of the modern State of Israel. Rather than Israel being the cause of anti-Semitism, it is more likely that dissatisfaction with Israeli behavior and the distorted media coverage of Israeli policies are reinforcing latent anti-Semitic views.

As writer Leon Wieseltier observed, "The notion that all Jews are responsible for whatever any Jews do is not a Zionist notion. It is an anti-Semitic notion." Wieseltier adds that attacks on Jews in Europe have nothing whatsoever to do with Israel. To blame Jews for anti-Semitism is similar to saying blacks are responsible for racism.[1]

> *"Israel is the only state in the world today, and the Jews the only people in the world today, that are the object of a standing set of threats from governmental, religious, and terrorist bodies seeking their destruction. And what is most disturbing is the silence, the indifference, and sometimes even the indulgence, in the face of such genocidal anti-Semitism."*
>
> **—Canadian Minister of Justice and Attorney General Irwin Cotler[2]**

MYTH

"Supporters of Israel only criticize Arabs and never Israelis."

FACT

Israel is not perfect. Even the most committed friends of Israel acknowledge that the government sometimes makes mistakes, and that it has not solved all the problems in its society. Supporters of Israel may not emphasize these faults, however, because there is no shortage of groups and individuals who are willing to do nothing but focus on Israel's imperfections. The public usually has much less access to Israel's side of the story of its conflict with the Arabs, or the positive aspects of its society; therefore, it is often important to put events in context.

Israelis themselves are their own harshest critics. If you want to read criticism of Israeli behavior, you do not need to seek out anti-Israel sources, you can pick up any Israeli newspaper and find no shortage of news and commentary critical of government policy. The rest of the world's media provides constant attention to Israel, and the coverage is far more likely to be unfavorable than complimentary.

The openness of debate in Israel has led some to conclude that Americans should not feel constrained from expressing similar critical views. America is not Israel, however; Israelis have a common narrative and shared experiences. Americans, even American Jews, do not have the same level of knowledge or experience with regard to Israel, so critics should be aware that their criticism may be subject to misinterpretation by those who do not know the history or context of the topic under discussion.

Criticism is also not justified by Israeli encouragement, as Israelis do not understand the American context and they typically only bless critics who agree with them (leftist Israelis are happy to encourage American Jews to speak out against rightist governments but are furious with criticism of leftist governments and vice versa).

MYTH

"Academic freedom means any criticism of Israel is permissible in a university."

FACT

The one place in America where anti-Semitism is still tolerated is in the university, where "academic freedom" is often used as a cover to sanction anti-Israel teachings and forums that are anti-Semitic.

In an address on the subject of academic freedom, Columbia President Lee Bollinger quoted from a report that described a professor as someone whom "'no fair-minded person' would even suspect of speaking other than as 'shaped or restricted by the judgment . . . of professional scholars.'" He also spoke about the need for faculty to "resist the allure of certitude, the temptation to use the podium as an ideological platform, to indoctrinate a captive audience, to play favorites with the like-minded, and silence the others."

Many faculty, however, do not resist temptation; rather, they embrace their position as an ideological platform. Those who abuse their rights, and insist they can say what they want, hypocritically denounce others who exercise their right to criticize them. To suggest that a professor's views are inappropriate, or their scholarship is faulty, is to risk being tarred with the charge of McCarthyism.

Legality is not the issue in evaluating the anti-Israel, sometimes anti-Semitic speeches and teachings of faculty and speakers on campus. No one questions that freedom of speech allows individuals to express their views. The issue is whether this type of speech should be given the cover of "academic" freedom, and granted legitimacy by the university through funding, publicity or use of facilities.

It is sometimes suggested critics seek to stifle legitimate criticism of Israel. There is a clear distinction, however, between criticism of Israeli policy, which you can read in any Israeli newspaper, and anti-Semitism, in which the attacks against Israel challenge its right to exist, or single Israel out among all other nations for opprobrium.

A related question is whether the presentations are in any way academic or scholarly. Few people would claim that a conference in which anti-black, anti-gay, or anti-woman sentiments were expressed would be protected by academic freedom, and yet that is the shield used to permit attacks on the Jewish people.

While criticism of Israel is allowed, when it crosses the line into hate speech or anti-Semitism, it may create a hostile environment that violates the civil rights of Jews. The U.S. Department of Education issued policy guidance in October 2010 clarifying that Jews are protected from discrimination and harassment under Title VI of the 1964 Civil Rights Act. The Office of Civil Rights specifies that school districts and institutions of higher education "may violate these civil rights statutes and the Department's implementing regulations when peer harassment based on race, color, national origin, sex, or disability is sufficiently serious that it creates a hostile environment and such harassment is encouraged, tolerated, not adequately addressed, or ignored by school employees."[3]

MYTH

"American universities should divest from companies that do business in Israel."

FACT

The word "peace" does not appear in divestment petitions, which makes clear the intent is not to resolve the conflict but to delegitimize Israel. Petitioners blame Israel for the lack of peace and demand that it make unilateral concessions without requiring anything of the Palestinians, not even the cessation of terrorism. Divestment advocates also ignore Israel's efforts to reach historic compromises with the Palestinians that would have created a Palestinian state. Even after Israel completely withdrew from the Gaza Strip, certain individuals and groups persisted in their campaign to undermine Israel and further demonstrated that they are interested in Israel's destruction rather than any territorial compromise.

The divestment campaign against South Africa was specifically directed at companies that were using that country's racist laws to their advantage. In Israel, no such racist laws exist; moreover, companies doing business there adhere to the same standards of equal working rights that are applied in the United States.

Harvard University President Lawrence Summers observed that the divestment efforts are anti-Semitic. "Profoundly anti-Israel views are increasingly finding support in progressive intellectual communities," said Summers. "Serious and thoughtful people are advocating and taking actions that are anti-Semitic in their effect, if not their intent."[4]

Peace in the Middle East will come only from direct negotiations between the parties, and only after the Arab states recognize Israel's right to exist, and the Palestinians and other Arabs cease their support of terror. American universities cannot help through misguided divestment campaigns that unfairly single out Israel as the source of conflict in the region. Divestment proponents hope to tar Israel through an association with apartheid South Africa, an offensive comparison that ignores the fact that all Israeli citizens are equal under the law.

MYTH

"Advocates for Israel try to silence critics by labeling them anti-Semitic."

FACT

Criticizing Israel does not necessarily make someone anti-Semitic. The determining factor is the intent of the commentator. Legitimate critics accept Israel's right to exist, whereas anti-Semites do not. Anti-Semites use double standards when they criticize Israel, for example, denying Israelis the right to pursue their legitimate claims while encouraging the Palestinians to do so Anti-Semites deny Israel the right to defend itself, and ignore Jewish victims, while blaming Israel for pursuing their murderers. Anti-Semites rarely, if ever, make positive statements about Israel. Anti-Semites describe Israelis using pejorative terms and hate-speech, suggesting, for example, that they are "racists" or "Nazis."

Natan Sharansky has suggested a "3-D" test for differentiating legitimate criticism of Israel from anti-Semitism. The first "D" is the test of whether Israel or its leaders are being demonized or their actions blown out of proportion. Equating Israel with Nazi Germany is one example of demonization. The second "D" is the test of double standards. An example is when Israel is singled out for condemnation at the United Nations for alleged human rights abuses while nations that violate human rights on a massive scale, such as Iran, Syria, and Saudi Arabia, are not even mentioned. The third "D" is the test of delegitimization. Questioning Israel's legitimacy, that is, its right to exist is always anti-Semitic.[5]

No campaign exists to prevent people from expressing negative opinions about Israeli policy. In fact, the most vociferous critics of Israel are Israelis themselves who use their freedom of speech to express their concerns every day. A glance at any Israeli newspaper will reveal a surfeit of articles questioning particular government policies. Anti-Semites, however, do not share Israelis' interest in improving the society; their goal is to delegitimize the state in the short-run, and destroy it in the long-run. There is nothing Israel could do to satisfy these critics.

> *"The view of Israel as a monolithic entity composed of racists and brutal oppressors is a caricature. Israel is a complex society, struggling with itself. The forces of good and evil, and many in between, are locked in a daily battle on many different fronts."*
>
> **—Uri Avnery**[6]

MYTH

"The Boycott, Divestment, Sanctions (BDS) movement originated with Palestinians seeking to promote peace and justice.

FACT

The Boycott, Divestment and Sanctions (BDS) campaign is a product of the NGO Forum held in parallel to the 2001 UN World Conference against Racism in Durban, South Africa. The NGO Forum was marked by repeated expressions of naked anti-Semitism by non-governmental organization (NGO) activists and condemned as such by United Nations High Commissioner for Human Rights Mary Robinson who chaired the Conference.

The Forum's final declaration described Israel as a "racist, apartheid state" that was guilty of "racist crimes including war crimes, acts of genocide and ethnic cleansing." The declaration established an action plan—the "Durban Strategy"—promoting "a policy of complete and total isolation of Israel as an apartheid state . . . the imposition of mandatory and comprehensive sanctions and embargoes, the full cessation of all links (diplomatic, economic, social, aid, military cooperation and training) between all states and Israel" (para. 424).[7]

The use of the apartheid accusation, which is the foundation of the BDS movement, is deliberate—drawing a false parallel to South Africa. According to BDS proponents, if apartheid South Africa was worthy of a boycott and sanctions campaigns that eventually led to the downfall of that despicable system, "apartheid Israel should be subject to the same kind of attack, leading to the same kind of result."[8]

"When people criticize Zionists, they mean Jews. You're talking anti-Semitism."

—Martin Luther King[9]

MYTH

"The Palestinian people are vigorous supporters of the BDS movement."

FACT

In 2005, anti-Israel activists issued the "Palestinian Civil Society Call for BDS against Israel" in an effort to create the false impression that BDS is endorsed by all Palestinians. In truth, despite the obvious tensions between Palestinian Arabs and Israelis, a great deal of dialogue and co-operation has been ongoing.

In 2008 the *Histadrut* (Israeli labor union) and the Palestine General Federation of Trades Unions (PGFTU) signed an agreement to base future relations on negotiation, dialogue and joint initiatives to advance "fraternity and co-existence." Palestinian Arab Universities—despite being hotbeds of anti-Israel activity—maintained links with their Israeli counterparts. Artist, doctors and businesspeople were amongst those who formed bonds of mutual benefit, cooperation and even occasional friendship across the divide of conflict. The severing of these ties were not an objective that Israelis or Palestinian Arabs sought and the move to isolate the two sides did not spring from popular opinion on the Palestinian Arab side. Rather it was a strategy of a self-appointed vanguard that expressed itself through a network of NGOs who put pressure on other elements in Palestinian Arab society to fall in behind the "Durban strategy."

MYTH

"Campus delegitimization campaigns are successful."

FACT

The campus divestment campaign was initiated in 2001 by Students for Justice in Palestine (SJP), a student group at the University of California, Berkeley, in conjunction with the San Francisco chapter of the American-Arab Anti-Discrimination Committee. A year later, following the Palestine Solidarity Movement's first conference, which was held in Berkeley, the delegitimization movement began to spread to other universities, including the University of Michigan, Yale, Princeton, Harvard and the Massachusetts Institute of Technology.

Campus divestment failed miserably. A huge blow came in 2002, when Harvard University President and former Treasury Secretary Lawrence Summers said the divestment campaign was anti-Semitic. Soon after, Columbia University President Lee Bollinger said he opposed divestment and considered the apartheid analogy "both grotesque and offensive."[10]

A newspaper study counted only 17 boycott or divestment efforts at 14 campuses during 2006–2011 that were significant enough to generate a response. "In no instance," the *Forward* concluded, "has BDS action led to a university in the U.S. or Canada divesting from any company or permanently ceasing the sale of any product."[11]

Another effort to push the Durban agenda has been for students to stage Israel "Apartheid Week" on campuses around the world. These events have typically been little more than hate fests in which students bring speakers and films to demonize Israel on campus. Though disturbing events, they have had virtually no impact on campus. Organizers have managed to stage these events on only about a dozen U.S. campuses in 2010–11 (out of roughly 4,000 colleges) and students report that they were marginal events. Meanwhile, pro-Israel students have staged Israel "Peace Week" and related positive programming on more than 80 campuses during the same period.

Even when they fail, BDS advocates often claim victory in the hope that the perception of winning will create momentum for their cause. Institutions that allow BDS initiatives to be launched on campus should be aware that BDS supporters may report success even when there is none, to the detriment of the university's reputation.

Perhaps the more serious delegitimization efforts on campus escape public notice because they take place in classrooms where professors around the country, predominantly in Middle East studies departments, use their positions to advance political agendas that are often hostile toward Israel and selective in their exploration of Islam.[12] As Princeton's Bernard Lewis observed, Middle East studies programs have been distorted by "a degree of thought control and limitations of freedom of expression without parallel in the Western world since the 18th century, and in some areas longer than that." He added, "It seems to me it's a very dangerous situation because it makes any kind of scholarly discussion of Islam, to say the least, dangerous. Islam and Islamic values now have a level of immunity from comment and criticism in the Western world that Christianity has lost and Judaism never had."[13]

Following a vote in 2007 by a British academic union to boycott Israeli universities (the decision was later rescinded), nearly 300 university presidents denounced the British boycott in a statement that said, "In seeking to Korantine Israeli universities and scholars, this vote threatens every university committed to fostering scholarly and cultural exchanges that lead to enlightenment, empathy, and a much-needed international marketplace of ideas."

The delegitimization movement on campus has to date had no impact on Israeli policy toward the Palestinians. Nevertheless, the mere discussion of BDS allows Israel's detractors to propagate a negative image of Israel that many fear will take root while, simultaneously, shifting the tenor of debate from the merits of Israeli policies to its right to exist.

"Israeli academics have never boycotted Palestinian professors, even in the worst days of terror. To the contrary: if you're organizing a conference in Israel, it's almost obligatory to have a Palestinian professor on the podium. Free exchange is what academic freedom means, and Israeli universities have done an admirable job of upholding it in trying times. In contrast, the academic boycott against Israel is itself a gross violation of academic freedom, because it explicitly imposes a political litmus test on Israelis scholars. It's radical-style McCarthyism. . . ."

—Professor Martin Kramer[14]

MYTH

"The BDS Movement advocates peace."

FACT

The BDS movement is based on coercion rather than democracy. Proponents imply that Israel is not open to persuasion and that the electorate is too stupid, immature or evil to know what is best for the society. Unable to convince the Israeli electorate of the merits of their views, BDS proponents demonize Israel and call for outsiders to punish the citizens of Israel until they capitulate.

Some students believe that pressure must be applied to stimulate the parties to make concessions that will make a peace agreement possible. While this is a debatable tactic, students genuinely interested in peace recognize that any pressure would have to be directed at both parties. BDS proponents, however, are interested only in pressuring Israel and hold the Palestinians blameless for the conflict. Many injustices have resulted from the ongoing failure to resolve the Israeli-Palestinian conflict, but seeking to present Palestinian grievances out of context and without consideration of parallel Israeli concerns is neither constructive nor fair. The advancement of Palestinian rights should not negate the legitimate rights of Israelis.

Unlike peace advocates fighting to hasten a two-state solution to the conflict, BDS proponents make partisan political demands that are clearly aimed at a different outcome.

"Our position is based upon the belief that it is through cooperation based on mutual respect, rather than through boycotts or discrimination, that our common goals can be achieved. Bridging political gulfs—rather than widening them further apart—between nations and individuals thus becomes an educational duty as well as a functional necessity, requiring exchange and dialogue rather than confrontation and antagonism. Our disaffection with, and condemnation of acts of academic boycotts and discrimination against scholars and institutions, is predicated on the principles of academic freedom, human rights, and equality between nations and among individuals."

—Joint Hebrew University–Al-Quds University Statement[15]

Israel does not need to be coerced to seek peace. The effort to reach a compromise between Jews and Arabs began nearly a century ago. Israel has repeatedly offered a variety of compromises that would have allowed the Palestinians to establish a state. They have already seen the size of the home they were promised reduced to a fraction of its original size. Still, Israelis express a willingness to do more if it will bring peace.

By contrast, the BDS Movement rejects the peace process. Its leaders routinely dismiss peace efforts ranging from the 1978 Camp David Peace Accords to the Oslo Process to President Barack Obama's peace initiatives. BDS advocates refuse to contemplate the negative effects their efforts will have on the peace process. With their zero-sum approach to everything Israeli, they make no attempt to address issues of reconciliation and coexistence. Moreover, they do not acknowledge any Palestinian responsibility or accountability.

BDS is modeled on the campaign against South Africa, which was not designed to promote peace, but to dismantle the state. Thus, BDS leaders abhor cooperation between Israelis and Palestinians. Perhaps the best example of their hypocrisy is BDS co-founder, Omar Barghouti, who advocates a boycott against Israeli universities even as he enjoys the benefits of participating in a Ph.D. program at Tel Aviv University.

The Arab League boycott, which has been in force since 1945, before the creation of the state, did nothing to help the Palestinians achieve independence nor did it prevent Israel from becoming one of the world's economic success stories. The BDS campaign will be similarly ineffective.

"If we are to look at Israeli society, it is within the academic community that we've had the most progressive pro-peace views and views that have come out in favor of seeing us as equals.... If you want to punish any sector, this is the last one to approach."

— **Al-Quds University President Sari Nusseibeh**
on academic boycotts of Israel[16]

Since BDS activities are indiscriminate, they harm those Israelis who are most actively campaigning for peace and strengthen those who are more skeptical of peace initiatives. BDS reinforces the views of the cynics who do not believe that any compromise will satisfy the Palestinians, and undermines the peace activists who believe the Palestinians would trade peace for land. Rather than encourage compromise, efforts to isolate Israel only make its citizens feel more vulnerable and raise the already high level of risk associated with evacuating additional territory.

MYTH

"The BDS movement advocates for a two-state solution."

FACT

Under the false premise of being "apolitical," BDS advocates claim they are not advocating any one solution. In reality, this is purposeful ambiguity, as their three demands clearly spell out a "one-state" outcome, which has no basis in international law and which is code for the destruction of Israel as the nation-state of the Jewish people. While disavowing any interest in a formula for concluding an Israeli-Palestinian agreement, their preconditions make it impossible to see an outcome whereby an independent state of Palestine would coexist beside a secure Jewish state. Meanwhile, BDS proponents use this ambiguity to try to recruit well-meaning people unaware of the movement's true agenda, BDS is, therefore, a recipe for disaster, not coexistence. Creating "one state" with the "right of return" would mean that there would be no Israel and no self-determination for the Jewish people. This is not a basis for peace but a formula for perpetual conflict.

"Good riddance! The two-state solution for the Palestinian-Israeli conflict is finally dead. But someone has to issue an official death certificate before the rotting corpse is given a proper burial and we can all move on and explore the more just, moral and therefore enduring alternative for peaceful coexistence between Jews and Arabs in Mandate Palestine: the one-state solution."

— **Omar Barghouti, Founder,**
Palestinian Campaign for the Academic and Cultural Boycott of Israel[17]

MYTH

"BDS activists promote unity on college campuses."

FACT

The BDS campaign does not advance the cause of Middle East peace, but does create unwanted and unnecessary turmoil on campus. At a time when real campus dialogue is needed more than ever, BDS is more of a barrier than a catalyst to such discussions.

Zionist Jews can handle criticism of Israeli policy, just as they are open to hearing criticism of American policy. Demonization, double standards, and delegitimization are a different story. Those who label Israel as a Nazi state, an apartheid state, or a colonial state are clearly trying to use these hurtful analogies to demonize Israel. These are not criticisms that are aimed at improving the lives of Israelis or Palestinians, but are rather attempts to convince people to ostracize, punish, and impugn the Jewish state. Likewise, questioning the Jewish connection to Israel or the right of the Jewish people to self-determination in their homeland are attacks on the identities of all Jews.

After many of the past campus divestment debates, Jewish students have left the room crying. They feel incredibly hurt when their peers become part of a movement that seeks to delegitimize their own identity. The ideas may be abstract, but the emotional alienation that many Jewish students feel from BDS is real.

Honest discussion about Israeli and Palestinian narratives is needed on college campuses. Divestment advocates seek to circumvent a real debate by promoting the Palestinian narrative and delegitimizing Israel's story. BDS proponents preempt dialogue by adopting an inherently anti-Israel position as their starting point. Instead of asking questions such as: "How did things get this way?" or "What should we do?" BDS supporters adopt the premise that Israel is guilty of misbehavior and therefore must be punished without taking into account historical context, alternative views, or Israel's side of the story.

If a BDS initiative is adopted, there is no incentive to hold any real discussion. The campus has already declared Israel guilty and alienated many Jewish and all pro-Israel students who are now falsely tarred as supporters of apartheid, colonialism, and racism.

MYTH

"Selective boycotts advance prospects
for Palestinian-Israeli peace."

FACT

A group of Israeli artists, academics and authors have called upon actors to avoid performing in a theater in the town of Ariel, which is located in the West Bank, as a form of protest against Israeli settlement policy. While the Israelis boycotting Ariel are primarily Zionists who believe strongly in the right of the Jewish people to self-determination and oppose the BDS agenda and creation of a binational state that replaces Israel, their tactics are similar identical to those used outside of Israel. The Ariel boycott, and similar targeted boycotts, do nothing to advance the cause of peace but do punish innocent Jews uninvolved in the political conflict and give unintentional legitimacy to the boycotters seeking to delegitimize Israel. As Rabbi Eric Yoffie, the President of the Reform Judaism movement, and a frequent critic of Israeli policy, observed:

> The most important reason to oppose the boycott, however, is simply that it is impossible to distinguish between different types of boycotts. There is a growing global BDS (boycott, divestment, sanctions) movement; its intention is to isolate and delegitimize the State of Israel. It is already a threat, and with time, could become a mortal threat to Israel's existence. Those who claim that they only support the boycott of Ariel but oppose the BDS movement are making distinctions that will not be clear to anyone but themselves. If an internal boycott in Israel is the way that Israelis deal with the question of settlement expansion, what is the basis for objecting when countries and groups hostile to Israel call for a boycott of Israel's academic institutions?[18]

The distinction between Israeli businesses and communities in the territories and the rest of their compatriots cannot be applied in practice. Any steps to isolate and exclude Israelis in settlements also impacts Israelis on both sides of the Green Line. Because the economies are interdependent, efforts to punish or damage the settlements also injure the broader economy and all Israelis. Both sweeping and targeted boycott campaigns are a form of collective-punishment that is fundamentally unfair.

"If Amos Oz, David Grossman, Meretz, Peace Now and other Zionist doves want the country to listen to them, they can't slap the settlers in the face, which is what this boycott does. It's not only a mistake, it's an insult. I, too, wish the settlements had never been built, and hope to see many of them evacuated one day, but in the meantime the people living there are entitled to a decent life, which includes such things as culture, entertainment and higher education."

—*Jerusalem Post* columnist Larry Derfner[19]

Boycotts and other punitive measures aimed solely at Israel do not address the real sources of the current political impasse, such as the Palestinian failure to reassure the Israeli public of the peacefulness of their intentions. Punishing Israelis for the "occupation" may even help entrench maximalist Palestinian claims, rather than encourage the moderation needed to reach a fair political accommodation.

The BDS movement is essentially a means of coercion. If it were meant to encourage peace, the measures would be directed against the Palestinians to pressure them to end terrorism and recognize the state of Israel. Peace and a two-state solution are not the intent, however, of most BDS advocates. They want to raise questions about the legitimacy of the State of Israel, to generate international pressure to force Israel to capitulate to Palestinian demands and to avoid the necessity of negotiations to arrive at a mutually agreed upon division of the land that will guarantee the rights of both Palestinians and Israelis.

While someone supporting a limited or selective boycott may think they are not engaging in an act of delegitimization, BDS proponents use and abuse any kind of BDS activity to claim support and momentum for their own, full-blown anti-Israel version of the strategy. No matter how good the intention may be, associating with BDS strengthens the delegitimizers who seek Israel's demise.

Notes

1. Leon Wieseltier, "Israel, Palestine, and the Return of the Binational Fantasy," *The New Republic,* (October 24, 2003).
2. *Jerusalem Post,* (February 6, 2004).
3. "Dear Colleague" letter from Russlyn Ali, the U.S. Department of Education's Assistant Secretary for Civil Rights, (October 26, 2010), http://www2.ed.gov/about/offices/list/ocr/letters/colleague-201010.html.
4. Address at morning prayers, Memorial Church, Cambridge, Massachusetts, (September 17, 2002), Office of the President, Harvard University.
5. Natan Sharansky, "Antisemitism in 3-D," *Forward,* (January 21, 2005), p. 9.
6. Uri Avnery, "The Boycott Revisited," Gush-Shalom.org, (September 6, 2009), http://zope.gush-shalom.org/home/en/channels/avnery/1252168050/.
7. NGO Forum, "World Conference Against Racism—Durban, South Africa," NGO Monitor, (August 27–September 1, 2001).
8. "NGO 'Apartheid State' Campaign: Deliberately Immoral or Intellectually Lazy," NGO Monitor, (March 22, 2010).
9. Seymour Martin Lipset, "The Socialism of Fools-The Left, the Jews and Israel," *Encounter,* (December 1969), p. 24.
10. Summers address at morning prayers, Memorial Church, Cambridge, MA, (September 17, 2002), Office of the President, Harvard University; Kim Kirschenbaum, "Israel, Gaza Student Groups Clash on Issues of Divestment, Apartheid," *Columbia Spectator,* (March 4, 2009).
11. Josh Nathan-Kazis, "Survey of Campus BDS Finds Few Serious Cases," *The Forward,* (May 4, 2011).

12. See, for example, Martin Kramer, *Ivory Towers on Sand,* (DC: The Washington Institute for Near East Policy), 2001, p. 16; Marla Braverman, "The Arabist Predicament," *Azure* (Summer 2003), pp. 176-184; Mitchell Bard, *The Arab Lobby: The Invisible Alliance That Undermines America's Interests in the Middle East,* (NY: HarperCollins, 2010), pp. 284-321.

13. Matt Korade, "Lack of Openness Makes Scholarly Discussion of Islam Dangerous, Says Bernard Lewis," *Congressional Quarterly's Homeland Security News and Analysis,* (April 26, 2008).

14. Martin Kramer, "Boycotting Israel at NYU," Sandstorm, (March 31, 2004).

15. Joint Hebrew University—Al-Quds University Statement on Academic Cooperation Signed in London, (May 22, 2005), accessed May 9, 2011, at http://www.hunews.huji. ac.il/articles.asp?cat=24&artID=449.

16. "Palestinian university president comes out against boycott of Israeli academics," Associated Press, (June 18, 2006).

17. Omar Barghouti, "Relative Humanity: The Essential Obstacle to a Just Peace in Palestine," Counterpunch.org, (December 13-14, 2003), http://www.counterpunch.org/barghouti12132003.html.

18. Eric H. Yoffie, "The Idiocy of the Ariel Boycott," *Jerusalem Post,* (November 15, 2010).

19. Larry Derfner, "Rattling the Cage: A little culture, comrades," *Jerusalem Post,* (September 6, 2010).

APPENDIX

The Military Balance in the Middle East (2010)

Country	Regular Troops	Reserve Troops	Total	Tanks	Aircraft*
Israel	176,500	445,000	621,500	3,770	875
Egypt	405,000	254,000	704,000	3,870	518
Jordan	100,700	60,000	160,700	1,217	101
Lebanon	61,400	15,000	76,400	350	5
Palestinian Authority[†]	~44,000	—	~44,000	—	—
Iran	520,000	350,000	870,000	1,620	341
Iraq	250,000		250,000	171	3
Syria	289,000	132,500	421,500	4,800	490
Saudi Arabia	214,500	—	214,500	1,015	330

*Refers to all combat aircraft, including those in "operational storage"; excludes combat helicopters

[†]Refers to total PA and Hamas troops in Gaza and West Bank.

Note: Data for Iraq as of 2008.

Sources: The Institute for National Security Studies

Suggested Reading

Aumann, Moshe. *Land Ownership in Palestine 1880-1948*. Jerusalem: Academic Committee on the Middle East, 1976.

Avineri, Shlomo. The Making of Modern Zionism: Intellectual Origins of the Jewish State. NY Basic Books, 1981.

Avner, Yehuda. The Prime Ministers: An Intimate Narrative of Israeli Leadership. NY: Toby Press, 2010.

Avneri, Arieh. The Claim of Dispossession. NJ: Transaction Books, 1984.

Bard, Mitchell G. and Moshe Schwartz. 1001 Facts Everyone Should Know About Israel. NJ: Jason Aronson, 2002.

Bard, Mitchell G. The Arab Lobby: The Invisible Alliance That Undermines America's Interests in the Middle East. HarperCollins, 2010.

Bard, Mitchell G. The Complete Idiot's Guide to Middle East Conflict. NY: Alpha Books, 2008.

Bard, Mitchell and David Nachmias. Israel Studies: An Anthology. MD: American-Israeli Cooperative Enterprise, 2011. http://www.jewishvirtuallibrary.org/jsource/isdf/text/anthologycvr.html.

Bard, Mitchell. Will Israel Survive? (NY: Palgrave Macmillan, 2007).

Becker, Jillian. The PLO. NY: St. Martin's Press, 1985.

Begin, Menachem. The Revolt. NY: EP Dutton, 1978.

Bell, J. Bowyer. Terror Out Of Zion. NJ: Transaction, 1996.

Gurion, David. Rebirth and Destiny of Israel. NY: Philosophical Library, 1954.

Ben Benvenisti, Meron. Intimate Enemies: Jews and Arabs in a Shared Land. CA.: University of California Press, 1995.]

Cohen, Hillel. Army of Shadows: Palestinian Collaboration with Zionism, 1917-1948. CA: University of California Press, 2008.

Collins, Larry and Dominique Lapierre. O Jerusalem!. NY: Simon and Schuster, 1972.

Dershowitz, Alan. The Case for Israel. NY: John Wiley & Sons, 2003

Eban, Abba. Heritage: Civilization and the Jews. NY: Summit Books, 1984.

Eban Abba. My Country: The Story of Modern Israel. NY: Random House, 1972.

Gilbert, Martin. Israel: A History. NY: William Morrow & Co., 1998.

Harel, Amos and Avi Issacharoff. 34 Days: Israel, Hezbollah and the War in Lebanon. NY: Palgrave Macmillan, 2009.

Hazony, Yoram. The Jewish State: The Struggle for Israel's Soul. NY: Basic Books, 2001.

Hertzberg Arthur. The Zionist Idea. PA: Jewish Publications Society, 1997.

Herzl, Theodore. The Diaries of Theodore Herzl. NY: Peter Smith Publishers, 1987.

Herzl, Theodore. The Jewish State. Dover Publications, 1989.

Herzog, Chaim. The Arab-Israeli Wars. NY: Random House, 1984.

Johnson, Paul. A History of the Jews. NY: HarperCollins, 1988.

Katz, Samuel. Battleground-Fact and Fantasy in Palestine. SPI Books, 1986.

Kollek, Teddy. Jerusalem. Washington, D.C.: Washington Institute For Near East Policy, 1990.

Lacquer, Walter and Barry Ru bin. The Israel-Arab Reader. NY: Penguin, 2001.

Lewis, Bernard. The Jews of Islam. NJ: Princeton University Press, 1984.

Lewis, Bernard. The Middle East: A Brief History of the Last 2000 Years. NY: Touchstone Books, 1997.Livingstone, Neil C., and David Halevy. Inside the PLO. NY: William Morrow and Co., 1990.

Lorch, Netanel. One Long War. NY: Herzl Press, 1976.

Meir, Golda. My Life. NY: Dell, 1975.

Netanyahu, Benjamin. A Place Among Nations: Israel and the World. NY: Warner Books, 1998.

Oren, Michael. Six Days of War: June 1967 and the Making of the Modern Middle East. NY: Oxford University Press, 2002.

Pipes, Daniel. The Hidden Hand: Middle East Fears of Conspiracy. Griffin Trade Paperback, 1998.

Pipes, Daniel. The Long Shadow: Culture and Politics in the Middle East. NJ: Transaction Publishers, 1990.

Porath Yehoshua. The Emergence of the Palestinian-Arab National Movement, 1918-1929. London: Frank Cass, 1996.

Porath Yehoshua. In Search of Arab Unity 1930-1945. London: Frank Cass and Co., Ltd., 1986.

Porath Yehoshua. Palestinian Arab National Movement: From Riots to Rebellion: 1929-1939. vol. 2. London: Frank Cass and Co., Ltd., 1977

Quandt, William B. Camp David: Peacemaking and Politics. DC: Brookings Institution, 1986.

Rabin, Yitzhak. The Rabin Memoirs. CA: University of California Press, 1996

Rabinovich, Itamar and Jehuda Reinharz. Israel in the Middle East: Documents and Readings on Society, Politics, and Foreign Relations, Pre-1948 to the Present. Waltham: Brandeis University Press, 2007

Sachar Howard. A History of Israel: From the Rise of Zionism to Our Time. NY: Alfred A. Knopf, 1998.

Safran, Nadav. Israel The Embattled Aly. MA: Harvard University Press, 1981.

Schiff Ze'ev and Ehud Ya'ari. Intifada. NY: Simon & Schuster, 1990.

Schiff Zeev and Ehud Yaari. Israel's Lebanon War. NY: Simon and Schuster, 1984.

Senor, Dan and Saul Singer. Start-Up Nation: The Story of Israel's Economic Miracle. Toronto: McClelland & Stewart, Ltd, 2009.

Stillman Norman. The Jews of Arab Lands. PA: The Jewish Publication Society of America 1989.

Stillman Norman. The Jews of Arab Lands in Modern Times. NY: Jewish Publication Society, 1991.

Weizmann Chaim. Trial and Error. NY: Greenwood Press, 1972.

Wigoder, Geoffrey, ed. New Encyclopedia of Zionism and Israel. NJ: Fairleigh Dickinson University Press, 1994.

Ye'or, Bat. *The Dhimmi.* NJ: Associated University Press, 1985.

Index of Myths

Alphabetical Index

American-Israeli Cooperative Enterprise (AICE)

The AMERICAN-ISRAELI COOPERATIVE ENTERPRISE (AICE) was established in 1993 as a nonprofit 501(c)(3), nonpartisan organization to strengthen the U.S.-Israel relationship by emphasizing the fundamentals of the alliance and the values our nations share. Tangibly, this means developing social and educational programs in the U.S. based on innovative, successful Israeli models that address similar domestic problems, and bringing novel U.S. programs to Israel. These cooperative activities, which stem from our common values, are called *Shared Value Initiatives*.

The objectives and purposes of AICE include:

- To provide a vehicle for the research, study, discussion and exchange of views concerning nonmilitary cooperation (*Shared Value Initiatives*) between the peoples and governments of the United States and Israel.
- To facilitate the formation of partnerships between Israelis and Americans.
- To publicize joint activities, and the benefits accruing to America and Israel from them.
- To explore issues of common historical interest to the peoples and governments of the United States and Israel.
- To sponsor research, conferences and documentaries.
- To serve as a clearinghouse on joint U.S.-Israeli activities.
- To provide educational materials on Jewish history and culture.
- To promote scholarship in the field of Israel studies.

AICE also runs the Jewish Virtual Library, a comprehensive online Jewish encyclopedia covering everything from anti-Semitism to Zionism (www.JewishVirtualLibrary.org).

BOARD OF DIRECTORS
Howard Rosenbloom President/Treasurer
Dr. Arthur Bard Vice President/Secretary
Mitchell G. Bard Executive Director

ADVISORY BOARD

Newton Becker	Andy Lappin
Henry Everett z"l	Stephen J. Lovell
Howard Friedman	Bernice Manocherian
Jerry Gottesman	Terry M. Rubinstein
Paula Gottesman	Alan Slifka z"l
Eugene M. Grant	Arnold Wagner

About the Author

Mitchell Bard is the Executive Director of the nonprofit American-Israeli Cooperative Enterprise (AICE) and one of the leading authorities on U.S.-Middle East policy. Dr. Bard is also the director of the Jewish Virtual Library (www.Jewish VirtualLibrary.org), the world's most comprehensive online encyclopedia of Jewish history and culture.

Dr. Bard has appeared on local and national television and radio outlets. His work has been published in academic journals, magazines and major newspapers. He is the author/editor of:

- *The Arab Lobby: The Invisible Alliance That Undermines America's Interests in the Middle East.*
- *Israel Matters: The Real Deal About Israel*
- *Israel Studies: An Anthology* (coeditor with David Nachmias)
- *Will Israel Survive?*
- *The Complete Idiot's Guide to Middle East Conflict* (4th edition)
- *48 Hours of Kristallnacht*
- *The Founding of Israel*
- *The Complete Idiot's Guide to World War II*
- *Myths And Facts: A Guide to the Arab-Israeli Conflict*
- *1001 Facts Everyone Should Know About Israel*
- *Forgotten Victims: The Abandonment of Americans in Hitler's Camps*
- *The Holocaust (Turning Points in World History)*
- *The Nuremberg Trials (At Issue in History)*
- *The Nuremberg Trials (Eyewitness to History)*
- *From Tragedy to Triumph: The Politics Behind the Rescue of Ethiopian Jews*
- *The Complete History of the Holocaust*
- *The Water's Edge And Beyond: Defining the Limits to Domestic Influence on U.S. Middle East Policy*
- *Partners for Change: How U.S.-Israel Cooperation Can Benefit America*
- *U.S.-Israel Relations: Looking to the Year 2000*
- *Building Bridges: Lessons For America From Novel Israeli Approaches To Promote Coexistence*
- *On One Foot: A Middle East Guide for the Perplexed or How to Respond on Your Way to Class When Your Best Friend Joins an Anti-Israel Protest*
- *The Complete Idiot's Guide to Understanding the Brain*

Bard holds a Ph.D. in political science from UCLA and a master's degree in public policy from Berkeley. He received his B.A. in economics from the University of California at Santa Barbara.